The Dilemma of Consent to International Arbitration in Investment Agreements without a Forum

International Investment Law and Arbitration

Volumes published in this Brill Research Perspectives title are listed at *brill.com/rpia*

The Dilemma of Consent to International Arbitration in Investment Agreements without a Forum

By

Fernando Tupa

BRILL

LEIDEN | BOSTON

This paperback book edition is simultaneously published as issue 4.3–4 of *International Investment Law and Arbitration*, DOI:10.1163/24055778-12340012.

Typeface for the Latin, Greek, and Cyrillic scripts: "Brill". See and download: brill.com/brill-typeface.

ISBN 978-90-04-54601-1 (paperback)
ISBN 978-90-04-54602-8 (e-book)

This book is printed on acid-free paper and produced in a sustainable manner.

Contents

The Dilemma of Consent to International Arbitration in Investment Agreements without a Forum

Fernando Tupa
Partner at the International Arbitration Department of Curtis, Mallet-Prevost, Colt & Mosle, Buenos Aires and New York
ftupa@curtis.com

Abstract

This monograph addresses the sometimes overlooked yet fundamental principle that consent to international arbitration is forum-specific, and explores its significance and practical consequences in investment arbitration. This monograph contends that if there is no arbitral forum mentioned in the relevant dispute settlement provision of an investment agreement, the forum specified therein becomes unavailable for some reason, or a subsequent agreement on a forum is required between the parties to the dispute, there is only consent "in principle" to international arbitration in the investment agreement. Such expression of "consent" is unenforceable and ineffective, which means that a foreign investor would not be entitled to unilaterally initiate an investment claim against the host State under said agreement absent a subsequent agreement between the foreign investor and the host State on an arbitral forum. This monograph also shows that there is an explicit requirement of a forum-specific consent in the arbitral rules of the often-used arbitral institutions. In addition, the most-favored nation clause in investment agreements could not be applied to overcome the lack of forum in dispute settlement provisions. Finally, this monograph proposes possible avenues to tackle the absence of an agreed-upon forum in an investor-State dispute settlement provision, draws some conclusions and warns against the dangerous consequences of ignoring this basic principle.

Keywords

arbitration – consent – dispute settlement provision – forum – forum-specific – investment agreement – investor-state arbitration – lack of forum – most-favored nation – treaty

 | DOI:10.1163/9789004546028_002

1 Introduction[1]

International arbitration is based on consent, and investment arbitration is no exception. Although one of the frequent features in investment agreements is the inclusion of dispute settlement provisions containing an offer by the host State to submit disputes with the foreign investor to international arbitration, not every investor-State dispute settlement provision contains an enforceable and effective consent to international arbitration. That is particularly so when there is no arbitral forum (*i.e.*, arbitral institution or arbitral rules)[2] mentioned in the relevant dispute settlement provision, when the one specified therein becomes unavailable for some reason, or when a subsequent agreement on a forum is required between the parties to a dispute.

Consent to international arbitration in investment agreements is forum-specific; there is no such thing as consent to international arbitration in the abstract. If either an arbitral institution or the application of specific arbitral rules are referred to in the investor-State dispute settlement provision (without requiring a subsequent agreement between the parties to the dispute), the expression of consent to international arbitration generally fulfills the requirement of providing for a "forum" (*i.e.*, is "forum-specific") and thus is enforceable and effective. However, in the event that the investor-State dispute settlement provision contains references to more than one forum, or to a "cafeteria style" menu of fora, and offers no default or fallback option to decide the competent forum in case of lack of agreement nor a method to determine the competent forum, there would only be an enforceable and effective consent to arbitration if the parties subsequently agree on a forum.

1 The author served as counsel in some of the cases mentioned in this monograph. The views expressed in this monograph do not reflect the views of the law firm or of its clients. The author thanks Belen Ibañez and Juan Jorge for their research assistance and Simon Batifort, Kabir Duggal, Borzu Sabahi, Fuad Zarbiyev and an anonymous peer reviewer for their insightful comments.

2 In this monograph, the term "forum" is used broadly. It could mean either arbitral institution or arbitral rules. If there is a submission to an arbitral institution (*e.g.*, International Centre for Settlement of Investment Disputes ("ICSID") or International Chamber of Commerce ("ICC")), the rules of that institution will determine the arbitral rules that are applicable in the arbitration (absent a contrary agreement by the parties, whenever that is possible according to the institution's rules). If the submission is to certain arbitral rules (*e.g.*, Arbitration Rules of the United Nations Commission on International Trade Law ("UNCITRAL Rules")), the arbitration could be either *ad hoc* or institutional. Certain arbitral institutions (such as the ICC) only allow the application of its own arbitral rules (with some modifications that the parties may agree upon), while other institutions (such as the Permanent Court of Arbitration ("PCA")) allow the application of other arbitral rules (such as the UNCITRAL Rules).

General references in investment agreements to the submission of disputes to "international arbitration," or similar vague formulations, without specifying a forum cannot be interpreted as an enforceable and effective offer of consent by a host State to submit disputes with foreign investors to international arbitration. This is due to two main factors: (i) those general references usually serve other purposes, such as to establish pre-conditions that must be fulfilled prior to submitting disputes to international arbitration or to limit the dispute settlement methods available to foreign investors to settle their investment claims with the host State; and (ii) even if the intention of the contracting States was to grant consent to international arbitration by means of a general and broad formulation, without specifying an arbitral forum (or by specifying an arbitral forum that later becomes unavailable for any reason), such consent could not be operative (and thus would not be enforceable and effective) without a subsequent agreement between the foreign investor and the host State on a specific arbitral forum. In other words, when there is no arbitral forum (either specified in the investment agreement or subsequently agreed upon by the parties to the dispute), a foreign investor does not have a unilateral right under an investment agreement to initiate an international arbitration against the host State, since it would have no forum under which it could do so.

The reason for this impossibility is simple and straightforward. Absent a forum and a choice to an arbitral seat (which is not found in investment agreements), the foreign investor has no means of making such general consent to "international arbitration" operative (*i.e.*, turning a purported offer of consent by the host State into an enforceable and effective consent), even if an arbitral tribunal were to uphold that consent to international arbitration exists "in principle" in the relevant investment agreement.[3] In order to apply, institutional arbitral rules require the submission of disputes not only to "international arbitration" in general, but specifically to that particular forum (namely, ICSID, ICSID Additional Facility, ICC, or UNCITRAL Rules, among others), which means that an arbitral tribunal constituted under any of those

3 The phrase consent "in principle" to international arbitration was used by Professor Boisson de Chazournes in her dissenting opinion in the *Garanti Koza v. Turkmenistan* case. *Garanti Koza LLP v. Turkmenistan*, ICSID Case No. ARB/11/20, Dissenting Opinion of Professor Boisson de Chazournes, 3 July 2013 ("*Garanti Koza*, Dissent"), ¶ 18. I will use that phrase to refer to situations in which there is a reference to submission of disputes to international arbitration or consent to international arbitration in general, without consent to a specific forum. Such offer of consent by the State thus would not be enforceable or effective without a subsequent agreement between the parties to the dispute on a competent forum. This situation could also be referred to as "inchoate" consent. Hence, strictly speaking, consent "in principle" to international arbitration is not in effect sufficient "consent," since the potential offer is unenforceable and ineffective without a further agreement on a forum.

arbitration rules or institutions could not find jurisdiction under such rules or institutions if there is no consent to submit the dispute at issue to international arbitration under those specific arbitral rules or institutions. In addition, as opposed to international commercial arbitration, in the absence of a choice of seat, in investment agreements there is no domestic court to which the foreign investor could resort to fill in the gap caused by the failure to specify a forum – by application of a domestic arbitration statute – in order to force the host State to go to international arbitration.[4]

4 A particular situation that is worth mentioning is the rare but possible scenario in which the investment agreement provides for the submission of the investment dispute to a "pure" *ad hoc* arbitration (*i.e.*, no arbitral institution or pre-existing arbitral rules), containing specific rules regarding the constitution of the arbitral tribunal, and delegating (explicitly or implicitly) the choice of procedural arbitral rules to the tribunal itself. *See* Organisation for Economic Co-operation and Development (OECD), *Dispute Settlement Provisions in International Investment Agreements: A Large Sample Survey* (2012), ¶¶ 50 ("[S]ome treaties order or allow that disputes be settled by an *ad hoc* arbitral tribunal, the setup of which is specified by the individual IIA."), 63 ("Many treaties that address the issue of applicable arbitration rules delegate the design of these rules entirely to the tribunals."); Chile-China BIT, Article 9 ("(3) If a dispute involving the amount of compensation for expropriation cannot be settled within six months after resort to negotiations as specified in Paragraph 1 of this Article, it may be submitted at the request of either party to an international arbitration of the International Centre for the Settlement of Investment Disputes (ICSID), created by the Convention on the settlement of investment disputes between States and Nationals of other States, opened for signature at Washington on March 18, 1965. Any dispute concerning other matters between an investor of either Contracting Party and the other Contracting Party may be submitted by mutual agreement to an *ad-hoc* arbitral tribunal. The provisions of this Paragraph shall not apply if the investor concerned has resorted to the procedure specified in Paragraph 2 of this Article. (4) Such an ad-hoc arbitral tribunal shall be constituted for each individual case in the following way; each party to the dispute shall appoint an arbitrator, and these two shall select a national of a third State which has diplomatic relations with the two Contracting Parties as Chairman. The first two arbitrators shall be appointed within two months of the written notice for arbitration by either party to the dispute to the other, and the Chairman be selected within four months. If within the period specified above, the tribunal has not been constituted, either party to the dispute may invite Secretary General of the International Centre for the Settlement of Investment Disputes to make the necessary appointments. If the Secretary General is a national of either Contracting Party or is otherwise prevented from discharging the said function, the next most senior member of the International Centre for the Settlement of Investment Disputes who is not a national of either Contracting Party shall be invited to make the necessary appointment(s). (5) That ad-hoc arbitral tribunal shall determine its own procedure. However, the tribunal may, in the course of determination of procedure, take as guidance the Arbitration Rules of the International Center for Settlement of Investment Disputes."); China-Nigeria BIT, Article 9 ("3. If a dispute cannot be settled within six months after resort to negotiations as specified in Paragraph 1 of this Article, it may be submitted at the request of either Party to an ad hoc arbitral tribunal … If within the period specified above, the tribunal has not been constituted; either Party to

Thus, in order to find an enforceable and effective offer of consent by a State to arbitrate disputes with foreign investors in an investment agreement, it is not only required that the relevant dispute settlement provision provides for submission of investment disputes to "international arbitration" in general or in the abstract, but also that those disputes be submitted to a specific forum or, in the absence of such forum (or a way of determining such forum or a default or fallback option in the dispute settlement provision itself), that the foreign investor and the host State subsequently agree on a forum. Simply put, without a forum indicated in the dispute settlement provision, or a subsequent agreement between the parties to the dispute on a competent forum, there is no enforceable and effective consent to international arbitration in the investment agreement.

Investment tribunals have taken different approaches when they have been called upon to construe investor-State dispute settlement provisions that do not specify a forum, or specify a forum that later becomes unavailable. Some tribunals have correctly held that there is no enforceable and effective consent to international arbitration without a forum, while others – through creative and questionable interpretations – have improperly found consent, even in the absence of a forum, and have affirmed jurisdiction. What is more, some tribunals have gone as far as to allow the importation of a forum through the application of most-favored nation ("MFN") clauses, *de facto* importing consent to international arbitration – despite disavowing to do so.

In a nutshell, if there is only consent "in principle" to international arbitration by the host State in an investment agreement due to the lack of a forum (or the unavailability of the forum contemplated therein), a foreign investor would not be entitled to unilaterally initiate an investment claim against the host State under said agreement, absent a subsequent agreement between the foreign investor and the host State on an arbitral forum. This is because the foreign investor would have to initiate an international arbitration based on an investment agreement at a specific forum, and the tribunal constituted under said forum would not be able to find consent by the State under the rules of that specific forum.

This monograph is divided into several parts. In Part 2, I will address the fundamental principle that consent to international arbitration is forum-specific, which seems to sometimes be overlooked by investment tribunals. In Parts 3

---

the dispute may invite the Secretary General of the [ICSID] to make the necessary appointments."). In those cases, there would be an "indirect" choice of forum by the parties to the dispute, and thus consent to international arbitration in the investment agreement would be enforceable and effective.

to 11, I will then address other related issues that explain the significance and practical consequences of this principle, including (i) the differences between investment arbitration and international commercial arbitration in the absence of a forum, (ii) the explicit requirement of a forum-specific consent in the arbitral rules of the often-used arbitral institutions, (iii) the applicable principles of interpretation to investor-State dispute settlement provisions and the standard of proof of State consent to international arbitration, (iv) how not every investor-State dispute settlement provision contains an enforceable and effective consent to international arbitration, (v) how general references to submission of disputes to international arbitration or the use of "shall" should not always be construed as enforceable and effective consent, (vi) the relevant investment cases to date that have dealt with this threshold issue, (vii) the inapplicability of the MFN clause to overcome the absence of a forum, (viii) the practical consequences of the lack of a forum, and (ix) possible avenues to tackle the absence of an agreed-upon forum in an investor-State dispute settlement provision. Finally, in Part 12, I will draw some conclusions and warn against the dangerous consequences of ignoring this basic principle.

2 Consent to International Arbitration in Investment Agreements Is Forum-Specific

A State's consent to international arbitration is forum-specific simply because consent to a specific forum (*e.g.*, ICSID arbitration) cannot be equated with consent to a different forum (*e.g.*, *ad hoc* UNCITRAL arbitration). In other words, consent to international arbitration under a specific forum is not interchangeable with consent to international arbitration under a different forum. An example to illustrate this situation is the case of an investment agreement that provides only for consent to international arbitration under ICSID, but after one of the contracting States to that investment agreement withdraws from the ICSID Convention, a foreign investor covered by the investment agreement initiates an international arbitration against the host State under the UNCITRAL Rules (which are not mentioned in said investment agreement, not even as a default or fallback option). Even if the UNCITRAL tribunal were to find that there is consent to international arbitration "in principle" in the investment agreement and that ICSID arbitration is not available to the foreign investor, the tribunal would not have jurisdiction since the host State has not given its specific consent to the application of the UNCITRAL Rules.[5]

5 *See* p. 14, *infra*.

Thus, in order to find jurisdiction over a particular dispute, an arbitral tribunal must find that, not only did the parties to the dispute consent to "international arbitration" in general, but that they also consented to the specific forum under which the tribunal was constituted.[6] Otherwise, the investment tribunal would not have the power to exercise jurisdiction over the dispute, even if it were to find that the relevant investor-State dispute settlement provision contains consent "in principle" to international arbitration.

It is virtually undisputed that an enforceable and effective arbitration clause, in addition to designating arbitration as a mandatory means of dispute resolution,

---

6 *See AHG Industry GmbH & Co. KG v. Republic of Iraq*, ICSID Case No. ARB/20/21, Award on the Respondent's Application under ICSID Rule 41(5), 30 September 2022 ("*AHG*"), ¶¶ 206 ("Given the nature of Law No. 64, which does not itself contain specific consent to ICSID arbitration in relation to the Claimant and its investment, the Claimant cannot rely on this law to establish this Tribunal's jurisdiction to hear the present dispute."), 210 ("What the Claimant needs to show is that, in addition to jurisdiction under the ICSID Convention, the Tribunal has jurisdiction under the specific instrument on the basis of which it has been constituted and the Claimant seeks to establish Iraq's liability on the merits. Thus, for this Tribunal to have jurisdiction to hear the dispute, the Claimant needs to establish both Iraq's consent to ICSID jurisdiction under the Convention (which is established, given that Iraq is a Contracting Party) and Iraq's consent to ICSID arbitration under a specific instrument – be it a contract, or a treaty."); *Case Concerning Mutual Assistance in Criminal Matters (Djibouti v. France)*, Judgment, 4 June 2008, ICJ REPORTS 177 (2008), ¶ 60 (stating that jurisdiction "is based on the consent of States under the conditions expressed" in the relevant treaties). On the other side of the coin, the tribunal constituted under a specific instrument (or forum) would only have jurisdiction to hear claims under that instrument (unless the parties agree otherwise or, arguably, when the dispute settlement provision has a broad scope encompassing claims beyond breaches of that instrument). Interestingly, in the case *Özer v. Lybia*, the tribunal decided that it was only duly constituted under the Turkey-Libya BIT, but not under the Agreement on the Promotion and Protection and Guarantee of Investments Among Member States of the Organization of the Islamic Conference ("OIC Agreement"), even if the claimants initiated an arbitration under both instruments. In a single notice of arbitration, the claimants commenced an arbitration under both the Turkey-Libya BIT and the OIC Agreement. Libya, however, agreed to appoint an arbitrator only in respect to the arbitration commenced under Article 8 of the Turkey-Libya BIT, as it considered the OIC Agreement to have been improperly invoked because it did not provide for investor-State arbitration. Once the tribunal was constituted, it ruled that it was duly constituted only under the Turkey-Libya BIT, limiting its power to the claims made under that instrument, and that it had not been constituted under the OIC Agreement. *See Mustafa Ohran Özer and Other v. State of Libya, Ad-hoc* arbitration, Decision on the Constitution of the Tribunal, 6 April 2022, ¶¶ 56, 57, 62. Thus, the fact that there is an arbitral tribunal properly constituted under a specific investment agreement cannot function as a means of supplying a missing forum to a purported consent "in principle" under a different investment agreement in order to make additional claims under that other investment agreement before the same tribunal.

needs to select the governing arbitral rules (either directly or indirectly).[7] The basic principle that consent is forum-specific – sometimes forgotten by investment tribunals when analyzing dispute settlement provisions – has also been recognized by commentators. For instance, Scott Vesel asserts that "[a] state's consent is both forum-specific and party-specific, so that consent to arbitration under UNCITRAL rules does not constitute consent to ICSID arbitration, nor does consent to ICSID arbitration of disputes with Finnish nationals constitute consent to arbitration with nationals of Cyprus."[8] Similarly, Zachary Douglas states that "arbitration rules such as the UNCITRAL Arbitration Rules, the ICC Rules of Arbitration and the LCIA Arbitration Rules can only be incorporated by reference into the arbitration if there is an agreement to arbitrate containing such a reference."[9]

A practical implication of this fundamental principle is that an arbitral tribunal constituted under a particular forum (namely, ICSID, ICC, UNCITRAL Rules) would not be able to find jurisdiction over a specific dispute if the relevant dispute settlement provision in the investment agreement at issue only

---

7 In general, any arbitration agreement must meet the following minimum requirements: "The first, which is common to all agreements, is to produce mandatory consequences for the parties. The second, is to exclude the intervention of state courts in the settlement of the disputes, at least before the issuance of the award. The third, is to give powers to the arbitrators to resolve the disputes likely to arise between the parties. The fourth, is to permit the putting in place of a procedure leading under the best conditions of efficiency and rapidity to the rendering of an award that is susceptible of judicial enforcement." Benjamin G. Davis, *Pathological Clauses: Frédéric Eisemann's Still Vital Criteria*, 7(4) ARBITRATION INTERNATIONAL 365 (1991), p. 366 (citing Frédéric Eisemann, *La clause d'arbitrage pathologique*, in COMMERCIAL ARBITRATION ESSAYS IN MEMORIAM EUGENIO MINOLI 129 (Unione Tipografico-editrice Torinese, 1974)). *See also* Paul Friedland, ARBITRATION CLAUSES FOR INTERNATIONAL CONTRACTS (2d. ed., JurisNet 2007), pp. 61–64 ("The elements *necessary* to an arbitration clause are those elements without which an arbitration clause will be ineffective and unenforceable ... [Leaving aside] the particular requirements of some national laws, there are three elements necessary to an effective arbitration clause": (i) it "cover[s] precisely the subject matter that the parties intend to be submitted to arbitration"; (ii) it "leave[s] no doubt as to either the designation of arbitration or the identity of the institution or rules chosen"; and (iii) it "provides clearly ... for arbitration as the exclusive dispute resolution mechanism."); M. Scherer, L. Richman & R. Gerbay, ARBITRATING UNDER THE 2014 LCIA RULES: A USER'S GUIDE (Kluwer Law International 2015), pp. 28–29 ("[T]he most critical elements that any Arbitration Agreement should address [are] (i) the parties' agreement to submit their disputes to arbitration; (ii) the scope of the disputes submitted to arbitration; and (iii) the choice of the institution and incorporation of its arbitration rules").

8 Scott Vesel, *Clearing a Path Through a Tangled Jurisprudence: Most-Favored Nation Clauses and Dispute Settlement Provisions in Bilateral Investment Treaties*, 32 YALE JOURNAL OF INTERNATIONAL LAW 125 (2007), pp. 185–186.

9 Zachary Douglas, THE INTERNATIONAL LAW OF INVESTMENT CLAIMS (Cambridge University Press 2009), pp. 75–76.

contains consent to international arbitration "in principle" (without referring to a particular forum), or contains consent to a different forum, but does not contain consent to the specific arbitral forum under which the tribunal is constituted.[10]

3 In the Absence of a Forum, Important Differences Exist between Investment Arbitration and International Commercial Arbitration

In order to fully understand the significance that a choice of forum has in an investment agreement for finding an enforceable and effective consent to international arbitration, and to appreciate the particularities of an international arbitration based on an investment agreement, it is important to draw a distinction between the consequences of the absence of a choice of forum in international commercial arbitration and in investment arbitration.[11]

---

10 Another related principle that reinforces the lack of an enforceable and effective consent to international arbitration in the absence of a forum in an investor-State dispute settlement provision is that, in order for an arbitration agreement to be perfected and come into existence, an investor has to accept a State's offer on the same terms and conditions on which the offer was made by the State. *See, e.g., Wintershall Aktiengesellschaft v. Argentine Republic*, ICSID Case No. ARB/04/14, Award, 8 December 2008 ("*Wintershall*"), ¶ 160(2) (indicating that "the 'standing offer' ('consent') of the Host State … must be accepted on the same terms by every individual investor who seeks recourse (ultimately) to ICSID arbitration for resolving its disputes with the Host State under the concerned BIT."); Z. Douglas, THE INTERNATIONAL LAW OF INVESTMENT CLAIMS, p. 76 ("If the investor claimant, in its notice of arbitration, purports to modify those terms [of the investment agreement] in any respect, then that would constitute a counter-offer and the respondent host state would have to accept those new terms concerning the arbitral tribunal's jurisdiction in a separate legal instrument."). Thus, if an investor purports to "accept" the offer of consent to international arbitration but proposes a different forum than the one provided for in the investor-State dispute settlement provisions of the investment agreement, it would only be considered a counter-offer, which the State by no means is obliged to accept.

11 For the general distinction between investment arbitration and international commercial arbitration, *see Abaclat and Others v. Argentine Republic*, ICSID Case No. ARB/07/5, Dissenting Opinion of Professor Georges Abi-Saab to Decision on Jurisdiction and Admissibility, 4 August 2011 ("*Abaclat*, Dissent"), ¶ 6 ("This is technically an international *ad hoc* arbitral Tribunal. It is '*ad hoc*' because specially established to hear one specific case, suit or action. It is 'international' because it is rooted in two layers of international treaties: the ICSID Convention and the Bilateral Investment Treaty between Italy and Argentina. As such it functions under, and is governed by international law, and has to be clearly distinguished from 'international' commercial arbitration tribunals, such as those established within the framework of the International Chamber of Commerce, which function under national law and ultimate national judicial control. It is necessary

In international commercial arbitration, in which the relevant arbitration clauses generally provide for an arbitral seat, even in the absence of a forum (arbitral institution or rules) in the arbitration clause itself, it is usually possible to resort to the arbitral law of the seat chosen by the parties to fill in the gap on the arbitral procedure and thus to proceed with the arbitration. A domestic arbitration law will typically provide for a default procedure in the absence of an agreement on arbitral rules (*ad hoc* or institutional), in some instances with the intervention of local courts when necessary (*e.g.*, in the appointment process of the arbitral tribunal). In other words, although the arbitration clause might not contain an explicit or direct selection of the governing arbitral rules, by selecting an arbitral seat, the parties are indirectly selecting the application of the arbitral laws of that seat, which in turn will fill in all necessary procedural gaps.[12] However, in the absence of a choice of forum (institution and/or

to keep this distinction in mind, as solutions may vary at these two distinct levels; and what is sometimes permissible in municipal law, is not necessarily acceptable in international law.").

12 In the context of international commercial arbitration, a particular situation arises when the forum selected in the arbitration clause is unavailable. In those cases, several solutions are possible. State courts could designate a substitute forum when the specified forum is unavailable, or could rigorously enforce the arbitration agreement according to its terms, since the forum is an integral part of the arbitration agreement, refusing to designate a substitute forum. *See* Gary Born, International Commercial Arbitration (Kluwer Law International 2021), pp. 836–838 ("[A] related set of problems concerns arbitration clauses that select arbitral institutions that once existed, but that have ceased operations; that select arbitrators who once were competent and available, but have since become incapacitated, or passed away, that provide procedures for selecting the arbitral tribunal that are no longer operative; or otherwise become unavailable; or that select appointing authorities which refuse to fulfill the contemplated functions. In these circumstances, most national courts again endeavor to preserve the parties' basic agreement to arbitrate, even if the particular mechanics that they have chosen to implement this agreement cannot function or cannot function as intended ... Nonetheless, in exceptional cases, where a party can show that it would not have agreed to arbitrate in any other manner than that in the parties' arbitration agreement, the unavailability of the specified arbitral institution, arbitrator, or appointing authority may be held to invalidate the agreement to arbitrate ... Similarly, a few other national courts have held that, where the parties' choice of a particular arbitral institution was an essential part of their agreement to arbitrate, the unavailability of the designated institution will result in invalidity of the arbitration agreement."). In the United States, there is circuit split as to whether a court should appoint substitute arbitrators and enforce arbitration, or simply excuse parties from their obligations to arbitrate when the agreed upon forum is no longer available. *See* C. Karacic & H. Suskin, *When the Arbitration Forum Is Unavailable: What Happens Next?*, American Bar Association, 6 February 2014.

arbitral rules) and of an arbitral seat (explicitly or implicitly[13]), it may not be possible to fill in such procedural gaps and the arbitration clause could be considered "pathological."[14]

---

13 In some instances, tribunals and courts might find that there is an implicit choice of an arbitral seat. *See, e.g.*, G. Born, INTERNATIONAL COMMERCIAL ARBITRATION, p. 2227 ("In many cases, these various references ['to the "situs," "venue" or "forum" of the arbitration'] are interpreted as implied specifications of the arbitral seat"), nn. 139 (citing several cases confirming this approach), 170 (citing "*Judgment of 26 June 2000, 8 SchH 01/00* (*Brandenburgisches Oberlandesgericht*)", where the "parties had impliedly agreed that the place of arbitration should be in Germany because contracts were in German, referred to German standard forms, were subject to German law, and obligations were to be performed in Germany"). Tribunals and courts might specifically resort to national laws to determine the arbitral seat in the absence of an arbitral institution. *See, e.g.*, UNCITRAL Model Law (2006), Article 20(1) ("The parties are free to agree on the place of arbitration. Failing such agreement, the place of arbitration shall be determined by the arbitral tribunal having regard to the circumstances of the case, including the convenience of the parties."). According to Gary Born, "[e]ven in the absence of arbitration legislation granting an arbitral tribunal default authority to select the arbitral seat, this authority should be implied (absent contrary agreement)". G. Born, INTERNATIONAL COMMERCIAL ARBITRATION, p. 2260. Moreover, according to the same author, "[a]bsent ... (implied) agreement [of the seat], the court should determine where the arbitral tribunal impliedly seated the arbitration ... This inquiry requires consideration of the conduct of the arbitration, rather than the parties' underlying contractual relationship. In particular, this inquiry is directed towards ascertaining the national arbitration law that was applied, or assumed to apply, in the arbitration. References to national arbitration legislation, judicial decisions, standards of national arbitration law, procedural requirements or practices, choice-of-law rules and the location of the arbitral hearings will be relevant in this analysis." G. Born, INTERNATIONAL COMMERCIAL ARBITRATION, pp. 2268–2269, n. 376.

14 Broadly speaking, a "pathological" arbitration clause is an arbitration agreement that is in some way defective. This term was coined by Frédéric Eisemann, former Secretary General of the ICC Court of Arbitration, in his often-cited publication "*La Clause d'arbitrage pathologique*" (1974). In his view, a "pathological" arbitration clause is "any arbitration clause which, by its wording[,] cannot fulfill its essential functions", which are the following: "(1) ... to produce mandatory consequences for the parties, (2) ... to exclude the intervention of state courts in the settlement of the disputes, at least before the issuance of the award, (3) ... to give powers to the arbitrators to resolve the disputes likely to arise between the parties, [and] (4) ... to permit the putting in place of a procedure leading under the best conditions of efficiency and rapidity to the rendering of an award that is susceptible of judicial enforcement." *See* G. Born, M. Angelini & C. Alcoberro Llivina, *Chapter 4: Rethinking "Pathological" Arbitration Clauses: Validating Imperfect Arbitration Agreements*, in S. Tung, F. Fortese, *et al.* (eds.), FINANCES IN INTERNATIONAL ARBITRATION: LIBER AMICORUM PATRICIA SHAUGHNESSY 35 (Kluwer Law International 2019), p. 35; Frédéric Eisemann, *La Clause d'arbitrage pathologique*, in COMMERCIAL ARBITRATION: ESSAYS IN MEMORIAM EUGENIO MINOLI 129 (Unione

In turn, in investment arbitration, where the relevant investment agreement contains a unilateral offer to submit disputes to international arbitration in its investor-State dispute settlement provision, the arbitration agreement is formed by a two-step process, which is generally referred to as "arbitration without privity": an offer made by the host State in the dispute settlement provision of the investment agreement followed by an acceptance by the foreign investor of the home State – either by a communication to the host State accepting the offer or by initiating an international arbitration against the host State. Thus, in bilateral or multilateral investment agreements, there are multiple offers to submit potential investor-State disputes to international arbitration by two or more States. Due to the particular nature of investment arbitration, such offers do not contain references to an arbitral seat.[15] Consequently, in the absence of a forum and an arbitral seat in the investment agreement, there is no default domestic arbitral law to apply, nor a domestic court to which the investor could resort to fill in the gaps caused by these absences in order to make the provision operative.[16]

Tipografico-Editrice Torinese 1974), p. 129. Truly "pathological" arbitration clauses could – at worst – "prevent the arbitration from taking place at all," "where it is impossible to infer an intention which is sufficiently coherent and effective to enable the arbitration to function," or – at best – "give rise to associated litigation, fueling the arguments of the party attempting to avoid arbitration and making the overall process more time-consuming and expensive." E. Gaillard & J. Savage, FOUCHARD GAILLARD GOLDMAN ON INTERNATIONAL COMMERCIAL ARBITRATION (Kluwer Law International 1999), p. 263. In other words, these "pathological" arbitration clauses could be "either incapable of enforcement or precursors to uncertain and costly litigation in national courts." G. Born, INTERNATIONAL COMMERCIAL ARBITRATION, p. 252.

15 In investment arbitration, the arbitral seat will typically be agreed upon by the parties at the beginning of the arbitration or, absent an agreement, will be determined by the arbitral tribunal itself. Often (but not always) the arbitral seat will be the place where the arbitral institution that administers the arbitration is located (*e.g.*, ICC, in Paris; PCA, in The Hague; ICSID, in Washington, D.C.). However, the parties could take into account other practical considerations when electing an arbitral seat at a different location. The arbitral seat will be of utmost importance in most arbitral proceedings (except for arbitrations conducted under the ICSID Convention, which provides a self-contained system) since it will determine the place where the non-prevailing party will have to apply to set aside the arbitral award if it considers that there are valid grounds to challenge it.

16 *See also* Convention on the Recognition and Enforcement of Foreign Arbitral Awards (1958) (New York Convention), Article II(1) ("1. Each Contracting State shall recognize an agreement in writing under which the parties undertake to submit to arbitration all or any differences which have arisen or which may arise between them in respect of a defined legal relationship, whether contractual or not, concerning a subject matter capable of settlement by arbitration. 2. The term 'agreement in writing' shall include an arbitral clause in a contract or an arbitration agreement, signed by the parties or contained in an exchange of letters or telegrams. 3. The court of a Contracting State, when seized of an action in a matter in respect of which the parties have made an agreement

4 Institutional Arbitral Rules Require Forum-Specific Consent

Institutional arbitral rules specifically require the submission of a dispute to that particular forum. For instance, for an ICC tribunal to find that there is consent to ICC arbitration, the parties must agree not only to submit disputes to international arbitration generally, but also to submit disputes to ICC arbitration in particular. Thus, if a dispute settlement provision in an investment agreement only provides for disputes to be submitted to international arbitration in general (or to a different forum, such as ICSID or UNCITRAL Rules), an arbitral tribunal constituted under the ICC Rules of Arbitration ("ICC Rules") would not be able to find that it has jurisdiction under the ICC Rules to hear the dispute since there is no specific submission to that particular forum. The same is true for other arbitration rules such as the UNCITRAL Rules, ICSID Additional Facility and ICSID (the latter of which also has additional requirements).

A survey of the frequently used arbitral rules in investment cases confirm this principle.[17] For instance, the jurisdiction of an ICSID tribunal is governed by Article 25 of the ICSID Convention, which provides that the parties to the dispute have to "consent in writing to submit to [ICSID]."[18] Likewise,

---

within the meaning of this article, shall, at the request of one of the parties, refer the parties to arbitration, unless it finds that the said agreement is null and void, inoperative or incapable of being performed.").

17 The most frequently used rules in investment arbitration cases are the arbitration rules of ICSID, ICSID Additional Facility, the ICC, the Stockholm Chamber of Commerce ("SCC"), and the UNCITRAL Rules. According to information compiled by the United Nations Conference on Trade and Development ("UNCTAD") (as of November 1, 2022), the arbitration rules applied to the 1190 known investment cases were the following: ICSID Rules (644 cases), UNCITRAL Rules (368 cases), ICSID Additional Facility Rules (66 cases), SCC Rules (53 cases) and ICC Rules (22 cases). *See* UNCTAD, Investment Poly Hub, *available at* investmentpolicy.unctad.org/investment-dispute-settlement. Other arbitration rules that were applied to investment cases in a few instances, or that could potentially be applied, are the rules of the London Court of International Arbitration ("LCIA"), the PCA and the Singapore International Arbitration Centre ("SIAC").

18 Accordingly, Rule 1(1) of the ICSID Arbitration Rules (2022) provides that "[t]hese Rules shall apply to any arbitration proceeding conducted under the [ICSID] Convention." *See also Planet Mining Pty Ltd. v. Republic of Indonesia*, ICSID Case No. ARB/12/14 and 12/40, Decision on Jurisdiction, 24 February 2014 ("*Planet Mining*"), ¶ 146 ("Article 25 of the ICSID Convention requires consent of the Parties to be bound to arbitrate under the ICSID regime."); Eric de Brabandere, *Importing Consent to ICSID Arbitration? A Critical Appraisal of Garanti Koza v. Turkmenistan*, 5(2) INTERNATIONAL INSTITUTE FOR SUSTAINABLE DEVELOPMENT INVESTMENT TREATY NEWS (2014), p. 15 ("[I]t should not be forgotten that consent to ICSID arbitration, as opposed to arbitration generally, is not only subject to the general rules of consent to jurisdiction applicable in international law, but is specifically addressed in Article 25 [of the] ICSID Convention which requires

jurisdiction of a tribunal constituted under the ICSID Additional Facility Rules (2022) requires "consent in writing" to the submission of disputes under those rules.[19]

In a similar vein, the UNCITRAL Rules (2021) address their "scope of application" in Article 1, which provides that if the "parties have agreed that disputes between them in respect of a defined legal relationship, whether contractual or not, shall be referred to arbitration under the UNCITRAL Arbitration Rules, then such disputes shall be settled in accordance with these Rules subject to such modification as the parties may agree."[20] In other words, in order

'consent in writing'."); *Garanti Koza*, Dissent, ¶ 47 ("Article 25 of the ICSID Convention requires that the parties to the dispute 'consent in writing' to submit that dispute to the Centre."); Andrea Steingruber, CONSENT IN INTERNATIONAL ARBITRATION (Oxford University Press 2012), p. 202 ("The vast majority of BITS contain clauses which make reference to investment arbitration. Numerous dispute settlement clauses in BITS offer several alternative forms of arbitration. However, only those that contain clear and unequivocal consent by the contracting State parties to ICSID dispute-settlement mechanism will automatically determine the existence of an ICSID arbitration clause and, by the same token, of ICSID jurisdiction, subject always to the proviso that consent in writing be given by the investor of a contracting State party in such a way as to amount to 'the act or result of coming into harmony or accord', *ie* of reaching mutual consent.").

19 Rule 1(1) of the ICSID Additional Facility Arbitration Rules (2022) states that "[t]hese Rules shall apply to any arbitration proceeding conducted pursuant to the ICSID Additional Facility Rules." It is important to stress that consent to international arbitration under the ICSID Convention is not equivalent to consent to international arbitration under the ICSID Additional Facility Rules. In those cases in which the ICSID Convention is no longer available (typically because one of the contracting parties to the investment agreement denounced the ICSID Convention and is no longer an ICSID contracting State), specific consent to the application of the ICSID Additional Facility Rules is required from the parties to the dispute, and thus a mere offer of consent to ICSID arbitration by the host State alone would not be sufficient. *See Kimberly-Clark Dutch Holdings, B.V., Kimberly-Clark S.L.U., and Kimberly-Clark BVBA v. Bolivarian Republic of Venezuela*, ICSID Case No. ARB(AF)/18/3, Award, 5 November 2021 ("*Kimberly-Clark*"), ¶¶ 228–229 ("[T]he provision for the submission of disputes to ICSID, which is established by the Convention, can only be understood as consent to arbitration under the Convention … [E]ven if one were to accept that ICSID is merely referenced as an arbitral institution, *quod non*, that would not suffice to establish consent to arbitration under the AF [Additional Facility] Rules. These Rules were issued in 1978 by the Administrative Council of ICSID to authorize the Secretariat to administer disputes falling outside ICSID's jurisdiction as it is defined by Article 25 of the Convention. The AF mechanism is thus a dispute settlement method that is distinct from ICSID Convention arbitration. It is governed by the national arbitration law of the seat of the arbitration and by the AF Rules, unlike ICSID arbitration that is subject to international law and to the ICSID Arbitration Rules. Hence, consent to AF arbitration must be manifested as such.").

20 *See also* J. Paulsson & G. Petrochilos, UNCITRAL ARBITRATION (Kluwer Law International 2017), p. 4, ¶ 1 ("Article 1 … [addresses] the scope of application of the Rules. It [stipulates]

for an UNCITRAL tribunal to find jurisdiction over a particular dispute based on an investment agreement, it should find that the host State consented not only to "international arbitration," but also specifically to international arbitration under the UNCITRAL Rules. Otherwise, even if an UNCITRAL arbitral tribunal were to conclude that the dispute settlement provision of the investment agreement should be construed as general consent to international arbitration, it would not have jurisdiction over that particular dispute unless it also finds that the host State consented specifically to the application of the UNCITRAL Rules.

The same is true with respect to the ICC Rules.[21] This principle has been acknowledged by Craig, Park and Paulsson in their famous commentary to the ICC Rules, expressing that "in order to be able to rely on the ICC arbitral mechanism irrespective of the defendant's attitude at the time of dispute, one must have a clear expression of intent not only to arbitrate, but also to have the arbitration take place under the ICC Rules."[22]

---

the fundamental principle that for the UNCITRAL Rules to apply, the parties must express their intent to arbitrate under the UNCITRAL Rules."); C. Croft, C. Kee & J. Waincymer, A GUIDE TO THE UNCITRAL ARBITRATION RULES (Cambridge University Press 2013), p. 12 ("Article 1 addresses the applicability of the UNCITRAL Arbitration Rules. Article 1(1) refers to their application based on an agreement between the parties to that effect."). The 2010 version of the UNCITRAL Rules is virtually identical and the 1976 version contains a similar provision. In addition, it should be noted that a potential procedural agreement between the parties in an arbitration proceeding about which version of the UNCITRAL Rules should apply in a particular case cannot not be construed as a substantive agreement on the application of the UNCITRAL Rules to that dispute. A distinction should be made between a "procedural agreement" to apply the UNCITRAL Rules (or any other rules) – for purposes of constituting an arbitral tribunal and agreeing on certain procedural issues in order to object to the jurisdiction of the tribunal – and a "substantive agreement" to apply those rules. *See* n. 232, *infra*.

21 There are multiple examples throughout the ICC Rules (2021) in support of this principle. For instance, Article 6(1) provides that if "the parties have agreed to submit to arbitration under the Rules, they shall be deemed to have submitted *ipso facto* to the Rules in effect on the date of commencement of the arbitration, unless they have agreed to submit to the Rules in effect on the date of their arbitration agreement." Similarly, Article 6(2) of the ICC Rules provides that "[b]y agreeing to arbitration under the Rules, the parties have accepted that the arbitration shall be administered by the Court." *See also* ICC Commission Report, *States, State Entities and ICC Arbitration* (2017), ¶ 12 ("In order to provide for ICC arbitration, a clause or provision should be incorporated into the relevant contract, BIT, investment treaty or domestic investment law.").

22 L. Craig, W. Park & J. Paulsson, INTERNATIONAL CHAMBER OF COMMERCE ARBITRATION (Oceana Publications, ICC Publishing 2000), p. 85, ¶ 6.01. *See also* E. Schwartz & Y. Derains, A GUIDE TO THE ICC RULES OF ARBITRATION (Kluwer Law International 2005), pp. 74–86.

Other arbitral rules which are sometimes used in investment cases, such as the arbitration rules of the SCC, the LCIA, the PCA or the SIAC, also embrace the same principle.[23]

---

23 *See* SCC Arbitration Rules (2017), p. 2 ("Under any arbitration agreement referring to the Arbitration Rules of the Arbitration Institute of the Stockholm Chamber of Commerce ... the parties shall be deemed to have agreed that the following rules, or such amended rules, in force on the date of the commencement of the arbitration, or the filing of an application for the appointment of an Emergency Arbitrator, shall be applied unless otherwise agreed by the parties."); J. Ragnwaldh, F. Andersson & C. Salinas Quero, A GUIDE TO THE SCC ARBITRATION RULES (Kluwer Law International 2019), pp. 26 ("Upon receipt of the Request for Arbitration, the SCC will examine the arbitration agreement under which the claims are brought. The arbitration agreement can consist of a clause included in the main contract or be in the form of a stand-alone arbitration agreement ... The arbitration agreement can also consist of a provision in a treaty giving investors the right to initiate SCC arbitration against the host state which, together with the consent by the investor, constitutes an agreement to arbitrate."), 37 ("The SCC's jurisdiction to administer a case derives from the arbitration agreement, where the parties consent to refer their disputes to the SCC, as opposed to referring their dispute to another arbitral institution or to ad hoc arbitration."); LCIA Arbitration Rules (2014) – Notes for Parties, ¶ 12 ("Since arbitration is a consensual process, a party who wishes to use the LCIA Arbitration Rules must first agree with the other parties to the transaction or the dispute (most usually at the time of contracting or once a dispute has arisen) that their dispute should be resolved by arbitration under the Rules. If there is no pre-existing agreement and one party wishes to refer a dispute to the LCIA, but the other does not, the LCIA will not be able to assist the parties with their dispute."); M. Scherer, L. Richman & R. Gerbay, ARBITRATING UNDER THE 2014 LCIA RULES: A USER'S GUIDE, p. 29 ("The parties are free to draft an Arbitration Agreement in their own words, referring their dispute to arbitration under the LCIA Rules ... At a strict minimum, the clause must contain ... [an] agreement to arbitrate, [a] definition of the scope of the disputes submitted to arbitration and [a] choice of the LCIA as the arbitral institution and incorporation of its Rules"); P. Turner & R. Mohtashami, A GUIDE TO THE LCIA ARBITRATION RULES (Oxford University Press 2009), ¶ 3.08 ("Upon its receipt, the Registrar reviews the Request (and any accompanying documents) in order to determine that it contains the information required to be included in a Request under the [LCIA] Rules, in particular, to determine the existence of an arbitration agreement providing for the adjudication of the parties' dispute under the [LCIA] Rules"); PCA Arbitration Rules (2012), Article 1(1) ("Where a State, State-controlled entity, or intergovernmental organization has agreed with one or more States, State-controlled entities, intergovernmental organizations, or private parties that disputes between them in respect of a defined legal relationship, whether contractual, treaty-based, or otherwise, shall be referred to arbitration under the Permanent Court of Arbitration Rules 2012 ..., then such disputes shall be settled in accordance with these Rules subject to such modification as the parties may agree."); SIAC Arbitration Rules (2016), Article 1.1 ("Where the parties have agreed to refer their disputes to SIAC for arbitration or to arbitration in accordance with the SIAC Rules, the parties shall be deemed to have agreed that the arbitration shall be conducted pursuant to and administered by SIAC in accordance with

5 Distinction between Interpretation of Dispute Settlement Provisions and Standard of Proof of State Consent to International Arbitration in Investment Agreements

The "pro-arbitration" stance that would typically guide an international commercial arbitration[24] is not applicable in investment arbitration, where the general rule is that the State exceptionally limits its sovereignty.[25] Moreover, the interpretation of treaty provisions should be distinguished from the interpretation of arbitration clauses in contracts. Pursuant to the Vienna Convention on the Law of Treaties ("Vienna Convention"), treaty provisions should be interpreted objectively – the alleged subjective intention of the contracting States being irrelevant[26] – while in contractual interpretation the

---

these Rules."); J. Choong, M. Mangan & N. Lingard, A GUIDE TO THE SIAC ARBITRATION RULES (Oxford University Press 2018), ¶ 5.03 ("Consent is a pre-condition of any arbitration. Thus, parties must agree to refer a dispute to SIAC for the SIAC Rules to apply. Where there is such an agreement, the version of the SIAC Rules in force at the time the arbitration commences will apply to the dispute, unless the parties have agreed otherwise.").

24 *See* G. Born, INTERNATIONAL COMMERCIAL ARBITRATION, pp. 1431–1448 (observing that, "[i]n a substantial majority of all jurisdictions, national law provides that international arbitration agreements should be interpreted in light of a 'pro-arbitration' presumption").

25 *See* pp. 24–27, *infra*. Some investment tribunals that have rendered questionable interpretations of dispute settlement provisions in investment agreements, finding consent to international arbitration even in the absence of a forum, seem to have surreptitiously relied in their reasonings on the "pro-arbitration" presumption generally applied in international commercial arbitration.

26 *See* Luigi Sbolci, *Interpretation of Treaties – Supplementary Means of Treaty Interpretation*, in Enzo Cannizzaro (ed.), THE LAW OF TREATIES BEYOND THE VIENNA CONVENTION 145 (Oxford University Press 2011), p. 146 ("Prior to the Vienna Convention, the debate on the general rules of treaty interpretation revolved around the identification of material criteria of interpretation that could be used to determine the precise content of a treaty rule … [T]he debate mainly focused on methodology, and above all on whether preference was to be accorded to a subjective or an objective method of treaty interpretation … The debate on these and other problematic aspects of treaty interpretation continued until the Vienna Conference, when states codified in Article 31 the objective method as the general rule of treaty interpretation. The main elements characterizing the subjective method were then incorporated, as supplementary means of interpretation, within the framework of Article 32"); ILC, *Draft Articles on the Law of Treaties with Commentaries*, p. 220, ¶ 11 ("The article as already indicated is based on the view that the text must be presumed to be the authentic expression of the intentions of the parties; and that, in consequence, the starting point of interpretation is the elucidation of the meaning of the text, not an *ab initio* into the intention of the parties. The Institute of International Law adopted this – the textual – approach to treaty interpretation. The objections to giving too large a place to the intentions of the parties as an independent basis of interpretation find expression in the proceedings of the Institute. The textual approach, on

subjective intention of the parties may be relevant depending on the applicable law.

Thus, the interpretation of treaty provisions, including dispute settlement provisions, should be conducted by following the interpretive rules of the Vienna Convention, starting from the textual interpretation of the provision

---

the other hand, commends itself by the fact that, as one authority has put it, '*the text signed is, save for rare exceptions, the only and most recent expression of common will of the parties*'. Moreover, the jurisprudence of the International Court contains many pronouncements from which it is permissible to conclude that the textual approach to treaty interpretation is regarded by it as established law. In particular, the Court has more than once stressed that it is not the function of interpretation to revise treaties or to reach into them what they do not, expressly or by implication, contain.") (partial translation); Sir Ian Sinclair, THE VIENNA CONVENTION ON THE LAW OF TREATIES (Manchester University Press 1984), p. 115 ("The Commission's proposals (which were adopted virtually without change by the Conference and are now reflected in Articles 31 and 32 of the Convention) were clearly based on the view that the text of a treaty must be presumed to be the authentic expression of the intentions of the parties; the Commission accordingly came down firmly in favor of the view that 'the starting point of interpretation is the elucidation of the meaning of the text, not an investigation *ab initio* into the intentions of the parties'."); Trinh Hai Yen, THE INTERPRETATION OF INVESTMENT TREATIES (Brill 2014), p. 79 ("Subjective interpretation of a treaty term, which is not based on interpretive guidance required or authorized under international law is very likely to result in inconsistent awards with unintended findings on the matter of laws."); Anthony Aust, MODERN TREATY LAW AND PRACTICE (Cambridge University Press 2013), p. 217 ("[Article 31] is limited to the primary purpose for interpreting a treaty; an elucidation of the meaning of the text, not a fresh investigation as to the supposed intentions of the parties."); *Land, Island and Maritime Frontier Dispute* (*El Salvador v. Honduras: Nicaragua intervening*), Separate Opinion of Judge Torres Bernárdez, ICJ REPORTS 629 (1992), p. 718, ¶ 189 ("[The] rules of treaty interpretation disregard any intentions of the parties to the treaty as a subjective element distinct from the text of the treaty. Subjective intentions alien to the text of the treaty, particularly *a posteriori* subjective intentions, should play no role in the interpretation."); *Case Concerning Right of Passage over Indian Territory* (*Portugal v. India*), Decision on Preliminary Objections, Dissenting Opinion of Judge Chagla, ICJ REPORTS 166 (1957), p. 167 ("No canon of construction is more firmly established than the one which lays down that the intention of a party to an instrument must be gathered from the instrument itself and not from what the party says its intention was."); *The Rompetrol Group N.V. v. Romania*, ICSID Case No. ARB/06/3, Decision on Respondent's Preliminary Objections on Jurisdiction and Admissibility, 18 April 2008, ¶ 109 (indicating that the question "is not what the Parties to this bilateral treaty might (or might not) conceivably have intended, but what they actually did, and the evidence for that is the terms of the treaty they concluded. That, so far as the Tribunal can see, is what the Vienna Convention requires."). The only exception in which the subjective interpretation is relevant under the Vienna Convention is in the case of Article 31(4), which provides that "[a] special meaning shall be given to a term if it is established that the parties so intended."

in its relevant context.[27] That means that words or phrases contained in the provision should not be interpreted in isolation. On the contrary, in order to capture the words' true meaning, they have to be interpreted taking into account their connection with the words or phrases found in the rest of the provision and the context in which they are found.[28]

On many occasions, investment tribunals that depart from the text of dispute settlement provisions in investment agreements in order to make extensive interpretations, or to find consent to international arbitration where there is none, have justified their decisions on the basis of: (i) the object and purpose of the investment agreement; (ii) the principle of good faith; and (iii) the principle of *effet utile*.[29] However, those are usually "red herrings" derived from

---

27 Vienna Convention on the Law of Treaties (1969), Article 31(1) ("A treaty shall be interpreted in good faith in accordance with the ordinary meaning to be given to the terms of the treaty in their context and in the light of its object and purpose."). *See Competence of the General Assembly for the Admission of a State to the United Nations*, Advisory Opinion, ICJ REPORTS 4 (1950), p. 8 ("[T]he first duty of a tribunal which is called upon to interpret and apply the provisions of a treaty, is to endeavor to give effect to them in their natural and ordinary meaning in the context in which they occur ... If the relevant words in their natural and ordinary meaning make sense in their context, that is an end of the matter."); *Wintershall*, ¶ 79 ("[W]here the ordinary meaning of words (the text) is clear and they make sense in the context, there is no occasion at all to have recourse to other means of interpretation."); Sir Humphrey Waldock, Special Rapporteur, *Third Report on the Law of Treaties*, A/CN.4/167, YEARBOOK OF THE IIC (1964-II), p. 54 (noting that, when construing a treaty, "the particular arrangement of the words and sentences" and "their relation to each other and to other parts of the document" are "considerations which have first to be appreciated by the interpreter."); *Garanti Koza*, Dissent, ¶ 64 ("The literal and ordinary meaning of Article 8(2) has to be given full effect to determine whether or not consent to ICSID arbitration exists. Any other interpretation would lead to an artificial construction.").

28 *See* pp. 38–39, *infra*.

29 *See, e.g.*, *Michael Anthony Lee-Chin v. Dominical Republic*, ICSID Case No. UNCT/18/3, Partial Award on Jurisdiction, 15 July 2020 ("*Lee-Chin*, Partial Award"), ¶ 152 ("The settlement of disputes arising between an investor and a Contracting Party to the Treaty is actually the object and purpose of Article XIII. These considerations do not imply that the majority of the Tribunal deems the drafting of Article XIII to be perfect. However, no good faith interpretation of the phrase under analysis, of paragraph 2, and of Article XIII in general can ignore the fact that those texts have been drafted so as to allow, not prevent, the settlement of disputes."); *Michael Anthony Lee-Chin v. Dominican Republic*, ICSID Case No. UNCT/18/3, Dissenting Opinion of Professor Marcelo Kohen, 10 July 2020 ("*Lee-Chin*, Dissent"), ¶¶ 38–40 ("The Treaty is an 'agreement on reciprocal promotion and protection of investments.' There is no preamble. Article II defines such object and purpose and provides that '[e]ach Party shall in its territory promote, as far as possible, the investment made in its territory by investors of the other Party and shall admit these investments in accordance with its laws.' ... [I]t does not follow from the object and

misapplications of these concepts and principles. First, the purported "object and purpose" of an investment agreement cannot be an excuse to override the explicit language of a dispute settlement provision.[30] Second, the principle

purpose of the Treaty that Article XIII should be interpreted as granting a right to the investor to decide which of the three dispute settlement mechanisms under Article XIII shall be used."), 42 ("The Partial Award refers repeatedly to the interpretation in good faith of different paragraphs of Article XIII in support of the arguments presented. It is unclear whether good faith adds something to the reasoning followed or it is mentioned to suggest that any other interpretation would not be in good faith."); *Lee-Chin*, Partial Award, ¶ 118 ("The *effet utile* of the provision that establishes the obligation to submit a dispute to arbitration ... is to serve as an offer of consent."); G. Lampo & G. Minervini, *Michael Anthony Lee-Chin v Dominican Republic: Interpreting the Consent to Arbitrate in the CARICOM–DR FTA*, 36(3) ICSID REVIEW 506 (2021), pp. 513–514 ("[T]he majority [in *Lee-Chin v. Dominican Republic*] supported its contention with three main arguments: (i) the *effet utile* doctrine, in the sense that the only way in which a provision establishing the obligation to submit a dispute to arbitration could be useful is to serve as an offer of consent ... [T]he reliance on the *effet utile* – or 'useful effect' – doctrine seems misplaced ... [T]he Tribunal appears to have disregarded the wording of the treaty (the 'may agree to refer', contained in the second paragraph of article XIII) by relying on the useful effect doctrine. Furthermore, the *effet utile*, according to the Tribunal, would be that of serving as an offer of consent; however, if the clause were to be interpreted as not containing an offer to arbitrate, it would not be inutile, inasmuch as it would still create an obligation, *ie* to later negotiate with the investor and eventually grant the consent to arbitrate the dispute. Thus, to argue that an obligation to submit a dispute to arbitration only makes sense if interpreted as an offer to arbitrate seems to distort the treaty's meaning. This is confirmed by the very existence of various IIAs whose arbitration clauses require case-by-case consent.").

30 *See, e.g., ICS Inspection and Control Services Limited (United Kingdom) v. Republic of Argentina*, UNCITRAL/PCA Case No. 2010-9, Award on Jurisdiction, 10 February 2012 ("*ICS*"), ¶ 281 ("A finding of no jurisdiction should not therefore be treated as a defect in a treaty scheme that runs counter to its object and purpose in providing for substantive investment protection".); Richard K. Gardiner, TREATY INTERPRETATION (Oxford University Press 2008), p. 219 ("[T]he object and purpose of a treaty cannot be used to alter the clear meaning of a term of treaty."); Mark E. Villiger, COMMENTARY ON THE 1969 VIENNA CONVENTION ON THE LAW OF TREATIES (Martinus Nijhoff 2009), p. 428 ("Interpretation in the light of a treaty's object and purpose finds its limits in the treaty text itself. One of the (originally many possible) ordinary meanings will eventually prevail. In other words, Article 31 avoids an extreme functional interpretation which may, in fact, lead to 'legislation' or the revision of a treaty."); J. Romesh Weeramantry, TREATY INTERPRETATION IN INVESTMENT ARBITRATION (Oxford University Press 2012), p. 68 (noting that international tribunals have consistently refrained from using the object and purpose of a treaty to arrive at an interpretation that displaces the clear meaning of a treaty's text); *United States v. Iran*, Dec. No. 130-A28-FT, Decision, 19 December 2000, 36 IRAN-US CLAIMS TRIBUNAL REPORTS 5, ¶ 58 ("The object and purpose is not to be considered in isolation from the terms of the treaty; it is intrinsic to its text. It follows that, under Article 31 of the Vienna Convention, a treaty's object and purpose is to be used only to clarify the text, not to provide independent sources of meaning that contradict the clear text.");

of good faith cannot have the effect of adding words or obligations that the provision does not contain.[31] Third, the principle of *effet utile* cannot be used

---

Venezuela US, S.R.L. v. Bolivarian Republic of Venezuela, PCA Case No. 2013-34, Dissenting Opinion of Professor Marcelo G. Kohen (on the Respondent's Objection to Jurisdiction *Ratione Voluntatis*), 26 July 2016 ("*Venezuela US*, Dissent"), ¶ 49 ("The promotion and protection of foreign private investment does not necessarily require the establishment of international arbitration at the disposal of investors as an inherent and indispensable element of BITs, as international conventional practice in general and contracts concluded between foreign investors and States demonstrate. Many of them do not establish international arbitration and constitute nevertheless BITs or contracts providing for other dispute settlement mechanisms, including domestic fora. Hence, the object and purpose of the BIT does not allow an interpretation of Article 8 as establishing that States parties consent to international arbitration with investors in other circumstances than those established in the Article itself."); *Plama Consortium Limited v. Republic of Bulgaria*, ICSID Case No. ARB/03/24, Decision on Jurisdiction, 8 February 2005 ("*Plama*"), ¶ 193 ("[T]he Tribunal is mindful of Sir Ian Sinclair's warning of the 'risk that the placing of undue emphasis on the "object and purpose" of a treaty will encourage teleological methods of interpretation [which], in some of its more extreme forms, will even deny the relevance of the intentions of the parties'."); A. Aust, MODERN TREATY LAW AND PRACTICE, p. 209 ("[A]lthough paragraph (1) [of Article 31 of the Vienna Convention] contains both the textual (or literal) and the effectiveness (or teleological) approaches, it gives precedence to the textual.").

31 *See, e.g.*, *Land and Maritime Boundary between Cameroon and Nigeria* (*Cameroon v. Nigeria*), Preliminary Objections, Judgment, 11 June 1998, ICJ REPORTS 275 (1998), ¶¶ 39, 59 (holding that "the principle of good faith ... relate[s] only to the fulfillment of existing obligations" and "is not in itself a source of obligation where none would otherwise exist."); *Border and Transborder Armed Actions* (*Nicaragua v. Honduras*), Jurisdiction and Admissibility, Judgment, 20 December 1988, ICJ REPORTS 69 (1988), ¶ 94 ("The principle of good faith ... is not in itself a source of obligation where none would otherwise exist."); *Regina v. Immigration Officer at Prague Airport and another* (*Respondents*) *ex parte European Roma Rights Centre* (*Appellants*), 9 December 2004, UKHL 55 (2004), ¶ 19 ("Taken together [*i.e.*, the good faith requirements of Articles 26 and 31(1) of the Vienna Convention], these rules call for good faith in the interpretation and performance of a treaty, and neither rule is open to question. But there is no want of good faith if a state interprets a treaty as meaning what it says and declines to do anything significantly greater than or different from what it agreed to do. The principle that *pacta sunt servanda* cannot require departure from what has been agreed. This is the more obviously true where a state or states very deliberately decided what they were and were not willing to undertake to do."); R. Gardiner, TREATY INTERPRETATION, p. 155 ("It seems clear that the approach indicated above and in the Vienna rules aims to elucidate what is unclear in the text of a treaty, not to invoke good faith in order to fill gaps in a manner which would impose additional obligations."); *Daimler Financial Services AG v. Argentine Republic*, ICSID Case No. ARB/05/1, Award, 22 August 2012 ("*Daimler*"), ¶ 173 ("While [Article 31(1) of the Vienna Convention] does not explicitly mention consent, the reference to 'good faith' nevertheless reinforces the duty of tribunals to limit themselves to interpretations falling within the bounds of the framework mutually agreed to by the contracting state parties."); T. Yen, THE INTERPRETATION OF INVESTMENT TREATIES, p. 46 ("The reason for the

to rewrite dispute settlement provisions or to render interpretations that are contrary to their clear and explicit terms.[32]

---

low number of decisions and awards resorting to this principle [of good faith] might be that if a tribunal has employed other interpretive aids under the [Vienna Convention] and has been able to deduce some meaning of a treaty term, it has complied with the requirement to interpret treaties in good faith, with or without explicit reference to it. On the contrary, if adjudicators rely solely on this principle and neglect other means of interpretation, they have not followed the required guidance under Article 31 of the [Vienna Convention] to ascertain intended meanings of treaty terms. Then the requirement of good faith interpretation would become a blanket authorization for subjective findings of legal issues. In this situation, the principle is misapplied because in the integrated formulation of Article 31(1), good faith must be accompanied with the application of the other interpretive elements. It is not a stand-alone guidance.").

32 *See, e.g.*, *ConocoPhillips Petrozuata B.V. and Others v. Bolivarian Republic of Venezuela*, ICSID Case No. ARB/07/30, Decision on Jurisdiction and Merits, 3 September 2013 ("*ConocoPhillips*"), ¶ 259 ("The principle of effective interpretation does not enable a court or tribunal to rewrite the provision that it is interpreting, in particular, by writing words out of the text."); G. Lampo & G. Minervini, *Michael Anthony Lee-Chin v Dominican Republic: Interpreting the Consent to Arbitrate in the CARICOM–DR FTA*, p. 514 ("[T]he use of the *effet utile* argument cannot serve the purpose of rewriting a poorly written treaty clause."); *Cemex Caracas Investments B.V. and Other v. Bolivarian Republic of Venezuela*, ICSID Case No. ARB/08/15, Decision on Jurisdiction, 30 December 2010 ("*Cemex*"), ¶ 114 ("In this respect one must recall that this principle does not require that a maximum effect be given to a text. It only excludes interpretations which would render the text meaningless, when a meaningful interpretation is possible."); *OPIC Karium Corp. v. Bolivarian Republic of Venezuela*, ICSID Case No. ARB/10/14, Award, 28 May 2013 ("*OPIC*"), ¶ 105 ("The Tribunal is of the view that the text of Article 22 is ambiguous. As there is more than one possible interpretation of Article 22, the principle of *effet utile* is not of itself capable of altering this conclusion or providing a clearer view one way or the other."); *Wintershall*, ¶ 84 (citing "*Interpretation of Peace Treaties with Bulgaria, Hungary and Romania*," (Second Phase), Advisory Opinion, 18 July 1950, ICJ REPORTS 221 (1950), p. 229) ("The ICJ said that the principle expressed in the maxim *Ut res magis valeat quam pereat*, often referred to as the rule of effectiveness, could not justify the Court in attributing to the provisions for settlement of disputes in the Peace Treaties a meaning which would be contrary to their letter and spirit. The Court then went on to say: 'The failure of machinery for settling disputes by reason of the practical impossibility of creating the Commission provided for in the Treaties is one thing; international responsibility is another. The breach of a treaty obligation cannot be remedied by creating a Commission which is not the kind of Commission contemplated by the Treaties. It is the duty of the Court to interpret the Treaties, not to revise them.' If this be the duty of an international court, the duty of an ICSID Tribunal is no different."); *Banro American Resources, Inc. and Societe Aurifere du Kivu et du Maniema S.A.R.L. v. Democratic Republic of the Congo*, ICSID Case No. ARB/98/7, Award of the Tribunal, 1 September 2000, ¶ 6 ("The Tribunal is certainly aware of the general principle of interpretation whereby a text ought to be interpreted in the manner that gives it effect – *ut magis valeat quam pereat*. However, this principle of interpretation should not lead to confer, a posteriori, to a provision deprived of its object and purpose a result that goes against its clear and explicit terms."); Sir Gerald

A different but intertwined question concerns the standard of proof that must be satisfied to establish the existence of State consent to international arbitration in an investment agreement. The standard of proof relates to how much evidence must be presented by the party who has the burden of proof in order to convince the adjudicator that it has satisfied that burden. As opposed to the interpretation of a treaty provision, it is a matter of fact and not a matter of law.[33] According to international law – which should be applied in determining the standard of proof for a State's consent to international arbitration – the standard of proof required is "clear and unequivocal,"[34]

Fitzmaurice, *Vae Victis or Woe to the Negotiators! Your Treaty or Our "Interpretation" of It*, 65 AMERICAN JOURNAL OF INTERNATIONAL LAW 358 (1971), p. 373 ("[T]he maxim *ut magis* is all too frequently misunderstood as denoting that agreements should always be given their *maximum possible effect*, whereas its real object is ('*quam pereat*') to prevent them failing altogether."); UNCTAD, Dispute Settlement, International Centre for Settlement of Investment Disputes, *2.3 Consent to Arbitration* (2003), pp. 33–34 ("Neither a principle of restrictive interpretation nor a doctrine of '*effet utile*' will do justice to a consent clause.").

33 Regrettably, tribunals often conflate the interpretation of dispute settlements provisions in investment agreements with the standard of proof required in order to find a State's consent to international arbitration. *See, e.g.*, *Planet Mining*, ¶ 146 ("Several arbitral tribunals have taken the position that the expression of consent to ICSID arbitration must be 'clear and unambiguous', or that consent must be proven through 'affirmative evidence'. Except for calling for a writing, the ICSID Convention contains no particular requirement of clarity or otherwise. Hence, the Tribunal will assess consent pursuant to the general rules on treaty interpretation.").

34 *See, e.g.*, *Sempra Energy International v. Argentine Republic*, ICSID Case No. ARB/02/16, Decision on Objections to Jurisdiction, 11 May 2005, ¶ 139 (noting that "a separate declaration by means of a treaty or other acts making such consent unequivocally clear" is required); *Plama*, ¶ 198 ("It is a well-established principle, both in domestic and international law, that [an agreement to arbitrate] should be clear and unambiguous."); *Wintershall*, ¶ 167; *Vladimir Berschader and Moïse Berschader v. The Russian Federation*, SCC Case No. 080/2004, Award, 21 April 2006 ("*Berschader*"), ¶ 177; *ConocoPhillips*, ¶ 254 (noting that consent should be "clear and unequivocal" and that the "necessary consent is not to be presumed," but "must be clearly demonstrated"); *Brandes Investment Partners, LP v. Bolivarian Republic of Venezuela*, ICSID Case No. ARB/08/3, 2 August 2011 ("*Brandes*"), ¶ 113 (noting that it is self-evident that consent "should be expressed in a manner that leaves no doubts"); *Pac Rim Cayman LLC v. Republic of El Salvador*, ICSID Case No. ARB/09/12, Decision on Respondent's Jurisdictional Objections, 1 June 2012, ¶ 5.38 (indicating that "[c]onsent must be evident in writing"); *Tidewater Inc. and Others v. Bolivarian Republic of Venezuela*, ICSID Case No. ARB/10/5, Decision on Jurisdiction, 8 February 2013 ("*Tidewater*"), ¶ 101 (indicating that "it will proceed to find that it has jurisdiction if, but only if, the existence of the consent in writing of both parties to its jurisdiction is clear"); *Professor Christian Doutremepuich and Other v. Republic of Mauritius*, CPA Case No. 2018-37 (UNCITRAL), Award on Jurisdiction, 23 August 2019 ("*Doutremepuich*"), ¶ 204 (establishing that consent "must be clear and unequivocal" and must not be presumed);

and thus consent should be proven with sufficient certainty.[35] That is the high threshold that has to be satisfied in order to find consent by a sovereign State to international arbitration; consent cannot be presumed.[36] Therefore, general references in investment agreements to the submission of disputes to

---

Manuel García Armas and Others v. Bolivarian Republic of Venezuela, PCA Case No. 2016-08, Award on Jurisdiction, 13 December 2019, ¶ 631 (stating that "jurisdiction on the international sphere necessarily assumes the existence of express consent, which cannot be presumed") (translation); *Ghella S.P.A. v. Bolivarian Republic of Venezuela and C.A. Metro de Valencia*, ICC Case No. 24776/JPA, Final Award, 16 March 2022 ("*Ghella*"), ¶ 137 (observing that "consent to jurisdiction cannot be presumed") (translation); *Case Concerning Mutual Assistance in Criminal Matters* (*Djibouti v. France*), Judgment, 4 June 2008, ICJ REPORTS 177 (2008), ¶ 62 (noting that consent to the ICJ "must be certain" and that "whatever the basis of consent, the attitude of the respondent State must be capable of being regarded as 'an unequivocal indication' of the desire of that State to accept the Court's jurisdiction in a 'voluntary and indisputable' manner"); F. Sourgens, K. Duggal & I. Laird, EVIDENCE IN INTERNATIONAL INVESTMENT ARBITRATION (Oxford University Press 2018), p. 86 ("Tribunals have also applied a heightened standard of proof for a wide range of issues ... Similarly, for matters like a state's consent (*ratione voluntatis*), tribunals have refused to infer or presume consent, instead requiring the consent to be clear."); C. McLachlan, L. Shore & M. Weiniger, INTERNATIONAL INVESTMENT ARBITRATION: SUBSTANTIVE PRINCIPLES (1st. ed., Oxford University Press 2007), ¶ 7.168 ("Jurisdiction in international law depends solely upon consent. This is a difficult concept in any event in investment arbitration. Given the absence of a meeting of minds between investor and host State, consent has to be constructed from the standing consent given by the State by treaty, and the subsequent consent given by the investor at the time the claim is submitted to arbitration. In those circumstances, it is particularly important to construe the ambit of the State's consent strictly.").

35 *See ICS*, ¶ 280 ("[A] State's consent to arbitration shall not be presumed in the face of ambiguity. Consent to the jurisdiction of a judicial or quasi-judicial body under international law is either proven or not according to the general rules of international law governing the interpretation of treaties. The burden of proof for the issue of consent falls squarely on a given claimant who invokes it against a given respondent. Where a claimant fails to prove consent with sufficient certainty, jurisdiction will be declined."). *See also Case Concerning Mutual Assistance in Criminal Matters* (*Djibouti v. France*), Judgment, 4 June 2008, ICJ REPORTS 177 (2008), ¶ 62 ("The consent allowing for the Court to assume jurisdiction must be certain. That is so, no more and no less, for jurisdiction based on *forum prorogatum*. As the Court has recently explained, whatever the basis of consent, the attitude of the respondent State must 'be capable of being regarded as 'an unequivocal indication' of the desire of that State to accept the Court's jurisdiction in a 'voluntary and indisputable' manner.").

36 *Wintershall*, ¶¶ 160(3), 161; *Daimler*, ¶ 175 ("[I]t is not possible to presume that consent has been given by a state. Rather, the existence of consent must be established. This may be accomplished either through an express declaration of consent to an international tribunal's jurisdiction or on the basis of acts 'conclusively establishing' such consent ... Non-consent is the default rule; consent is the exception. Establishing consent therefore requires affirmative evidence.").

international arbitration alone in the absence of a forum would not constitute "clear and unequivocal" evidence of an enforceable and effective consent by a State to international arbitration.[37] The burden is on the claimant (the foreign investor) to prove that the dispute settlement provision in an investment agreement contains an enforceable and effective offer of consent by the State to submit disputes to international arbitration – which would obviously not be satisfied if there is no forum or if that forum is not subsequently agreed upon by the parties to the dispute.

6 Not Every Investor-State Dispute Settlement Provision Embodies State Consent or Contains an Enforceable and Effective Offer of Consent to International Arbitration

As a general principle under international law, international courts and tribunals can exercise jurisdiction over a State solely based on the State's consent.[38]

---

37 Tribunals often overlook this requisite standard of proof and find consent even if there is ambiguity or unclear language in the relevant dispute-settlement provision. *See, e.g.*, *Hesham Talaat M. Al-Warraq v. Republic of Indonesia*, UNCITRAL, Award on Respondent's Preliminary Objections to Jurisdiction and Admissibility of the Claims, 21 June 2012 ("*Al-Warraq*"), ¶ 75 (observing that "[t]he opening phrase of Article 17 is ambiguously drafted;" "the reference to 'disputes' lacks a subject, so it is not clear whether Contracting Parties or investors, or both, are entitled to seek to resolve their disputes through conciliation or arbitration" and concluding that it was implicit in the language of Articles 16 and 17 that Article 17 of the OIC Agreement provides for investor-State arbitration); *Lee-Chin*, Dissent, ¶ 117 ("It takes a lot of imagination to believe that the Parties to the Treaty have 'clearly and unambiguously' consented to the possibility that the investor alone decided to choose to refer the dispute to international arbitration.").

38 *See, e.g.*, *Abaclat*, Dissent, ¶¶ 7–8 ("In international law, all tribunals – not only arbitral, but even judicial – are tribunals of attributed, hence limited jurisdiction ... This is because, in the absence of a centralized power on the international level that exercises the judicial function through a judicial system empowered from above (or rather incarnating the judicial power as part of the centralized power), all international adjudicatory bodies are empowered from below, being based on the consent and agreement of the subjects (*i.e.* the litigants, *les justiciables*) themselves ... This is the reason why, the fundamental principle and basic rule in international adjudication, is that of the consensual basis of jurisdiction ... It explains as well the widely shared perception that the first task of an international tribunal is to ascertain its jurisdiction; and the great care international tribunals take in establishing from the outset, the existence and limits of the consent of the parties before them, on which their jurisdiction is founded."); Z. Douglas, THE INTERNATIONAL LAW OF INVESTMENT CLAIMS, p. 125 ("Arbitral tribunals constituted to hear international or transnational disputes are creatures of consent. Their source of authority must ultimately be traced to the consent of the parties to the arbitration itself."); *Daimler*, ¶ 168 ("Stepping back from the specific case of bilateral treaties,

In fact, the default state of affairs under international law is the absence of an available forum to submit investment claims.[39] Only exceptionally, when a State expressly consents that certain disputes can be submitted to a particular international court or tribunal, is a particular international court or tribunal vested with power and can exercise jurisdiction over a specific dispute.[40] This

---

all international treaties – whether bilateral, plurilateral or multilateral – are essentially expressions of the contracting states' consent to be bound by particular legal norms. They encapsulate voluntarily accepted restraints upon the universally recognized principle of state sovereignty. Consent is therefore the cornerstone of all international treaty commitments."); *Interpretation of Peace Treaties with Bulgaria, Hungary and Romania* (*First Phase*), Advisory Opinion, 30 March 1950, ICJ REPORTS 65 (1950), p. 71 ("The Court cannot, it is said, give the Advisory Opinion requested without violating the well-established principle of international law according to which no judicial proceedings relating to a legal question pending between States can take place without their consent.").

39 *See ICS*, ¶ 281 ("This principle follows from the lack of a default forum for the presentation of claims under international law. Whereas the inherent jurisdiction or hermetic division of competence over claims before general courts is a common feature of municipal judicial systems, the default position under public international law is the absence of a forum before which to present claims. The absence of a forum before which to present valid substantive claims is thus a normal state of affairs in the international sphere. A finding of no jurisdiction should not therefore be treated as a defect in a treaty scheme that runs counter to its object and purpose in providing for substantive investment protection."); *Menzies Middle East and Africa S.A. and Aviation Handling Services International Ltd. v. Republic of Senegal*, ICSID Case No. ARB/15/21, Award, 5 August 2016 ("*Menzies*"), ¶ 130 ("Thus, pursuant to international law in general, and pursuant to investment arbitration in particular, a sovereign State cannot be subject to international jurisdiction without its clearly expressed and unequivocal consent. This requirement stems from respect for the sovereignty of States and the principle that in international law the consent of States to arbitration is the exception, not the rule.") (translation); *President Allende Foundation, Victor Pey Casado and Other v. Republic of Chile II*, PCA Case No. 2017-30/AA662, Award, 28 November 2019, ¶ 244 ("A State's consent to arbitration under an investment treaty is an exception to the public international law rule that individuals may not bring international claims against States based on norms of public international law. Therefore, the Tribunal has a duty to satisfy itself that it is competent to hear Claimants' claim based on the Treaty.").

40 *See, e.g., Ambatielos Case* (*Greece v. United Kingdom*), Judgment, 19 May 1953, ICJ REPORTS 10 (1953), p. 19 ("The Court is not departing from the principle which is well established in international law and accepted by its own jurisprudence as well as that of the Permanent Court of International Justice, to the effect that a State may not be compelled to submit its disputes to arbitration without its consent."); *Wintershall*, ¶ 160(3); *Status of Eastern Carelia case*, PCIJ, Series B, No. 5 (1923), p. 27 ("It is well established in international law that no State can, without its consent, be compelled to submit its disputes ... either to mediation or to arbitration, or to any other kind of peaceful settlement."); *ST-AD GmbH v. Republic of Bulgaria*, PCA Case No. 2011-06, Award on Jurisdiction, 18 July 2013 ("*ST-AD*"), ¶ 337 ("At the outset, the Tribunal wants to restate that it is of the utmost importance

fundamental principle is derived from the notion that consent to investment arbitration implies "a specific and qualified derogation" from the host State's sovereignty and that "any restriction upon the independence of a State (not agreed to) cannot be presumed by courts."[41]

Not every investment agreement contains the consent of the contracting States to submit investor-State disputes to international arbitration.[42] Some

---

not to forget that no participant in the international community, be it a State, an international organisation or a physical or a legal person, has an inherent right of access to a jurisdictional recourse. For such right to come into existence, specific consent has to be given. As far as investment arbitration is concerned, such consent can be given in a contract, a domestic law or an international bilateral or multilateral treaty. In all these different hypotheses, the State can shape its consent as it sees fit by providing the conditions under which it is given – in other words, the conditions subject to which an 'offer to arbitrate' is made to the foreign investors."); *Enrique Heemsen and Jorge Heemsen v. Bolivarian Republic of Venezuela*, Paris Court of Appeals, Judgment, 20 September 2022, ¶ 68 ("It is established in international law that no State can be compelled to submit its disputes with other States either to mediation, or to arbitration, or finally to any process of peaceful settlement, without its consent.") (translation).

41 *See Tulip Real Estate Investment and Development Netherlands B.V. v. Republic of Turkey*, ICSID Case No. ARB/11/28, Decision on Bifurcated Jurisdictional Issue, 5 March 2013, ¶ 44; *Wintershall*, ¶ 160(3).

42 Some investment agreements do not even provide for binding arbitration. *See, e.g.*, OECD, *Dispute Settlement Provisions in International Investment Agreements: A Large Sample Survey*, ¶ 16 (according to this survey of 1660 BITs, 108 of such treaties do not provide for international arbitration); UNCTAD, BILATERAL INVESTMENT TREATIES 1995–2006: TRENDS IN INVESTMENT RULEMAKING (2007), p. 107 ("Yet another approach is to reserve the right of the host country to consent to arbitration. Within this group of agreements, some BITs include an explicit reservation. The BIT between Argentina and New Zealand (1999) is an example ... This approach allows a contracting party to decide on a case-by-case basis whether to consent to the submission of an investment-related dispute to international arbitration. This clause not only explicitly states that the contracting parties have to consent to submit a dispute to ICSID, but also provides for the possibility of settling a dispute under the UNCITRAL rules if both parties to the dispute so wish."); Aron Broches, *Bilateral Investment Protection Treaties and Arbitration of Investment Disputes*, in J. Schultsz & A. van den Berg, THE ART OF ARBITRATION 63 (Kluwer 1982), pp. 64–65 ("The treaties entered into by Sweden with Malaysia and Yugoslavia provide in their Article 6 that a dispute between an investor of one contracting party and the other contracting party in connection with an investment in the territory of the latter 'shall upon the agreement by both parties be submitted for arbitration to [ICSID].' Such a provision does not, of course, constitute consent to arbitration by the States concerned as required by Article 25(1) of the Convention. Nor does it impose a legal obligation on these States to give such consent."). This is true not only for older investment agreements. Some of the most recent investment agreements do not even contemplate the possibility of resorting to investment arbitration. *See, e.g.*, Mozambique-Brazil Cooperation and Investment Facilitation Agreement (2015), Article 15 (establishing a Joint Committee and providing

investment agreements – even if they mention international arbitration as the only dispute settlement method or one of the potential dispute settlement methods to resolve disputes between the foreign investor and the host State – do not contain an expression of consent.[43] In many of those investment

---

for potential State-to-State arbitration to settle disputes with investors); Angola-Brazil Cooperation and Investment Facilitation Agreement (2015), Article 15 (equally establishing a Joint Committee and providing for potential State-to-State arbitration to settle disputes with investors); United States-Mexico-Canada Agreement, Chapter 14, Article 14 (providing for investor-State arbitration only between the United States and Mexico, but not between the Canada and the United States or Mexico – in the latter case, investor-State arbitration would only be possible under the Comprehensive and Progressive Agreement for Trans-Pacific Partnership).

43 *See* UNCTAD, *Dispute Settlement, International Centre for Settlement of Investment Disputes, Consent to Arbitration* (2003), p. 18 ("Not all references to the ICSID Convention in BITS constitute binding offers of consent by the host State. Some clauses contain promises of future consent or hold out a general prospect of sympathetic consideration. Still others simply state that consent may be given by way of agreements with the investor."); Christoph Schreuer, *Consent to Arbitration*, in P. Muchlinski, F. Ortino & C. Schreuer (eds.), THE OXFORD HANDBOOK OF INTERNATIONAL INVESTMENT LAW 830 (Oxford University Press 2008), p. 836 ("Not all references to investor/State arbitration in BITS constitute binding offers of consent by the host State. Some clauses in BITS referring to arbitration amount to an undertaking by the host State to give consent in the future. For instance, the States may promise to accede to a demand by an investor to submit to arbitration by stating that the host State 'shall consent' to arbitration in case of a dispute … An even weaker reference to consent is contained in some BITS that provide for the host State's sympathetic consideration of a request for dispute settlement through arbitration. Obviously, a clause of this kind does not amount to consent by the host State. Some BITS merely envisage a future agreement between the host State and the investor containing consent to arbitration."); Stephan W. Schill (ed.), SCHREUER'S COMMENTARY ON THE ICSID CONVENTION, Vol. 1 (3d. ed., Cambridge University Press 2022), p. 363, ¶ 828 ("Not every reference to the Convention in a BIT constitutes an offer of consent by the host State. While some clauses amount to an unequivocal commitment, others contain undertakings to give consent or hold out a general prospect of sympathetic consideration. Still others simply state that consent may be given by way of agreements with the investor."); C. Dugan, D. Wallace, Jr., N. Rubins & B. Sabahi, INVESTOR-STATE ARBITRATION (2d. ed., Oxford University Press 2019), pp. 316–317 ("[Some] treaty consent clauses [*e.g.*, Australian BITS] … [do] not contain the unconditional consent of the state party to submit to arbitration. Rather, the state party has an obligation to provide its consent to arbitrate when asked by a foreign investor … [Other] BITS just foresees a future agreement between the host state and the investor, or refer to arbitration as a possible way to handle a dispute. In certain Swedish BITS, for example, the dispute resolution provision appears to constitute a mere agreement to agree: Disputes 'shall upon the agreement by both parties be submitted for arbitration to [ICSID]' … Instead, this language merely establishes ICSID arbitration as the preferred means for the resolution of investment disputes, and provides notice to foreign investors that the host state may be prepared to consider such an avenue.");

agreements, it is clear that a further agreement between the foreign investor and the host State – after the particular dispute arises – is necessary in order to submit such dispute to international arbitration under a specific competent forum.[44] An example of an investment agreement in which a further agreement between the parties to the dispute is required is Article XI of the Australia-Indonesia BIT, which provides that the foreign investor may submit the dispute to ICSID, in which case the host State "shall consent in writing within 45 days" after the investor's request.[45] The tribunal in *Planet Mining v.*

A. Steingruber, CONSENT IN INTERNATIONAL ARBITRATION, p. 204 ("There are BITS provisions which, although referring to investor – State arbitration, do not constitute binding offers of consent by the host State."); *Lee-Chin*, Dissent, ¶ 32 ("Numerous treaties refer to the 'settlement of disputes' but contain mechanisms that do not ultimately allow settling them if the disputing parties subsequently fail to decide which means they will use to do so. It would be pointless to list all bilateral or multilateral treaties under which judicial or arbitral means of dispute settlement may be used only if the disputing parties so decide afterwards. Those are the treaties that contain dispute settlement clauses referring to arbitration or judicial means with *opt-in* or *opt-out* mechanisms. That is, the clause is not sufficient to use arbitration or judicial settlement. Another step must be taken (act or omission) so that the State accepts or refuses to resort to a court or arbitral tribunal. Or those treaties that do not even consider the possibility of using compulsory means leading to binding decisions").

44 *See, e.g.*, R. Dolzer & M. Stevens, BILATERAL INVESTMENT TREATIES (Martinus Nijhoff Publishers 1995), p. 132 ("It must however be emphasized that not every reference in a BIT to arbitration under the ICSID Convention will qualify as an advance consent by the States parties to resort to such arbitration. A handful of BITs provide ... that investment disputes 'shall' be submitted to ICSID arbitration only if there is a subsequent agreement to that effect between the disputing parties."); A. Steingruber, CONSENT IN INTERNATIONAL ARBITRATION, p. 205 ("Some BITS only foresee a future agreement between the host State and the foreign investor containing consent to ICSID's jurisdiction."); Jeswald Salacuse, THE LAW OF INVESTMENT TREATIES (2d. ed., Oxford University Press 2021), p. 531 ("Some clauses, found principally in older BITs, simply state that investor-state arbitration will be resorted to if the parties agree to it. This requires the creation of a subsequent, specific agreement to arbitrate between the investor and the host state.").

45 The text of the relevant part of Article XI of the Australia-Indonesia BIT is as follows: "1. In the event of a dispute between a Party and an investor of the other Party relating to an investment, the parties to the dispute shall initially seek to resolve the dispute by consultations and negotiations. 2. In the event that such a dispute cannot be settled through consultations and negotiations, the investor in question may submit the dispute for settlement: a. In accordance with the laws and regulations of the Party which has admitted the investment to the competent judicial or administrative bodies of that Party; or b. To the International Centre for the Settlement of Investment Disputes ('the Centre') for the application of the conciliation or arbitration procedures provided by the 1965 Convention on the Settlement of Investment Disputes between States and Nationals of Other States ('the Convention'). 3. If both Parties are not at the same time the

Indonesia – when interpreting this provision – reasoned that if consent has to be given in writing within 45 days after the initial request, "it follows that consent cannot be located in the Treaty itself and that a separate act is needed," and thus concluded that "Article XI does not express Indonesia's advance consent to ICSID proceedings."[46]

In the majority of investment agreements that contain some form of consent to investor-State arbitration, treaties either provide for a specific forum to submit those disputes, contain a "cafeteria style" menu of alternative fora from which the foreign investor could choose, or alternatively list different fora on which the parties could agree, but contemplate a default or fallback option in case the parties could not reach an agreement on a forum. In all such cases, the consent of the host State to international arbitration is enforceable and effective. Conversely, in some situations, either there is no mention of a forum in the investor-State dispute settlement provision at issue, the forum mentioned is no longer available for some reason, or there is a list of potential fora but no default or fallback option in case the parties could not reach an agreement on a forum. In those cases, although the investor-State dispute settlement provision arguably contains consent "in principle" to international arbitration, the purported offer does not constitute an enforceable and effective consent without a further agreement on a competent forum.

Accordingly, there are two types of investor-State dispute settlement provisions in investment agreements where it is theoretically possible to merely find consent "in principle" to international arbitration without a forum: (i) dispute settlement provisions in which there is general consent to the submission of disputes to international arbitration without specifying a forum, or in which there is a list of potential fora but a subsequent agreement on a forum between the

---

dispute arises party to the Convention, the dispute may be submitted to such procedures for settlement as may be agreed between the parties to the dispute. If no such procedures have been agreed within a three month period from written notification of the claim, the parties to the dispute shall be bound to submit it to arbitration under the Arbitration Rules of the United Nations Commission on International Trade Law as then in force. The arbitral tribunal shall have the power to award interest. The parties to the dispute may agree in writing to modify those Rules. 4. Where a dispute is referred to the Centre pursuant to sub-paragraph 2(b): a. Where that action is taken by an investor of one Party, the other Party shall consent in writing to the submission of the dispute to the Centre within forty-five days of receiving such a request from the investor; or b. If the parties to the dispute cannot agree whether conciliation or arbitration is the more appropriate procedure, the investor affected shall have the right to choose."

46 *Planet Mining*, ¶¶ 161, 167. This is also the opinion of several doctrinal writings and studies that were referred to by the tribunal in that case. *Id.*, ¶¶ 176–180.

foreign investor and the host State is required, and no default or fallback option is contemplated; or (ii) investment agreements in which the forum specified is no longer available for some reason (*e.g.*, the investment agreement provides submission of investor-State disputes to ICSID arbitration but one contracting party to the investment agreement is no longer an ICSID contracting State) and no alternative forum is envisaged. I will next analyze each of those types of dispute settlement provisions.

6.1 *Investor-State Dispute Settlement Provisions Containing General Consent to International Arbitration without Specifying a Forum or Requiring a Subsequent Agreement on a Forum*

An example of this first type of dispute settlement provision is the one contained in the investment chapter of the free trade agreement between the Community of the Caribbean (CARICOM) and the Dominican Republic. Article XIII of Annex III of the free trade agreement provides as follows:

> 1 Disputes between an investor of one Party and the other Party concerning an obligation of the latter under this Agreement in relation to an investment of the former which have not been amicably settled shall, after a period of three months from written notification of a claim, be submitted to the courts of that Party or to national or international arbitration.
>
> 2 Where the dispute is referred to international arbitration, the investor and the Party concerned in the dispute may agree to refer the dispute to an international arbitrator or *ad hoc* arbitration tribunal to be appointed by a special agreement or established under the Arbitration Rules of the United Nations Commission on International Trade Law.

The first paragraph of this provision merely establishes the pre-conditions to international arbitration and limits the different dispute settlement methods to which the parties to disputes under that investment agreement could potentially resort (including international arbitration), without specifying whether any of the parties to the dispute could unilaterally choose among those alternatives or if there has to be an agreement on a single method. The second paragraph provides that, if a particular dispute is referred to international arbitration, the parties to that dispute may agree on one of the arbitral fora mentioned therein (international arbitrator or an *ad hoc* arbitration tribunal, appointed by special agreement or established under UNCITRAL Rules), without contemplating a default or fallback option in case of a failure to agree on a forum.[47] In other words, even assuming that the investor would have the right to unilaterally choose among the dispute settlement methods mentioned therein (which is not clear), there would be only consent "in principle" to international arbitration, subject to a subsequent agreement between the parties to a particular dispute on a competent forum. However, absent an agreement between the parties to a dispute on a specific forum (and absent a default or fallback option in case of failure to agree on a forum in the provision), there is no enforceable and effective consent to international arbitration.[48]

47 Although this provision is very similar to the alternative version of the UK model BIT (and was possibly inspired by that model), Article XIII of Annex III of the CARICOM-DR FTA does not contemplate a default or fallback option as the alternative version of the UK model BIT does. *Compare with* UK Model BIT (2005) (alternative version), Article 8(2) ("Where the dispute is referred to international arbitration, the investor and the Contracting Party concerned in the dispute may agree to refer the dispute either to: (a) the International Center for the Settlement of Investment Disputes (having regard to the provisions, where applicable, of the Convention on the Settlement of Investment Disputes between States and Nationals of other States, opened for signature at Washington DC on 18 March 19651 and the Additional Facility for the Administration of Conciliation, Arbitration and Fact-Finding Proceedings); or (b) the Court of Arbitration of the International Chamber of Commerce; or (c) an international arbitrator or *ad hoc* arbitration tribunal to be appointed by a special agreement or established under the Arbitration Rules of the United Nations Commission on International Trade Law. If after a period of three months from written notification of the claim there is no agreement to one of the above alternative procedures, the dispute shall at the request in writing of the investor concerned be submitted to arbitration under the Arbitration Rules of the United Nations Commission on International Trade Law as then in force. The Parties to the dispute may agree in writing to modify these Rules."). *See also* A. Steingruber, CONSENT IN INTERNATIONAL ARBITRATION, p. 204 ("The provision [of the alternative version of the UK model BIT] contains a fallback clause providing for arbitration under the UNCITRAL Arbitration Rules in the case that the disputing parties should not reach an agreement with regard to the form of arbitration to be adopted."); G. Lampo & G. Minervini, *Michael Anthony Lee-Chin v Dominican Republic: Interpreting the Consent to Arbitrate in the CARICOM–DR FTA*, p. 515 ("The very presence of the last sentence – which explicitly entitles an investor to use UNCITRAL Rules to start an arbitration in lack of a special agreement on the procedure to be followed – is significant. Indeed, one can infer from it that such a faculty of the investor cannot be derived solely from article 8(2)(c) (which, in turn, is identical to article XIII(2) of the CARICOM–DR FTA). Quite the contrary, if the interpretation of the *Lee-Chin* Tribunal were to be followed, this last part of the quoted provision would be deprived of any *effet utile* as the application of UNCITRAL Rules would stem directly from article 8(2)(c).").

48 The majority of the tribunal in the case *Michael Lee-Chin v. Dominican Republic* reached a different conclusion when it was called upon to interpret this provision. *Lee-Chin*, Partial Award, ¶¶ 86–135, 138–144, 150–156, 164–174, 185–194. Professor Kohen disagreed and issued a strong dissenting opinion. *Lee-Chin*, Dissent, ¶¶ 3–97. For the reasons that will be explained below, the tribunal's majority reasoning is flawed and contrary to the language

6.2 *Investor-State Dispute-Settlement Provisions Where the Agreed-upon Forum Is No Longer Available*

The second type of dispute settlement provision could be found in cases where one of the contracting parties to an investment agreement withdraws from the ICSID Convention and thus is no longer an ICSID contracting State. The situation will typically arise in cases in which the investor-State dispute settlement provision of the investment agreement only contemplates the possibility of submission to ICSID arbitration, without offering any alternative fora (or merely provides for an alternative forum for the period before both contracting parties to the investment agreement became parties to the ICSID Convention).[49] An example of this type of provision is Article 8 of the Barbados-Venezuela BIT, which provides as follows:

> (1) Disputes between one Contracting Party and a national or company of the other Contracting Party concerning an obligation of the former under this Agreement in relation to an investment of the latter shall, at the request of the national concerned, be submitted to the International Centre for Settlement of Investment Disputes for settlement by arbitration or conciliation under the Convention on the Settlement of Investment Disputes between States and Nationals of other States, opened for signature at Washington on March 18, 1965.
>
> (2) As long as the Republic of Venezuela has not become a Contracting State of the Convention as mentioned in paragraph 1 of this Article, disputes as referred to in that paragraph shall be submitted to the International Centre for Settlement of Investment disputes under the Rules Governing the Additional Facility for the Administration of Proceedings by the Secretariat of the Centre (Additional Facility Rules). If for any reason the Additional Facility is not available the investor shall have the right to submit the dispute to arbitration under the rules of the United Nations Commission on International Trade Law (UNCITRAL).

---

of Article XIII of Annex III of the CARICOM-DR FTA. *See* pp. 53–58, *infra*. *See also* G. Lampo & G. Minervini, *Michael Anthony Lee-Chin v Dominican Republic: Interpreting the Consent to Arbitrate in the CARICOM–DR FTA*, p. 515 ("[I]t seems that article XIII does not contain any offer to arbitrate.").

49 *See* M. Nolan & F. Sourgens, *The Interplay Between State Consent to ICSID Arbitration and Denunciation of the ICSID Convention: The (Possible) Venezuela Case Study*, 4(5) TRANSNATIONAL DISPUTE MANAGEMENT (2007), n. 57 ("Existing consent [in the case of a State's ICSID withdrawal] would be deprived of the arbitral regime, thus making it 'inchoate' consent analogous to a law that failed to specify the respective arbitral institution and seat of arbitration.").

(4) Each Contracting Party hereby gives its unconditional consent to the submission of disputes as referred to in paragraph 1 of this Article to international arbitration in accordance with the provisions of this Article.

In this provision, ICSID arbitration is the mechanism contemplated to resolve investment disputes.[50] Other alternative fora are envisaged only for the pre-ICSID period, but there is no alternative fora for the post-ICSID period. After Venezuela denounced the ICSID Convention, the Barbados-Venezuela BIT only contained consent to a specific forum (ICSID) which was no longer available, since both contracting parties were no longer ICSID contracting States, as required by Article 25 of the ICSID Convention (among other requirements) for ICSID jurisdiction to exist.[51] Thus, under the current state of affairs, the consent "in principle" to international arbitration contained in this provision

50 The same is true for other BITs entered into by Venezuela and Bolivia, two States which denounced the ICSID Convention. *See, e.g.*, Article 9(2) of the Netherlands-Venezuela BIT (signed in 1991 and terminated in 2008, which provided for ICSID arbitration and only alternatively provided for ICSID Additional Facility arbitration for the pre-ICSID period); Article 9 of The Netherlands-Bolivia BIT (signed in 1992 and terminated in 2009, also provided for ICSID arbitration, but alternatively contemplated the option of an *ad hoc* arbitration (without indicating any forum)).

51 This was precisely the tribunal's interpretation of Article 8 of the Barbados-Venezuela BIT in the case *Venezuela US v. Venezuela*. *See Venezuela US S.R.L. v. Bolivarian Republic of Venezuela*, PCA Case No. 2013-34, Interim Award on Jurisdiction (on Respondent's Objection to Jurisdiction *Ratione Voluntatis*), 26 July 2016 ("*Venezuela US*, Interim Award"), ¶¶ 85, 88 ("The Additional Facility was an option in the pre-ICSID period. And only if 'for any reason' during this period it was not available did arbitration under the UNCITRAL Rules provide a substitute arbitral forum. The continued validity of Venezuela's consent to arbitration under Article 8(4) as long as it is a Contracting Party to the BIT would provide for ICSID jurisdiction in the future if Venezuela one day decides to accede once again to the ICSID Convention."). However, as analyzed below, the majority of the tribunal tried to overcome the lack of an available forum by improperly applying the MFN clause of the treaty and, in effect, importing consent to international arbitration into the Barbados-Venezuela BIT from a treaty entered into by Venezuela with a third country. *See* pp. 76–79, *infra*. Likewise, the tribunal in *Heemsen v. Venezuela*, while interpreting a similar provision (Article 10.2 of the Germany-Venezuela BIT, together with *Ad* Article 10 of its Protocol), found that the option of submitting investment disputes to UNCITRAL arbitration existed only in the pre-ICSID period and provided that ICSID Additional Facility was not available. *Enrique Heemsen and Jorge Heemsen v. Bolivarian Republic of Venezuela*, PCA Case No. 2017-18, Award on Jurisdiction, 29 October 2019 ("*Heemsen*, Award"), ¶¶ 359–367. Such interpretation was confirmed by the Paris Court of Appeals when it dismissed the claimants' attempt to set aside the award. *Enrique Heemsen and Jorge Heemsen v. Bolivarian Republic of Venezuela*, Paris Court of Appeals, Judgment, 20 September 2022, ¶ 43.

is not operative,[52] at least without a subsequent agreement between the parties on a competent forum.[53]

•••

In sum, in these two types of dispute-settlement provisions, it might be possible to argue that there is consent "in principle" by the State to submit disputes to international arbitration, but there is no "complete" consent to international arbitration.[54] Even if it were possible to sustain that there is a general

52 *Venezuela US*, Interim Award, ¶ 88 ("Paragraph 1 envisages ICSID arbitration, which at present is not available as Venezuela ceased to be bound by the ICSID Convention on 25 July 2012."); *Venezuela US*, Dissent, ¶ 47 ("Under these circumstances, the 'standing offer' of Article 8 will become operational if Venezuela becomes party to the ICSID Convention again and if Barbados does not withdraw from it in the meantime."). Actually, that is what happened in the case of Ecuador, which denounced the ICSID Convention but later rejoined ICSID.

53 The possibility of a subsequent agreement on a forum is not merely a hypothetical scenario. In effect, when Bolivia withdrew from ICSID, E.T.I. Euro Telecom International N.V. ("E.T.I.") and Bolivia entered into an *ad hoc* arbitration agreement to conduct an arbitration initiated under the Netherlands-Bolivia BIT (which provided for ICSID arbitration) pursuant to the UNCITRAL Rules (in addition to other specific procedural rules to which the parties to the dispute agreed). *E.T.I. Euro Telecom International N.V. v. Plurinational State of Bolivia (II)*, PCA Case No. 2009-16, Procedural Order No. 1, 21 October 2009. A few days before Bolivia's denunciation of the ICSID Convention took effect, E.T.I. commenced an ICSID arbitration against Bolivia under the Netherlands-Bolivia BIT. *See E.T.I. Euro Telecom International N.V. v. Plurinational State of Bolivia*, ICSID Case No. ARB/07/28. E.T.I. and Bolivia subsequently agreed to remove their investment arbitration from the auspices of ICSID and agreed to resolve the dispute by the same arbitral tribunal in an *ad hoc* arbitration under the UNCITRAL Rules. *See* L. Peterson, *Telecom Italia Subsidiary Agrees to Withdraw ICSID Claim Against Bolivia, but Case to Proceed under Other Auspices*, INVESTMENT ARBITRATION REPORTER, 30 October 2009. Interestingly, Article 9 of the Netherlands-Bolivia BIT provided for ICSID arbitration in the event that both contracting parties were ICSID contracting States, but also contained rules for the constitution of an *ad hoc* arbitration, even contemplating the role of the President to the ICC Court of Arbitration as appointing authority.

54 This possibility was even recognized by the tribunal in *Michael Lee-Chin v. Dominican Republic*, despite the fact that the tribunal then questionably found that there was consent to UNCITRAL arbitration in the absence of an agreement between the parties to submit the dispute to a tribunal under the UNCITRAL Rules, as was expressly required by the provision at issue (*see* pp. 53–58, *infra*). *Lee-Chin*, Partial Award, ¶ 139 ("A potential scenario in which a State's intent – clearly expressed – to submit to a given dispute settlement mechanism is frustrated by the inability to put it in practice should not be ruled out. Such inability may be based, for example, on the failure to meet one or several of particular conditions or definitions included in the body of rules containing consent. There could also be incurable drafting defects.").

commitment or obligation by the State in the relevant investment agreement to submit disputes to international arbitration, such a commitment or obligation is not operative without a further agreement between the foreign investor and the State on a competent forum. Put differently, absent a subsequent agreement on a forum, there is no enforceable and effective consent to international arbitration.[55]

7 General References to Submission of Disputes to "International Arbitration" or Use of "Shall" in Investor-State Dispute Settlement Provisions Should Not Always Be Construed as Enforceable and Effective Consent to Arbitration

A consequence stemming from this forum-specific requirement is that not every general reference to "international arbitration" or use of words such as "shall" in an investor-State dispute settlement provision should necessarily be construed as an expression of an enforceable and effective offer of consent by the State to international arbitration. This is particularly so where there is no reference to a specific forum (or a further agreement of the parties to the dispute on a competent forum is required, but there is no agreement and no fallback option contemplated in the provision in the event of failure to

55 A different but related question is when the dispute settlement provision of the investment agreement has a hierarchical or multi-tiered structure and thus the investor cannot freely choose among the different fora contemplated therein, but only can resort to a specific forum under certain circumstances. In those cases, consent to a specific arbitral forum may be subject to certain conditions, and only when those conditions are fulfilled is there an enforceable and effective consent to an international arbitration under that forum. For instance, if consent to arbitration under the UNCITRAL Rules is conditioned upon both ICSID and ICSID Additional Facility not being available, a tribunal constituted under the UNCITRAL Rules could not find that it has jurisdiction over a specific dispute when either ICSID or the ICSID Additional Facility are available. *See Nova Scotia Power Inc. v. Bolivarian Republic of Venezuela*, PCA Case No. 2009-14, Award on Jurisdiction, 22 April 2010, ¶¶ 90–91, 147 (dismissing the case for lack of jurisdiction by noting that there is a hierarchy in Article XIII(4) of the Canada-Venezuela BIT and that, according to the intention of the provision's drafters, an investor would be entitled to resort to UNCITRAL arbitration when ICSID or ICSID Additional Facility were not available); *Kimberly-Clark*, ¶¶ 155 ("In conclusion, in the Tribunal's opinion, the ordinary meaning of the words used in Article 9(2) of the [Netherlands-Venezuela] BIT indicates that the offer to arbitrate under the AF [Additional Facility] Rules was only valid until Venezuela (first) acceded to the ICSID Convention."), 199 ("This context thus corroborates that access to AF arbitration was only open [under the Spain-Venezuela BIT] until both Spain and Venezuela had completed the process to adhere to the ICSID Convention.").

agree). These clauses might serve other purposes, such as simply establishing pre-conditions to submission of disputes to international arbitration[56] or limiting the alternative dispute settlement methods that could be resorted to by the investor to resolve investment disputes. In certain cases, these clauses might only entail consent "in principle" to international arbitration, subject to a subsequent agreement between the parties to the dispute on a competent forum.

In some instances, it is clear that there is no consent of the State to international arbitration at all and that a subsequent agreement between the parties to the dispute is required, in which case the investor-State dispute settlement provision serves other purposes. An example is the dispute settlement provision that was at issue in *Biwater v. Tanzania* (requiring an agreement between the parties to the dispute),[57] where the tribunal held that "a subsequent agreement between the parties is required – which is very different from a standing unilateral offer that simply requires acceptance by an investor."[58]

Similarly, in the recent award in *Ghella v. Venezuela*, the tribunal found that Article XV of the 2001 Italy-Venezuela framework cooperation agreement (a dispute settlement provision contained in that international agreement), which provided for the resolution of disputes "between Companies of the Parties," did not constitute an offer of consent of the State to international

56 *See, e.g.*, *Garanti Koza*, Dissent, ¶ 18 ("The legal purpose of Article 8(1) is to fix pre-conditions or what is commonly referred to as 'conditions precedent' to international arbitration, *i.e.*, negotiations during four months. There lies the *ratio legis* of Article 8(1). It is meant to govern the pre-conditions of consent to arbitration under Article 8 of the U.K.-Turkmenistan BIT. In other words, Article 8(1) contains, subject to the condition of four months of negotiations, consent in principle to international arbitration, and such consent in principle must still be read in light of the further specific conditions governing consent to arbitration by virtue of Article 8(2).").

57 Section 23.2 of the Tanzania Investment Act provides: "A dispute between a foreign investor and the [Tanzania Investment] Centre … may be submitted to arbitration in accordance with any of the following methods as may be mutually agreed by the parties, that is to say – … (b) in accordance with the rules of procedure for arbitration of the International Centre for the Settlement of Investment Dispute." *Biwater Gauff (Tanzania) Ltd. v. United Republic of Tanzania*, ICSID Case No. ARB/05/22, Award, 24 July 2008, ¶ 326. Although the tribunal was construing a domestic investment law, the same reasoning would apply in the case of an investment agreement.

58 *Id.*, ¶ 329. *See also ConocoPhillips*, ¶ 259 ("There is the further consideration, to quote from the ICSID decision in the *Biwater Gauff* case, that a provision such as Article 22 may have some effect by clearing the way for the State to conclude specific types of dispute resolution agreements without internal issues such as *ultra vires* arising and as such it provides a sense of certainty for investors.").

arbitration.[59] The tribunal concluded that Article XV of the framework agreement merely established that Venezuelan and Italian companies could resort to ICC arbitration if they so wished, but that the provision itself did not constitute a commitment.[60] It reasoned that "the ordinary meaning of the terms of Article XV within their context leads the Tribunal to reject that Article XV is an unilateral offer of the Republic to Italian investors (and vice versa) to settle disputes."[61]

Thus, it is important to properly construe the meaning and scope of each dispute settlement provision in an investment agreement – analyzing the ordinary meaning of terms used in their context – in order to determine whether the provision actually embodies a standing offer of consent to international arbitration. A good example of the importance of construing words or phrases in context is the meaning of the word "shall" – frequently found in dispute settlement provisions in investment agreements. The use of the word "shall" in a dispute settlement provision of an investment agreement should not always be interpreted as a "complete" offer of consent to international arbitration. The use of the word "shall" could mean an obligation, but could also mean a future action, depending on the context in which it is employed. That dual function of the word "shall" was stressed by the tribunal in *Churchill v. Indonesia*:

59 *Ghella*, ¶¶ 160, 172. Article XV ("Dispute Settlement Between Companies of the Parties") of the 2001 Italy-Venezuela Framework Cooperation Agreement provides: "All differences and disputes that may arise between Venezuelan and Italian companies, which derive from the performance of this Agreement, shall be settled amicably. In case the differences or disputes indicated in the previous paragraph cannot be solved amicably within six (6) months from the date of the written request for consultations, it will be possible to resort to the mechanisms of dispute settlement provided in the Arbitration and Conciliation Rules of the International Chamber of Commerce of Paris, and pursuant to the norms established in these Rules. The proceedings shall be defined by the International Chamber of Commerce of Paris." (translation). *Id.*, ¶ 112.

60 *Id.*, ¶ 160. *See also ConocoPhillips*, ¶ 216 ("As the Tribunal has already indicated, the ordinary meaning of the terms of Article 22 leads it strongly to the conclusion that Venezuela has not consented to ICSID jurisdiction by enacting that provision."). The *Ghella* tribunal did find that Article XVII of the framework agreement – a State-to-State dispute settlement provision for the resolution of disputes arising out of the interpretation or application of the framework agreement – contained consent by the State to international arbitration. *Ghella*, ¶ 161.

61 *Ghella*, ¶ 157 (translation). Among other reasons, the tribunal observed that: (i) although the phrase "will be possible to resort to" – which is commonly used in BITs – was employed, the Framework Agreement refers to companies (not investors) of both countries, but not to States as counterparties, as generally BITs do; (ii) the provision does not establish arbitration as the specific dispute settlement mechanism nor does it constitute a unilateral offer of the State to resort to arbitration, as it only referred to the "dispute settlement mechanisms provided" in the ICC Rules. *Id.*, ¶¶ 157–158.

"As to the word 'shall', it can either imply an obligation (suggesting that the Respondent's submission to ICSID is mandatory) or refer to a future action (suggesting the contrary)."[62] Similarly, the tribunal in the parallel case *Planet Mining v. Indonesia* found that, although "[i]t is common ground, and rightly so, that the word 'shall' implies an obligation, 'shall' can also be understood as implying a future action. In this sense, the use of the word 'shall' does not necessarily imply automaticity in the achievement of the contemplated result."[63] In short, the use of the word "shall" by itself does not necessarily mean that there is an enforceable and effective offer of consent to international arbitration in a dispute settlement provision of an investment agreement. There are cases in which the use of such language could not be interpreted as consent to international arbitration taking into account the context in which it is used, or could merely be construed as consent "in principle" to international arbitration (due to the absence of a forum). Such a provision, however, would not constitute an enforceable and effective offer to arbitrate.

In addition, it is necessary to assess whether the language of a purported offer of consent to international arbitration is subject to certain substantive conditions. If those conditions are not fulfilled, there may not be an enforceable and effective consent to international arbitration.[64]

---

62 *Churchill Mining Plc v. Republic of Indonesia*, ICSID Case No. ARB/12/14 and 12/40, Decision on Jurisdiction, 24 February 2014, ¶ 162.

63 *Planet Mining*, ¶ 163; Tarcisio Gazzini, INTERPRETATION OF INTERNATIONAL INVESTMENT TREATIES (Hart Publishing 2016), pp. 76–79 ("The interpreter must always be vigilant on the different meanings that can be attached to the very words depending on the specific circumstances of its use. The same word may assume different meaning in different provisions of the same treaty or in different treaties. The use of the modal 'shall' provides a useful example. In some cases, the modal 'shall' obviously indicates the existence of legally binding obligations ... In some cases, the literal interpretation of the meaning of a provision based on 'shall' has been inconclusive. The decision on jurisdiction in two parallel cases [*Churchill* and *Planet Mining*] confirm the versatility of the modal 'shall' ... In both cases, the Tribunal pointed out the double function of 'shall', which can either indicate that the parties have consented to submit to international arbitration their dispute with their respective investors, or be understood as implying some future action leading to the expression of such consent (or assent).").

64 *See, e.g.*, *ST-AD*, ¶ 361 ("[S]pecific consent has to be given within the treaty. The State can shape this consent as it sees fit, by providing for the basic conditions under which it is given, or, in other words, the conditions under which the 'offer to arbitrate' is made to the foreign investors."); *Venezuela US*, Interim Award, ¶ 88 ("Although consent to international arbitration is expressed in Article 8(4) and is still valid, in order to generate legal consequences in relation to different arbitral fora, the conditions specified in paragraphs 1 and 2 of Article 8 have to be met."); *ConocoPhillips*, ¶ 257 ("The Tribunal considers that those four words – if it [*i.e.*, the treaty or agreement] so provides [should it so provide] – present the essential issue to be determined. They do state a condition – as

In conclusion, general references to international arbitration, or the use of specific words such as "shall," should not necessarily be translated into a finding of an enforceable and effective consent to international arbitration in investment agreements, particularly when the forum is missing (or a subsequent agreement on a forum is required) in the dispute settlement provision.

8 Analysis of Investment Cases Discussing the Issue of Consent to International Arbitration without Forum

Some arbitral tribunals and domestic courts have had to grapple with the issue of the lack of forum in dispute settlement provisions contained in investment agreements. In some cases, tribunals rejected the proposition that general references to "international arbitration" or to an "arbitration proceeding," without specifying a forum, could be construed as enforceable and effective consent by the State to submit disputes to international arbitration. However, in other cases, tribunals unfortunately overlooked this basic principle and – through creative and expansive interpretations of dispute settlement provisions – found an enforceable and effective offer of State's consent to international arbitration despite the lack of forum (or an agreement on a forum when one was required).

8.1 *Cases Upholding the Principle that Consent Is Forum-Specific*

In *Metal-Tech v. Uzbekistan*, the arbitral tribunal was called upon to interpret Article 10 of the Law of Guarantees of Uzbekistan, which merely contained a

indeed the Claimants' expert on Venezuelan law accepted. In the Tribunal's opinion, that condition has not been satisfied. It is not enough, as the Claimants contend, that the ICSID Convention provides for international arbitration. That treaty must itself manifest Venezuela's consent to arbitration; but that treaty does not do that, as its Article 25 and preamble make clear. The ordinary meaning of the terms of Article 22, and especially of the condition, leads the Tribunal to the conclusion that Venezuela does not by that means consent to international arbitration under the ICSID Convention."); *Tidewater*, ¶¶ 132–133 ("[I]n the Tribunal's view, all of Article 22 is concerned with cases where, by operation of the relevant treaty, there is, for the purpose of the dispute itself, a consent to submission to international arbitration. In the case of the ICSID Convention, that can only be achieved if and to the extent that the requirements of Article 25, including consent of both parties, are met ... [T]he argument that Article 22 itself supplies consent is circular, since the condition stated in Article 22 expressly refers to the respective treaty – here the ICSID Convention – for determination of whether it establishes or provides for a submission to international arbitration.").

reference to multiple dispute resolution methods,[65] but no reference to the specific forum invoked by the claimant (ICSID arbitration). The tribunal ruled that the provision did not embody the State's consent to international arbitration, stating:

> To the Tribunal, Article 10 does not embody Uzbekistan's consent to submit disputes to ICSID arbitration independently of the BIT. Paragraph (1) of Article 10 merely states that a dispute which the Parties are unable to resolve amicably may be resolved by the Economic Court of Uzbekistan or through arbitration. It contains no expression of consent to a particular arbitral mechanism. More specifically, it embodies no offer by the State to submit to dispute settlement in the ICSID framework; ICSID is not even mentioned.[66]

---

65 Article 10 of the Uzbekistan Law of Guarantees provides the following: "Disputes associated with foreign investments (investment dispute) directly or indirectly, can be settled on agreement of the parties by consultation between them. If the parties will not be able to achieve agreed settlement, then [sic] such dispute should be settled either by an economic court of the Republic of Uzbekistan or by arbitration in accordance with the rules and procedures of international agreements (conventions) on settlement of investment disputes, to which the Republic of Uzbekistan has been joined. The parties involved in investment dispute can, on mutual agreement, determine the authority settling such dispute, as well as a county which can execute arbitration legal procedure of investment dispute." *Metal-Tech Ltd. v. Uzbekistan Republic*, ICSID Case No. ARB/10/3, Award, 4 October 2013 ("*Metal-Tech*"), ¶ 382. Although this case involved a domestic law and not an investment agreement, the same principle remains applicable.

66 *Metal-Tech*, ¶ 383. The tribunal also noted that "statutory provisions more specific than Article 10 – even provisions expressly naming ICSID – have been held not to contain state consent to ICSID arbitration." *Metal-Tech*, ¶ 383. The *Metal-Tech* tribunal referred to the decisions in *Mobil v. Venezuela* and *CEMEX v. Venezuela*, in which two arbitral tribunals held that there was no State consent to ICSID arbitration, when the provision at issue in those cases (Article 22 of the Venezuelan Investment Law) was "more specific than Article 10," including "even provisions expressly naming ICSID." Article 22 of the Venezuelan Investment Law provides: "Disputes arising between an international investor whose country of origin has in effect with Venezuela a treaty or agreement on the promotion and protection of investments, or disputes to which are applicable the provision of the Convention Establishing the Multilateral Investment Guarantee Agency (OMGI – MIGA) or the Convention on the Settlement of Investment Disputes between States and National of other States (ICSID), shall be submitted to international arbitration according to the terms of the respective treaty or agreement, if it so provides, without prejudice to the possibility of making use, when appropriate, of the dispute resolution means provided for under the Venezuelan legislation in effect." *Venezuela Holdings, B.V. and Others v. Bolivarian Republic of Venezuela*, ICSID Case No. ARB/07/27, Decision on Jurisdiction, 10 June 2010 ("*Mobil*"), ¶ 68. Despite expressly mentioning ICSID, six tribunals ruled that this provision does not constitute a standing offer of consent by Venezuela

The tribunal went on to observe that the second paragraph of Article 10 made it clear that a "mutual agreement" between the parties was required to determine the arbitral authority to settle the dispute, but did not entitle the investor to commence arbitral proceedings before ICSID unless the State consented to ICSID beyond the general mention of arbitration in the first paragraph.[67] Thus, the *Metal-Tech* tribunal found that Uzbekistan had not consented to

---

to international arbitration. *See Mobil*, ¶¶ 111, 140 (noting that the text is "ambiguous and obscure," and "it cannot conclude from the ambiguous text of Article 22 that Venezuela, in adopting the 1999 Investment Law, consented in advance to ICSID arbitration for all disputes covered by the ICSID Convention"); *ConocoPhillips*, ¶¶ 257, 261 ("The Tribunal considers that those four words – if it [*i.e.* the treaty or agreement] so provides [should it so provide] – present the essential issue to be determined. They do state a condition – as indeed the Claimants' expert on Venezuelan law accepted. In the Tribunal's opinion, that condition has not been satisfied. It is not enough, as the Claimants contend, that the ICSID Convention provides for international arbitration. That treaty must itself manifest Venezuela's consent to arbitration; but that treaty does not do that, as its Article 25 and preamble make clear. The ordinary meaning of the terms of Article 22, and especially of the condition, leads the Tribunal to the conclusion that Venezuela does not by that means consent to international arbitration under the ICSID Convention ... [T]he ordinary meaning of the terms of Article 22 leads it strongly to the conclusion that Venezuela has not consented to ICSID jurisdiction by enacting that provision."); *Cemex*, ¶ 138 ("[I]t cannot conclude from the obscure and ambiguous text of Article 22 that Venezuela, in adopting the 1999 Investment Law, consented unilaterally to ICSID arbitration for all disputes covered by the ICSID Convention in a general manner. That article does not provide a basis for jurisdiction of the Tribunal in the present case."); *Brandes*, ¶¶ 86, 92, 118 ("Its conclusion is that the wording of Article 22 of the Investment Law is confusing and imprecise, and that it is not possible to affirm, based on a grammatical interpretation, whether or not it contains the consent of the Bolivarian Republic of Venezuela to ICSID jurisdiction ... The clarity of most provisions of the [Venezuelan Investment Law] contrast with the confusing and ambiguous wording of Article 22 ... [I]t is obvious that Article 22 of the Law on Promotion and Protection of Investments does not contain the consent of the Bolivarian Republic of Venezuela to ICSID jurisdiction."); *Tidewater*, ¶ 137 ("In the Tribunal's view, such a construction would require clearer words in the Investment Law indicating the intention of Venezuela to give such general standing consent. Such words are not to be found in the text of Article 22."); *OPIC*, ¶¶ 105, 107 (observing that "the text of Article 22 is ambiguous" and concluding that "the plain meaning of Article 22 does not point to the conclusion that Venezuela intended to give its consent to arbitrate at ICSID"). *See also AHG*, ¶ 167 ("The Claimant states that, under international law, 'a host State may provide advance consent to ICSID Convention arbitration through a unilateral declaration in the form of its national legislation'. However, for such advance consent to exist, as in any investment protection treaty, it must be expressed specifically and unequivocally. It is not enough, for purposes of consent, that the law in question generally refers to international agreements which, in turn, may include such consent.").

67 *Metal-Tech*, ¶ 384.

ICSID jurisdiction through Article 10 of the Law of Guarantees and that, consequently, it lacked jurisdiction over the claims brought on that basis.

Similarly, in *Heemsen v. Venezuela*, the claimant argued that Venezuela consented to international arbitration, without any limitation or condition, when it accepted to submit disputes to an "arbitration proceeding" in the investment treaty at issue.[68] The relevant provision – Article 10.2 of the Germany-Venezuela BIT – provides that "[if] a dispute could not be resolved within a period of six months from the date in which one of the parties to the dispute notified it, it shall be submitted, at the request of the national or the company, to an arbitration proceeding."[69] The same provision specifies that if the parties to the dispute could not agree otherwise, then the dispute shall be submitted to an arbitration proceeding before ICSID. However, since Venezuela had withdrawn from ICSID several years before the notification of the dispute, ICSID arbitration was not available in that case.[70] Faced with this problem, the UNCITRAL tribunal that was called upon to hear the claim rejected the proposition that the phrase "arbitration proceedings" embodied an unlimited and unconditional consent to international arbitration, reasoning as follows:

---

68 *Heemsen*, Award, ¶ 370.

69 *Id.*, ¶ 354 (translation).

70 In addition, the Protocol to the Germany-Venezuela BIT provides in *Ad* Article 10 as follows: "(a) As long as the Republic of Venezuela has not become a Party to the Convention on the Settlement of Investment Disputes between States and Nationals of Others States of March 18, 1965, the dispute shall be submitted to an arbitration proceeding before the International Centre for Settlement of Investment Disputes under the Rules Governing the Additional Facility for the Administration of Proceedings by the Secretariat of the Centre (Additional Facility Rules), insofar as the parties to the dispute have not reached another arrangement. (b) In the event that recourse to arbitration under the Additional Facility Rules is not possible, the dispute shall be submitted, at the request of the national or of the company, to an *ad hoc* arbitration proceeding under the Arbitration Rules of the United Nations Commission on International Trade Law." *Id.*, ¶ 355 (translation). The claimants in *Heemsen* argued that under the Germany-Venezuela BIT they could opt for an arbitration proceeding under ICSID or ICSID Additional Facility, and when ICSID was not available, then to an arbitration proceeding under the UNCITRAL Rules. *Id.*, ¶ 357. The tribunal rejected this argument, since it held that subparagraphs (a) and (b) of *Ad* Article 10 of the Protocol were connected, and thus the option of UNICTRAL arbitration in subparagraph (b) was linked to the condition established in subparagraph (a); namely, "[a]s long as the Republic of Venezuela has not become a Party to [ICSID]." *Id.*, ¶¶ 359–360. Accordingly, the tribunal held that ICSID was the primary forum (absent a different agreement) and that both ICSID Additional Facility and UNCITRAL were options only during the pre-ICSID period. *Id.*, ¶ 367. The Paris Court of Appeals upheld this interpretation. *Enrique Heemsen and Jorge Heemsen v. Bolivarian Republic of Venezuela*, Paris Court of Appeals, Judgment, 20 September 2022, ¶¶ 52–54.

> The Tribunal considers very exaggerate the scope that Claimants want to give to the phrase "arbitral proceeding" that, according to them, would allow them to imply the existence of consent by Venezuela to submit disputes to arbitration without any condition or limitation, to any existing arbitral mechanism ... Consequently, the consent of the State to resolve the present dispute under the UNCITRAL Rules cannot be found in the general reference to an arbitration proceeding captured in article 10 of the Treaty.[71]

Russian courts have also addressed this issue in a few cases involving the setting aside of arbitral awards against Kyrgyzstan, upholding the principle that consent is forum-specific. This was first specifically discussed in the setting aside proceedings of the case *State Energy Corp. and Other v. Kyrgyz Republic* submitted before Russian courts, in the context of an application to set aside an award rendered against Kyrgyzstan based on the State's alleged general consent to international arbitration pursuant to the Convention on the Protection of Investors' Rights (known as the "Moscow Convention").[72]

Two investors filed a claim against Kyrgyzstan in the arbitration court of the Moscow Chamber of Commerce and Industry based on the Moscow Convention, which provides in Article 11 that "the disputes on investments under the present Convention shall be decided by courts or by arbitration courts of the states-participants to the disputes, by the Economic Court of the Commonwealth of Independent States and/or other international courts or international arbitration courts."[73] This provision does not identify the arbitral institution or applicable arbitration rules. The claimants argued that such provision allowed them to apply to any competent arbitral institution of their choice. The arbitral tribunal of the Moscow Chamber of Commerce and Industry – which was called upon to hear the dispute – found itself competent and entered an award against the State. Kyrgyzstan applied to the Arbitrazh Court of Moscow to set aside the award and, during the setting aside proceedings, applied for an advisory opinion to the Economic Court

71 *Heemsen*, Award, ¶¶ 371–373 (translation). The tribunal also rejected the claimant's attempt to import consent through the MFN clause. *See* pp. 66–67, *infra*.

72 Natalia Ivanova, *Consent to Treaty Arbitration Should Be Specific, Not General*, CIS ARBITRATION, 2 September 2015. The Convention on the Protection of Investors' Rights entered into by the Commonwealth of Independent States ("CIS") – and that is currently in force among Armenia, Belarus, Moldova, Tajikistan, Kazakhstan and Kyrgyzstan – was signed on 28 March 1997 and entered into force on 21 January 1999.

73 N. Ivanova, *Consent to Treaty Arbitration Should Be Specific, Not General*, 2 September 2015.

of the Commonwealth of Independent States (the "CIS Court")[74] concerning Article 11 of the Moscow Convention. The relevant question was whether Article 11 as such amounted to consent to arbitration. According to the decision of the CIS Court, the Moscow Convention only specifies possible dispute resolution procedures, but does not contain consent to arbitration. The court of first instance upheld Kyrgyzstan's position on three main grounds: lack of arbitration agreement, non-respect of state sovereignty, and doubts as to the arbitrators' impartiality. The investors then applied to the Arbitrazh Court of the Moscow Circuit to repeal the ruling of the court of first instance. The court of second instance upheld the court judgment, holding that the decision of the CIS Court on the interpretation of the Moscow Convention was final. The court also affirmed that the arbitration court of the Moscow Chamber of Commerce did not have jurisdiction over the dispute in question.[75] According to one commentator, the Moscow court "confirmed that the treaty clause which provides that a state will resolve disputes by arbitration (but does not specify the arbitral institution or rules) does not enable an investor to apply to arbitration without an explicit arbitration clause."[76]

Finally, the tribunal in *Itisaluna v. Iraq*, in an arbitration initiated under the ICSID Convention, rejected the proposition that Article 17 of the OIC Agreement constituted by itself consent to ICSID arbitration.[77] Although the

74 The CIS Court is an international judicial organ located in Minsk, Belarus, and is empowered to resolve disputes within the framework of the CIS and to interpret legal instruments of the CIS organs and international treaties. The Moscow Convention provides that "controversies related to interpretation of this Convention shall be resolved by ... application to [the CIS Court]." *Id.*

75 Other cases that have also involved claims based on an alleged consent to arbitration contained in Article 11 of the Moscow Convention had similar outcomes. For instance, in the case *Lee John Beck and Other v. Kyrgyz Republic*, the arbitration court also upheld the investors' claims and Kyrgyzstan had to apply to the Russian courts to reverse the decision. A Russian court reversed the arbitral award after receiving the decision on an interpretation of the CIS Court, which ruled that Article 11 of the Moscow Convention does not amount to consent to arbitration, but merely stipulates possible means of resolving disputes under the Moscow Convention. *See id.*

76 *Id.*

77 *Itisaluna Iraq LLC and Others v. Republic of Iraq*, ICSID Case No. ARB/17/10, Award, 3 April 2020 ("Itasaluna"). The Organisation of the Islamic Conference has over 50 member States. Article 17 of the OIC Agreement provides: "Until an organ for the settlement of disputes arising under the agreement is established, disputes that may arise shall be entitled through conciliation or arbitration in accordance with the following rules of procedure: ... 2. Arbitration. (a) If the two parties to the dispute do not reach an agreement as a result of their resort to conciliation, or if the conciliator is unable to issue his report within the prescribed period, or if the two parties do not accept the solutions proposed therein, then each party has the right to resort to the Arbitration Tribunal for a

tribunal found that Article 17(2)(b) of the OIC Agreement established a "right" to resort to investor-State arbitration and that it constituted "consent to arbitration in general terms," it held that "this general consent to arbitration does not constitute consent to ICSID arbitration."[78] The tribunal observed that in the OIC Agreement "there is no basis whatsoever to establish clear, specific and intended consent to ICSID arbitration."[79] Ultimately, the tribunal rejected the claimants' attempt to import consent to ICSID arbitration from the Iraq-Japan BIT through the application of the MFN clause of the OIC Agreement.[80]

8.2 *Cases Disregarding the Principle that Consent Is Forum-Specific*

On the other hand, there are certain investment tribunals that have overlooked the fundamental principle that consent to international arbitration is forum-specific, stretching the language of dispute settlement provisions in investment agreements to find consent where there is none due to the fact that no forum is mentioned in those provisions or a subsequent agreement on a forum is required.

In *Garanti Koza v. Turkmenistan*, the dispute settlement provision at issue – Article 8 of the UK-Turkmenistan BIT, which followed the UK alternative model BIT – provides in its first paragraph that disputes between a national or

---

final decision on the dispute. (b) The arbitration procedure begins with a notification by the party requesting the arbitration to the other party to the dispute, clearly explaining the nature of the dispute and the name of the arbitrator he has appointed. The other party must, within sixty days from the date on which such notification was given, inform the party requesting arbitration of the name of the arbitrator appointed by him. The two arbitrators are to choose, within sixty days from the date on which the last of them was appointed arbitrator, an umpire who shall have a casting vote in case of equality of votes. If the second party does not appoint an arbitrator, or if the two arbitrators do not agree on the appointment of an Umpire within the prescribed time, either party may request the Secretary General to complete the composition of the Arbitral Tribunal. (c) The Arbitration Tribunal shall hold its first meeting at the time and place specified by the Umpire. Thereafter the Tribunal will decide on the venue and time of its meetings as well as other matters pertaining to its functions. (d) The decisions of the Arbitration Tribunal shall be final and cannot be contested. They are binding on both parties who must respect and implement them. They shall have the force of judicial decisions. The contracting parties are under an obligation to implement them in their territory, no matter whether it be a party to the dispute or not and irrespective of whether the investor against whom the decision was passed is one of its nationals or residents or not, as if it were a final and enforceable decision of its national courts."

78 *Id.*, ¶ 191.

79 *Id.*, ¶ 222.

80 The discussion of the majority of the tribunal in *Itisaluna* rejecting the importation of consent to ICSID arbitration through the application of the MFN clause of the OIC Agreement can be found at pp. 69–73, *infra*.

company of one Contracting Party and the other Contracting Party concerning an obligation of the latter under said investment agreement "shall … be submitted to international arbitration if the national or company concerned so wishes," provided that the dispute had not been amicably settled after a period of four months from the written notification of the claim. The second paragraph contains a menu of arbitral fora (ICSID, ICC, special agreement, UNCITRAL Rules) to which the parties may agree to refer the dispute, as well as a fallback option (UNCITRAL arbitration) if the parties cannot agree on an arbitral forum after a period of four months from the written notification of the claim.[81]

The majority of the tribunal conceded that the first paragraph of Article 8 did not provide consent to ICSID, but found that it contained a general consent to international arbitration, even if it lacked the mention of a forum, and upheld jurisdiction.[82] The dissenting opinion of Professor Boisson de Chazournes disagreed with the majority and properly reasoned that both paragraphs of Article 8 of the UK-Turkmenistan BIT should be read together. She affirmed that the first paragraph contained only "consent in principle to international arbitration," which was subject to the specific conditions governing consent in the second paragraph. In other words, Turkmenistan's

81 *Garanti Koza LLP v. Turkmenistan*, ICSID Case No. ARB/11/20, Decision on the Objection to Jurisdiction for Lack of Consent, 3 July 2013 ("*Garanti Koza*, Decision on Jurisdiction"), ¶ 17. Article 8 of the UK-Turkmenistan BIT provides: "Disputes between a national or company of one Contracting Party and the other Contracting Party concerning an obligation of the latter under this Agreement in relation to an investment of the former which have not been amicably settled shall, after a period of four [months] from written notification of a claim, be submitted to international arbitration if the national or company concerned so wishes. Where the dispute is referred to international arbitration, the national or company and the Contracting Party concerned in the dispute may agree to refer the dispute either to: (a) the International Centre for the Settlement of Investment Disputes (having regard to the provisions, where applicable, of the Convention on the Settlement of Investment Disputes between States and Nationals of other States, opened for signature at Washington DC on 18 March 1965 and the Additional Facility for the Administration of Conciliation, Arbitration and Fact-Finding Proceedings); or (b) the Court of Arbitration of the International Chamber of Commerce; or (c) an international arbitrator or *ad hoc* arbitration tribunal to be appointed by a special agreement or established under the Arbitration Rules of the United Nations Commission on International Trade Law. If after a period of four months from written notification of the claim there is no agreement to one of the above alternative procedures, the dispute shall at the request in writing of the national or company concerned be submitted to arbitration under the Arbitration Rules of the United Nations Commission on International Trade Law as then in force. The parties to the dispute may agree in writing to modify these Rules."

82 *Id.*, ¶ 37. The majority of the tribunal then proceeded to import consent to ICSID arbitration through the application of the MFN clause of the relevant treaty. *See* pp. 73–75, *infra*.

consent to international arbitration was not contained in the first paragraph, but only in the second paragraph of the relevant provision, where an agreement on a forum was required and there was a fallback selection of a forum absent an agreement. In addition, the dissenting arbitrator pointed out that "[t]he legal purpose of Article 8(1) is to fix pre-conditions or what is commonly referred to as 'conditions precedent' to international arbitration, *i.e.*, negotiations during four months. There lies the *ratio legis* of Article 8(1). It is meant to govern the pre-conditions of consent to arbitration under Article 8 of the UK-Turkmenistan BIT."[83]

The majority's interpretation of Article 8 of the UK-Turkmenistan BIT, finding consent to international arbitration in the first paragraph where no forum is mentioned, has been criticized. As noted by one commentator, the first paragraph of the relevant dispute settlement provision could not be construed as a self-standing consent to international arbitration – as the majority did – precisely due to the lack of an arbitral forum:

> The dissenting arbitrator's interpretation is clearly to be preferred. Article 8(1) is not a self-standing provision providing for consent to arbitration. Its *ratio legis* is merely to fix the precondition for international arbitration. It contains no standing offer by the contracting parties simply because the putative arbitral tribunal is not indicated. The expression of consent must be established in Article 8(2) which prospected two alternatives: either the parties to the dispute reach an agreement on referral to one of the three tribunals listed, or the investor can rely on the default option, namely a tribunal established under UNCITRAL [R]ules.[84]

Another commentator also underscored that the majority's interpretation "run[s] counter to the exact wording and logic of the clause."[85] He observed "that the very fact that the second paragraph of Article 8 includes a 'default' option in case no agreement is reached on any of the listed options seems to clearly indicate that specific consent is required in order to initiate arbitral proceedings under the ICSID Convention, and that consent in fact is only given for arbitration under the UNCITRAL arbitration rules – the default option."[86]

---

83 *Garanti Koza*, Dissent, ¶ 18.

84 T. Gazzini, INTERPRETATION OF INTERNATIONAL INVESTMENT TREATIES, p. 87.

85 Eric de Brabandere, *Importing Consent to ICSID Arbitration? A Critical Appraisal of Garanti Koza v. Turkmenistan*, p. 14.

86 *Id.*

In line with the dissenting arbitrator, he opined that the first paragraph of Article 8 of the UK-Turkmenistan BIT only contains pre-arbitration requirements, and that "reading into that paragraph a general consent to arbitrate seems to be overly inventive."[87]

By the same token, in *Krederi v. Ukraine*, while interpreting Article 8 of the UK-Ukraine BIT[88] (a provision almost identical to the one at issue in *Garanti Koza*), the majority of the tribunal followed the reasoning of the majority in *Garanti Koza* without further analysis.[89] Although the parties to the dispute agreed that the dispute settlement clause "provides for investor-State arbitration as a matter of principle," it was disputed whether Article 8 contains an offer of consent to ICSID. The tribunal observed that the first paragraph of the provision, "[i]n spite of the use of obligatory ('shall') ... does not provide for a choice between different types of investment arbitration to investors," and that the second paragraph makes clear that there are three options and a fallback option in case the parties cannot agree.[90] The tribunal concluded that Ukraine could not be regarded as having consented to ICSID arbitration via Article 8 of the UK-Ukraine BIT alone.[91] However, the majority reasoned that consent to

87 *Id.*

88 *Krederi Ltd. v. Ukraine*, ICSID Case No. ARB/14/17, Award, 2 July 2018 (excerpts) ("*Krederi*"), ¶ 264. Article 8 of the UK-Ukraine BIT provides: "(1) Disputes between an investor of one Contracting Party and the other Contracting Party concerning an obligation of the latter under this Agreement in relation to an investment of the former which have not been amicably settled, shall, after a period of three months from written notification of a claim, be submitted to international arbitration if the investor concerned so wishes. (2) Where the dispute is referred to international arbitration, the investor and the Contracting Party concerned in the dispute may agree to refer the dispute either to: (a) the International Centre for the Settlement of Investment Disputes (having regard to the provisions, where applicable, of the Convention on the Settlement of Investment Disputes between States and Nationals of other States, opened for signature at Washington DC on 18 March 1965 and the Additional Facility for the Administration of Conciliation, Arbitration and Fact-Finding Proceedings); or (b) the Court of Arbitration of the International Chamber of Commerce; or (c) an international arbitrator or ad hoc arbitration tribunal to be appointed by a special agreement or established under the Arbitration Rules of the United Nations Commission on International Trade Law. If after a period of three months from written notification of the claim there is no agreement to one of the above alternative procedures, the dispute shall at the request in writing of the investor concerned be submitted to arbitration under the Arbitration Rules of the United Nations Commission on International Trade Law as then in force. The parties to the dispute may agree in writing to modify these Rules."

89 *Id.*, ¶¶ 327–330.

90 *Id.*, ¶¶ 275–276.

91 *Id.*, ¶ 280.

arbitration was already contained in Article 8(1) of the UK-Ukraine BIT, which did not mention any forum.[92]

The dissenting arbitrator in *Krederi* agreed with the dissenting opinion of Professor Boisson de Chazournes in *Garanti Koza* and advanced that the first paragraph of Article 8 "does not provide the requisite consent under the BIT to refer claims by investors to 'international arbitration'," and that "[a]bsent express consent given within three months, the requisite Contracting Party's consent solely arises under [the second paragraph] where Ukraine's consent to international arbitration is confined to UNCITRAL Rules."[93]

A number of tribunals that were called upon to interpret Article 17 of OIC Agreement – which is a confusingly-drafted dispute settlement provision that has no reference to a specific forum (but that contains certain rules on the constitution of the arbitral tribunal, the arbitral procedure and the role of the OIC Secretary General as appointing authority[94]) – also had to deal (directly or indirectly) with the issue of consent to international arbitration without a forum.

In *Al-Warraq v. Indonesia*, the first case of this saga, the tribunal held that Article 17 of the OIC Agreement established an effective investor-State dispute settlement provision, finding that it had jurisdiction to hear the case under the UNCITRAL Rules.[95] The claimant in that case commenced an investment arbitration against Indonesia pursuant to Article 17(2) of the OIC Agreement and the UNCITRAL Rules. By letter, Indonesia accepted that the tribunal be constituted for the sole purpose of determining the issue of whether Article 17 of the OIC Agreement contained an offer of consent to arbitrate disputes. Indonesia further agreed that the UNCITRAL Rules in effect on the date of the letter be applicable to the arbitration proceedings, except to the extent it varied by the terms of such letter and without prejudice to the conditions imposed by Article 17 of the OIC Agreement.[96]

Indonesia objected to the jurisdiction of the tribunal, arguing that Article 17 of the OIC Agreement did not contain the State's consent to investor-State

92 The majority of the *Krederi* tribunal then proceeded to apply the MFN clause of the UK-Ukraine BIT to import consent to ICSID arbitration. *See* p. 76, *infra*.

93 *Krederi*, ¶ 343. In the award, the name of the dissenting arbitrator is not disclosed. Although the analysis of the majority of the tribunals in *Garanti Koza* and *Krederi* was flawed (since there was no consent to international arbitration in the first paragraphs of the relevant provisions, where there was no forum even mentioned), the reality is that both provisions at issue in those cases contained consent to UNCITRAL arbitration in their second paragraphs (but not to ICSID arbitration).

94 *See* n. 77, *supra*.

95 *Al-Warraq*, ¶ 93.

96 *Id.*, ¶ 13.

arbitration, but merely stated "the procedure to be followed in case both state parties agree to refer their dispute to conciliation in a separate instrument or agreement." In its view, the provision only provided recourse to conciliation or arbitration (in the event the conciliation failed) until an OIC organ for dispute settlement had been established, which, according to the respondent, happened when the International Islamic Court of Justice ("IICJ") was created in 1987, thereafter excluding recourse to the OIC Agreement.[97] In turn, the claimant argued that Article 17 of the OIC Agreement constituted a plain offer to arbitrate, permitting the investor to choose the forum, and that no additional consent expressed in a separate agreement was required.[98]

The tribunal sided with the claimant and concluded that Article 17 provides for investor-state arbitration. Although the tribunal recognized that "[t]he opening phrase of Article 17 is ambiguously drafted," it reasoned that "it is implicit in the language of Article[s] 16 and 17, and consistent with the object and purpose of OIC Agreement, to conclude that Article 17 provides for investor-state arbitration."[99] In addition, the tribunal ruled that Article 17 does not mandate conciliation to precede arbitration; rather, conciliation and arbitration are separate forms of dispute resolution which may be used either sequentially or alternatively.[100] The tribunal found that "Article 17 constitutes an investor-state arbitration provision, and there is nothing in this Article inconsistent with the modern practice to interpret these clauses as constituting an open offer by the state parties to investors, that can be accepted and the arbitration initiated without any separate agreement by the state party."[101] Although Indonesia argued that at the time the OIC Agreement was made there was no concept of investor-state arbitration based on an international investment treaty, the tribunal held that the Vienna Convention required an interpretation of *mens legis*, given that "the language of Article 17 can and should be interpreted from a contemporary perspective and that it constitutes an open offer to arbitrate that can be accepted by an investor."[102]

97 *Id.*, ¶¶ 49, 52–53. The tribunal also noted that the Secretary General of the OIC did not accept the arbitration when notified because he contended that the OIC Agreement only covered State-to-State disputes. *Id.*, ¶ 50.

98 *Id.*, ¶ 59.

99 *Id.*, ¶¶ 75–76.

100 *Id.*, ¶ 79.

101 *Id.*, ¶ 81.

102 *Id.*, ¶ 81. The tribunal went on to state that it "considers that the intention of the Contracting Parties to the OIC Agreement was to create a dispute resolution mechanism that might develop with international law," emphasizing that "an interpretation of a treaty that recognizes the evolution of international law since the signature of the treaty is recognized in the rule of inter-temporal law, accords with the interpretation provisions

It is worth highlighting that the tribunal did not have to address the question as to whether Indonesia specifically consented to the submission of the investment dispute to an UNCITRAL arbitration, since it is apparent from the jurisdictional award that Indonesia consented by letter to the application of the UNCITRAL Rules.[103]

Similarly, in *Kontinental Conseil v. Gabon*, the tribunal concluded – citing the *Al-Warraq* award – that the investor was entitled to avail itself of the offer to arbitration that was contained in Article 17 of the OIC Agreement.[104] In that case, Gabon participated in the constitution of the tribunal and appointed its arbitrator. At the beginning of the arbitration, the tribunal chose the 2010 UNCITRAL Rules and the PCA as the administering institution. Gabon later indicated that it accepted the administration of the case by the PCA, but that

---

of the [Vienna Convention], and has also been recognized in the International Court of Justice." *Id.*, ¶ 82. Notably, the tribunal did not cite any support for that proposition. The "evolutionary" interpretation of the tribunal in *Al-Warraq* was contrary to a well-settled principle under international law, the principle of contemporaneity, which the tribunal simply decided to cast aside. *See, e.g., Dispute Regarding Navigational and Related Rights* (*Costa Rica v. Nicaragua*), Judgment, 13 July 2009, ICJ REPORTS 213 (2009), ¶ 63 ("[T]he terms used in a treaty must be interpreted in light of what is determined to have been the parties' common intention, which is, by definition, contemporaneous with the treaty's conclusion."); *Wintershall*, ¶ 129 (indicating that this principle implies "that the terms of a treaty have to be interpreted according to the meaning they possessed (and in the circumstances prevailing), at the time the treaty was concluded"), n. 147 ("[I]n the interpretation of treaties one important principle is contemporaneity: *i.e.*, it must be construed as at the time it was entered into."); *ICS*, ¶ 289 ("[I]t is appropriate and helpful to resort to the principle of contemporaneity in treaty interpretation, particularly pertinent in the case of bilateral treaties. This principle requires that the meaning and scope of this term be ascertained as of the time when the UK and Argentina negotiated their BIT."). As to the temporal limitation contained in Article 17 of the OIC Agreement ("until the Organ for the settlement of disputes arising under the Agreement is established"), the tribunal observed that no document designated the IICJ as the dispute resolution organ contemplated in Article 17, and that its competence was expressly limited to inter-State disputes. *Al-Warraq*, ¶ 86. Thus, the *Al-Warraq* tribunal concluded that it had not been established in evidence that the IICJ was the organ contemplated by Article 17: it is a judicial organ, it does not provide conciliation or arbitration services, it is not competent to decide investor-State disputes and, last but not least, it is not operational. *Id.*, ¶¶ 88–89.

103 *Id.*, ¶ 13.

104 *Kontinental Conseil Ingénierie v. Gabonese Republic*, PCA Case No. 2015-25, Award, 23 December 2016 ("*Kontinental Conseil*"), ¶ 157. In another non-public arbitration in which jurisdiction was also based on Article 17 of the OIC Agreement, *Navodaya Trading v. Gabon*, PCA Case No. 2018-23, it was reported that the tribunal also found that the provision contained consent to arbitration and that Gabon had consented to the tribunal's jurisdiction. *See* Damien Charlotin, *Uncovered: Kaufmann-Kohler Chaired Tribunal Confirms That OIC Agreement Contains Consent to Arbitration, but Ultimately Dismisses Mining Claims on the Merits*, INVESTMENT ARBITRATION REPORTER, 17 February 2021.

it wanted the arbitration proceedings to be conducted under the ICC Rules. However, the tribunal confirmed its initial choice of the 2010 UNCITRAL Rules and the PCA as the administering institution.[105] The tribunal ultimately found that Gabon breached the obligation to provide fair and equitable treatment to investors, which was imported from the Belgium/Luxembourg Economic Union-Gabon BIT by application of the OIC Agreement's MFN clause.[106] As in *Al-Warraq*, the respondent in this case consented to the application of the UNCITRAL Rules.[107]

105 *Kontinental Conseil*, ¶¶ 32–33, 35, 48–49, 52, 54–55.

106 *Id.*, ¶ 170. In contrast, the tribunal rejected the claimant's attempt to import umbrella clauses from the Belgium/Luxembourg Economic Union-Gabon BIT and the Germany-Gabon BIT to bring claims related to the contracts it had concluded with Gabon. *Id.*, ¶¶ 172–189. The claimant later applied to the Paris Court of Appeals for a partial set aside of the award, but the application was dismissed. *Kontinental Conseil Ingénierie v. Gabonese Republic*, Paris Court of Appeals, Judgment, 25 June 2019, ¶ 16. Interestingly, the Paris Court of Appeals noted that the MFN clause of the OIC Agreement did not extend to procedural provisions included in these other treaties (which arguably included the umbrella clause) – particularly to the provisions that delimit the arbitral tribunal's jurisdiction. *Id.*, ¶¶ 16–18.

107 Indonesia's explicit agreement to the application of the UNCITRAL Rules in the *Al-Warraq* case, as well as Gabon's agreement to the application of the UNCITRAL Rules in the *Kontinental Conseil* case, could be regarded as a subsequent agreement on a forum between the parties to the dispute (which turns consent "in principle" to international arbitration into an enforceable and effective consent). This key distinction with other cases involving Article 17 of the OIC Agreement (in which there was no similar agreement) was precisely underscored by the Paris Court of Appeals in its decision to set aside the partial award in *D.S. Construction FZCO v. Libya* (*see* pp. 68–70, *infra*). *See D.S. Construction FZCO v. Libya*, Paris Court of Appeals, Judgment, 23 March 2021, ¶ 103 ("In this respect, if DS Construction relies on the position of certain State parties to the OIC Agreement having accepted the possibility of submitting their dispute to the Permanent Court of Arbitration such as in the case of *Al-Warraq v. Republic of Indonesia* (award of June 21, 2012) and in the *Kontinental Conseil Ingenierie SARL v. Gabon* case (award of December 23, 2016) relating to two claims for arbitration based on the OIC Agreement, it should be noted that in these two cases, which did not concern [Libya], there was no agreement between the parties to derogate from the application of Article 17 in the absence of the appointment of arbitrators by the States concerned. On the contrary, in these two cases, only once the arbitral tribunal has been duly constituted, the States concerned having accepted to appoint an arbitrator, is that the parties have agreed to apply the UNCITRAL Rules, so that these precedents do not allow to draw the interpretative conclusion that DS Construction intends within the meaning of the aforementioned article 31.") (translation). It should also be highlighted that the tribunal in *Itisaluna v. Iraq* reached the conclusion that the general consent to international arbitration contained in Article 17 of the OIC Agreement did not constitute consent to a specific forum (*see* pp. 45–46, *supra*).

More recently, in *Michael Lee-Chin v. Dominican Republic*, the majority of the tribunal completely disregarded the fundamental principle that there is no consent without a forum and found jurisdiction under Article XIII of Annex III of the CARICOM-DR FTA, even in the absence of an agreement to arbitrate under the UNCITRAL Rules.[108]

The Dominican Republic objected to the jurisdiction *ratione voluntatis* of the UNCITRAL tribunal on the grounds that the first paragraph of Article XIII could not be interpreted as a standing offer of consent, and that the second paragraph of Article XIII expressly required a subsequent agreement on a forum (and no agreement was reached with the claimant on the establishment or composition of the tribunal, since the State only appeared before the arbitral tribunal to object to its jurisdiction). In turn, the claimant argued that the first paragraph of Article XIII contained an offer to arbitrate on the part of the State and that the second paragraph only addressed the issue of how to appoint the arbitrators (*i.e.*, dealing only with procedural issues once an arbitral proceeding had already been initiated). In addition, the claimant contended that the Dominican Republic agreed to apply the 1976 version of the UNCITRAL Rules, but that in any event an agreement was not necessary since, in the absence of an agreement, the UNCITRAL Rules could be applied by default.

In its decision upholding jurisdiction, the majority of the tribunal stated that the wording of the first paragraph of Article XIII ("shall ... be submitted") was unambiguous, expressed a duty, and represented an offer to arbitrate, which could be unilaterally accepted by the investor.[109] To justify its conclusion, the majority relied on the *effet utile* principle, alleging that the effective use of the provision was to "serve as an offer of consent."[110] The majority also opined that the third paragraph of Article XIII, which provides that the investor who has consented to submit a dispute to international arbitration cannot

108 Article XIII of Annex III the CARICOM-DR FTA states as follows: "1. Disputes between an investor of one Party and the other Party concerning an obligation of the latter under this Agreement in relation to an investment of the former which have not been amicably settled shall, after a period of three months from written notification of a claim, be submitted to the courts of that Party or to national or international arbitration. 2. Where the dispute is referred to international arbitration, the investor and the Party concerned in the dispute may agree to refer the dispute to an international arbitrator or ad hoc arbitration tribunal to be appointed by a special agreement or established under the Arbitration Rules of the United Nations Commission on International Trade Law." *See* pp. 30–32, *supra*. The author of this monograph was counsel for respondent in this case.

109 *Lee-Chin*, Partial Award, ¶¶ 94, 97, 109.

110 *Id.*, ¶ 118.

benefit from diplomatic protection and implied that the investor's unilateral act was sufficient, confirmed its interpretation.[111]

As to the interpretation of the second paragraph of Article XIII, the majority believed that it "establishes what happens when a choice is made to institute an international arbitration,"[112] particularly pointing to the sentence "[w]here the dispute is referred to international arbitration," which, in its view, "indicate[s], in a clear, straightforward and unambiguous manner, that the entire content of paragraph 2 is circumscribed to the case in which the claimant selects that option."[113]

Moreover, the majority held that the expression "may agree to refer the dispute to an international arbitrator or *ad hoc* arbitration tribunal to be appointed by a special agreement or established under the [UNCITRAL Rules]" alluded to the possibility to conclude a subsequent agreement to choose between a sole arbitrator and a three-member tribunal, which had to be constituted in one of the ways provided for, holding that "it is apparent that the Parties have opted for a three-member tribunal for the constitution of which they have followed the precepts of the UNCITRAL Rules, even if considering that Respondent has done so for procedural reasons and reserving its objections to the Tribunal's jurisdiction."[114]

Despite the foregoing, the majority confusingly stated that "assuming that Article XIII offers two options to constitute the tribunal and that both options are equally valid, the fact that the parties do not reach any special agreement to appoint the arbitral tribunal necessarily leads to the other option, specified in this provision after the disjunctive conjunction 'or', that is, the establishment of the tribunal under the UNCITRAL Rules."[115] It added that "[t]he distinction between the verbs 'appointed' and 'established' respectively used for each of them is important," and that "[t]he fact that the tribunal may be established under the UNCITRAL Rules clearly indicates that such rules are applicable."[116] Oddly, the majority then held that "the Parties could have agreed to appoint the sole arbitrator (an international arbitrator) or provided for a special mechanism to appoint arbitrators," and that "[t]hey did neither, relying on the provisions of the UNCITRAL Rules."[117] It went on to say that "the Parties did not question the applicability of the UNCITRAL Rules to the constitution

111 *Id.*, ¶ 126.
112 *Id.*, ¶ 144.
113 *Id.*, ¶ 152.
114 *Id.*, ¶¶ 164–174.
115 *Id.*, ¶ 186.
116 *Id.*, ¶ 187.
117 *Id.*, ¶ 189.

of the Tribunal or to any of the actions taken so far," concluding that "[e]ven accepting Respondent's allegation that it accepted the application of these rules in order to object to the jurisdiction, since, according to Respondent, the Republic had never consented to international arbitration, the truth is that it did so on the basis of the UNCITRAL Rules without proposing the application of any other arbitral instrument."[118]

Those statements on the purported "agreement" to apply the UNCITRAL Rules are in stark contradiction to what the tribunal said immediately thereafter: "In the Tribunal's view, Respondent is correct to state – consistently with the expert proposed by Claimant – that the involvement of a party in the constitution of an arbitral tribunal cannot be interpreted as a consent to the jurisdiction of such tribunal."[119] The majority ultimately held that the UNCITRAL Rules applied to the arbitration and thus declared that the dispute was within the jurisdiction of the tribunal.[120]

In short, the majority resorted to a series of confusing (and sometimes even contradictory) arguments and undertook an interpretation mainly based on factors such as alleged good faith, the object and purpose of the provision and the doctrine of *effet utile* to override the clear wording of Article XIII.[121] It is striking that the majority did not focus at all on the terms "may agree," effectively reading those terms out of the relevant dispute settlement provision, and simply found – without any basis – that the disjunctive conjunction "or" meant that the second option (UNCITRAL Rules) was the default or fallback option.[122]

---

118 *Id.*, ¶ 192.

119 *Id.*, ¶ 193. *See also* G. Lampo & G. Minervini, *Michael Anthony Lee-Chin v Dominican Republic: Interpreting the Consent to Arbitrate in the CARICOM–DR FTA*, p. 509 ("The [Dominican Republic], however, noted that it had not reached an agreement with the Claimant on the establishment and the composition of the Tribunal, as it had only appeared before the arbitrators to object to their jurisdiction. Hence, its involvement in the arbitration proceedings could not have been construed as consent to the use of the UNCITRAL Rules.").

120 *Lee-Chin*, Partial Award, ¶¶ 194, 222.

121 *See, e.g.*, nn. 29, 32, *supra*.

122 *See* G. Lampo & G. Minervini, *Michael Anthony Lee-Chin v Dominican Republic: Interpreting the Consent to Arbitrate in the CARICOM–DR FTA*, p. 514 ("[T]he Tribunal neglected to notice that both the options of 'having an *ad hoc* tribunal appointed' or 'an UNCITRAL tribunal established' do follow the only verb 'may agree to refer'. Hence, also the application of UNCITRAL Rules requires the subsequent agreement of the parties. Furthermore, the fact that the verb 'to establish' conveys the idea that the UNCITRAL Rules operate as the automatic and default arbitration rules is contrasted by several BITs whose arbitration clauses – despite being very similar to article XIII of the CARICOM-DR FTA – explicitly allow investors to initiate an arbitration using the UNCITRAL Rules when a different agreement is lacking."). *See* n. 47, *supra*.

In his dissenting opinion, Professor Kohen observed that, under Article XIII, "the State bound itself to submit disputes not to international arbitration, but to one of three different options, which include international arbitration, but without consenting to the investor having the power to choose which of the three shall be used to settle the dispute."[123] He added that "[i]f there is no unilateral possibility of choice, there is no unilateral consent by the State that can be perfected when the investor makes his/her choice. An *ex post* agreement between the parties is necessary."[124] While analyzing the first paragraph of Article XIII, Professor Kohen emphasized that "[i]t is undeniable that the text fails to state who shall proceed to the election of one of the three adjudicatory dispute settlement means mentioned therein or how this is to be done."[125] He considered that the majority's interpretation "seriously affects the principle of equality of the parties in dispute settlement."[126] As to the second paragraph of Article XIII, he opined that it "establishes what happens or may happen 'where the dispute is referred to international arbitration'," only regulating "the scenarios *where* this happens," but it did not arise from the text of the provision "that it is the investor who has the ability to choose international arbitration."[127] Professor Kohen stated that the reasoning of the majority was the result of a series of inferences, concluding that "[i]t takes a lot of imagination to believe that the Parties to the Treaty have 'clearly and unambiguously' consented to the possibility that the investor alone decide to choose to refer the dispute to international arbitration."[128] In his view, an interpretation of Article XIII of the treaty in accordance with the interpretive principles enshrined in the Vienna Convention showed that "there are three dispute settlement options between a State and an investor, that none if preferred, and that the Parties did not consent to either one of the disputing parties or only the investor deciding which of the three dispute settlement means shall apply."[129]

Notably, both the majority and the dissenting arbitrator shared the view that, absent an agreement between the parties with respect to the election of a sole arbitrator or a tribunal, the UNCITRAL Rules shall apply.[130] However, the

123 *Lee-Chin*, Dissent, ¶ 4.
124 *Id.*, ¶ 4.
125 *Id.*, ¶ 6.
126 *Id.*, ¶ 10.
127 *Id.*, ¶¶ 17–18, 22.
128 *Id.*, ¶¶ 91, 117.
129 *Id.*, ¶ 80.
130 *Lee-Chin*, Partial Award, ¶¶ 187, 189, 192 ("The fact that the tribunal may be established under the UNCITRAL Rules clearly indicates that such rules are applicable … [T]he Parties could have agreed to appoint a sole arbitrator ('an international arbitrator') or provided for a special mechanism to appoint arbitrators. They did neither, relying on the provisions

language of the provision clearly requires an agreement between the parties to the dispute on a forum; it does not contemplate UNCITRAL arbitration as the default or fallback option, as the tribunal wrongly stated. In fact, this decision has been criticized precisely for not taking into account that the second paragraph of the provision expressly requires a subsequent agreement on the arbitral forum and on the procedure to be followed.[131]

As two commentators have observed, the conclusion reached by the tribunal is "unconvincing inasmuch as it is based on a reading of [A]rticle XIII(2) which seems to disregard the wording providing that the parties 'may agree to refer' the dispute to a sole arbitrator or to a tribunal (either appointed by a special agreement or established under the UNCITRAL Rules)."[132]

In short, from an analysis of the relevant precedents, it is apparent that some investment tribunals reached incorrect conclusions primarily because they overlooked the basic principle that consent to international arbitration is forum-specific.

9 The Invocation of the Most-Favored Nation Clause Does Not Do the "Trick" in the Absence of a Forum

Investors often invoke the MFN clause of an investment agreement to overcome the absence of a forum in the relevant dispute settlement provision. However, the MFN clause cannot be used to provide for an arbitral forum where one does

of the UNCITRAL Rules … [T]he express inclusion of the UNCITRAL Rules in Article XIII does not seem unremarkable."); *Lee-Chin*, Dissent, ¶ 21 ("I agree with Claimant and my colleagues' interpretation of the meaning of the reaming part of this paragraph … absent an agreement between the parties with respect to the election of a sole arbitrator or a tribunal, then the UNCITRAL Arbitration Rules shall apply. This shows as well that the Parties to the Treaty know how to draft an option by default when they want to include it.").

131 *See* G. Lampo & G. Minervini, *Michael Anthony Lee-Chin v Dominican Republic: Interpreting the Consent to Arbitrate in the CARICOM–DR FTA*, p. 517 ("[A]rticle XIII cannot serve as a jurisdictional basis for tribunals and thus the conclusion reached by Prof Kohen in his Dissenting Opinion is to be shared. However, contrary to what Prof Kohen argued, this conclusion would not derive from an interpretation of [A]rticle XIII(1) according to the principle of equality of the parties. Rather, it would follow from the wording of the second paragraph of the provision, which specifies that the parties 'may agree to refer' a dispute to arbitration, thus imposing a subsequent agreement on the arbitral forum and on the procedure to be followed.").

132 *Id.*, p. 517. *See also id.* ("The Dissenting Opinion did not properly highlight this formulation either.").

not exist.[133] Without a forum, there is no enforceable and effective consent to international arbitration. The MFN clause cannot serve the function of supplying the missing forum in order to "supplement" or "perfect" consent to arbitration. If an MFN clause were allowed to be used in this way (*i.e.*, to supply the missing arbitral forum), it would have the practical effect of importing consent to arbitration – that is not present in the basic treaty – from another investment agreement entered into by the host State with a third State. Such an expansive application of an MFN clause should be frowned upon by arbitral tribunals since it would be contrary to basic principles of international law.[134]

As a preliminary matter, applying the MFN obligation (which is a substantive obligation) prior to establishing the existence of consent to arbitration under an investment agreement would in effect mean putting the cart before the horse. Put simply, if there is no consent to international arbitration in an investment agreement, an arbitral tribunal constituted under said investment agreement would not be empowered to apply the MFN obligation contained therein in the first place – a problem that has been described as a "sequential issue."[135]

---

133 This monograph does not intend to discuss the meaning and scope of the MFN clause in investment agreements, and to what extent, if any, the MFN clause could be used to import better procedural rights or substantive protections from other investment agreements. In the present monograph, the discussion on the role of the MFN clause is limited to dealing with the impossibility of using an MFN clause to import consent to international arbitration (including consent to a specific forum) from another investment agreement.

134 *See* pp. 24–27, *supra*.

135 *See, e.g.*, *ST-AD*, ¶ 344 ("[B]efore a tribunal can apply an MFN clause, ... above all, the tribunal must have jurisdiction *ratione voluntatis*."); *Kimberly-Clark*, ¶¶ 165–167 ("As a matter of principle, a Tribunal which lacks jurisdiction (*ratione voluntatis*) is barred from applying the treaty's substantive guarantees, including the MFN clause ... Like for other substantive protections, an arbitral tribunal can only assess whether the host state breached the MFN clause of a treaty if it has jurisdiction to do so."); *Hochtief AG v. Argentine Republic*, ICSID Case No. ARB/07/31, Decision on Jurisdiction, 24 October 2011, Separate and Dissenting Opinion of J. Christopher Thomas, Q.C., ¶¶ 81–82 ("Seeking the application of a particular rule of treatment in the Treaty in order to create jurisdiction seems to me to be putting the cart before the horse ... A tribunal cannot adjudicate someone's rights if they have not met the threshold jurisdictional requirements to be able to claim such rights."); *Venezuela US*, Dissent, ¶ 28 ("One of the contradictions in applying a MFN provision to issues of jurisdiction is that the Tribunal, instead of determining first that it has jurisdiction under the ISDS provision in the BIT and then analysing a claim of a breach under an MFN provision, has begun the analysis the other way around."); C. McLachlan, L. Shore & M. Weiniger, INTERNATIONAL INVESTMENT ARBITRATION: SUBSTANTIVE PRINCIPLES (2d. ed., Oxford University Press 2017), ¶ 7.333 ("It is also a basic principle of international law that the existence and application of a substantive obligation is a separate question to the conferral of jurisdiction upon an international tribunal. Whatever the source or

In addition to this "sequential issue," it is generally recognized that consent to international arbitration could never be imported through an MFN clause.[136] This fundamental limitation on the application of an MFN clause was even underscored by the tribunal in the seminal case on MFN, *Maffezini v. Spain*, in which it stated that a forum agreed by the contracting parties to an investment agreement could not be replaced by another.[137] In fact, as the late Professor Orrego Vicuña (who chaired the *Mafezzini* tribunal) asserted in an article he published after the decision, the role of the MFN clause "is not to substitute consent for a lack of consent."[138]

---

nature of the substantive obligation, 'jurisdiction always depends upon consent.'"); T. Gazzini, INTERPRETATION OF INTERNATIONAL INVESTMENT TREATIES, pp. 305–306 ("[T]he majority [in *Garanti Koza*] conflate[d] two questions that must be kept distinct: the consent to ICSID arbitration and the functioning of the MFN clause ... It is after – and only after – establishing its competence on the basis of the relevant procedural provisions that a tribunal can interpret and apply [the MFN clause] ... The tribunal conflates the two questions and lets the unsettled jurisprudence on the functioning of the MFN clause upset the sacrosanct principle that no international tribunal is competent unless all concerned parties have agreed, one way or another, to the exercise of its jurisdiction. In this case, therefore, the task before the Tribunal was first to interpret Article 8 of the BIT in order to determine whether it could exercise its jurisdiction. Having answered in the negative, there was no need to interpret Article 3 of the BIT, containing the MFN.").

136 In some decisions, tribunals have focused on the language of the relevant MFN provisions in investment agreements to accept or reject the importation of consent to international arbitration or to a forum other than the one provided in the basic treaty. However, the fact that an MFN clause explicitly applies to dispute settlement, or to "all matters" covered by an investment agreement, is not sufficient to conclude that consent to international arbitration or to a different forum could be imported.

137 *Emilio Agustín Maffezini v. Kingdom of Spain*, ICSID Case No. ARB/97/7, Decision of the Tribunal on Objections to Jurisdiction, 25 January 2000, ¶¶ 62–63 ("[T]here are some important limits that ought to be kept in mind. As a matter of principle, the beneficiary of the clause should not be able to override public policy considerations that the contracting parties might have envisaged as fundamental conditions for their acceptance of the agreement in question ... [I]f the agreement provides for a particular arbitration forum, such as ICSID, for example, this option cannot be changed by invoking the [MFN] clause, in order to refer the dispute to a different system of arbitration.").

138 Francisco Orrego Vicuña, *Reports of [Maffezini's] Demise Have Been Greatly Exaggerated*, 3 JOURNAL OF INTERNATIONAL DISPUTE SETTLEMENT 299 (2012), pp. 302–303 ("The issue concerning the application of the MFN clause, however, is not that consent has not been given, it is that once given there might be more favourable conditions for the exercise of rights under a different treaty to which also consent was given and MFN treatment granted. No rights different from those in the original treaty are created by the MFN clause, only the treatment accorded to such rights is the relevant element of comparison ... The role of the MFN clause ... is not to substitute consent for a lack of consent but to ensure that the consent given is implemented in the most favorable manner to the individual investor entitled to protection as compared to the treatment given

After the *Maffezini* decision, this principle was reaffirmed by many tribunals. For instance, in *Hotchief v. Argentina*, the tribunal emphasized that the MFN clause "cannot create a right to go to arbitration where none otherwise exists under the BIT."[139] Similarly, in *EURAM v. Austria*, the tribunal unequivocally stated that "[i]f a BIT has no provision for investor-State arbitration, there is no offer of arbitration and thus no scope for the creation of an arbitration agreement."[140] More recently, the tribunal in *Doutremepuich v. Mauritius* noted that arbitral tribunals have consistently concluded that "consent to arbitrate could not be imported via the MFN clause from a third State treaty."[141]

A distinction must be made between those cases in which the claimants tried to enlarge an existing consent via an MFN clause in the basic treaty and cases in which the claimants were trying to import non-existing consent in

---

to other such individuals in treaties with third countries."). Other commentators have also underscored this basic principle. *See, e.g.*, S. Vesel, *Clearing a Path Through a Tangled Jurisprudence: Most-Favored-Nation Clauses and Dispute Settlement Provisions in Bilateral Investment Treaties*, pp. 127–128 ("[A]n MFN clause cannot be made to substitute for a state's consent to jurisdiction, either to gain access to arbitration in the first instance or to gain access to what might be perceived as a more favorable arbitral forum.").

139 *Hochtief AG v. Argentine Republic*, ICSID Case No. ARB/07/31, Decision on Jurisdiction, 24 October 2011, ¶¶ 79, 81 ("It might be argued that the MFN clause requires that investors under the Argentina-Germany BIT be given MFN treatment during the conduct of an arbitration but that the MFN clause cannot create a right to go to arbitration where none otherwise exists under the BIT. The argument can be put more generally: the MFN clause stipulates how investors must be treated when they are exercising the rights given to them under the BIT but does not purport to give them any further rights in addition to those given to them under the BIT ... [I]t cannot be assumed that Argentina and Germany intended that the MFN clause should create wholly new rights where none otherwise existed under the Argentina-Germany BIT ... The MFN clause is not a *renvoi* to a range of totally distinct sources and systems of rights and duties: it is a principle applicable to the exercise of rights and duties that are actually secured by the BIT in which the MFN clause is found.").

140 *European American Investment Bank AG v. Slovak Republic*, PCA Case No. 2010-17 (UNCITRAL), Award on Jurisdiction, 22 October 2012 ("*EURAM*"), ¶ 447. *See also id.* ("Even if that BIT contains a broadly worded MFN clause, that clause cannot substitute for the arbitration provision and make it possible for an investor successfully to bring arbitration proceedings against a State Party to the BIT, no matter what provisions for arbitration that State Party might have agreed to include in its other BITs."); *Accession Mezzanine Capital L.P. and Danubius Kereskedöház Vagyonkezelö Zrt. v. Hungary*, ICSID Case No. ARB/12/3, Decision on Respondent's Objection under Arbitration Rule 41(5), 16 January 2013, ¶ 74 ("[A]n investor may properly rely only on rights set forth in the basic treaty, meaning the BIT to which the investor's home state and the host state of the investment are directly parties, but not more than that.").

141 *Doutremepuich*, ¶ 223.

the basic treaty through the MFN clause from a different treaty with a third State that had consent. In the first line of cases (save for those tribunals that claimed not to be importing consent but in effect did so[142]), tribunals rejected importing consent to arbitration that did not exist in the basic treaty.[143] In the second line of cases, although the majority of tribunals rejected enlarging an existing consent in the basic treaty,[144] a few tribunals improperly allowed the

---

142 *See* pp. 73–79, *infra*.

143 *See* pp. 64–73, *infra*.

144 *See Salini Costruttori S.p.A. and Italstrade S.p.A. v. Hashemite Kingdom of Jordan*, ICSID Case No. ARB/02/13, Decision on Jurisdiction, 9 November 2004, ¶¶ 102–119 (rejecting the claimants' argument that the MFN clause of the Italy-Jordan BIT could expand the tribunal's jurisdiction to cover contractual claims by relying on the Jordan-US BIT and UK-Jordan BIT); *Berschader*, ¶¶ 159–208 (rejecting by majority the claimants' argument that the MFN clause contained in the Belgium/Luxembourg-Russia BIT – whose dispute resolution clause only covered arbitration of claims relating to expropriation – could incorporate a more favorable dispute settlement mechanism contained in the Norway-Russia BIT); *Telenor Mobile Communications v. Republic of Hungary*, ICSID Case No. ARB/04/15, Award, 13 September 2006, ¶¶ 83–101 (rejecting the claimant's argument that in order to make an fair and equitable claim it could invoke, pursuant to the MFN clause of the Norway-Hungary BIT (which limited the tribunal's jurisdiction to claims of expropriation and of breach of the BIT's transfer clause), other more favorable dispute resolution provisions in other (unspecified) BITS); *Quasar de Valors SICAV S.A., Orgor de Valores SICAV S.A., GBI 9000 SICAV S.A. and Alos 34 S.L. v. The Russian Federation*, SCC Case No. 24/2007, Award on Preliminary Objections, 20 March 2009, ¶¶ 68–120 (holding by majority that the particular MFN clause of the Spain-Russia BIT – providing investors a no less favorable level of fair and equitable treatment – precluded recourse to the broader arbitration provision of the Denmark-Russia BIT, but finding that it had jurisdiction pursuant to Article 10 of the Spain-Russia BIT to determine whether there had been an expropriation); *Señor Tza Yap Shum v. The Republic of Peru*, ICSID Case No. ARB/07/6, Decision on Jurisdiction and Competence, 19 June 2009, ¶¶ 207–216 (holding that it had jurisdiction over claimant's expropriation claim but rejecting additional claims for breach of other treaty provisions, including FET, as the China-Peru BIT did not provide for arbitration of such claims and its MFN clause could not be used in search of more generous arbitration terms); *Austrian Airlines (AUA) v. Slovak Republic*, UNCITRAL, Final Award, 9 October 2009, ¶¶ 135–140 (rejecting by majority the claimant's argument that it could rely on the MFN clause in the Austria-Slovakia BIT to circumvent a restrictive arbitration clause contained in the BIT – which limited arbitration to the amount and conditions of payment of compensation for expropriation and free transfer obligations contained in that treaty); *Les Laboratoires Servier, S.A.A., Biofarma, S.A.S., Arts et Techniques du Progres S.A.S. v. Republic of Poland*, UNCITRAL, Award, 14 February 2012 (redacted) (though the Interim Award on Jurisdiction of 3 December 2010 is not public, it is referred to in the Award, and rejects the claimant's attempt to use an MFN clause to expand the tribunal's jurisdiction beyond claims relating to expropriation), ¶ 511 ("[T]he MFN provisions in Article 4(1) of the France-Poland BIT do not expand arbitral competence in the present proceedings, with the consequence that BIT Article 8(2) applies to restrict the Tribunal's jurisdiction to disputes relating to alleged divestment under Article 5(2), to the exclusion of the Claimants' Non-Expropriation

use of MFN clauses to expand or enlarge consent to international arbitration in the basic treaty *via* an MFN clause.[145] Those expansive interpretations of MFN

Claims. Moreover, the Tribunal has not been persuaded that the applicable law provisions of the BIT, including Article 8(3), operate to expand its jurisdiction in these proceedings."); *EURAM*, ¶¶ 441–455 (rejecting the claimant's argument that the MFN clause of the Austria-Slovakia BIT could be used in a way that completely transformed the scope of its arbitration provision, which only covered disputes concerning the mode or amount of compensation owed in case of an expropriation, and disputes over the transfers clause of the BIT); *ST-AD*, ¶¶ 376–403 (rejecting the claimant's contention that the MFN provision of the Bulgaria-Germany BIT allowed the claimant to circumvent the treaty's narrow arbitration clause, which only covered the question of compensation owed in cases of (already-established) expropriations); *Sanum Investments Limited v. The Government of the Lao People's Democratic Republic*, PCA Case No. 2013-13, Award on Jurisdiction, 13 December 2013 ("*Sanum*"), ¶¶ 343–358 (rejecting the claimant's contention that the MFN clause of the China-Laos BIT permitted the claimant to reach into other Laotian BITs in search of an even more generous investor-state arbitration mechanism, since the dispute resolution clause in the China-Laos BIT only covered disputes concerning "the amount of compensation for expropriation"); *A11Y LTD v. Czech Republic*, ICSID Case No. UNCT/15/1, Decision on Jurisdiction, 9 February 2017, ¶¶ 93–107 (rejecting the claimant's attempt to expand the scope of the arbitration clause in the UK-Czech Republic BIT – which only covered disputes concerning the umbrella clause, compensation for losses, expropriation and transfer provisions – by invoking the MFN clause of the treaty and the more favorable dispute resolution clause contained in the Netherlands-Czech BIT); *Ivan Peter Busta and James Peter Busta v. Czech Republic*, SCC Case No. V 2015/014, Final Award, 10 March 2017, ¶¶ 163–169 (rejecting the claimant's attempt to use an MFN clause to invoke dispute settlement provisions that permitted arbitration over a broader range of issues than did the basic treaty); *Anglia Auto Accessories Ltd. v. Czech Republic*, SCC Case No. V2014/181, Final Award, 10 March 2017, ¶¶ 191–194 (rejecting the claimant's attempt to use an MFN clause to invoke dispute settlement provisions that permitted arbitration over a broader range of issues than the basic treaty, since the basic treaty did not provide consent to arbitrate claims based on fair and equitable treatment, full protection and security, or on the MFN clause itself); *Beijing Urban Construction Group Co. Ltd. v. Yemen*, ICSID Case No. ARB/14/30, Decision on Jurisdiction, 31 May 2017, ¶¶ 116–121 (rejecting the investor's attempt to rely on the China-Yemen BIT's MFN clause to widen the tribunal's jurisdiction so that claims other than expropriation could also be arbitrated).

145 *See RosInvest v. Russia*, SCC Case No. V079/2005, Award on Jurisdiction, 1 October 2007, ¶¶ 124–139 (holding that the arbitration clause contained in the United Kingdom-Russia BIT did not confer the tribunal with jurisdiction to determine whether an expropriation had occurred – providing only for arbitration of disputes over the amount of compensation in cases where an expropriation has been established or in relation to other matters dependent upon an act of expropriation – and, instead, relying on the MFN clause of that treaty to resort to the more favorable arbitration clause contained in the Denmark-Russia BIT); *UP and C.D. Holding Internationale (formerly Le Chèque Déjeuner) v. Hungary*, ICSID Case No. ARB/13/35, Decision on Preliminary Issues of Jurisdiction, 3 March 2016, ¶¶ 221–222 (holding that the claimants could validly import a more favorable arbitration clause from the Hungary-Lithuania BIT to bypass the France-Hungary BIT's provision that limited arbitration to "dispossession" (expropriation) claims, and thus allowing for

clauses are highly questionable and, in effect, also result in importing consent to issues that were not covered by the scope of the consent granted in the basic treaty.[146] In the words of the tribunal in *Sanum v. Laos*, to use an MFN clause to expand the dispute settlement provision to "cover all protections under the Treaty when the Treaty itself provides for very limited access to international arbitration would result in a substantial re-write of the Treaty and an extension of the States Parties' consent to arbitration beyond what may be assumed to have been their intention, given the limited reach of the Treaty protection and dispute settlement clauses."[147]

9.1 *Cases Rejecting the Importation of Consent to a Forum through an MFN Clause*

The importation of consent through an MFN clause has been expressly rejected in several cases. In *Plama v. Bulgaria*, the tribunal expressly dismissed an attempt to create consent to ICSID jurisdiction where none existed, holding that a specific agreement on a dispute settlement mechanism could not be replaced by the application of the MFN clause. The tribunal observed that "dispute resolution provisions in a specific treaty have been negotiated with a view to resolving disputes under that treaty."[148] It further noted that "[i]t is also not evident that when parties have agreed in a particular BIT on a specific dispute resolution mechanism, as is the case with the Bulgaria-Cyprus BIT (*ad hoc* arbitration), their agreement to most-favored nation treatment means that they intended that, by operation of the MFN clause, their specific agreement on such a dispute settlement mechanism could be replaced by a totally different dispute resolution mechanism (ICSID arbitration)."[149] The tribunal

---

the investors' fair and equitable treatment claims to be heard on the basis of the arbitration clause in the Hungary-Lithuania BIT).

146 *See* Facundo Perez-Aznar, *The Use of Most-Favoured-Nation Clauses to Import Substantive Treaty Provisions in International Investment Agreements*, 20 J. INT'L ECON. L. 777 (2017), p. 781 ("[T]ribunals have consistently rejected the use of MFN clauses to alter the scope of the ISDS provisions or to create consent, with only three exceptions (the tribunals in *RosInvest v Russia*, *Garanti Koza v Turkmenistan* and *Venezuela US v Venezuela*). This shows that, in general, tribunals have rejected the application of MFN provisions to broaden the jurisdiction of investment tribunals *ratione temporis*, *materiae*, *personae* or *voluntatis*."); A. Steingruber, CONSENT IN INTERNATIONAL ARBITRATION, p. 317 ("The consensual nature of arbitration should not make it possible to enlarge the jurisdictional basis of an investment tribunal or to invoke the host State's consent to a different arbitral forum.").

147 *Sanum*, ¶ 358.

148 *Plama*, ¶ 207.

149 *Id.*, ¶ 209. The *Plama* tribunal mentioned Article 3(3) of the UK Model BIT (which provides that, "[f]or avoidance of doubt[,] it is confirmed that the treatment provided for

also made a distinction between providing more favorable treatment and replacing a negotiated forum for another: "It is one thing to add to the treatment provided in one treaty more favorable treatment provided elsewhere. It is quite another thing to replace a procedure specifically negotiated by parties with an entirely different mechanism."[150] Ultimately, the *Plama* tribunal concluded that the MFN provision of the Bulgaria-Cyprus BIT could not be interpreted as providing consent to submit a dispute under the Bulgaria-Cyprus BIT to ICSID jurisdiction.[151]

A similar reasoning was applied by the tribunal in *Menzies v. Senegal*, where the claimant strangely attempted to use the MFN clause of the General Agreement on Trade in Services ("GATS") to import consent from the offers of arbitration contained in the investment agreements concluded between

in paragraphs (1) and (2) above shall apply to the provisions of Articles 1 to 11 of this Agreement.") as an example of a provision in which the "intention to incorporate dispute settlement provisions [is] clearly and unambiguously expressed." *Id.*, ¶ 204. However, even if the language of the MFN clause is broad and explicitly encompasses dispute settlement provisions, it is still not possible to import consent to a different arbitral forum. *See Garanti Koza*, Dissent, ¶ 71(v) ("The MFN clause contained in Article 3(3) of the U.K.-Turkmenistan BIT cannot be interpreted as allowing the 'import' of consent to ICSID arbitration to a treaty regime that does not contain such consent.").

150 *Plama*, ¶ 209.

151 *Id.*, ¶ 227. *See also Yaung Chi oo Trading Pte Ltd. v. Republic of the Union of Myanmar*, ASEAN I.D. Case No. ARB/01/1, Award, 31 March 2003, ¶ 83 (rejecting the claimant's reliance on the MFN clause contained in Article 8 of the 1998 Framework Agreement for the ASEAN Investment Area in order to import a jurisdictional basis from the Myanmar-Philippines BIT); *Wintershall*, ¶ 176 ("[T]he MFN clause in Article 3 (even assuming it were to be so interpreted as to extend to Article 10), cannot avail the Claimant, since what the Claimant seeks to invoke in its Request for Arbitration ... is a different system of arbitration under a different BIT. Systems of arbitration in two treaties can never be the same when, under one treaty, the dispute is to be ultimately resolved only by ICSID arbitration (if both Contracting States are parties to the ICSID Convention), and under the other treaty (Argentina-US BIT) the dispute is to be resolved at the choice of the investor either under ICSID arbitration or under UNCITRAL arbitration: the latter is undoubtedly "a different system of arbitration."); C. McLachlan, L. Shore & M. Weiniger, INTERNATIONAL INVESTMENT ARBITRATION: SUBSTANTIVE PRINCIPLES (1st. ed.), ¶¶ 7.162, 7.168. ("[I]t is essential when applying an MFN clause to be satisfied that the provisions relied upon as constituting more favourable treatment in the other treaty are properly applicable, and will not have the effect of fundamentally subverting the carefully negotiated balance of the BIT in question ... [T]he balance struck in investment treaties between the various dispute settlement options is often the subject of careful negotiation between the State parties, selecting from a range of different techniques. It is not to be presumed that this can be disrupted by an investor selecting at will from an assorted menu of other options provided in other treaties, negotiated with other State parties and in other circumstances.").

Senegal and third States.[152] The tribunal dismissed the claimant's attempt since Senegal had not granted such consent through the GATS. In its reasoning, the tribunal observed that the purported consent was not "express, clear and unambiguous," given that the MFN clause under the GATS is silent on dispute resolution, and that its general wording could not be "considered a current, express and unequivocal consent to arbitration."[153] The tribunal also observed that, even if it were to accept that the MFN clause includes investment arbitration (which it did not), doing so would only "create an obligation for the State concerned to offer arbitration," but the "States still have the option of refusing to respect an obligation, which remains an inescapable prerogative of their sovereignty."[154] Thus, the tribunal concluded that if Senegal would be "in breach" of the MFN clause, it could not be compelled to arbitration because of the lack of consent.[155] In the tribunal's view, in the hypothetical case that the MFN clause of the GATS applied to investment arbitration, "this would only be of a nature to create an obligation for the signatory States to offer arbitration in the future and does not represent a consent to arbitration or the extension of an offer to arbitrate."[156]

In *Heemsen v. Venezuela*, the tribunal also rejected the claimants' attempt to rely on the MFN clause of the Germany-Venezuela BIT to import consent to UNCITRAL arbitration from Venezuela's BITs with third parties, which did

152 *Menzies Middle East and Africa S.A. and Aviation Handling Services International Ltd. v. Republic of Sénegal*, ICSID Case No. ARB/15/21, Award, 5 August 2016 ("*Menzies*"). *See also* Facundo Pérez-Aznar, *Menzies Middle East and Africa SA and Aviation Handling Services International Ltd v Senegal: Consent to International Jurisdiction and the Limits of Most-Favoured-Nation Clauses*, 34(1) ICSID REVIEW 190 (2019).

153 *Menzies*, ¶¶ 130, 132.

154 *Id.*, ¶¶ 136–137.

155 *Id.*, ¶ 143.

156 *Id.*, ¶ 140. In a similar fashion, the tribunal in *AHG v. Iraq* rejected the attempt of a claimant to access consent to ICSID arbitration from the State's consent in the France-Iraq BIT through the MFN clause of the Partnership and Cooperation Agreement Between the European Union and the Republic of Iraq ("EU-Iraq PCA"). Although the EU-Iraq PCA contained an MFN clause, the tribunal held that the relevant section of the treaty was limited to "measures affecting trade in services and establishment in all economic activities," and that Ad Article 23(2) of Annex 4 specifically excluded investor-State protection, including investor-State dispute settlement procedures, from the scope of Section II. In the tribunal's view, the "clear and unequivocal" language of Ad Article 23(2) belied the claimant's assertion, since the provision "says the exact contrary," excluding investment protection. Thus, the tribunal, by majority, concluded that the claimant's argument that consent to ICSID arbitration contained in the Iraq-France BIT could be imported through the MFN clause of the EU-Iraq PCA was manifestly without legal merit. *AHG*, ¶¶ 98–100, 111.

not limit access to UNCITRAL arbitration to a specific temporal period.[157] First, the tribunal held that the MFN clause of the Germany-Venezuela BIT did not explicitly cover the treaty's dispute-settlement provisions; rather, the MFN clause strictly applied to the treatment with regard to the investors' "activities related to their investments."[158] Second, it observed that it was not true that the claimants were trying to merely import more favorable procedural requirements, as the issue of the applicability of the MFN clause had to be resolved precisely because the tribunal concluded that the contracting parties did not consent to an UNCITRAL arbitration except for the interim period during which Venezuela had not become a party to the ICSID Convention.[159] Although the claimants argued that the temporal condition relates to a non-existent period (as in reality there was no interim period), the tribunal held that "nothing in the text of the Treaty indicates that the Contracting Parties would have consented to submit disputes to an *ad hoc* arbitration under UNCITRAL Rules if they had not contemplated the existence of an interim period."[160] Thus, "if the MFN Clause would be applied to the dispute settlement provision, without any indication that such was the will of the Contracting Parties, Respondent's consent would be imported in an artificial manner."[161] In rejecting importation, the tribunal stressed that the MFN clause could not have a "neutralizing effect" over the conditions of access *ratione voluntatis* of the BIT, and in particular indicated that the elected fora could not be affected by the MFN clause.[162] Recently, the Paris Court of Appeals dismissed a setting aside application and upheld the tribunal's decision.[163]

Likewise, the tribunal in *Kimberly-Clark v. Venezuela* rejected importing consent to international arbitration through MFN clauses when consent granted in the basic treaties was limited to a specific period of time that had already elapsed.[164] The claimants submitted a dispute to arbitration under the ICSID Additional Facility Rules on the basis of three separate investment agreements: the Spain-Venezuela BIT, the Netherlands-Venezuela BIT and the Belgium/Luxembourg-Venezuela BIT. Venezuela objected to the jurisdiction *ratione voluntatis* of the tribunal on the ground that the Spain-Venezuela

157 *Heemsen*, Award, ¶¶ 407–408. *See* pp. 42–43, *supra*.
158 *Heemsen*, Award, ¶ 405.
159 *Id.*, ¶ 406. *See* n. 70, *supra*.
160 *Heemsen*, Award, ¶ 406.
161 *Id.*, ¶ 407.
162 *Id.*, ¶ 408.
163 *Enrique Heemsen and Jorge Heemsen v. Bolivarian Republic of Venezuela*, Paris Court of Appeals, Judgment, 20 September 2022, ¶¶ 67–78.
164 *Kimberly-Clark*, ¶ 213.

BIT and the Netherlands-Venezuela BIT contained only a time-limited offer to arbitrate under the ICSID Additional Facility Rules – which had expired when Venezuela became a party to the ICSID Convention. The Belgium/Luxembourg-Venezuela BIT, moreover, never contained any offer of arbitration under the ICSID Additional Facility Rules. The tribunal sided with Venezuela and held that none of the treaties at issue contained consent to arbitration under the ICSID Additional Facility Rules.[165] Alternatively, the claimants argued that they could rely on the MFN clauses of the three treaties and invoke more favorable dispute resolution provisions found in a treaty concluded by Venezuela with third States, specifically seeking to import Article 8(2) of the UK-Venezuela BIT, which offers investors the option to pursue arbitration under the ICSID Additional Facility Rules. The tribunal rejected the claimants' attempt to import this dispute settlement provision, affirming the general principle that "a tribunal has no power to incorporate into the treaty more favorable dispute resolution terms so as to create or expand the Contracting States' consent to arbitrate."[166] After analyzing the terms of the MFN clauses of the treaties at issue, the tribunal reasoned that the importation requested by the claimants was not possible on two main grounds. First, "as a matter of principle, a Tribunal which lacks jurisdiction (*ratione voluntatis*) is barred from applying the treaty's substantive guarantees, including the MFN clause."[167] Second, the tribunal rejected incorporating a more favorable dispute resolution provision through the MFN clauses of the relevant treaties because it found that, even if it had jurisdiction, the MFN clauses at issue had limitations and would not cover dispute settlement.[168] Thus, the tribunal concluded that the claimants were not entitled to benefit from more favorable dispute resolution terms through the MFN clauses of other treaties.[169]

165 *Id.*, ¶¶ 161, 212, 231.

166 *Id.*, ¶ 167.

167 *Id.*, ¶ 165.

168 *Id.*, ¶¶ 169, 212, 233, 235. It is interesting to note that the tribunal found that the MFN clause of the Belgium/Luxembourg-Venezuela BIT (Article 3(3)) did not apply to procedural matters, but only to substantive treatment, because of the words "in the territory of the other Contracting Party" contained in that provision. The tribunal reasoned that the settlement of investment disputes could not qualify as "treatment in the territory of Venezuela," and that even if arbitration could be characterized as "treatment," it would not be located in the host State. *See Kimberly-Clark*, ¶ 235. In comparison, the language of the MFN clause (Article 3(2)) in the Barbados-Venezuela BIT at issue in *Venezuela US v. Venezuela*, also uses the words "in its territory" and has arguably even more limiting language than the MFN clause of the Belgium/Luxembourg-Venezuela BIT. *See Venezuela US*, Interim Award, ¶ 47; pp. 76–79, *infra*.

169 *Kimberly-Clark*, ¶¶ 172, 212, 236.

Similarly, in *Doutremepuich v. Mauritius*, the tribunal rejected the claimant's attempt to import the offer of arbitration contained in Article 9 of the Finland-Mauritius BIT on the basis of the MFN clause of France-Mauritius BIT, which does not contain an offer to arbitrate investor-State disputes. After analyzing the specific language of the MFN clause, discarding its extension to investor-State arbitration and acknowledging the principle of *ejusdem generis* as a limit to the application of MFN clauses, the tribunal underscored that "where the Basic Treaty does not contain consent to arbitrate investor-State disputes at all, the Tribunal cannot imagine any circumstances in which the *ejusdem generis* rule would be met," since "[t]he subject matter of the provision to be imported from a third-State treaty containing consent to arbitrate would be different from the one in the Basic Treaty containing no consent."[170] Accordingly, the tribunal dismissed the case, finding that the claimants could not invoke the MFN clause to import consent.[171]

Several tribunals were faced with requests to import consent to international arbitration through the MFN clause of the OIC Agreement. In *D.S. Construction FZCO v. Libya*, the claimant invoked the MFN clause of the OIC Agreement to import the provisions allowing the application of the UNCITRAL Rules from the Austria-Libya BIT. Given that Libya failed to appoint an arbitrator, the claimant requested the OIC Secretary General to make a default appointment. However, since the OIC Secretary General did not make the appointment, the claimant resorted to the PCA and requested that it designate another appointing authority, relying on the MFN clause of the OIC Agreement to import Libya's consent to the UNCITRAL Rules – which entrusts the Secretary General of the PCA with appointing authority in case of failure by a previous appointing authority – as expressed in the Austria-Libya BIT. The PCA held that it had authority under the OIC Agreement, the Austria-Libya BIT and the UNCITRAL Rules to designate an appointing authority, and accordingly designated Pierre-Marie Dupuy as appointing authority, who in turn appointed Nassib Ziade as Libya's arbitrator. Although Libya objected to the constitution of the tribunal, the arbitral tribunal issued a partial award on 15 February 2018 affirming that it had been properly constituted.[172]

After the tribunal rendered its partial award, Libya resorted to the Court of Appeals of Paris (the seat of the arbitration) requesting the setting aside of that partial award on the basis that the tribunal had been improperly constituted.

170 *Doutremepuich*, ¶ 229.

171 *Id.*, ¶ 236.

172 Katia Bennadji, *The PCA's Assistance in the Constitution of an Arbitral Tribunal: Last Breath for Investor-State OIC Arbitrations?*, Kluwer Arbitration Blog, 15 April 2019.

In its decision dated 23 March 2021, the Paris Court of Appeals sided with Libya and annulled the tribunal's partial award.[173] Libya argued that Article 17 of the OIC Agreement had no reference to the UNCITRAL Rules and that the application of the UNCITRAL Rules required a written agreement between the parties, which did not exist.[174] In addition, Libya contended that the tribunal could not import that consent to UNCITRAL arbitration through the MFN clause of the OIC Agreement.[175] The Court observed that Article 17 did not provide for any rules in the case that the OIC Secretary General refused to designate an arbitrator, nor expressly provided recourse to other arbitral rules, and in particular to the UNCITRAL Rules.[176] In rejecting the importation of the UNCITRAL Rules through the MFN clause of the OIC Agreement, the Court viewed the OIC Agreement's investor-State arbitration provisions, meant as a gap filler pending the institution of a permanent court (which never occurred), as relevant. It followed that the "intent of the OIC parties was manifestly not to rely on a dispute-settlement procedure imported from another treaty, but to the contrary to provide for an *ad hoc* procedure."[177] In addition, the Court did not consider that the MFN clause of the OIC Agreement covered the right to arbitrate.[178] Accordingly, in the absence of Libya's express agreement to either submit the constitution of the tribunal to the PCA or to the application of the UNCITRAL Rules, the Paris Court of Appeals concluded that the tribunal was improperly constituted and proceeded to set aside the partial award.[179]

More recently, the majority of the tribunal in the *Itisaluna v. Iraq* case mentioned above rejected the importation of consent to international arbitration through an MFN clause.[180] The claimants initiated a case against Iraq

---

173 D.S. Construction FZCO v. Libya, Paris Court of Appeals, Judgment, 23 March 2021, Dispositif (2).

174 *Id.*, ¶¶ 53–54.

175 *Id.*, ¶ 58.

176 *Id.*, ¶ 82.

177 *Id.*, ¶ 97 (translation).

178 *Id.*, ¶ 101.

179 *Id.*, ¶ 107, IV – Dispositif (2). There are other pending cases in which the PCA accepted that it had authority under the MFN clause of the OIC Agreement to designate an appointing authority. *See* Luke Peterson, *OIC Round Up: An Update on Pending Arbitration Cases Lodged under the OIC Investment Agreement*, INVESTMENT ARBITRATION REPORTER, 11 August 2020 (reporting that in the case *Omar Bin Sulaiman Abdul Aziz AL Rajhi v. Oman*, PCA Case No. 2017-32, the PCA designated late judge James Crawford as appointing authority, who in turn appointed Ms. Jean Kalicki to serve as Oman's arbitrator, and that the tribunal rejected Oman's jurisdictional objections).

180 *Itisaluna*, ¶¶ 223, 225. In another case involving the interpretation of Article 17 of the OIC Agreement, *Al-Warraq v. Indonesia* (*see* pp. 49–52, *supra*), the claimant alternatively argued that, if Article 17 of the OIC Agreement did not contain the required consent to

for alleged violations of the OIC Agreement, on the basis that Article 17 of the OIC Agreement constituted Iraq's consent in writing to submit a dispute to arbitration in general terms and that, by operation of the MFN clause of the OIC Agreement, Iraq's consent in writing to submit the dispute to ICSID arbitration in Article 17(4)(a) of the Iraq-Japan BIT could be read into the OIC Agreement.[181] In other words, the claimants' case was "rooted in a claim to a general consent to arbitration founded in Article 17 of the OIC Agreement, supplemented by consent to ICSID arbitration, derived, via de OIC Agreement MFN clause, from the Iraq-Japan BIT."[182] Iraq objected to the jurisdiction *ratione voluntatis* of the tribunal, arguing that Article 17 of the OIC Agreement made no reference to ICSID arbitration and written consent could not be imported from the Iraq-Japan BIT by operation of the MFN clause of the OIC Agreement.[183]

The majority of the tribunal concluded that the MFN clause of the OIC Agreement could not be relied upon by the claimants to incorporate the consent in writing to submit the dispute to ICSID arbitration found in the Iraq-Japan BIT into the OIC Agreement.[184] Given that the OIC Agreement is a multilateral agreement, the tribunal underscored that it had "to exercise considerable caution when it comes to a (proposed) interpretation of the Agreement that neither follows clearly and necessarily from the plain and ordinary meaning of its terms[,] nor derives from the clear and dispositive practice of all of its Contracting Parties, resting rather on the contested practice of one of its Contracting Parties alone."[185] Although the tribunal concluded that Article 17(2) of the OIC Agreement constituted consent to arbitration in general terms, but not specific consent to ICSID arbitration, it proceeded to analyze whether

arbitrate, then the claimant was entitled to seek resolution of disputes by virtue of the MFN clause in Article 8 of the OIC Agreement. *Al-Warraq*, ¶ 59. However, since the tribunal considered that consent to arbitrate existed under Article 17 of the OIC Agreement, it held that no decision was required as to the application of the MFN clause. *Al-Warraq*, ¶ 103. Furthermore, there are other non-publicly available cases in which the MFN clause of the OIC Agreement had been invoked to import consent from other investment treaties. *See* Luke Peterson, *Libya Wins One And Loses One, As New Bilateral Investment Treaty Awards Are Rendered*, INVESTMENT ARBITRATION REPORTER, 18 February 2020 (reporting on the case *Tekfen TML Joint Venture et al. v. Libya*, ICC Case No. 21371 (2015), where the claimants invoked the provisions of the OIC Agreement and the Libya-Turkey BIT – which contains a clause providing for ICC arbitration, among other options – and in which the tribunal held that it had jurisdiction, but dismissed all claims on the merits).

181 *Itisaluna*, ¶ 21.

182 *Id.*, ¶ 79.

183 *Id.*, ¶¶ 20–21, 40.

184 *Id.*, ¶ 148.

185 *Id.*, ¶ 153.

consent to ICSID arbitration contained in Article 17(4)(a) of the Iraq-Japan BIT could be imported into the OIC Agreement by operation of Article 8(1) of the OIC Agreement, the MFN clause.[186]

The *Itisaluna* tribunal observed that the MFN clause was "subject to exception and limitation, both express and by necessary implication, that exclude its application to incorporate an ICSID consent to arbitration clause from another treaty."[187] The tribunal also appreciated the public policy framework on which the claimants were seeking to rely, particularly the incorporation of a principle from another treaty without regard to the bargain that was struck when the other treaty was adopted, stressing that it had to strike the balance that preserved the MFN principle but guarded against the risks of overreach.[188] It reasoned that the MFN clause could not be properly relied upon to incorporate into the OIC Agreement the consent to ICSID arbitration found in an unrelated bilateral treaty concluded by an OIC Agreement contracting party and a non-contracting party.[189] In addition, the tribunal held that the OIC Agreement established "a clearly defined and particular dispute settlement regime with institutional elements that include an arbitration forum with bespoke characteristics" and that "nowhere provides for ICSID arbitration."[190] The tribunal also noted that "the OIC Agreement establishes a systemic framework for investor protection and facilitation with unique characteristics," which could be described as "public policy considerations," that compelled "a conclusion that the MFN clause in the OIC Agreement cannot be relied upon to incorporate into the OIC Agreement an ICSID consent to arbitration clause from an unrelated bilateral investment treaty."[191] Interestingly, the tribunal observed that, while it may be said "that the MFN principle is capable of enlarging the reach of ICSID arbitration to which consent has already been given in the principal treaty, the Tribunal does not consider that the MFN principle can properly be used to derive from another treaty consent to ICSID arbitration that is not only absent from the principal treaty but evidently intentionally

186 *Id.*, ¶ 191.

187 *Id.*, ¶ 197.

188 *Id.*, ¶ 208. Seeking guidance from *Maffezini*, the *Itisaluna* tribunal noted that "three of the situations expressly envisages in abstract terms … as limiting the application of the MFN principle to dispute settlement arrangements on grounds of public policy either address or approach the situation with which the Tribunal is faced in the circumstances of the present case." *Id.*, ¶ 212.

189 *Id.*, ¶ 213.

190 *Id.*, ¶ 216.

191 *Id.*, ¶¶ 218, 220.

so."[192] Ultimately, the majority of the tribunal concluded that the claimant could not rely on the MFN clause in the OIC Agreement to incorporate into the OIC Agreement the respondent's consent to ICSID arbitration derived from Article 17(4)(a) of the Iraq-Japan BIT, and upheld Iraq's jurisdictional objection *ratione voluntatis*.[193]

Arbitrator Peter reached the opposite conclusion and issued a dissenting opinion. He believed that the tribunal was entitled to assume jurisdiction by operation of the MFN clause included in the OIC Agreement. In his view, "Article 17 of the OIC Agreement contains a general consent to arbitration, that is supplemented by ICSID arbitration through the incorporation of Article 17 of the Iraq-Japan BIT via Article 8(1) of the OIC Agreement."[194] He considered that giving effect to the MFN clause of the OIC Agreement was "consistent with an active and straightforward interpretation and application of this clause," and that, as opposed to the examples given in *Maffezini* referring to situations where clear rules regarding arbitration had been included in the agreement, "the OIC Agreement sometimes lacks clarity and difficulties of interpretation and application arise in the analysis of its dispute resolution provisions."[195] Thus, he opined that the importation of Iraq's consent to ICSID arbitration from the Iraq-Japan BIT by virtue of the MFN clause should have been allowed, as the MFN clause had been invoked "simply to substitute an efficient procedure for a defective one and an effective appointing authority for a dysfunctional one."[196]

---

192 *Id.*, ¶ 221. *See also* Mohamed Abdel Wahab, *Itisaluna and Others v Iraq: The OIC Agreement Conundrum: Consent to ICSID Arbitration and the MFN Clauses Saga*, 36(1) ICSID REVIEW 1 (2021), p. 13 ("[T]he majority does provide a compelling argument that the absence of any reference to ICSID arbitration in the OIC Agreement was based on a conscious decision by the Contracting Parties, especially because many of the OIC Contracting Parties were members of the ICSID Convention at the time of conclusion of the OIC Agreement.").

193 *Itisaluna*, ¶¶ 223, 225.

194 *Id.*, ¶ 231.

195 *Id.*, ¶ 241.

196 *Id.*, ¶ 242. In some reported cases, arbitrations were discontinued due to the failure of the OIC Secretary-General to make default appointments. *See* J. Hepburn & L. Peterson, *Investigation: As new cases emerge under Islamic investment treaty, initial viability of claims seems to hinge on willingness of respondents to appoint arbitrators*, INVESTMENT ARBITRATION REPORTER, 2 March 2017 (reporting that, in the three cases initiated by Hashem Al Mehdar. Mohamed Al Mehdar, Badr Al Mehdar and Betoul Al Mehdar against Egypt, the claims did not proceed since Egypt failed to nominate an arbitrator and the OIC Secretary-General did not make the default appointment). In such cases, the fact that the procedure is "defective" or that the appointing authority is "dysfunctional" could not be used as an excuse to import consent to a specific forum through the MFN clause where there is none.

9.2 *Cases Allowing the Importation of Consent to a Forum through an MFN Clause*

On the other hand, in three cases – *Garanti Koza v. Turkmenistan*, *Krederi v. Ukraine* and *Venezuela US v. Venezuela* – even while acknowledging the basic principle that consent to arbitration could not be imported, the majority of those arbitral tribunals – regrettably and despite disavowing to do so – ended up importing consent to international arbitration through the application of an MFN clause. In all of these cases, one of the arbitrators dissented.

In *Garanti Koza v. Turkmenistan*, the majority of the tribunal imported consent to ICSID arbitration, accepting the claimant's argument that the MFN clause of the UK-Turkmenistan BIT – which did not contain consent to ICSID arbitration, and only contained consent to UNCITRAL arbitration – permitted it to reach into other Turkmenistan BITs (such as the Switzerland-Turkmenistan BIT) that contained consent to ICSID arbitration. Article 8(2) of the UK-Turkmenistan BIT restricts the investor to submitting a dispute to UNCITRAL arbitration unless Turkmenistan reaches an agreement with said investor to submit a particular dispute to either ICSID or ICC arbitration. After establishing that Turkmenistan had generally consented to international arbitration in the first paragraph of Article 8(1) of the UK-Turkmenistan BIT (which did not mention any forum) but stressing that Turkmenistan had not consented to ICSID arbitration,[197] the majority of the tribunal found that the MFN clause of the UK-Turkmenistan BIT was broadly worded and could be applied to the investor-State arbitration provision in the manner invoked by the claimant.[198] The claimant argued that it was entitled to invoke the MFN clause of the UK-Turkmenistan BIT to benefit from what it considered to be more favorable treatment accorded by Turkmenistan to Swiss investors under Article 8(2) of the Switzerland-Turkmenistan BIT, insofar as a Swiss investor may choose to submit an investment dispute to either ICSID or UNCITRAL arbitration. According to the majority's reasoning, consent to international arbitration did not need to be imported, since Turkmenistan consented "generally" to arbitration. The only provision to be imported was "the choice between ICSID arbitration and UNCITRAL arbitration."[199] Thus, the majority concluded that the choice given to investors between ICSID and UNCITRAL arbitrations in the Switzerland-Turkmenistan BIT respecting dispute settlement was more favorable than the UK-Turkmenistan BIT that restricted the submission of a claim

197 *Garanti Koza*, Decision on Jurisdiction, ¶ 37. *See* pp. 46–48, *supra*.

198 *Garanti Koza*, Decision on Jurisdiction, ¶¶ 51, 64.

199 *Id.*, ¶ 75.

to one system of arbitration.[200] Consequently, the tribunal found that the claimant had availed itself of that more favorable treatment by commencing an ICSID arbitration, holding that it had jurisdiction to hear the claim.[201]

The dissenting opinion of Professor Boisson de Chazournes rightly pointed out that "[l]ack of consent cannot be remedied by the so-called 'import' of consent" through an MFN clause.[202] She stressed that the right to MFN treatment "can only be exercised if the foreign investor and the host State are subject to a dispute settlement relationship under one of the dispute settlement options that are provided in Article 8(2)" of the UK-Turkmenistan BIT.[203] In that regard, she noted that, under Article 8(2) of the UK-Turkmenistan BIT, ICSID arbitration is deemed applicable only "if the foreign investor has *mutually* agreed with the respondent state to have recourse to ICSID arbitration," and, therefore, "there is simply no issue of treatment under ICSID arbitration that arises, since ICSID arbitration is deemed inexistent in the absence of a mutual agreement."[204] Professor Boisson de Chazournes emphasized that, in that case, it "is clear that no mutual agreement *in writing* was reached between Garanti Koza and Turkmenistan to submit the dispute to ICSID arbitration," adding that, since "consent to ICSID cannot be identified, Article 3.3 on MFN treatment is not applicable."[205] Moreover, she found that consent to ICSID arbitration could not be provided by the MFN clause read together with the dispute settlement clause of the UK-Turkmenistan BIT, underscoring that "no investment award or decision has since then decided that an MFN provision would

200 *Id.*, ¶¶ 89–95.

201 *Id.*, ¶ 97. The decision of the majority has been criticized. E. de Brabandere, *Importing Consent to ICSID Arbitration? A Critical Appraisal of Garanti Koza v. Turkmenistan*, p. 15 ("[E]ven if one assumes that the MFN clause applies and may be invoked by the claimant, it is doubtful that, through operation of that clause, consent to a particular form of arbitration may be 'imported' from another treaty. Here, the relative ease with which the majority discarded the paramount need for consent to a specific form of arbitration is very much open to criticism. Indeed, and this is of course peculiar to international law and the involvement of a State, the default principle is that international courts and tribunals have no jurisdiction unless States have given explicit consent. As such, the choice of the specific dispute settlement method made by the States needs to be respected.").

202 *Garanti Koza*, Dissent, ¶ 8. It should be recalled that Professor Boisson de Chazournes had previously found that there was no consent to international arbitration in Article 8(1) of the UK-Turkmenistan BIT, and that the majority's reasoning in finding that the first paragraph contained consent to arbitration "generally" while the second paragraph merely contained the arbitration system which could be used, disregarding the need to interpret the provision as a whole, was wrong. *See* pp. 46–48, *supra*.

203 *Garanti Koza*, Dissent, ¶ 41.

204 *Id.*, ¶¶ 43–44 (emphasis in original).

205 *Id.*, ¶ 51 (emphasis in original).

allow the import of consent to ICSID arbitration from another treaty."[206] She observed that, granting the MFN clause "such extensive effect as to allow for consent to ICSID through incorporation by reference in the frame of a treaty that does not allow this, would have the effect of 'replac[ing] a procedure specifically negotiated by parties with an entirely different mechanism' or 'system of arbitration'," which "would involve a forum-shopping attitude that bypasses the consent requirement of the Respondent while running against the fundamental principles of international adjudication."[207] Accordingly, she reasoned that the MFN clause "cannot bypass the requirement of consent to ICSID arbitration," highlighting that "[n]o attempt to establish consent to ICSID arbitration under an MFN clause is possible, since it will have the perverse effect of replacing *actual* non-consent by *virtual* consent."[208] Finally, Professor Boisson de Chazournes concluded that "[i]t is the absence of a mutual agreement that prevents the 'import' of ICSID arbitration into a treaty that does not provide for ICSID arbitration."[209]

Similarly, in *Krederi v. Ukraine*, a majority of the tribunal found that the possibility to opt for ICSID arbitration could be imported through the UK-Ukraine BIT's MFN clause.[210] Article 8 of the UK-Ukraine BIT only contained a choice for an investor to unilaterally initiate UNCITRAL arbitration (which was the fallback option contemplated in the treaty absent a mutual agreement between the foreign investor and the respondent State on other fora, such as ICSID). The majority found that consent to arbitration was already contained in Article 8(1) of the UK-Ukraine BIT – which did not mention UNCITRAL arbitration – and that the MFN clause did apply to dispute settlement provisions, stating that the application of the MFN clause "did not serve to import consent, but merely the choice between different arbitration systems."[211] Accordingly, the majority concluded that "the MFN clause of the UK-Ukraine BIT, which expressly extends to dispute settlement, can be relied upon to import the more favorable choice of different forms of investment arbitration given to third party investors than only UNCITRAL arbitration as provided for in Article 8(2)

206 *Id.*, ¶ 61. *See also id.*, ¶ 61 ("The role of the MFN clause is not to substitute for a lack of consent, but to ensure that the consent given is implemented in the most favourable manner to the individual investor entitled to protection, as compared to the treatment given to other such individuals in treaties with third countries.").

207 *Id.*, ¶ 63.

208 *Id.*, ¶¶ 62, 64 (emphasis in original).

209 *Id.*, ¶ 68.

210 *Krederi*, ¶¶ 283–341.

211 *Id.*, ¶ 334. *See* pp. 48–49, *supra*.

of the Treaty."[212] One of the arbitrators dissented, finding that the MFN provision could "not abrogate the limitations to jurisdiction arising under the last paragraph of Article 8(2) [of the UK-Ukraine BIT] as an alternative," excluding "the possibility of jurisdiction being found to arise under the MFN clause."[213]

Another case in which consent was improperly imported via the MFN clause – albeit the majority of the tribunal disavowed doing so – is *Venezuela US v. Venezuela*. Although the tribunal unanimously stated that "the MFN clause cannot serve the purpose of importing consent to arbitration when none exists under the BIT,"[214] that was in fact what the majority did. The Barbados-Venezuela BT contained only a time-limit offer to arbitrate under the UNCITRAL Rules (for a period before Venezuela became an ICISD contracting State, if for any reason the ICSID Additional Facility Rules were not available) that had already elapsed – and, in reality, was a possibility that never existed because both contracting parties were already ICSID contracting States when the treaty entered into force.[215] Thus, by incorporating through the MFN clause a consent to UNCITRAL arbitration that did not exist at the time the case was commenced, the majority in effect imported consent to UNCITRAL arbitration.

The tribunal unanimously concluded that "Article 8 alone does not provide a basis for its jurisdiction in the case at hand as arbitration under the UNCITRAL Rules was contemplated by the BIT's Contracting Parties for the period during which Venezuela had not yet become a Contracting State of the ICSID Convention."[216] However, the majority of the tribunal surprisingly allowed the importation of UNCITRAL arbitration, through the application of the MFN clause, from the Venezuela-Ecuador BIT. According to the majority, that was because the MFN clause of the Barbados-Venezuela BIT applied to the provisions on settlement of investment disputes, and, since Venezuela had given its unconditional consent to the submission of investment disputes with Barbadian investors to international arbitration, Barbadian investors could have recourse to UNCITRAL arbitration through the application of the MFN clause under conditions which are not less favorable than the conditions granted to Ecuadorian investors.[217]

---

212 *Krederi*, ¶ 341.

213 *Id.*, ¶ 343(ii).

214 *Venezuela US*, Interim Award, ¶ 105. *See also Venezuela US*, Dissent, ¶ 1. The author of this monograph was counsel for respondent in this case.

215 *See* pp. 32–35, *supra*.

216 *Venezuela US*, Interim Award, ¶ 89.

217 *Id.*, ¶¶ 100, 109, 128.

The majority explained that, since Article 8(4) of the Barbados-Venezuela BIT provides that the unconditional consent was given "in accordance with the provisions of this Article," the submission to international arbitration is subject to the conditions specified in paragraphs (1) and (2) of Article 8, which determines the arbitration forum to which the dispute can be submitted – either ICSID, ICSID Additional Facility or UNCITRAL Rules. It reaffirmed that "consent covers three different arbitral fora (ICSID, Additional Facility, UNCITRAL [Rules]) under the conditions specified in Article 8."[218] In the majority's view, Article 8(4) expresses the contracting parties' consent to international arbitration, and "[t]here is thus no question of importing Venezuela's consent to international arbitration with Barbadian investors through the operation of Article 3(2) of the BIT from another of Venezuela's BITs concluded with a third State." Rather, the question "is that of the conditions from resorting to international arbitration."[219] Next, the majority observed that recourse to arbitration under the UNCITRAL Rules in the Barbados-Venezuela BIT was subject to a temporal condition (namely, that it has been envisaged for the period prior to Venezuela becoming a contracting State to the ICSID Convention, if the ICSID Additional Facility was not available for any reason), and that, in order to apply the MFN clause, it was sufficient that one of the other treaties entered into by Venezuela with third countries "provides more favourable treatment of investors in relation to the conditions under which they can have recourse to arbitration under the UNCITRAL Rules than Barbadian investors."[220] In the majority's view, if one of those other BITs contains temporal conditions that are less stringent, "then Barbadian investors relying on Article 3(2) of the BIT can claim not to be subjected to the conditions in Article 8(2) of the BIT."[221] Ultimately, since the Ecuador-Venezuela BIT "gives a right to the investor to submit a dispute to an *ad hoc* tribunal under the UNCITRAL Rules not only when the Additional Facility is for any reason not available, but also when ICSID itself is for any reason not available," the majority concluded that Venezuela had to "accept that Barbados' investors shall have recourse to UNCITRAL arbitration ... under

218 *Id.*, ¶ 109.

219 *Id.*, ¶ 111.

220 *Id.*, ¶¶ 113, 115.

221 *Id.*, ¶ 115. Conversely, while interpreting a very similar provision, the Paris Court of Appeals in *Heemsen v. Venezuela* rejected the invocation of the MFN clause to import consent when the offer to arbitrate had a temporal limitation. *Enrique Heemsen and Jorge Heemsen v. Bolivarian Republic of Venezuela*, Paris Court of Appeals, Judgment, 20 September 2022, ¶ 76 ("The [G] consorts could therefore not invoke the benefit of the MFN clause of the Treaty for the purpose of importing a new consent to arbitration by the Venezuelan State under the BIT when the arbitration offer had been expressly limited in time and subject to conditions.") (translation).

conditions which are not less favorable than the conditions under which Ecuadorian investors have such recourse to UNCITRAL arbitration."[222]

In his dissenting opinion, Professor Kohen convincingly noted that the approach taken by the majority of tribunal was meant "to import the consent Venezuela has made regarding UNCITRAL arbitration in other BITs to the present case in which there is none."[223] He observed that "MFN clauses do not possess the power to express consent" and could not be used for "creating *ratione voluntatis* jurisdiction."[224] Professor Kohen reasoned that "Article 8 does not provide to investors of the other party *options* for having recourse to international arbitration" or "establish *mere temporal conditions* for having recourse to one or other of the three possibilities mentioned," but "contains an unconditional consent to international arbitration only to the extent of this article and nothing else."[225] There was no arbitration available in the post-ICSID period and, in his view, "[t]he majority's decision tries to bring back to life a consent to UNCITRAL arbitration that was envisaged at the time of the signature of the BIT (when Venezuela was not a party to the ICSID Convention) but that it *has never been available*."[226] In others words, Professor Kohen noted that the MFN clause "cannot operate with regard to UNCITRAL arbitration and allegedly improve the conditions of the Barbados-Venezuela BIT, simply because the possibility to have recourse to UNCITRAL arbitration under the BIT has never existed."[227] He further observed that "[i]t is a serious mistake to consider that the three different arbitral proceedings mentioned in those paragraphs are simply subject to 'temporal conditions,'" stressing that there are "important differences between a mere 'temporal condition' and the determination of the existence of a given situation."[228] Professor Kohen concluded that, "in spite of an explicit assertion to the contrary," "the majority decided not to follow what is a clear position sustained by different arbitral tribunals in not importing consent when none exists," and its decision resulted in "bring[ing] back to life consent to an arbitral means that had since disappeared, and which has never been applicable."[229]

222 *Venezuela US*, Interim Award, ¶¶ 124, 128.
223 *Venezuela US*, Dissent, ¶ 1.
224 *Id.*, ¶¶ 32, 36 (emphasis in original).
225 *Id.*, ¶ 41 (emphasis in original).
226 *Id.*, ¶ 42 (emphasis in original).
227 *Id.*, ¶ 42.
228 *Id.*, ¶ 48.
229 *Id.*, ¶¶ 54, 58. It should be highlighted that the tribunal in *Kimberly-Clark v. Venezuela*, while interpreting almost identical provisions, reached the opposite conclusion to the one reached by the majority in *Venezuela US*. *See* pp. 67–68, *supra*.

• • •

In sum, the application of the MFN clause of an investment agreement (regardless of its language and scope) cannot function as a tool that would enable a foreign investor to "supplement" or "complete" a general expression of consent, or consent "in principle," to international arbitration in an investment agreement (without a forum), since doing so would in effect result in importing consent – absent in the basic treaty – from another investment agreement entered into by the host State with a third State.

10 What Are the Practical Consequences of the Lack of Forum?

The crux of the matter is that, even if an investment tribunal were to find that there is "consent" by the host State to international arbitration in a broad and general dispute settlement provision of an investment agreement – which only refers to the submission of disputes to international arbitration but does not mention a forum – such general (non-forum-specific) consent could not be considered an enforceable and effective consent to international arbitration that would allow a foreign investor to unilaterally initiate an investment claim against the host State under said investment agreement.

Why? Simply because the foreign investor would have to initiate an international arbitration at a specific forum (*e.g.*, ICSID, ICSID Additional Facility, UNCITRAL Rules, ICC) and a tribunal constituted under those rules would not be able to find State consent to submit disputes to international arbitration under the rules of that specific forum, absent consent to that forum in the relevant investment agreement or a subsequent agreement between the foreign investor and the host State on an arbitral forum.

This problem of lack of forum would have no solution without a subsequent agreement between the parties to the particular dispute on a competent forum. As previously explained, since investment agreements do not contain a choice of arbitral seat, there is no domestic court that could theoretically force or mandate the host State to agree on a forum, or whose domestic arbitral rules could potentially provide a default option on a forum. In practical terms, that would mean that such general consent to international arbitration found in the investment agreement would be unenforceable and ineffective and would merely qualify – at best – as consent "in principle" to international arbitration, which is no more than an incomplete or inchoate expression of consent.[230]

230 Some States have taken note of this pitfall and in their recent model investment treaties have addressed the problem by including more than one forum in their investor-State

It should also be underscored that an arbitral tribunal could not force the State to agree on a forum (either the one under which the arbitration was commenced or a different one) if the State is not willing to do so. As observed by the tribunal in *Planet Mining*, "[b]e as it may, even if 'shall' expresses an obligation of the State to give its consent, the sanction for a failure to do so would not be to supply the missing consent or to deem that constructive consent exists."[231]

In those cases in which the dispute settlement provision in an investment agreement contains merely consent "in principle" to international arbitration, it is always theoretically possible (though unlikely) that the host State would agree on a forum to submit a particular dispute to international arbitration after such dispute has arisen.[232] In fact, where a subsequent agreement on a competent

---

dispute settlement provisions for the investor to choose from. *See, e.g.*, 2019 Dutch Model BIT, Article 19.1 ("If a request for consultations has been submitted according to the procedures laid down in Article 18 and where such consultations do not result in a resolution of the claim within six months from the date of the written request for consultations, the investor may submit a claim under one of the following sets of rules on dispute settlement: a) the Convention on the Settlement of Investment Disputes between States and Nationals of Other States of 18 March 1965 (ICSID Convention) or in accordance with the Rules on the Additional Facility for the Administration of Proceedings by the Secretariat of the Centre (ICSID Additional Facility), where the conditions for proceedings pursuant to the ICSID Convention do not apply; b) the arbitration rules of the United Nations Commission on International Trade Law (UNCITRAL Arbitration Rules), with the understanding that the Permanent Court of Arbitration (PCA) shall administer the proceedings."); 2021 Canada Model FIPA, Article 6 ("An investor of a Party may submit a claim to dispute settlement under: (a) the ICSID Convention, provided that both Parties are parties to the ICSID Convention; (b) the ICSID Additional Facility Rules, if only one Party is a party to the ICSID Convention; (c) the UNCITRAL Arbitration Rules; or (d) any other rules on agreement of the disputing parties."); 2022 Italy Model BIT, Article 24.2 ("In the event that such dispute cannot be settled as provided for in paragraph 1 of this Article within six (6) months from the date of a written application for settlement, the investor in question may submit at its choice the dispute for settlement to one of the following fora (hereinafter collectively referred as 'The Arbitration Tribunal'): (a) an ad hoc Arbitration Tribunal, in compliance with the Arbitration Rules of the UN Commission on International Trade Law (UNCITRAL) as in force at that time, unless another set of rules is agreed by the Parties to the dispute; (b) an arbitral tribunal which is established pursuant to the Dispute Resolution Rules of the International Chamber of Commerce (ICC), the London Court of International Arbitration (LCIA) or the Arbitration Institute of the Stockholm Chamber of Commerce (SCC); (c) the International Centre for Settlement of Investment Disputes (ICSID), for the implementation of an arbitration procedure, under the Washington Convention of 18 March, 1965, on the Settlement of Investment Disputes between State and National of other State, if this had entered into force for both of the Parties to the dispute, or, alternatively, in accordance with the ICSID Additional Facility Rules, if the Washington Convention has entered into force only for one the Parties.").

231 *Planet Mining*, ¶ 162.

232 *See* n. 53, *supra*. It is worth noting that the mere participation in an arbitration or in the constitution of the arbitral tribunal (when done under reservation) cannot be regarded

forum exists between the parties to a dispute, consent to international arbitration under that specific forum would be formed by the general offer to submit disputes to international arbitration in the dispute settlement provision of the investment agreement, accepted by the investor, coupled with the subsequent agreement between the parties to the dispute on a specific forum.

Hence, the practical consequence of the absence of a choice of arbitral forum in a dispute settlement provision of an investment agreement is that such provision is unenforceable and ineffective as a "complete" offer of consent by a State to submit disputes to international arbitration. A subsequent agreement on a forum is required to transform that purported consent "in principle" into an enforceable and effective consent to international arbitration.

11 What Are the Possible Avenues if No Forum Is Subsequently Agreed upon?

As discussed above, investment tribunals cannot find an enforceable and effective unilateral offer of State consent to international arbitration when there is no forum specified in the investment agreement, nor can they mandate or force the State to agree on an arbitral forum without its consent. This is a corollary of States' sovereignty.[233]

---

as "substantive consent" to international arbitration or as a subsequent agreement to a specific forum (*i.e.*, an arbitral institution or rules). Rightly, an ICSID tribunal in *AHS Niger v. Niger* affirmed that "it is an established principle in arbitration that the simple fact of participating in the constitution of a tribunal does not constitute consent to its jurisdiction or a renunciation to submit objections to that effect." *AHS Niger and Menzies Middle East and Africa SA v. Republic of Niger*, ICSID Case No. ARB/11/11, Decision on Jurisdiction, 13 March 2013, ¶ 184. Strangely, although the tribunal in *Lee-Chin v. Dominican Republic* acknowledged this general and well-settled principle, it then held that the State accepted the application of the UNCITRAL Rules, even if it did so only for the limited purpose of objecting to the jurisdiction of the tribunal, by not proposing an alternative arbitral instrument. *Compare Lee-Chin*, Partial Award, ¶ 193 ("In the Tribunal's view, Respondent is correct to state ... that the involvement of a party in the constitution of an arbitral tribunal cannot be interpreted as a consent to the jurisdiction of such tribunal.") *with* ¶ 192 ("Strictly speaking, the Parties did not question the applicability of the UNCITRAL Rules to the constitution of the Tribunal or to any of the actions taken so far. They only argued about the applicable version, with the 1976 original version prevailing. Even accepting Respondent's allegation that it accepted the application of these rules in order to object to the jurisdiction, since, according to Respondent, the Republic had never consented to international arbitration the truth is that it did so on the basis of the UNCITRAL Rules without proposing the application of any other arbitral instrument.").

233 *See* nn. 39–40, *supra*.

However, if the parties to the dispute do not subsequently agree on a forum (including the possibility of the constitution of an *ad hoc* tribunal), that does not mean that the foreign investor is necessarily left with no recourse or remedy.[234] Some potential avenues might be worth exploring. First, the foreign investor could always try to find another investment agreement that contains the State's consent to arbitration in order to initiate an investment arbitration against the host State, by taking advantage of its network of subsidiaries and the broad and encompassing language contained in most investment agreements.[235] Second, the relevant investment agreement could contemplate other dispute settlement mechanisms to which the foreign investor may resort, such as national arbitration or the submission of disputes to domestic courts.[236]

---

234 It is also possible that, in a specific dispute, the State agrees with the claimant on the method to constitute an *ad hoc* arbitral tribunal under an investment agreement (relying on the provisions on the constitution of an arbitral tribunal contained in the investment agreement itself or simply by accepting an offer of constitution of an arbitral tribunal proposed by the claimant). *See* n. 53, *supra* (discussing the *E.T.I. v. Bolivia* case, where the parties to the dispute entered into an *ad hoc* forum agreement). In that scenario, even when there is no direct agreement on a forum, given that the parties agreed on the constitution of the arbitral tribunal, it could be sustained that they "indirectly" agreed on a forum. The reason for this is that, if the parties to the dispute subsequently fail to agree on arbitral rules or an arbitral institution, the constituted tribunal would have inherent powers to select a forum to conduct the arbitration (*i.e.*, to choose arbitral rules and an administering institution). That was precisely the case in the *Kontinental Conseil v. Gabon* arbitration discussed above (*see* p. 52, *supra*). Obviously, this situation has to be distinguished from the State's participation in an arbitration under a particular forum (by participating in the constitution of the arbitral tribunal) for the sole purpose of objecting to that tribunal's jurisdiction (and reserving its rights).

235 The possibility of initiating an arbitration under another investment agreement would depend on the definitions of "investor" or "national" and "investment" in the relevant instrument (for instance, whether the treaty requires a company to have substantial business activity in the country in order to qualify as a national, or contains a denial of benefits clause, or does not protect indirect investments), and would always be subject to treaty abuse arguments by the State – in particular, when several entities within the same corporate chain initiate the same claim or when there is a corporate restructuring at the time that the dispute is foreseeable in order to take advantage of the protection of an investment agreement.

236 Even when the dispute settlement provision in an investment agreement does not contemplate the submission of an investment dispute to the local courts of the host State, those courts might still be competent to hear the foreign investor's claims when domestic courts have jurisdiction over potential breaches of investment agreements – which is generally the case in many civil law jurisdictions that adopt a monist approach. *See* David Sloss, *Domestic Application of Treaties*, in D. Hollis (ed.), THE OXFORD GUIDE TO TREATIES 355 (2d. ed., Oxford University Press 2020), p. 363 ("All monist States recognize the possibility, at least theoretically, that domestic courts can apply (at least some) treaties directly as law.").

Third, even in the absence of an alternative investor-State dispute settlement mechanism, if the host State does not agree with the foreign investor on an arbitral forum, leaving the foreign investor with no recourse against the host State, it could be analyzed whether that conduct constitutes a violation of an obligation of the host State to resolve the investment dispute through investor-State arbitration or to negotiate in good faith a dispute settlement method.[237] If an obligation were found to exist, a breach of such obligation could potentially trigger an inter-State dispute under the State-to-State dispute settlement provision of the relevant investment agreement (depending on the scope and language of such a provision),[238] or even open up the possibility of

---

237 *See, e.g.*, *Lee-Chin*, Dissent, ¶ 95 ("[I]f the investor's State considers that the host State failed to comply in good faith with its obligation to negotiate the selection of the adjudicative means indicated in paragraph 1 of Article XIII, it may rely on Article XIV of the Treaty [State-to-State dispute settlement provision] and submit the dispute to arbitration without the need for its investor to exhaust all domestic remedies."); J. Salacuse, THE LAW OF INVESTMENT TREATIES, pp. 531–532 ("In other treaties, contracting states promise 'sympathetic consideration' of requests to arbitrate disputes by investors of another contracting party. Such a provision is much less than a firm, unequivocal consent to arbitration; however, it can be interpreted as an implied obligation not to withhold consent unreasonably."); A. Steingruber, CONSENT IN INTERNATIONAL ARBITRATION, p. 205 ("The refusal of the host State to give its consent would amount to a breach of its obligation under the BIT for which remedy must, in the first place, lie with the contracting States parties to the BIT.").

238 *See* Nathalie Bernasconi-Osterwalder, *State-to-State Dispute Settlement in Investment Treaties* (International Institute for Sustainable Development, Best Practices Series, October 2014), p. 7 ("Most state-state dispute settlement clauses in investment treaties provide that any disputes between the parties 'concerning the interpretation or application' of the treaty be brought to arbitration … 'Application' relates to the extent to which the actions or measures taken or proposed by the contracting parties comply with the terms of an agreement, its object and purpose … The scope set by these two phrases is 'all-encompassing' regarding the interpretation of a treaty provision in an abstract manner or a specific case, whether an act amounts to a treaty violation either based on direct claims or indirect, diplomatic protection claims."); Michele Potestà, *State-to-State Dispute Settlement Pursuant to Bilateral Investment Treaties: Is There Potential?*, in N. Boschiero, T. Scovazzi, C. Pitea & C. Ragni (eds.), INTERNATIONAL COURTS AND THE DEVELOPMENT OF INTERNATIONAL LAW: ESSAYS IN HONOUR OF TULLIO TREVES 753 (T.M.C. Asser Press 2013), pp. 766–767 ("For certain authors the inter-State arbitration option should be characterized as a guarantee 'of last resort' for the protection of foreign investors should they encounter difficulties in investor-State proceedings. In a similar vein, State-to-State dispute settlement could be viewed as an 'additional tool' in case investor-State arbitration fails, for example due to a lack of co-operation by the host State … In contrast, ordinary difficulties encountered in the course of investment proceedings (deriving, for example, from the refusal by the host State to take part in the arbitration or to appoint their party-appointed arbitrators, or from other dilatory tactics, etc.) should not be viewed as a sufficient reason for discontinuing (or failing to initiate) investor-State proceedings

resorting to diplomatic protection through a State-to-State dispute settlement provision.[239]

12 Conclusion

Investment tribunals must exercise great care when interpreting a dispute settlement provision in an investment agreement and, in particular, when exercising jurisdiction over a sovereign State. Consent to international arbitration must be clear and unequivocal, and has to be proven with a sufficient degree of certainty. When interpreting an investor-State dispute settlement

---

and for 'elevating' the dispute to an inter-State level. That is so because investor-State provisions in BITs are normally drafted so as to avoid such scenarios, either by referring to arbitration administered by an institution (*in primis*, ICSID) which will therefore ensure that the arbitration is not derailed, or by providing for procedural safeguards in case of *ad hoc* arbitration. The room for resorting to inter-State arbitration would thus not seem to be too wide in practice. Things, however, may change in the future if the backlash, perceived in certain quarters, against investor-State arbitration should succeed in convincing States to discard this mechanism in their future treaties. It is still early to attempt to identify trends in this area. But it appears significant that certain countries, such as Australia, have recently expressed the firm resolution to avoid investor-State dispute settlement mechanisms in their future investment treaties (or in the investment chapter of their free trade agreements). If this choice is effectively pursued in future treaty negotiations, the so far dormant inter-State dispute settlement mechanisms are likely to experience renewed interest."); A. Steingruber, CONSENT TO INTERNATIONAL ARBITRATION, p. 204–205 ("The investor's home State can nevertheless request that the host State gives its consent and, if necessary, resort to such procedures as are available between the States parties to the BIT. Thus, any remedy must, in the first place, lie with the treaty partner to the BIT. In such a case, several remedies for breach of treaty on the level of public international law may be available to the investor's home State.").

239 In one publicly-known case, the *Italy v. Cuba ad hoc* arbitration, a diplomatic protection claim was brought by Italy against Cuba, asserting the protection of Italian investors' investments under the State-to-State dispute settlement provision of the Cuba-Italy BIT. Cuba argued that the existence of investor-State provisions in the investment agreement barred Italy from bringing a diplomatic protection claim. However, the majority of the tribunal rejected Cuba's argument because it decided that – in the absence of any provision dealing with the relationship between investor-State and State-to-State dispute settlement mechanisms in the Cuba-Italy BIT – the investor's home State could exercise diplomatic protection as long as the investor had neither consented to arbitrate with the host State nor submitted the dispute to investor-State arbitration. Thus, the tribunal ultimately found that, since no investor-State claim had been commenced by the purportedly affected Italian investors against Cuba, Italy was entitled to bring diplomatic protection claims. *Italian Republic v. Republic of Cuba*, Ah-Hoc State-to-State Arbitration, Interim Award, 15 March 2005, ¶ 65. *See also* N. Bernasconi, *State-to-State Dispute Settlement in Investment Treaties*, p. 9.

provision in an investment agreement, an arbitral tribunal should take into account the objective intention of the contracting parties as embodied in the text of the provision itself, even if such interpretation leads to a result that the tribunal finds undesirable.[240]

Consent to international arbitration is forum-specific, which means that consent is not granted in the abstract, but is specific to a particular arbitral tribunal under a particular forum. Therefore, general or vague references in investor-State dispute settlement provisions to the submission of disputes to international arbitration, without specifying a forum or any indication as to how the competent forum must be determined, are not sufficient to constitute an enforceable and effective offer of consent to international arbitration that would allow a foreign investor to unilaterally initiate a claim against the host State. Such broad, general language could be potentially interpreted in four ways:

- Some dispute settlement provisions could be interpreted as simply acknowledging the possibility of submitting disputes to international arbitration provided a subsequent agreement is entered into by the foreign investor and the host State.
- In certain circumstances, those provisions could be interpreted as merely establishing certain pre-conditions prior to the submission of disputes to international arbitration, or even limiting the different alternative dispute settlement methods available to the parties to resolve their investment dispute, but without embodying State consent to international arbitration.
- In other cases, dispute settlement provisions might contain only general or vague references to the submission of disputes to international arbitration, without any mention of an arbitral forum (or might require an agreement on a forum and not contemplate a default or fallback option in case of lack of agreement). Even if in those cases it were possible to conclude that there is consent "in principle" to international arbitration, such consent is not an enforceable and effective offer to arbitrate an investment dispute without

240 *See Planet Mining*, ¶ 169 ("It is also noteworthy that a failure to abide by the requirements of Article XI(4)(a) does not open the door to UNCITRAL arbitration as a default mechanism. Thus, if one follows Indonesia's interpretation, Planet could well be barred from ICSID arbitration (because Indonesia does not consent under Article XI(4)(a)) and from UNCITRAL arbitration (because both Contracting States are ICSID members). This is undoubtedly a surprising and unsatisfactory result. Yet, it is the result that derives from the text of the Treaty and the Tribunal cannot change the text, especially not in the absence of *travaux* that would shed a different light on the words. As was stated in *Renta 4*, the Tribunal's task is to discover, not to invent, meaning.").

a subsequent agreement on a competent forum between the parties to the dispute.

- Finally, in some cases, there was initially consent to international arbitration in the investor-State dispute settlement provision, but the relevant forum contemplated by the contracting parties to the investment agreement is no longer available (typically because one of the contracting parties withdrew from ICSID). That situation could be equated to the prior case: there is arguably consent "in principle" to international arbitration, but a subsequent agreement on a competent forum is required in order to have an enforceable and effective offer of consent to international arbitration.

The lack of a supranational investment court or arbitral tribunal means that there is no authority that could solve the dilemma or somehow "fix" or "supplement" an incomplete, unenforceable or ineffective offer of consent to international arbitration contained in an investment agreement if the State is not willing to subsequently agree on a forum. As frustrating as it may be for the foreign investor, the host State cannot be forced to agree on a competent forum, let alone be mandated to go to international arbitration, without its consent.[241] The language of dispute settlement provisions in investment agreements cannot be "stretched" or "supplemented" to fabricate consent to international arbitration where there is no forum indicated or where there are multiple fora mentioned but no fallback option in case of lack of agreement on a competent forum.

In some recent cases, a handful of investment tribunals have resorted to contorted and questionable interpretations of dispute settlement provisions in investment agreements in order to overcome the lack of a forum. Those tribunals, while asserting that they were merely "interpreting" those dispute settlement provisions in accordance with the interpretive principles laid down in the Vienna Convention, clearly departed from the language of those provisions, either by reading words into them that those provisions do not contain – for instance, by invoking the purported "object and purpose" of the investment agreement, vague notions of good faith or the malleable principle of *effet utile* – or by applying MFN clauses in a way that results in supplying the

241 *See, e.g.*, *Planet Mining*, ¶ 171 ("It is correct that an inter-State tribunal would not be in a position to procure Indonesia's missing consent. It could only order specific performance. It would be left to Indonesia to abide by such an order with the result that the investor might still be left without recourse to ICSID arbitration ... For that tribunal's jurisdiction to exist consent is needed; an obligation to consent is insufficient."); *Ghella*, ¶ 183 ("As international law does not offer a jurisdictional solution to remedy alleged breaches without an expression of consent, it would be 'unfair', as the Respondents indicated at the Hearing, that the Arbitral Tribunal accepts to decide the present case.") (translation).

missing forum. Investment tribunals should not lose sight of the fact that it is not their task to rewrite dispute settlement provisions in investment agreements, but simply to interpret and apply them.[242] It is a core principle of international law that a State cannot be forced to surrender or limit its sovereignty or to be taken without its consent to an international tribunal.[243] Those questionable and expansive interpretations of dispute settlement provisions, and particularly some "creative" findings of jurisdiction, are some of the main reasons that give investment arbitration a bad name and undermine the confidence of States in the system.[244]

---

242 *See, e.g.*, *Interpretation of Peace Treaties with Bulgaria, Hungary and Romania* (Second Phase), Advisory Opinion, 18 July 1950, ICJ REPORTS 221 (1950), p. 221 ("It is the duty of the Court to interpret the Treaties, not to revise them."); *Wintershall*, ¶¶ 82 ("[I]t is not the function of interpretation to revise treaties or to read into them what they do not contain expressly or by implication; that the terms (the text) of a treaty must always be adhered to, for the reason that a treaty expresses the mutual will of the Contracting States."), 84 ("If this be the duty of an international court, the duty of an ICSID Tribunal is no different."); *Lee-Chin*, Dissent, ¶ 96 ("[I]t is not [the tribunal's] task to evaluate the dispute settlement mechanisms agreed upon by the Parties, but to strictly apply the Treaty, rather than forcing the Treaty to state what it fails to state."); *Enrique Heemsen and Jorge Heemsen v. Bolivarian Republic of Venezuela*, Paris Court of Appeals, Judgment, 20 September 2022, ¶ 55 ("[U]nder Article 31 of the Vienna Convention, it is not for the arbitral tribunal, under the guise of interpretation, to modify the clear terms of the Treaty.") (translation); *Quasar de Valors SICAV S.A. et al. (Formerly Renta 4 S.V.S.A. et al.) v. Russian Federation*, SCC Case No. 24/2007, Award on Preliminary Objections, 20 March 2009, ¶ 93 ("The duty of the Tribunal is to discover and not to create meaning."); *Gabčíkovo-Nagymaros Project (Hungary/Slovakia)*, Separate Opinion of Judge Bedjaoui, 25 September 1997, ICJ REPORTS 7 (1997), p. 123 ("'*[I]nterpretation*' is not the same as the '*substitution*' for a negotiated and approved text, of a completely different text, which has neither been negotiated nor agreed.") (emphasis in original); Robert Jennings & Arthur Watts (eds.), OPPENHEIM'S INTERNATIONAL LAW, VOL. I (9th. ed., 1992), pp. 1271–1272 ("That such a textual approach – on which the International Law Commission was unanimous – is an accepted part of customary international law is suggested by many pronouncements of the International Court of Justice, which has also emphasised that interpretation is not a matter of revising treaties or of reading into them what they do not expressly or by necessary implication contain, or of applying a rule of interpretation so as to produce a result contrary to the letter or spirit of the treaty's text.").

243 This warning was expressly made by Professor Kohen in his dissenting opinion in *Lee-Chin v. Dominican Republic*: "International courts and tribunals must be extremely cautious in analyzing the existence of their jurisdiction. The exercise of jurisdiction over a dispute in which a State has not given its consent entails a serious disregard for the sovereignty of the State(s) concerned." *Lee-Chin*, Dissent, ¶ 118. *See also Venezuela US*, Dissent, ¶ 2 ("[A]n exercise of jurisdiction in a dispute by which consent has not been given constitutes a serious infringement of the sovereignty of the State or States concerned.").

244 *See, e.g.*, E. de Brabandere, *Importing Consent to ICSID Arbitration? A Critical Appraisal of Garanti Koza v. Turkmenistan*, p. 15 ("From a systemic perspective, it should also not be forgotten that creative findings of jurisdiction may well be counterproductive for the

Bibliography

Books

Andrea Steingruber, CONSENT IN INTERNATIONAL ARBITRATION (Oxford University Press 2012).

Anthony Aust, MODERN TREATY LAW AND PRACTICE (Cambridge University Press 2013).

Campbell McLachlan, Laurence Shore & Matthew Weiniger, INTERNATIONAL INVESTMENT ARBITRATION: SUBSTANTIVE PRINCIPLES (1st. ed., Oxford University Press 2007).

Campbell McLachlan, Laurence Shore & Matthew Weiniger, INTERNATIONAL INVESTMENT ARBITRATION: SUBSTANTIVE PRINCIPLES (2d. ed., Oxford University Press 2017).

Christopher F. Dugan, Don Wallace, Jr., Noah D. Rubins & Borzu Sabahi, INVESTOR-STATE ARBITRATION (2d. ed., Oxford University Press 2019).

Clyde Croft, Christopher Kee & Jeff Waincymer, A GUIDE TO THE UNCITRAL ARBITRATION RULES (Cambridge University Press 2013).

Emmanuel Gaillard & John Savage, FOUCHARD GAILLARD GOLDMAN ON INTERNATIONAL COMMERCIAL ARBITRATION (Kluwer Law International 1999).

Eric A. Schwartz & Yves Derains, A GUIDE TO THE ICC RULES OF ARBITRATION (Kluwer Law International 2005).

Frédéric Gilles Sourgens, Kabir Duggal & Ian A. Laird, EVIDENCE IN INTERNATIONAL INVESTMENT ARBITRATION (Oxford University Press 2018).

---

system of investment treaty arbitration. Considering the recent criticism of the system, and the denunciation by several States of the ICSID Convention and certain BITs, tribunals should adhere to the general principles governing consent of States to arbitration, in order to avoid creating mistrust amongst States towards [investment treaty] arbitration"); G. Lampo & G. Minervini, *Michael Anthony Lee-Chin v Dominican Republic: Interpreting the Consent to Arbitrate in the CARICOM–DR FTA*, p. 513 ("[I]t has been argued that one of the problems of investment arbitration which has led to its current crisis has been the tendency of tribunals to interpret in an extensive manner the provisions grounding their jurisdiction. The [Partial] Award [of *Lee-Chin v. Dominican Republic*] under scrutiny could well be part of this trend."); *Venezuela US*, Dissent, ¶ 59 ("The way to promote the acceptance of, recourse to and reliance on international investment arbitration is not by imposing it without the fundamental requirement of State consent. On the contrary, this would only serve to undermine its credibility."); *Garanti Koza*, Dissent, ¶ 6 ("The trust and confidence in third-party adjudication is dependent on the respect by international courts and tribunals of the limits to the jurisdiction conferred upon them. Tribunals should not create a *de facto* system of compulsory jurisdiction, which in the present stage of positive international law remains the exception. The international legal order still rests largely on a system of facultative jurisdiction, and because of that essential characteristic, a tribunal should never attempt to impose its jurisdiction and adjudicate the merits of a dispute when the parties have not consented to its jurisdiction.").

Gary Born, INTERNATIONAL COMMERCIAL ARBITRATION (Kluwer Law International 2021).

J. Romesh Weeramantry, TREATY INTERPRETATION IN INVESTMENT ARBITRATION (Oxford University Press 2012).

Jakob Ragnwaldh, Fredrik Andersson & Celeste E. Salinas Quero, A GUIDE TO THE SCC ARBITRATION RULES (Kluwer Law International 2019).

Jan Paulsson & Georgios Petrochilos, UNCITRAL ARBITRATION (Kluwer Law International 2017).

Jeswald Salacuse, THE LAW OF INVESTMENT TREATIES (2d. ed., Oxford University Press 2021).

John Choong, Mark Mangan & Nicholas Lingard, A GUIDE TO THE SIAC ARBITRATION RULES (Oxford University Press 2018).

Laurence Craig, William W. Park & Jan Paulsson, INTERNATIONAL CHAMBER OF COMMERCE ARBITRATION (Oceana Publications, ICC Publishing 2000).

Mark E. Villiger, COMMENTARY ON THE 1969 VIENNA CONVENTION ON THE LAW OF TREATIES (Martinus Nijhoff 2009).

Maxi Scherer, Lisa Richman & Rémy Gerbay, ARBITRATING UNDER THE 2014 LCIA RULES: A USER'S GUIDE (Kluwer Law International 2015).

Paul Friedland, ARBITRATION CLAUSES FOR INTERNATIONAL CONTRACTS (2d. ed., JurisNet 2007).

Peter Turner & Reza Mohtashami, A GUIDE TO THE LCIA ARBITRATION RULES (Oxford University Press 2009).

Richard K. Gardiner, TREATY INTERPRETATION (Oxford University Press 2008).

Rudolf Dolzer & Margrete Stevens, BILATERAL INVESTMENT TREATIES (Martinus Nijhoff Publishers 1995).

Sir Ian Sinclair, THE VIENNA CONVENTION ON THE LAW OF TREATIES (Manchester University Press 1984).

Stephan W. Schill (ed.), SCHREUER'S COMMENTARY ON THE ICSID CONVENTION, Vol. 1 (3d. ed., Cambridge University Press 2022).

Tarcisio Gazzini, INTERPRETATION OF INTERNATIONAL INVESTMENT TREATIES (Hart Publishing 2016).

Trinh Hai Yen, THE INTERPRETATION OF INVESTMENT TREATIES (Brill 2014).

Zachary Douglas, THE INTERNATIONAL LAW OF INVESTMENT CLAIMS (Cambridge University Press 2009).

Journal/Book Articles

Aron Broches, *Bilateral Investment Protection Treaties and Arbitration of Investment Disputes*, in Jan C. Schultsz & Albert J. van den Berg, THE ART OF ARBITRATION 63 (Kluwer 1982).

Benjamin G. Davis, *Pathological Clauses: Frédéric Eisemann's Still Vital Criteria*, 7(4) ARBITRATION INTERNATIONAL 365 (1991).

Christoph Schreuer, *Consent to Arbitration*, in Peter T. Muchlinski, Federico Ortino & Christoph Schreuer (eds.), THE OXFORD HANDBOOK OF INTERNATIONAL INVESTMENT LAW 830 (Oxford University Press 2008).

David Sloss, *Domestic Application of Treaties*, in Duncan B. Hollis (ed.), THE OXFORD GUIDE TO TREATIES 355 (2d. ed., Oxford University Press 2020).

Eric de Brabandere, *Importing Consent to ICSID Arbitration? A Critical Appraisal of Garanti Koza v. Turkmenistan*, 5(2) INTERNATIONAL INSTITUTE FOR SUSTAINABLE DEVELOPMENT INVESTMENT TREATY NEWS (2014).

Facundo Pérez-Aznar, *Menzies Middle East and Africa SA and Aviation Handling Services International Ltd v Senegal: Consent to International Jurisdiction and the Limits of Most-Favoured-Nation Clauses*, 34(1) ICSID REVIEW 190 (2019).

Facundo Perez-Aznar, *The Use of Most-Favoured-Nation Clauses to Import Substantive Treaty Provisions in International Investment Agreements*, 20 J. INT'L ECON. L. 777 (2017).

Francisco Orrego Vicuña, *Reports of [Maffezini's] Demise Have Been Greatly Exaggerated*, 3 JOURNAL OF INTERNATIONAL DISPUTE SETTLEMENT 299 (2012).

Frédéric Eisemann, *La Clause d'arbitrage pathologique*, in COMMERCIAL ARBITRATION: ESSAYS IN MEMORIAM EUGENIO MINOLI 129 (Unione Tipografico-Editrice Torinese 1974).

Gary Born, Matteo Angelini & Carolina Alcoberro Llivina, *Chapter 4: Rethinking "Pathological" Arbitration Clauses: Validating Imperfect Arbitration Agreements*, in Sherlin Tung, Fabricio Fortese, *et al.* (eds.), FINANCES IN INTERNATIONAL ARBITRATION: LIBER AMICORUM PATRICIA SHAUGHNESSY 35 (Kluwer Law International 2019).

Giuliana Lampo & Gustavo Minervini, *Michael Anthony Lee-Chin v Dominican Republic: Interpreting the Consent to Arbitrate in the CARICOM–DR FTA*, 36(3) ICSID REVIEW 506 (2021).

Luigi Sbolci, *Interpretation of Treaties – Supplementary Means of Treaty Interpretation*, in Enzo Cannizzaro (ed.), THE LAW OF TREATIES BEYOND THE VIENNA CONVENTION 145 (Oxford University Press 2011).

Michael Nolan & Frédéric G. Sourgens, *The Interplay Between State Consent to ICSID Arbitration and Denunciation of the ICSID Convention: The (Possible) Venezuela Case Study*, 4(5) TRANSNATIONAL DISPUTE MANAGEMENT (2007).

Michele Potestà, *State-to-State Dispute Settlement Pursuant to Bilateral Investment Treaties: Is There Potential?*, in Nerina Boschiero, Tullio Scovazzi, Cesare Pitea & Chiara Ragni (eds.), INTERNATIONAL COURTS AND THE DEVELOPMENT OF INTERNATIONAL LAW: ESSAYS IN HONOUR OF TULLIO TREVES 753 (T.M.C. Asser Press 2013).

Mohamed Abdel Wahab, *Itisaluna and Others v Iraq: The OIC Agreement Conundrum: Consent to ICSID Arbitration and the MFN Clauses Saga*, 36(1) ICSID Review 1 (2021).

Scott Vesel, *Clearing a Path Through a Tangled Jurisprudence: Most-Favored Nation Clauses and Dispute Settlement Provisions in Bilateral Investment Treaties*, 32 Yale Journal of International Law 125 (2007).

Sir Gerald Fitzmaurice, *Vae Victis or Woe to the Negotiators! Your Treaty or Our "Interpretation" of It*, 65 American Journal of International Law 358 (1971).

Reports

Nathalie Bernasconi-Osterwalder, *State-to-State Dispute Settlement in Investment Treaties* (International Institute for Sustainable Development, Best Practices Series, 2014).

Organisation for Economic Co-operation and Development (OECD), *Dispute Settlement Provisions in International Investment Agreements: A Large Sample Survey.*

Sir Humphrey Waldock, Special Rapporteur, *Third Report on the Law of Treaties*, A/CN.4/167, Yearbook of The IIC (1964-II).

United Nations Conference on Trade and Development (UNCTAD), Bilateral Investment Treaties 1995–2006: Trends in Investment Rulemaking (2007).

United Nations Conference on Trade and Development (UNCTAD), Dispute Settlement, International Centre for Settlement of Investment Disputes (2003).

United Nations Conference on Trade and Development (UNCTAD), Investment Policy Hub.

Press Articles/Web Articles

Christopher J. Karacic & Howard S. Suskin, *When the Arbitration Forum Is Unavailable: What Happens Next?*, American Bar Association, 6 February 2014.

Damien Charlotin, *Uncovered: Kaufmann-Kohler Chaired Tribunal Confirms That OIC Agreement Contains Consent to Arbitration, but Ultimately Dismisses Mining Claims on the Merits*, Investment Arbitration Reporter, 17 February 2021.

Jarrod Hepburn & Luke Peterson, *Investigation: As new cases emerge under Islamic investment treaty, initial viability of claims seems to hinge on willingness of respondents to appoint arbitrators*, Investment Arbitration Reporter, 2 March 2017.

Katia Bennadji, *The PCA's Assistance in the Constitution of an Arbitral Tribunal: Last Breath for Investor-State OIC Arbitrations?*, Kluwer Arbitration Blog, 15 April 2019.

Luke Peterson, *Libya Wins One And Loses One, As New Bilateral Investment Treaty Awards Are Rendered*, Investment Arbitration Reporter, 18 February 2020.

Luke Peterson, *OIC Round Up: An Update on Pending Arbitration Cases Lodged under the OIC Investment Agreement*, INVESTMENT ARBITRATION REPORTER, 11 August 2020.

Luke Peterson, *Telecom Italia Subsidiary Agrees to Withdraw ICSID Claim Against Bolivia, but Case to Proceed under Other Auspices*, INVESTMENT ARBITRATION REPORTER, 30 October 2009.

Natalia Ivanova, *Consent to Treaty Arbitration Should Be Specific, Not General*, CIS ARBITRATION, 2 September 2015.

www.ingramcontent.com/pod-product-compliance
Lightning Source LLC
Chambersburg PA
CBHW031330230926
51848CB00001B/173

Preface

Wars annihilate. Death and demolition are the most visible and immediate outcomes of wars. In wars, the destruction of some buildings, statues, or books may appear insignificant when compared to the loss of human lives, but some of these buildings, statues, and books represent the endeavour of generations of the local population in various fields. They symbolise the evolution of humanity. With the destruction of such valuable assets, we lose connection with our past, and indeed the evolution clock rests to zero. We need to begin again and redefine our culture and ethos. In wars, in the long run, mankind has suffered the most from the destruction of cultural heritage.

For almost 800 years, Nalanda was a major hub for educational and intellectual exchange and dissemination of knowledge among Asian societies. In its glorious days, from approximately 425 CE onwards, with over 2000 teachers and 10,000 students, it had the best library in the world. In 1193, on their conquest march, Bakhtiyar Khilji commanded forces to attack the university complex and the library to obliterate local culture and identity. The Nalanda Library was set on fire and millions of books and manuscripts were burnt to ashes.[1] The burning of Nalanda University was India's biggest singular loss of cultural heritage.

Fast forward another millennium. Things have not changed much. When a state adopts a strategy to defeat its enemy by obliterating its culture and

1 The library at Nalanda comprised three huge buildings called Ratnasagara (Ocean of Jewels), Ratnadadhi (Sea of Jewel), and Ratnaranjaka (Jewel-adorned), of which Ratnasagara was a nine-storied building, was one of the world's oldest skyscrapers and was specialized in the collection of rare sacred works. The library had a rich stock of manuscripts (over 9 million) on philosophy and religion and contained text relating to grammar, logic, literature, the Vedas, the Vedanta, the Samkhya philosophy, the Dharmasastras, the Puranas, Astronomy, Astrology, and Medicine. Bhatt, R. K., Academic libraries in India: A historical study (in International Conference on Academic Libraries organized by Delhi University Library System from 5th–8th October 2009), University of Delhi, Delhi.

identity, the scope of such destruction can be relatively wide and has been called "urbicide," a concept used during the Bosnian Wars.

In August 1992, the National and University Library in Sarajevo was repeatedly attacked over three days, until its rich collection, including many rare books and manuscripts testifying to the cultural, religious, and linguistic diversity within the Sarajevo society, was almost entirely devoured by flames. In 2001, two huge ancient Buddha statues of the Bamiyan Valley in Afghanistan were dynamited by the Taliban. Their obliteration was announced in advance and carried out and recorded with a camera, despite pleas from the international community. In Libya, Salafi-jihadist groups have pillaged, plundered, and destroyed Sufi cultural sites across the country – including shrines, mosques, and libraries. Some estimates suggest that more than 530 Sufi religious sites were destroyed between 2011 and 2020.

Cultural property is often understood as artefacts, historical monuments, and buildings, as well as archaeological sites. But the concept of cultural heritage is even wider than that and has gradually grown to include all evidence of human creativity and expression: photographs, documents, books and manuscripts, and instruments, etc. either as individual objects or as collections. Practically, cultural property is a subset of cultural heritage.

International humanitarian law, dedicated to wartime protection of cultural property, is contained in the 1954 Hague Convention and its two Protocols. The Convention and its protocols apply during international and non-international armed conflicts. The 1998 Rome Statute of the International Criminal Court (ICC) criminalises as a war crime the intentional destruction of cultural property in both international and non-international armed conflict. When the destruction of cultural heritage targets a particular ethnic, racial, or religious group with discriminatory intent, it is categorised as a crime against humanity. Several sources of law now link cultural heritage to human rights.[2]

2 The International Court of Justice (ICJ) linked human rights and cultural heritage in *Cambodia v. Thailand*, a dispute concerning which country had sovereignty over the Temple of Preah Vihear included in the World Heritage List. The border dispute had resulted in the loss of human life and endangered the historical structure. The court viewed the temple as having religious and cultural significance for all the people in the region and, as a site of continuing religious significance, the local people had a right to free access. In the opinion of ICJ, it encompassed the human rights to life and personal integrity, as well as cultural and spiritual world heritage. Chechi Alessandro, The 2013 Judgment of the ICJ in the Temple of Preah Vihear Case and the Protection of World

Destruction of cultural heritage in ongoing armed conflict in Syria, Gaza, and Ukraine has raised doubt about whether this legal regime is defunct in limiting damage to the cultural heritage of mankind. An attempt has been made in this book to analyse international humanitarian law (IHL), which is expected to provide a framework of protection for cultural heritage in the event of armed conflict. In this context, the authors would also analyse the role of the armed forces in the protection of cultural property; since the concept of military necessity entails that violence must be limited to what is strictly necessary to achieve the only legitimate aim of the belligerent parties: to weaken the military capacities of the enemy.

Arrangement of the Chapters

This book has been divided into three sections containing nine chapters. The first section covers definitions and history with the opening chapter focussed on definitions, their interpretations and analysis and the overarching legal framework. There are many definitions of cultural heritage and cultural property in international law. Cultural property is defined in Article 1 of the 1954 Hague Convention. Another definition of cultural property is contained in the 1972 World Heritage Convention, which relates to heritage having "outstanding universal value". The first chapter covers a brief comparative analysis of the term's cultural heritage and cultural property.

A look into the history of armed conflicts shows that the warring parties have made serious efforts to destroy and erase culture during wars. Deliberate attacks on cultural property in an armed conflict, including efforts to erase culture, by state and non-state actors, are not new. Although several militaries have devised special operational arrangements for the protection of cultural sights when deploying forces in conflict-affected areas, including "no-strike lists" (UNESCO, 2020; Clack, 2022)[3] yet history is replete with examples to the contrary. The second chapter looks at the destruction of cultural property during the armed conflict in eight situations, including the ongoing Gaza and Ukraine wars.

Cultural Heritage Sites in Wartime, *Asian Journal of International Law*, Vol. 6(2), 2016, pp. 353-378.

3 Clack Timothy, Cultural Heritage on the Frontline: the destruction of peoples and identities in war, University of Oxford, October 4, 2022; Dzerowich Julie, History and Identity Under Attack: Protecting Cultural Heritage in Conflict, Committee in Democracy and Security (CDS), NATO Parliamentary Assembly, Preliminary Draft Special Report, March 29, 2024, p. 17.

The Second Section covers the evolution of legal framework for protection of cultural property during conflict starting with the existing IHL that provides for a comprehensive set of rules when it comes to protecting cultural property from the effects of armed conflict. Not only does it restrict the behaviour of the warring parties during hostilities, but also purports to prepare for the protection of valuable cultural property in peacetime. Chapters three to five of the book critically examine legal regimes relating to the protection of cultural property in armed conflict. Since the concept of international law of war law goes back to ancient history and exists in every culture, religion, and tradition; Chapter three covers the classical law relating to the protection of cultural property in war and its development until the Second World War. After World War II, international organisations recognised the need to create conventions or laws to help protect cultural sites and materials in conflict zones, so that the devastating destruction would not happen again. Chapter four of the book covers the 1954 Hague Convention for the Protection of Cultural Property in the Event of Armed Conflict (with Regulations for the Execution of the Convention for the Protection of Cultural Property in the Event of Armed Conflict annexed thereto) and its First Protocol. The purpose of the First Protocol is to prevent the exportation of cultural property and to provide for the restitution of illegally exported objects. Chapter four also covers in brief the functions and responsibilities of the United Nations Educational, Scientific and Cultural Organization (UNESCO), the standard-setter and guardian of world heritage and culture. International law concerning the protection of cultural property in the event of armed conflict has continued to develop after the 1954 Hague Convention. Chapter Five of the book discusses the Second Protocol to the 1954 Hague Convention adopted in the March 1999 Hague Diplomatic Conference. This protocol strengthens the protection of cultural property in times of war.

The Rome Statute of the International Criminal Court (ICC), adopted in July 1998, heralded a new era in the fight against the deliberate destruction of cultural property during armed conflict. Chapter six of the book examines provisions relating to the protection of cultural property under international criminal law. On December 17, 2015, Mr Ahmad Al Faqi Al Mahdi was charged by the ICC for the intentional direction of attacks against ten buildings of a religious and historical character in Timbuktu, Mali. This trial is critically examined being the first, and the only one that has revolved exclusively around the war crime of intentionally directing attacks against religious and cultural buildings.

The last section covers various operational and functional facets of the protection of cultural property starting with the role of combatants. International humanitarian law obliges combatants to respect and protect cultural property. Therefore, it is paramount that every military officer in the field is aware of his obligations during operations. The intentional destruction, damage, or misappropriation of cultural property in armed conflict can result in prosecution for war crimes. Chapter seven of the book covers these aspects in detail and makes a recommendation for a Military Manual on the Laws of War, with explicit provisions relating to the protection of cultural property. Only a few training manuals or programmes exist like the 2004 US Army cultural property training manual and the Training military personnel on cultural property protection in the USA: 2017–2018.

Chapter eight covers a few additional issues relating to the protection of cultural property during armed conflict. These include the impact of explosive weapons on cultural property; nuclear disarmament and the protection of cultural property; protection of cultural property in UN peacekeeping operations; the impact of social media; the destruction of cultural property as a weapon of war; and the protection of cultural property versus combatants lives in armed conflict. The concluding chapter makes certain recommendations for improving ratification and implementation of the existing treaty system by the states. A serious monitoring mechanism by international organisations is needed to facilitate states parties to improve their implementation mechanism. Future efforts to avoid the loss of cultural heritage will certainly rely on the international community's political will and vision. And this book is a primer for policymaking on the protection of cultural property during peace and war.

The authors are grateful to M/S Vij Books for bringing out this edition.

New Delhi — Umesh Chandra Jha

15 September 2024 — Kishore Kumar Khera

Section I

Definitions and History

Chapter 1

Defining Cultural Property

In 2012, a Malian jihadist was prosecuted at the International Criminal Court (ICC) for destruction and looting of cultural property in Timbuktu.[1] This prosecution was the first of its kind.[2] Earlier, in 1998, the United Nations Compensation Commission awarded close to USD 19,000,000 to an individual Kuwaiti collector for the destruction and pillage by invading and occupying Iraqi forces of his collections of Islamic art and rare books, which Iraq was compelled by the United Nations Security Council to pay. In 2009, the Eritrea Ethiopia Claims Commission ordered Ethiopia to pay Eritrea USD 50,000 for wilful damage caused by Ethiopian troops to an ancient Eritrean monument during the war between those two states.[3]

Cultural property, which includes monuments, archaeological sites, works of art, buildings and historical centres containing them, has constituted one of the basic elements of local, national, or regional cultures, leading to the creation of a cohesive society. Cultural properties are a unique, irreplaceable resource[4] deserving of the highest standards of protection so that they can

1 The 1998 ICC Rome Statute, which constitutes a landmark treaty on individual responsibility in international crimes, contains important provisions for crimes against cultural property. The ICC can prosecute individuals responsible for deliberate destruction, and Mali is a party to the Rome Statute. These legal instruments only complement the national legislations of affiliated State Parties; they do not override them. For instance, when criminal laws in each State Party to the ICC Statute cannot be enforced, the statute can function as a substitute.

2 Archibong James E., Destruction of cultural property as a war crime: Breaking new ground in the quest for accountability, *International Journal of Law*, Volume 5, Issue 2, March 2019, pp. 126-132.

3 O'Keefe Roger, et.al., Protection of Cultural Property: Military Manual, UNESCO, 2016, p. 91.

4 Cultural property is unique if there is no other comparable cultural property that is of the same cultural significance. The unique character may be deduced from a variety of

be enjoyed by present and future generations alike. Unfortunately, cultural property is targeted with impunity in both peace and armed conflict. Recent examples can be found in the peacetime destruction of the statue of the Bamiyan Buddha in Afghanistan,[5] in the looting of the Baghdad Museum during the occupation of Iraq,[6] and the destruction in the ongoing armed conflicts in Syria, Gaza, and Ukraine. Also, cultural objects have been looted and pillaged from museums, galleries, and religious buildings, while important archaeological sites and monuments have been destroyed during armed conflict. Once destroyed, these items of immense historical and cultural value can never be recreated. This is accentuated by criminality. According to an estimate, the illicit trade in cultural objects

---

indicative criteria including age; history; community; representativity; location; size and dimension; shape and design; purity and authenticity in style; integrity; context; artistic craftsmanship; aesthetic and scientific value. The criterion of irretrievable loss for humanity is met if the damage or destruction of the cultural property in question would result in the impoverishment of the cultural diversity or cultural heritage of humankind.

5 In 2001, the Taliban ordered the destruction of the Buddhas of Bamiyan in Afghanistan. These monumental sculptures, carved into sandstone cliffs during the third through fifth centuries AD, were among the most significant treasures in Afghan cultural heritage. Despite public outcry over the cultural and historical value of the sculptures, the Taliban deemed them insulting to Islam. In an act of cultural terrorism, the statues were blown up following the orders of the Taliban's supreme leader. After the destruction of the Buddhas, Afghanistan's ruling Taliban sacrificed dozens of cows as an act of atonement for not acting sooner in destroying these statues and others, and Buddhist art and antiquities from Afghanistan found their place in the illegal international market. Passas Nikos and Blythe Bowman Proulx, "Overview of Crimes and Antiquities," in Manacorda Stefano and Chappell Duncan, (eds.), 2011, *Crime in the Art and Antiquities World: Illegal Trafficking in Cultural Property*, New York: Springer, pp. 51-68.

6 The US had not ratified the 1954 Hague Convention when it attacked Iraq on March 20, 2003. The US rejected the 1954 Hague Convention. The position of the Department of State was that "the major difficulty [with Hague 1954] is that adherence to the Convention would seriously limit the options of the United States in the event of nuclear war or even in some cases of conventional bombardment." The US government did not want to sign on to a convention unless it could live up to its terms. Nonetheless, US military personnel have been continually briefed on their responsibility to preserve and protect cultural property since World War II. According to General Eisenhower, in 1943, "military necessity" justifying the destruction of cultural property should be interpreted as narrowly as possible. Hanson Anne Coffin and Bettauer Ronald J, Protection of Cultural Property, *Art Journal*, Vol. 31, No. 4, 1972, p. 488. The State Department position was presented by Ronald J. Bettauer, Attorney, Office of the Legal Adviser Department of State, in response to a letter urging US ratification of the Convention by Anne Coffin Hanson, President, College Art Association of America.

is one of the most profitable forms of transnational organised crime.[7] This trafficking in cultural property damages cultural heritage worldwide deprives people of their history and culture and weakens social cohesion in the long term.[8] Our right to enjoy the arts and participate in the cultural life of the community is a component of human rights.[9]

In 1954, under the aegis of the United Nations Educational, Scientific and Cultural Organization (UNESCO), the Hague Convention for the Protection of Cultural Property in the Event of Armed Conflict was adopted in the wake of the large-scale destruction of cultural heritage carried out during the Second World War. The Hague Convention is the first multilateral treaty to focus exclusively on the protection of cultural heritage during hostilities. The 1954 Hague Convention was supplemented by an optional protocol, now known as the First Protocol. In a view to enhancing the protection of cultural property during armed conflict, a Second Protocol was added in 1999. This 'Hague' regime, including international criminal law, remains the cornerstone of the protection of tangible cultural heritage under international humanitarian law (IHL). Recent conflicts have shown that cultural property has been subjected to wide and indiscriminate

7 The retail value of illicit trafficking in cultural property is estimated to be between US $1.2 billion to 1.6 billion, annually. Such criminal activities encompass a range of illicit actions, including the theft of cultural property from museums, the illegal excavation and looting of archaeological sites, and the illicit transfer of ownership. Mazzini Marina and E. Ayhan, International Atomic Energy Agency (IAEA), UNICRI Propose Cooperation Platform on Using Nuclear Techniques to Combat Illicit Trafficking in Cultural Goods, IAEA News Letter, May 16, 2023.

8 Illicit trade in cultural goods happens clandestinely and takes many different forms, including but not limited to theft from cultural heritage institutions or private collections; looting of archaeological sites; and displacement of artefacts due to war. Held every year on 14 November, the International Day against Illicit Trafficking in Cultural Property reminds the world that theft, looting and illicit trafficking of cultural property take place in every country, robbing people of their culture, identity, and history and that we must work together to combat this crime. The International Day was adopted by the UNESCO during its 40th General Conference in 2019.

9 In recent years, the link between cultural heritage and human rights has been strengthened. This connection between cultural heritage and human rights is recognized by States in the Human Rights Council and confirmed by the UN Special Rapporteur on Cultural Rights, who emphasized that considering access to and enjoyment of cultural heritage as a human right is a necessary and complementary approach to the preservation/ safeguard of cultural heritage. Francesco Francioni, "Culture, Heritage and Human Rights: An Introduction," in Francesco Francioni and Martin Scheinin (eds), 2008, *Cultural Human Rights*, Brill, p. 7; UN Human Rights Council, Report of the Independent Expert in the Field of Cultural Rights, Farida Shaheed, March 21, 2011; UN Doc A/HRC/17/38, 3, paras 4–7.

assaults, sometimes even tending to destroy the identity of a people. Social media and new technologies have been successful in bringing out in detail information relating to damage, destruction, and pillage of cultural property in recent armed conflicts. Public outbursts in response to these acts of cultural destruction have challenged the deficiencies in, or lack of, national, regional, and international responses and the ineffectiveness of the laws relating to the protection of cultural property.[10]

The states parties to the 1954 Hague Convention and/or its Protocols have additional obligations and special institutions and mechanisms for the enforcement of these obligations come into play. For example, state parties must prepare in times of peace for the safeguarding of cultural property situated within their territory against the foreseeable effects of an armed conflict by taking appropriate measures. These measures include the preparation of inventories, the planning of emergency measures for protection against fire or structural collapse, the preparation for the removal of movable cultural property or the provision of adequate in situ protection of such property, and the designation of competent authorities responsible for the safeguarding of cultural property. Under the Second Protocol, a state party in occupation of the whole or part of the territory of another must prohibit and prevent any archaeological excavation in the occupied territory, save where this is strictly required to safeguard, record, or preserve cultural property. The same applies concerning any alteration to, or change of use of, cultural property which is intended to conceal or destroy cultural, historical, or scientific evidence.[11]

Direct and intentional attacks on cultural property may constitute a crime under international criminal law. The 1998 Rome Statute, confers upon the ICC jurisdiction over crimes against or affecting cultural heritage. The ICC can prosecute individuals responsible for the deliberate destruction of cultural property. International humanitarian law (IHL) provides that, in cases where they are not 'cultural property' in the formal sense, buildings such as educational institutions, libraries, archives and places of worship and objects such as artworks and books, civilian objects and private property will be protected during armed conflict.[12]

10 Vrdoljak Ana Filipa and Francesco Francioni, "Introduction," in S-42, p. 1.

11 O'Keefe Roger, 2006, The Protection of Cultural Property in Armed Conflict, *Amicus Curiae*, Issue 71, Autumn 2007, pp. 3-7.

12 Article The 1977 Additional Protocol I to the Geneva Conventions of 1949.

The 1954 Convention and its Protocols provide for elaborate implementation and compliance mechanisms, in which the armed forces play an important role. The protection of cultural property under the Convention is not absolute. If cultural property is used for military purposes, or in the event of imperative military necessity, the protection afforded by the Convention is waived. The Convention does not prevent military commanders from doing what is necessary to accomplish their missions. Protections are lost if the cultural objects are put to military use, and legitimate military actions may be taken even if collateral damage is caused to cultural property. At the same time, if cultural property protection is planned and executed correctly by a military commander, it can be a force multiplier.

The looting of the Baghdad Museum in April 2003 triggered international attention.[13] The US strategists failed to plan for the proper identification and protection of the cultural heritage in Iraq before the invasion; no ground forces were allocated responsibility to protect museums and sites post-invasion; when pressed, no invading troops appeared to even know where the Iraq Museum was in Baghdad as it seems not to have been marked on their maps.[14] This massive loss of cultural property could have been avoided or ameliorated, and the archaeologists who worked with the military during the invasion planning were held at least morally responsible for failing to prevent the loss. The disparity between the planned protection of heritage sites and their eventual destruction has led some of those involved in this planning process to reconsider the impact of their role.[15]

We have entered a new era of urban warfare. On October 7, 2023, a coordinated attack by more than 1,000 members of the Hamas military wing and other Palestinian armed groups was launched against southern Israel, near the border with Gaza. Attackers killed more than 1,200 persons and at least 252 people were abducted to Gaza as hostages. In the Israeli

13 Looting manifests itself in a variety of guises such as mob looting, systematic looting, and flash looting. All have different causes and catalysts. The whole complex of the looting, stealing, and smuggling of artefacts is, of course, market-driven and based on the international rising demand for antiquities. Since there is only a limited supply of legal objects that are available for trade, any increase can only come from illegal sources.

14 Stone P., Review of: The Rape of Mesopotamia: Behind the Looting of the Baghdad Museum by Lawrence Rothfield, *Public Archaeology*, Vol. 8(4), 2009, pp. 378-81.

15 Stone P., The Identification and Protection of Cultural Heritage during the Iraq Conflict: a Peculiarly English Tale, *Antiquity*, Vol. 79, 2005, pp. 933-943; Also see: Rothfield Lawrence, 2009, *The Rape of Mesopotamia: Behind the Looting of the Iraq Museum*, University of Chicago Press, pp. 228.

counter-attack, at least 37,765 people have been killed and 86,429 wounded in Gaza since October 7, 2023. In the Russo-*Ukrainian War, which* began on February 24, 2022, nearly 100,000 troops have been killed or wounded from both sides.[16] These urban armed conflicts have also caused immense destruction of cultural heritage, monuments, and libraries. Archaeological sites and artefacts in both places of armed conflict are vulnerable to trafficking and exploitation, as the chaos of war can enable illicit actors and terrorist groups to illegally excavate sites and obtain artefacts, circumvent due diligence practices, and, ultimately, profit from the sale of antiquities abroad.[17] The destruction of cultural heritage can also hinder post-conflict recovery. The loss can make it difficult to bind together a fragile society emerging from conflict.

The Preamble to the 1954 Hague Convention reminds us that damage to cultural property belonging to any people whatsoever means damage to the cultural heritage of all mankind since each person contributes to the culture of the world. Further, considering that the preservation of the cultural heritage is of great importance for all peoples of the world, this heritage must receive international protection. The destruction of cultural property/ heritage may appear trivial in the face of other war crimes and crimes against humanity. However, the connection between cultural heritage and identity and the utilisation of its destruction to eliminate cultures reinforces the need to prioritise its protection.

Cultural Property v Cultural Heritage

According to the rules of customary international law, each party to the armed conflict must respect and protect cultural property. Any form of theft, pillage, or misappropriation of, and any acts of vandalism directed against, property of great importance to the cultural heritage of every

16 These are estimates and no authentic official figure is available. Typically, Ukrainia officials do not make casualty figures public. Armstrong Kathryn Ukraine war: Zelensky says 31,000 troops killed since Russia's full-scale invasion, BBC News, February 25, 2024.

17 The notorious private military company, 'Wagner Group' provides an apt example. Cultural heritage experts have noted that the group has engaged in the illicit trafficking of antiquities in Syria since 2016, as well as in other regions of north and northeast Africa and Ukraine. Wagner demonstrates not only the ability of illicit actors to take advantage of instability to profit from the trafficking of antiquities but also the relative impunity with which they operate in the trade. Millender Michaela, Identities Destroyed, Histories Revised: The Targeting of Cultural Heritage and Soft Targets by Illicit Actors, The Soufan Centre, January 2014, pp. 26.

people is prohibited.[18] Although the opening sentence appears clear and correct, doubt may arise as to the meaning of the term "cultural heritage" in the second sentence, and hence the scope of the protection granted by the relevant international law rules. The scope of international legal protection cannot be determined without defining and distinguishing the scope of the two terms: 'cultural property' and 'cultural heritage.' There is little consensus as to the boundaries between "cultural property" and "cultural heritage," and many scholars use these two terms interchangeably.[19]

Cultural heritage was first addressed in international law in 1907 and a body of international treaties and texts for its protection has been developed by UNESCO and other intergovernmental organisations since the 1950's.[20] The concept of cultural heritage, if compared to that of cultural property, is broader in scope, as it expresses a form of inheritance to be kept in safekeeping and handed down to future generations. Conversely, the concept of cultural property is "inadequate and inappropriate for the range of matters covered by the concept of the cultural heritage", which includes, *inter alia*, the non-material cultural elements like dance, folklore, etc. entitled to legal protection at the international level.[21] For instance, Article 2 of the UNESCO Convention for the Safeguarding of the Intangible Cultural Heritage of 2002, includes in the definition of "intangible cultural heritage" the practices, expressions, knowledge, skills — as well as the

18 According to the ICRC study on Customary IHL, Rules 38 and 40 of the Customary IHL provide that each party to the conflict must respect cultural property. Special care must be taken in military operations to avoid damage to buildings dedicated to religion, art, science, education or charitable purposes and historic monuments unless they are military objectives. Property of great importance to the cultural heritage of every people must not be the object of attack unless imperatively required by military necessity. Each party to the conflict must protect cultural property. All seizure of or destruction or wilful damage done to institutions dedicated to religion, charity, education, the arts and sciences, historic monuments and works of art and science is prohibited. Any form of theft, pillage, or misappropriation of, and any acts of vandalism directed against, property of great importance to the cultural heritage of every people is prohibited. Henckaerts Jean-Marie and Doswald-Beck Louise, 2005, Customary International Humanitarian Law, Vol I Rules, ICRC/ Cambridge University Press, pp. 127-135.

19 O'Keefe Roger, The Meaning of 'Cultural Property' Under the 1954 Hague Convention, *Netherlands International Law Review*, Vol. 46, Issue 1, May 1999, pp. 25-56.

20 Blake Janet Blake, On Defining the Cultural Heritage, *International and Comparative Law Quarterly*, Vol. 49, No. 1, 2000, pp. 61-85.

21 Frigo Manlio, Cultural Property v. Cultural Heritage: A 'Battle of Concepts' in International Law? *International Review of the Red Cross*, Vol. 86, No. 854, 2004, pp. 367-378.

instruments, objects, artefacts and cultural spaces associated therewith — that communities, groups and in some cases individuals recognise as part of their cultural heritage.

In theory, cultural heritage embodies a form of community in its manifestation and usage, while the term cultural property lends itself to a more formal ownership discourse. Heritage creates a perception of something handed down; something to be cared for and cherished. These cultural manifestations have come down to us from the past; they are our legacy from our ancestors. Similarly, cultural heritage is inherited to safeguard and pass on to future generations. The real sense of heritage is not so much in the possession of an object but in the act of passing on and receiving memories and knowledge. The real grief of losing one's heritage comes from the loss of the opportunity to pass it on, and the role it plays as both prop and prompt in the stories about one's heritage. Cultural property, on the other hand, has a narrower definition and can be described as a "sub-group" to cultural heritage which is capable of encompassing this within its much broader range of possible elements, including the intangibles. Indeed, cultural property may be limited in scope, as it can prove inadequate and inappropriate for the range of matters covered by the concept of 'cultural heritage'. Different international instruments use both the terms cultural property and cultural heritage.

The protection of cultural property is governed by the rules laid down in the international agreements on the circulation of movables, i.e. works of art and objects of artistic, historic, and archaeological interest.[22] Such property has been conceived as a sub-group within the notion of cultural heritage, the protection of cultural heritage being capable of encompassing within its much broader range of possible elements, including the intangibles. On the other hand, the "equivalent" of the term cultural property certainly includes not only immovables but also intangibles and/or non-material elements, at least for civil law countries.[23]

22 This includes the 1954 Hague Convention for the Protection of Cultural Property in the Event of Armed Conflict, followed by the 1970 United Nations Educational, Scientific and Cultural Organization (UNESCO) Convention on the Means of Prohibiting and Preventing the Illicit Import, Export and Transfer of Ownership of Cultural Property; and the 1999 Second Protocol to the Hague Convention of 1954 for the Protection of Cultural Property in the Event of Armed Conflict, which applies to both international and non-international armed conflicts.

23 Frigo Manlio, Cultural Property v. Cultural Heritage: A 'Battle of Concepts' in International Law? *International Review of the Red Cross*, Vol. 86, No. 854, 2004, pp. 367-378.

Cultural property cannot be defined purely by description. An object that is "cultural property" and one that is not may be exactly alike in all particulars of workmanship, materials, and provenance. In the 1954 Hague Convention and the 1970 UNESCO Convention, cultural property is defined straightforwardly. For example, the Hague Convention, Article 1, defines cultural property as objects, buildings containing objects, and collections of buildings containing objects. However, it does not articulate the heart of the definition: "great importance to the cultural heritage of every people." In the past seven decades, Conventions and Treaties have expanded the definition of cultural property because of the increased interest in "heritage" of all kinds. Like any object, an object defined as a "cultural property" can be redefined, mis-defined, or forgotten. The definition attaches great value to the object, at least for the moment in which a culture claims the object as its property.[24] Several definitions exist to describe cultural property. Cultural property has also been referred to as the "fourth estate" of property, along with real property, intellectual property, and personal property. Cultural property encompasses several different ideas and shifting concepts and has suffered from insufficient definitions. John Merryman (1990) has defined cultural property as "objects that embody the culture."[25]

Within both national and international legislative frameworks, the definitions of cultural property become increasingly specific, and as a result longer and more complicated. For example, Article 2, para 2 of the 2017 Council of Europe Convention on Offences Relating to Cultural Property [26] lists eight categories of properties having importance for archaeology, prehistory, ethnology, history, literature, art, or science.[27] This includes

24 Tatiana Flessas, Cultural Property Defined, and Redefined as Nietzschean Aphorism, *Cardozo Law Review*, Vol. 24:3, 2003, pp. 1070–73; O'Keefe Roger, The Meaning of 'Cultural Property' Under the 1954 Hague Convention, *Netherlands International Law Review*, Vol. 46, Issue 1, May 1999, pp. 25-56.

25 John Henry Merryman, "Protection" of the Cultural "Heritage"? *American Journal of Comparative Law*, Vol. 38, 1990 (Supplement), pp. 513, 529.

26 The 2017 Council of Europe Convention on Offences Relating to Cultural Property Convention, is the only international treaty specifically dealing with the criminalisation of the illicit trafficking of cultural property, establishes many criminal offences, including theft; unlawful excavation, importation, and exportation; and illegal acquisition and placing on the market. CEST No. 221.

27 This includes (a) rare collections and specimens of fauna, flora, minerals and anatomy, and objects of palaeontological interest; (b) property relating to history, including the history of science and technology and military and social history, to the life of national leaders, thinkers, scientists and artists and events of national importance; (c) products

products of archaeological exploration and excavation, documents, works of fine and decorative art, tools, archaeological artefacts, musical instruments, and rare manuscripts. Further, the European Convention goes on to list what may be considered more modern cultural property, including the life of national leaders, thinkers, scientists, and artists to events of national importance, property relating to history, rare collections and specimens of fauna, flora, minerals, anatomy, property of paleontological, anthropological, ethnological, philatelic, and numismatic interest.[28]

Fincham (2011) defines heritage as the physical and intangible elements associated with a group of individuals which are created and passed from generation to generation. Heritage may take many forms. There exists material heritage, intangible heritage, and natural heritage.[29] Heritage law now governs a wide range of activities, some of which include preventing the destruction of works of art, preventing the theft of art and antiquities, preventing the illegal excavation of antiquities, preventing the mutilation and destruction of ancient structures and sites, creating a means for preserving sites and monuments, and even righting past wrongs. This allows us to distinguish heritage from other traditional notions of property. In many cases, objects which we would classify as heritage may be owned as property. This class of objects can be described as cultural property. The phrase "the protection of cultural property in armed conflict" is a component of international obligation under the laws of war, there is

---

of archaeological excavations (including regular and clandestine) or archaeological discoveries; (d) elements of artistic or historical monuments or archaeological sites which have been dismembered; (e) antiquities more than one hundred years old, such as inscriptions, coins and engraved seals; (f) objects of ethnological interest; (g) property of artistic interest. The Properties of 'artistic interest' further include (i) pictures, paintings and drawings produced entirely by hand on any support and in any material (excluding industrial designs and manufactured articles decorated by hand); (ii) original works of statuary art and sculpture in any material; (iii) original engravings, prints and lithographs; (iv) original artistic assemblages and montages in any material; (h) rare manuscripts and incunabula, old books, documents and publications of special interest (historical, artistic, scientific, literary, etc.) singly or in collections; (i) postage, revenue and similar stamps, singly or in collections; (j) archives, including sound, photographic and cinematographic archives; (k) articles of furniture more than one hundred years old and old musical instruments. Article 2, para 2, the Council of Europe Convention on Offences Relating to Cultural Property, 2017.

28 Tatiana Flessas, Cultural Property Defined, and Redefined as Nietzschean Aphorism, *Cardozo Law Review*, Vol. 24:3, 2003, pp. 1070–73.

29 Fincham Derek, The Distinctiveness of Property and Heritage, *Penn State Law Review*, Vol. 115, 2011, pp. 641-684.

no agreed understanding of what the terms "cultural property," and "protection," represent.[30]

Cultural heritage includes tangible places (such as historic sites and buildings), and moveable artefacts (like archives, libraries, art, and museum collections). These are collectively often referred to as cultural property.[31] In this book, the terms "cultural property" and "cultural heritage", have been used interchangeably, unless otherwise specified.

Urbicide

The destruction of cities has historically been an act of punishment, retribution, and projection of absolute power. The term "urbicide" is formed by two words: "urbs," which is city, and "cide", meaning death - hence, violence against the city or the death of the city. Not a natural decrease or a general homicide, though, but truly a murder. Urbicide is the liturgical murder of the city, a premeditated and ordered one, with an explicit form.[32] The term 'urbicide' was first used in the 1990s during the war involving the territories of the former Yugoslavia. The war conflict at the time brought attention to the phenomenon of material, cultural, and urban identity destruction. Urbicide is the end of the violence continuum, where guardians become raiders, opting for ultimate forms of purposeful violence perpetrated within and against 'the city'.[33] It is the result of actions that wipe out systems of common life's meaningful places (squares, monuments, libraries), ravage the city's material basis (infrastructure and services), exterminate society and citizenship (the civitas), and annihilate institutional marks of the government (privatisation, deregulation, centralisation). Urbicidal violence deliberately strives to kill, discipline, or

30 Lostal Marina, 2017, *International Cultural Heritage Law in Armed Conflict: Case-Studies of Syria, Libya, Mali, the Invasion of Iraq, and the Buddhas of Bamiyan*, Cambridge: Cambridge University Press, p. 4.

31 Cunliffe Emma, et al. (ed.), The Protection of Cultural Property in the Event of Armed Conflict: Unnecessary Distraction or Mission-Relevant Priority? NATO OPEN Publications, Volume 2, No. 4, Summer 2018, p. 29.

32 Mena F.C., Urbicide, or the city's liturgical death, *Oculum Ensaios*, Vol. 15(1), 2018, pp. 5–12.

33 For more details see: Graham Stephen (ed.), 2004, *Cities, War and Terrorism: Toward an Urban Geopolitics*, Oxford: Blackwell Publishing Ltd, p. 384.

deny the city to its inhabitants by targeting and then reordering the socio-material urban assemblage.[34]

In total disregard for international humanitarian law, urbicide is undergirded by a logic of collective punishment, targeting civilian populations and the built infrastructure on which their lives depend. Russia's campaign of urbicide has been most intense in Ukraine's south and east, particularly since the Kremlin's retreat from around Kyiv and the north. From the onset of the Russian invasion of Ukraine, Russia has engaged in a sustained and systematic campaign of urbicide. Both targeted and indiscriminate attacks by air, land, and sea continue to destroy vital civilian infrastructure, systematically denying Ukrainians access to basic needs and essential services.[35]

There is a plethora of causes that might drive actors to target cultural property. The destruction of cultural property in eight situations during armed conflict or otherwise has been discussed in the next chapter.

34 Stanely Bruce, The City-Logic of Resistance: Subverting Urbicide in the Middle East City, Journal of Peacebuilding & Development, Vol. 12, No. 3, December 2017, pp. 10-24.

35 Clements-Hunt Aaron, Russia's Campaign of Urbicide in Ukraine, New Lines Institute, June 7, 2022. https://newlinesinstitute.org/rules-based-international-order/russias-campaign-of-urbicide-in-ukraine/.

Chapter 2

History of Annihilation of Cultural Property

In the early hours of September 1, 1939, German bombers attacked Warsaw. The two historic streets of the city and the Nowy Swiat, with several fine old buildings, were reduced to a mass of debris.[1] Although the losses of both human life and cultural heritage during World War II are beyond comprehension, evidence suggests that as many as fourteen libraries were lost because of the German occupation of various European countries between 1939 and 1945. For example, the National Library in Warsaw lost about 700,000 volumes, including all its manuscripts and its map collections. On the "eve of liberation," the German army burned the main stacks of the Warsaw Public Library and approximately 15 million of the 22.5 million volumes in all Polish libraries were destroyed. The Germans also took possession of 24,000 volumes after they burned the Jewish Theological Seminary in Lublin. In France in 1944, German troops blew up the Dieppe Municipal Library, and the Municipal Library of Douai lost over 95 per cent of its holdings. Moreover, because the extent of losses of private libraries and collections is unknown, these numbers represent only a fraction of the total European losses during the Second World War.

During the War, as the Nazi occupation of Europe began, the German army seized cultural objects, library materials, and artworks, and destroyed what the regime did not need. Many museums and libraries were destroyed and their collections looted, while other museums and libraries were able to move their collections into safe storage. While the world lost untold numbers of books and manuscripts during the Second World War, a significant number were preserved and repatriated through the collective efforts of librarians, scholars, and ordinary citizens. By the end of the war,

1 Spaight J.M., 1947, *Air Power and War Rights*, London: Longmans, Green, p. 265.

the Allied strategic bombing campaign had devastated Germany and Japan. High explosives and incendiaries weapons were used indiscriminately destroying rained civilian districts and the civilian population, and with them monuments and works of art.[2]

Britain and France made a joint declaration on September 3, 1939, publicising instructions to their respective armed forces which prohibited 'the bombardment whether from the air, or the sea or by artillery on the land of any except strictly military objectives'. British and French governments expressed a firm desire to preserve in every way possible those monuments of human achievement which are treasured in all civilised countries. However, it was not possible by air, with the UK's secretary of state for air explaining the policy: "We cannot be prevented from bombing important military targets because, unfortunately, they happen to be close to ancient monuments. The same principles are applied to all centres. We must bomb important military objects. We must not be prevented from bombing important military objects, because beautiful or ancient buildings are near them."[3] The orthodox view throughout the war was that the intensive and indiscriminate aerial bombing of German cities was a necessary means to Allied victory. Area bombing was the predominantly British aerial practice of destroying numerous distinct military objectives scattered over an urban concentration by levelling the whole concentration indiscriminately. General area bombing worked almost on the principle that to destroy anything it was necessary to destroy everything.[4] Military necessity was invoked to justify the destruction of irreplaceable treasures of art, culture and history. And the US nuclear attacks on Japan in 1945 obliterated a part of humanity along with all signs of culture.

Armed conflict kills, but its consequences extend far beyond these direct deaths. In addition to human casualties, armed conflict often leads to collateral damage in the form of forced migration, refugee flows, and the destruction of societies' infrastructure, including cultural property. However, deliberate attacks on cultural property in an armed conflict,

2 Telford Taylor, in his subsequent role as Chief Counsel for War Crimes at Nuremberg, had concluded that 'the ruins of German and Japanese cities were the results not of reprisal but of deliberate policy'. O'Keefe Roger, 2006, *The Protection of Cultural Property in Armed Conflict*, Cambridge University Press, p. 63.

3 O'Keefe Roger, 2006, *The Protection of Cultural Property in Armed Conflict*, Cambridge University Press, p. 64.

4 Webster C. and Frankland N., 1961, *The Strategic Air Offensive Against Germany 1939-1945*, Vol. III, London: HMSO, p. 44.

including efforts to erase culture, by state and non-state actors, are not new. It is a tactic that has been used throughout history and has occurred in many conflict zones. A look into the history of armed conflicts shows that the warring parties have made serious efforts to destroy and erase culture during wars. The examples are many: The bombing of Guernica, a Basque town in northern Spain, by the German air force in support of General Franco during the Spanish Civil War; the systematic destruction of Polish libraries and archives by the Nazis during World War II; the deliberate destruction of the statue of the Bamiyan Buddha in Afghanistan; destruction of religious and cultural properties in Bosnia; attacks on cultural heritage sites, including Palmyra in Syria; and intentional attacks against religious and historic buildings in Timbuktu, Mali. This intentional destruction is not limited to states, as terrorists and organised criminal groups have also been known to target and pillage/ destroy cultural heritage.

Monuments and historic sites play an important role in the building of a national identity. Cultural property in certain contexts can stymie reconciliation through history and provide a challenge for conflict resolution initiatives.[5] In addition to their importance as sources of cultural information, the tangible remains of human cultural heritage are also a critical component of national identity. Antiquities and archaeological resources are finite and irreplaceable; once they are gone, they are gone forever. Art, antiquities, and cultural heritage thus play an integral role in the formation and perpetuation of national identity and self-image, and the destruction of such resources contributes to the destruction of a people's identity.[6] Connected to the problem of destruction of cultural property is the illegal trade in antiquities, an issue that is a source of revenue to non-state armed groups and has the same effect as the destruction of antiquities, for once an item is sold on the black market, it is rarely recovered and is lost to the world.

The destruction of cultural property during armed conflict in eight situations in the last four decades has been briefly discussed in this chapter.

5 Defreese Michelle, Kosovo: Cultural Heritage in Conflict, *Journal of Conflict Archaeology*, Vol. 5, No. 1, June 2009, pp. 257-270.

6 Passas Nikos and Proulx B.B., "Overview of Crimes and Antiquities," in Manacorda Stefano, Duncan Chappell (Ed.), 2011, *Crime in the Art and Antiquities World: Illegal Trafficking in Cultural Property*, New York: Springer, pp. 51-68.

Sri Lanka (1983-2009)

Sri Lanka is very rich in cultural heritage[7] and home to six cultural UNESCO World Heritage Sites, covering exquisite ancient cities, forts, and temples, all housing innumerable artefacts. Ever since Western intervention started by way of the Portuguese (1505-1658), Dutch (1658-1796), and British (1796-1948), these cultural objects have been exported *end masse* [8] and little hope of their repatriation.[9] Here is a case study of The Dutch Fort of Jaffna and the impact of the Civil War on it.

The Dutch Fort of Jaffna is situated in the Northern Province of Sri Lanka and is the second-largest fort in Sri Lanka. It was first built by the Portuguese and subsequently fortified by the Dutch and archaeologists believe that it was built in 1680.[10] Before the civil war began, the Tamils of Jaffna used this fort for their social and cultural events. With an administrative building, God temple (*Kovil*) and Roman Catholic church in the Fort, it was used for both official and religious activities. The Fort was built with advanced technology, while its large size, independent location, isolation from the local population for administrative functions, coupled with a strategic defensive position, indicate the value of this monument. It spread over an area of 14 acres, constructed in the shape of a star. The Fort has two walls which are separated by a deep moat, with evidence of five guard towers on

7 The largest removal of Sri Lankan cultural property occurred during the British era. There are more than 3,000 recorded items in 16 UK museums. A notable example is the 10th-century bronze statue of Tara, who is considered an embodiment of the female Buddha. This statue was taken from the last King of Kandy and given to the British Museum by Governor Brownrigg in 1830. Kamardeen N., The Role of Cultural Diplomacy in Addressing Loss of Cultural Property: Perspectives from Sri Lanka, November 18, 2019.

8 Smith Emiline, The Ongoing Looting of Sri Lanka's Cultural Heritage, March 10, 2022. Available at: https://hyperallergic.com/716524/the-ongoing-looting-of-sri-lankas-cultural-heritage/.

9 The British government has not responded positively to requests made by the Sri Lankan government in 1970 and again in 2013 to return property taken during the colonial era. This may be due to a concern that this will encourage requests from many other former colonies.

10 The land-side entrance to the fort bears the number 1680, which archaeologists believe to be the year it was built. Samanthi Ranjith Priyanga Dissanayaka Mudiyanselage, *"Sri Lankan archaeological heritage damaged by war: The restoration of the Dutch Fort of Jaffna," in* Simon Lambert and Cynthia Rockwell (ed.), Protecting Cultural Heritage in Times of Conflict, International Centre for the Study of the Preservation and Restoration of Cultural Property, 2010-2011, pp. 72-78.

top. Inside the walls are separate administrative complexes. An armoury, church and housing for senior officers can be identified.

In 1948, Sri Lanka gained its independence from British colonial rule, and the Jaffna Fort came under the administration of the Sri Lankan government. After independence, the Fort was preserved and remained in good condition for a long period. Its internal buildings were still suitable for occupation. Until the first half of the 1990s, the ramparts and interior officers' quarters were still in good condition. Since the early 1970s, there had been an army camp (now moved out) located inside the Fort, but there had been no damage to any part of the interior or the outer walls. In 1971, the government declared this Fort as a listed monument for its safety, but it did not survive the fallout from the decades of war.

The civil war in this island nation from 1983-2009 has destroyed not only the lives of thousands of citizens and their property but also a good amount of cultural property. The civil war originated when the Liberation Tigers of Tamil *Eelam* (LTTE), a guerrilla organisation, sought to establish an independent Tamil state, Eelam, in northern and eastern parts of Sri Lanka.

The on-and-off insurgency of the early 1980s against the Sri Lankan government by the LTTE intensified in the early 1990s when militants attacked the army camp inside the Fort. These attacks and counter-attacks by the Sri Lankan Army caused heavy damage to the Fort: the northern and south-eastern sectors were destroyed, while the internal buildings were heavily damaged and the Dutch church was damaged extensively.

The prevailing war situation prevented any archaeological work to restore the damaged parts of the buildings. Even though an army camp was located inside the Fort, they could not intervene to prevent the degradation of the site, which allowed this fort to turn into an abandoned monument. The non-intervention of the army to protect the site allowed trees to grow on the ramparts and other buildings. Plant roots penetrated and weakened buildings, and the unattended moat filled with silt. Over three decades of civil war, the occupation of the Fort changed hands several times – back and forth between the Sri Lankan army and the LTTE. Parts of the damaged buildings were used as building materials for bunkers, and mining of the area caused further damage.

A fort's primary purpose is to house an army garrison and establish power to protect its surroundings. Thus, maintaining an army camp inside the fort met this basic strategy, and during the conflict this fact was evident. Even though this was an archaeological monument, during war situations it reverted to its original function. The events that unfolded during the conflict led to the destruction of this monument, but it is unclear who was directly responsible. The activities of both sides led to the fort's unfortunate fate. In the civil war that lasted two and a half decades, both sides were accused of all manner of war crimes. Reportedly, during the 30 years of civil war, the LTTE traded in cultural objects to raise funds.[11]

Restoration of the Dutch Fort of Jaffna

In 2009, the Sri Lankan Army defeated the LTTE and won the war, leading to the return of a peaceful atmosphere and enabling long-neglected archaeological interests and enthusiasm to be revived. The Dutch Fort was the first project of the post-war period undertaken by archaeologists, and they encountered many challenges. The Sri Lanka–Netherlands Cultural Cooperation Program provided the funds for conserving the Jaffna Dutch Fort. The fort's restoration comes under a programme launched by the National Heritage and Cultural Affairs Ministry to renovate and preserve national heritage sites in the north and the east. The project would include the armoury and barracks used by Dutch soldiers in the 17th century, the tunnels that were destroyed during the war, a canal used for inner security, as well as the Queen's House and a damaged Roman Catholic church.

Iraq (1991-2003)

A tale written on twelve stone tablets, which archaeologists discovered in Nineveh, Iraq, amidst ruins of the library of an Assyrian king who ruled from 669-633 BC, goes as follows:

> There is a plant which grows at the bottom of the ocean that, when eaten, returns man to his youth. One man, Gilgamesh, tied rocks to his feet, sank deep below the waves of the sea and plucked the plant from the ocean floor. When he returned to the surface, he was afraid to eat it and decided to travel home, to the city of Uruk, to test the plant's powers on an old man living there. He crossed many mountains and oceans during his trip, and one night while he lay sleeping a snake slithered up to Gilgamesh and ate the magic plant. When the snake slipped away, he left his old skin behind, and ever since that day, snakes have shed their skin reclaiming their youth.

11 Kamardeen, N., The Protection of Cultural Property: Post-Colonial and Post-Conflict Perspectives from Sri Lanka. *International Journal of Cultural Property, Vol. 24*(4), 2017, pp. 429-450.

The foregoing is an excerpt from the Epic of Gilgamesh, which art historians consider the oldest written story on Earth, even pre-dating the Iliad. Nobody knows where are these tablets now. They are just some of the thousands of artefacts stolen or destroyed in April 2003 during the widespread looting and destruction following the invasion of Iraq. Most experts believe that the truly priceless relics of Iraq's lost civilisations might never return.[12]

The present-day Iraq occupies the territory that historians traditionally have considered the site of the earliest civilisations of the ancient West Asia. The land of ancient Mesopotamia (the land between two rivers), was settled in approximately 6000 BC along the Tigris and Euphrates rivers. The Sumerians[13] who inhabited southern Mesopotamia created many innovations, including written languages imprinted on clay tablets, which made civilisation possible. The Sumerians were responsible for the development of the wheel and sophisticated irrigation techniques to assist in farming in the fertile river valley. They also created a complex mathematical system, used for everything from basic counting to predictions of astronomical occurrences.[14] Organised archaeological excavations of ancient Mesopotamia have been ongoing since the late 19th century and extensive excavations have been conducted at Baylon, Nimrud, and other major sites. It is believed that Iraq may be as rich and concentrated a cultural heritage of humankind as can be found anywhere.[15]

12 Quoted in: Miller Amy E., Looting of Iraqi Art: Occupiers and Collectors Turn away Leisurely from the Disaster, *Case Western Reserve Journal of International Law*, Vol 37, Issue 1, 2005, pp. 49-84.

13 Sumer is the ancient name for southern Mesopotamia.

14 Sumer also pioneered advances in warfare technology. By the middle of the third millennium B.C., the Sumerians had developed the wheeled chariot. At approximately the same time, the Sumerians discovered that tin and copper when smelted together produced bronze—a new, more durable, and much harder metal. The wheeled chariot and bronze weapons became increasingly important as the Sumerians developed the institution of kingship and as individual city-states began to vie for supremacy. Metz Helen Chapin (ed.), 1990, *Iraq: A Country Study*, Department of Army, United States Government, p. 302.

15 Iraq has rightly been called the cradle of urban civilization. It was here that the world's first cities, with perhaps as many as 50,000 inhabitants, emerged in the fourth millennium B.C. along with monumental architecture and the beginnings of writing. Epic literature, codes of laws, and contributions to astronomy and mathematics all followed in succeeding millennia. The processes by which mercantile economic practices gradually infiltrated into redistributive state institutions are still of contemporary relevance. Ninth-century Baghdad under the caliphs may well have been the greatest city of that age. Thousands of archaeological sites of every size

Iraq is divided into four major regions: desert in the west and southwest; rolling upland between the upper Euphrates and Tigris rivers; highlands in the north and northeast; and alluvial plain in central and southeast sections. A military revolution in 1958 led to the establishment of the government ruled by the Baath's Revolutionary Command Council (RCC) and created the Provisional Constitution of July 16, 1970, that institutionalised the RCC's role. Iraq gained success in the Iran-Iraq war by compelling Iran in August 1988 to request a cease-fire in the eight-year-old Iran-Iraq War.

Iraq had one of the most successful cultural property protection schemes in West Asia. Iraqi national law has considered all immovable and movable antiquities to be owned by the state. Any trade in antiquities is illegal, and it is also illegal to break, mutilate, destroy, or damage antiquities whether movable or immovable. The Iraqi government outlawed the export of antiquities and established severe criminal penalties for the looting of archaeological sites. The government required that antiquities be reported within one week of discovery, and no excavations were allowed without permits from the national government.[16] In the years after Saddam Hussein came to power, the Iraqi Ba'ath Party nearly doubled its funding for archaeological projects. Saddam encouraged scientific excavation by local and international teams of archaeologists. The regime established new local archaeological museums in most provinces that showcased local finds and treasures so that they would be more accessible to Iraqis living throughout the country. Saddam also encouraged museum system educational programmes that taught Iraqi citizens to value their rich archaeological heritage both above and below ground and to safeguard these vestiges of the past. Through a large-scale archaeological project and cultural reconstruction of the ancient Mesopotamian civilisation, Saddam

---

and era crowd one another, not only across the alluvial plain between the Tigris and Euphrates Rivers in the south but also in the hilly uplands of the north. Robert McC. Adams, *Iraq's Cultural Heritage: Collateral Damage*, Science, July 6, 2001, p. 13.

16 The Antiquities Law 1936 (Law No. 55), as amended in 1974 and 1975. Some private ownership was allowed under Article 3 if the object was in private hands when the legislation was enacted and the property was registered with the state. Export of movable and immovable possessions which were erected, made, produced, sculptured, written, drawn, or photographed by man, if they are 200 years old or more was also prohibited. The penalties for violating the Law may include incarceration of up to 10 years in prison and a fine of 100,000 Iraqi Dinars. Illegal excavation (looting) may result in imprisonment for a period of up to 15 years and a fine of two times the value of the damages sustained. Trafficking in antiquities is punishable with a term of imprisonment for a period not to exceed 10 years and a fine of up to 1,000,000 Iraqi Dinars.

tried to gain cultural confidence for the modern Iraqi state from the ancient Mesopotamian civilisation before the rise of Islamic civilisation.[17] As a result of these policies, there was virtually no illicit trade in Iraqi antiquities before 1991.[18]

The 1991 Gulf War and Looting of Cultural Objects

The Gulf War and its aftermath shattered cultural heritage research and protection schemes in Iraq.[19] During the first Gulf War, Allied bombings and ground forces directly damaged several important archaeological sites in Iraq. Particularly, the damage was done at the Ur of the Chaldees, where cannon holes and bomb craters riddle the site.[20] In the early 1990s, the Iraq State Board of Antiquities and Heritage (SBAH), was suffering from the effects of economic hardship caused both by debts from the war with Iran and by comprehensive sanctions imposed by the United Nations in response to the invasion of Kuwait. The Oil-for-Food Programme had not yet been established. Hunger, unemployment and poverty were increasing, particularly in southern Iraq.

The reduced security at archaeological sites was caused by a lack of funds to pay guards who invited looters. It was also fuelled by the strong demand of a Western market that had not had easy access to Mesopotamian artefacts

17 Qian Xuming and Xu Ziqing, The Cultural Heritage Protection in Iraq: History, Development and Challenges, *Cultural and Religious Studies*, July 2022, Vol. 10, No. 7, pp. 372-378.

18 Forsyth Marion, Casualties of War: The Destruction of Iraq's Cultural Heritage as a Result of US Action During and after the 1991 Gulf War, *DePaul Jour of Art, Technology & Intellectual Property Law*, Vol. 14, Issue 1, 2016, pp. 73-108.

19 Funds that had previously gone to the Antiquities Department were diverted to the war effort, and the preservation of archaeological sites took on a low priority in comparison to national defence. Foreign excavation teams were forced to leave the country, and they took with them the funds required to protect many of the sites. The Antiquities Department was left to disperse its scarce resources to safeguard the thousands of archaeological sites in the country. The United Nations sanctions also adversely impacted academic activities for those studying to be archaeologists as they were unable to receive academic books and new information on excavations. Forsyth Marion, Casualties of War: The Destruction of Iraq's Cultural Heritage as a Result of US Action During and after the 1991 Gulf War, *DePaul Jour of Art, Technology & Intellectual Property Law*, Vol. 14, Issue 1, 2016, p. 78-79.

20 The archaeological site of Ur of the Chaldees, the reputed birthplace of Abraham, was bombed and strafed by Allied aircraft, with over 400 cannon holes reported in the temple tower and at least 4 bomb craters on the site. The unexcavated major site of Tell el-Lahm was trenched and bulldozed by American forces. Sue Williams, *Iraq: Robbers of the Cradle*, UNESCO SOURCES, May 2000, p. 11-12.

in several years. This was also an unfortunate time of several high-profile auctions of Iraqi antiquities where artefacts were purchased for substantial amounts of money, showing that there was an unexpectedly strong demand for this material.[21] Looters received special orders for certain pieces from collectors. Organised and armed groups conducted illicit excavations, sometimes using bulldozers. They even attacked established museums as early as April 1991, when the museum at Babylon was robbed of its treasures. Those who attempted to challenge the looters were met with violence and machine guns.[22]

The looting over two to three days at Iraq's National Museum in April 2003, was quite different from the rest of the pillaging and vandalism in Baghdad. The looted antiquities included ancient stone carvings of bulls and kings and princesses; copper shoes and cuneiform tablets; tapestry fragments and ivory figurines of goddesses and women and Nubian porters; friezes of soldiers and ancient seals and tablets on geometry; and ceramic jars and urns and bowls, all dating back at least 2,000 years, some more than 5,000 years.[23]

Extensive looting of cultural property in Iraq was stimulated by the international market in illicit antiquities that supplies US, European, and Japanese collectors.[24] Recent studies evaluating the looting of archaeological sites across Iraq have shown that looting after the Gulf War was directly linked to the prosperity of the international market for cultural relics. For example, in Iraq at that time, cultural relics needed to pass relatively fixed routes and organisations to flow to the international market.[25] Wealthy

21 Russel John M., "Efforts to Protect Archaeological Sites and Monuments in Iraq 2003-2004," in Emberling Geoff and Hanso Katharyn (ed.), 2008, *The Looting and Destruction of Iraq's Past*, The Oriental Institute Museum of the University of Chicago, p. 29.

22 Reportedly, Mesopotamian objects were available on Portobello Road in London that were not available before the Gulf War. It is widely known that of particular interest to antiquities, buyers are cylinder seals, cuneiform tablets, sculptural reliefs, and jewellery of any kind. Forsyth Marion, Casualties of War: The Destruction of Iraq's Cultural Heritage as a Result of US Action During and after the 1991 Gulf War, *DePaul Jour of Art, Technology & Intellectual Property Law*, Vol. 14, Issue 1, 2016, p. 80-81.

23 Burns John F., A Nation at War: Looting; Pillages Strip Iraqi Museum of Its Treasure, *New York Times*, April 13, 2003.

24 Robert McC. Adams, *Iraq's Cultural Heritage: Collateral Damage*, SCIENCE, July 6, 2001, p. 13.

25 A survey of archaeological sites showed that the cities that suffered more looting in the years following the Gulf War were concentrated around these three cities, while

cultural relic collectors in Europe and the United States could even directly book a specific type of cultural relic, for example, a relief sculpture from the Neo-Assyrian period. Then they could hire someone to steal directly from the Nineveh ruins, rather than passively selecting goods in the cultural relic market.[26] The transformation of site looting after the Gulf War has caused irreversible damage to Iraq's historical heritage.[27]

The Gulf War in 1991 and the Iraq War in 2003 caused devastating blows to the country's archaeology and cultural property protection. Besides being directly damaged in armed conflict, its other main causes were the robbery of ruins, the smuggling of cultural relics, and the destruction of museums. Decades of neglect, sanctions, and conflict – including factors such as the US occupation and the rise of Islamic State (ISIS) – have taken a heavy toll on Iraq's cultural heritage.[28] The incidents of looting of cultural property also focused international attention on an important issue of international law, namely the protections afforded cultural property during armed conflicts. The Iraq National Archive and Library's Jewish Archive, having a collection of artefacts, manuscripts, and books from Iraq's Jewish communities; was removed to the US, supposedly for conservation. It has not yet been returned.[29] In 2014, ISIS also carried out attacks on places

archaeological sites in Northern Iraq, even as famous as the ancient city of Babylon, were less damaged than those in the south. Stone E. C., 2008, "Archaeological site looting: The destruction of cultural heritage in Southern Iraq," in G. Emberling and K. Hanson (Eds.), 2008, *Catastrophe: The looting and destruction of Iraq's past. Oriental Institution Museum Publications*, No. 28, Chicago: The University of Chicago Press, pp. 65-80. Not only did Iraqi civilians contribute a large amount of goods to the cultural relic market by directly robbing the ruins, but even the high-level officials of Saddam's government also participated in the sale of cultural relics to make huge profits. Saddam's son, Uday Hussein, for example, sold stone bowls stolen from Roman-era strata at the ruins of the ancient city of Babylon. Foster B. R., Foster K. P., and Gerstenblith P., 2005, *Iraq beyond the headlines: History, archaeology, and war. Series on the Iraq war and its consequences*, Vol. 2. Singapore: World Scientific Publishing, p. 208.

26 Gottlieb Martin and Barry Meier, Aftereffects: The Plunder; Of 2000 treasures stolen in Gulf War of 1991, only 12 have been recovered, *New York Times*, May 1, 2003.

27 Qian Xuming and Xu Ziqing, The Cultural Heritage Protection in Iraq: History, Development and Challenges, *Cultural and Religious Studies*, July 2022, Vol. 10, No. 7, p. 376.

28 Kathem Mehiyar, Eleanor Robson and Lina G. Tahan, Cultural Heritage in Iraq: The sectarian appropriation of Iraq's past, Research Paper, Middle East and North Africa Programme, Chatham House, March 2022, pp. 45.

29 Kathem Mehiyar, Eleanor Robson and Lina G. Tahan, Cultural Heritage in Iraq: The sectarian appropriation of Iraq's past, Research Paper, Middle East and North Africa Programme, Chatham House, March 2022, p. 13.

of worship, cemeteries, and other representations of Iraqi communities to destabilise the country.

In 2003, the United States invaded Iraq and occupied the Iraqi capital, Baghdad. The fall of Baghdad coincided with the looting of the Iraq National Museum. The US military forces stood idle as a rampaging mob ravaged the collection. Initial reports noted that 170,000 objects had been taken including some of the world's most priceless ancient treasures.[30] The looting of the Museum and several other important cultural sites in Baghdad and throughout Iraq raised four important political, moral, and legal questions: (i) Whether the US had an obligation to protect the greatest cultural assets of the Iraqi people. (ii) Does the US have an obligation to protect the greatest cultural assets of the Iraqi people? (iii) Does the US military policy provide adequate guidance to ensure that the cultural property of the occupied territory will be preserved? (iv) At what point is the responsibility to protect cultural property waived by countervailing principles of military necessity?[31]

Immediately after the looting began, the curator of the museum, Mr. Muhammed, appealed to invading military forces in the area to stop the looting. Around noon, several soldiers and a tank accompanied Mr Muhammed to the Museum and opened fire over the heads of looters, temporarily bringing a halt to the destruction. Unfortunately, the American soldiers did not stay there and looters soon returned to the Museum where they continued picking over the collection for the next day and a half.[32] The National Museum was not the only victim of rampaging Iraqi mobs in the days following the destabilisation of the Hussein regime. The regional museum at Mosul was ransacked, the National Library in Baghdad burned to the ground (and nearly all its rare books, historical maps, and photos

30 The National Museum of Iraq recorded a history of civilizations that began to flourish in the fertile plains of Mesopotamia more than 7,000 years ago. But once American troops entered Baghdad in sufficient force to topple Saddam Hussein's government this week, it took only 48 hours for the museum to be destroyed, with at least 170,000 artefacts carried away by looters. 28 galleries of the museum and vaults with huge steel doors guarding storage chambers that descend floor after floor into unlighted darkness had been completely ransacked. Burns John F., A Nation at War: Looting; Pillages Strip Iraqi Museum of Its Treasure, *New York Times*, April 13, 2003.

31 Thurlow Matthew D., Protecting Cultural Property in Iraq: How American Military Policy Comports with International Law, *Yale Human Rights and Development Law Journal*, Vol. 8, 2005, pp. 153-187.

32 John F. Burns, Pillagers Strip Iraqi Museum of Its Treasure, *New York Times*, April 13, 2003.

were lost) and an archive of ancient Korans also fell victim to looters.[33] One cannot rule out the involvement of some of the US military personnel in smuggling antiquities out of the country. It is believed that many artefacts taken out of Iraq during the occupation period were stolen by coalition officers and privates, including at the request of concerned US agencies and private collectors.

For the US military, the laws of war provide a model code of behaviour. It forbids the US forces from committing abuses against individuals and property, but it does not create affirmative duties to prevent these acts from occurring in the theatre of war. The laws of war also focus on the legal obligations and policies of the United States military as described under the four Geneva Conventions of 1949. Despite referring to nearly every major treaty and international convention on cultural property, the US Department of Defence military manuals provided very limited protections for cultural property. The manual provides that the US has virtually no affirmative commitments (including those regarding cultural property) to civilian populations in occupied territories. The military manual held that soldiers must take all necessary precautions to spare cultural sites from bombardment, and are also forbidden from targeting undefended cities, towns, villages, dwellings, or buildings. American troops have no greater obligation to spare a national museum than to spare a privately owned car dealership. Both are forbidden targets, but if the enemy uses either site for military purposes, it can be destroyed. The United States military also absolves itself from any broader collective obligation to protect or preserve cultural property in times of war.[34]

The reaction from military authorities and the Bush Administration in the immediate aftermath was slow and defensive. On April 16, 2003, almost a full week after the looting began, an American tank platoon was finally assigned to protect the National Museum. As reported, the US commanders did not instruct local commanders to protect the National Museum or National Library. The members of the Bush Administration downplayed the destruction of cultural property as either unforeseeable

33 The museum, which housed a priceless collection dating back 7,000 years to the Sumerian civilization, was looted over two days following the fall of Saddam Hussein's government. The pillaging infuriated Iraqis who complained that American troops here did little to stop it. Fisher Ian, Museum Pillage Described as Devastating but Not Total, *New York Times*, April 17, 2003.

34 Thurlow Matthew D., Protecting Cultural Property in Iraq: How American Military Policy Comports with International Law, *Yale Human Rights and Development Law Journal*, Vol. 8, 2005, pp. 153-187.

or unpreventable. In the face of an angry international community, the US government took some action and the US military appointed guards to keep watch over the remnants of the National Museum. The US government also sent a team of cultural experts to Iraq. As regards, the responsibility toward the protection of cultural property on occupied territory, the US defines the concept of "military occupation" narrowly. Before it adheres to the obligations of an occupying authority, the US contends that "occupation" must be both actual and effective. Therefore, in regions not immediately under the direct control of American troops, the military can claim a lack of jurisdiction.[35] According to the April 1992 US Department of Defence (DOD) report, the US Armed Forces acted by the international laws of war throughout the conflict.[36]

The 1954 Hague Convention affirms general principles that cultural property should be above the fray of war and special efforts should be made to safeguard these treasures during hostilities. Parties to the Convention agree to offer protection, including both not using cultural property for military purposes and safeguarding cultural property by stopping theft and vandalism during times of war. The Convention allows a party to waive its duty to protect in the case of military necessity, such as if an enemy uses the property as a shield or a military planning facility. In times of occupation, the Convention imposes upon an occupying party an obligation to assist the occupied country in protecting its cultural property by providing the most necessary aid. The Convention also prohibits reprisals directed at cultural property. Although the US has not formally ratified the treaty in 2003, [37] in practice, the US follows its tenets. The US military personnel are trained in the law of war and the Hague Convention, and they are instructed to respect the Hague emblem. During the Gulf War bombing campaign, the US Defence Department maintained that it was doing all it could to ensure that bombs were not targeting important cultural sites.

35 Thurlow Matthew D., Protecting Cultural Property in Iraq: How American Military Policy Comports with International Law, *Yale Human Rights and Development Law Journal*, Vol. 8, 2005, pp. 153-187.

36 The report states that the Department of Defence mandated instruction and training in the law of war were reflected in US operations, which were in keeping with historic US adherence to the precepts of the law of war. Adherence to the law of war impeded neither Coalition planning nor execution; Iraqi violations of the law provided Iraq with no advantage. The US Department of Defence Report to Congress on the Conduct of the Persian Gulf War, April 10, 1992, [31 I.L.M. 612 (1992)].

37 On March 13, 2009, the United States deposited its instrument of ratification of the 1954 Hague Convention for the Protection of Cultural Property in the Event of Armed Conflict with UNESCO.

In its final report to Congress, the Defence Department stated, "Some targets were specifically avoided because the value of destruction of each target was outweighed by the potential risk to nearby civilians or, as in the case of certain archaeological and religious sites, to civilian objects."[38] By failing to take the necessary measures to prevent looters from ransacking Iraqi artefacts; the US war planners, executioners as well as legal advisers, breached the international obligation to protect cultural property under occupation law.[39] According to Miller (2005), when the US failed to prevent the looting of antiquities in Iraq, it not only allowed the destruction of Iraqi art - it allowed the destruction of the world's history.[40]

The US Department of Defence Law of War Manual (June 2015, updated July 2023) now provides:

> Certain types of property receive additional protection as cultural property. Cultural property, the areas immediately surrounding it, and appliances in use for its protection should be safeguarded and respected. There are also obligations concerning cultural property during occupation and peacetime. Certain treaty obligations concerning cultural property may only apply on the territory of Parties to the 1954 Hague Cultural Property Convention, but the US has previously identified some of these obligations as customary international law. Department of Defence personnel, therefore, in the absence of contrary guidance by competent authority, should act as if they were legally bound by the rules for the protection of cultural property in the 1954 Hague Cultural Property Convention during hostilities even when conducting operations in the territory of a State that is not a Party to the 1954 Hague Cultural Property Convention.

38 The military judge advocates and civilian attorneys with international law expertise provided advice on the law of war and other legal issues at every level of command in all phases of Operations Desert Shield and Desert Storm. The US Department of Defence Report to Congress on the Conduct of the Persian Gulf War, April 10, 1992, [31 I.L.M. 612(1992)].

39 The United States had an obligation to protect the cultural property of Iraq as an occupying power under international occupation law. The Fourth Geneva Convention and the 1907 Hague Convention require an occupying power to refrain from the destruction of private property in the occupied territory. The Geneva Protocol I expands the occupying power's obligation to include the specific protection of cultural property by classifying any wilful destruction of the cultural heritage of a people, including historic monuments and works of art, as a grave breach of the Protocol.

40 Miller Amy E., Looting of Iraqi Art: Occupiers and Collectors Turn away Leisurely from the Disaster, *Case Western Reserve Journal of International Law*, Vol 37, Issue 1, 2005, pp. 49-84.

Military commanders must take reasonable measures to prevent or stop any form of theft, pillage, or misappropriation of, and any acts of vandalism directed against cultural property. This obligation may also be viewed as part of the obligation to take feasible precautions to reduce the risk of harm to cultural property.[41]

Bosnia (1992-95)

The wars of the 1990s that accompanied the dissolution of Yugoslavia with violent conflicts taking place in Croatia, Bosnia-Herzegovina, and Kosovo. The 1992–95 Bosnian War was the most violent and destructive of the wars of Yugoslav Succession resulting in ethnic cleansing and the destruction of cultural and religious property. The devastation wreaked on cultural and religious property during the Bosnian War was the greatest destruction of cultural heritage in Europe since World War II. The destruction was not collateral damage but a well-planned and systematic destruction of cultural property. The attacks on iconic structures like the National Library in Sarajevo and the Old Bridge (Stari Most) at Mostar provoked worldwide condemnation. The obliteration of structures from the landscape went hand in hand with forced expulsion, imprisonment in concentration camps, torture, mass rape, the sexual enslavement of women and mass murder. [42]

The Bosnian War began in earnest after Slovenia and then Croatia declared independence from federal Yugoslavia in 1991, and Bosnia-Herzegovina followed suit in March 1992. Bosnia-Herzegovina was home to three principal ethno-national groups: Bosnian Muslims (Bosnia's), Bosnian Serbs and Bosnian Croats. After a referendum held on February 29 and March 1, 1992, the Republic of Bosnia-Herzegovina declared independence on March 3, 19992 and received international recognition as a state. It became a member of the United Nations on May 22, 1992. A war broke out immediately which was followed by a well-planned ethnic cleansing of the non-Serb population, targeting both Muslims and Croats to create a contiguous mono-ethnic territory. By autumn 1992 the Bosnian Serbs

41 The US Department of Defence Law of War Manual (June 2015, updated July 2023), Para 5.18 Protection of Cultural Property During Hostilities, pp. 301-310.

42 Walasek Helen, Cultural heritage, and memory after ethnic cleansing in post-conflict Bosnia-Herzegovina, *International Review of the Red Cross*, Vol. 101(1), 2019, pp. 273-294.

controlled over 70 percent of Bosnia-Herzegovina.[43] War among the Serb, Croat and Muslim populations in Bosnia and Herzegovina began in 1992 and lasted until late 1995. The signing of the Dayton Peace Agreement (DPA) on December 14, 1995, marked the legal conclusion of the Bosnian War.

The destruction of two prominent cultural properties: Sarajevo's Austro-Hungarian era National Library in August 1992 by Bosnian Serb forces, and the destruction of Mostar's graceful 16th century Ottoman Old Bridge (Stari Most) in November 1993 by Bosnian Croat forces is covered in greater details.

On the night from August 25 to 26, 1992, Bosnia's National and University Library built in 1890 on the Sarajevo riverfront was shelled and burned.[44] Before the fire, the library held 1.5 million volumes, including over 155,000 rare books and manuscripts; the country's national archives; deposit copies of newspapers, periodicals and books published in Bosnia, and the collection of the University of Sarajevo. It was bombarded with incendiary grenades from Serbian nationalist positions across the river, the library burned for three days and was reduced to ashes with most of its content. A few librarians and volunteer citizens formed a human chain to pass books out of the burning building. During the whole course of the conflict, four library staff members lost their lives, mostly through sniper fire.[45] It was a clear attack on the cultural identity of a people in which millions of books and countless artefacts were destroyed.[46]

43 Walasek Helen (ed), 2017, *Bosnia and the Destruction of Cultural Heritage*, London: Routledge, pp. 4-5.

44 Twenty-five mortar shells struck the building, along with forty shells that were dropped on nearby streets to prevent the fire department from reaching the library…The next day the sky was dark with smoke, while across the city, pages and small bits of burned books sailed through the air…Over 1,200,000 books and 600,000 serials, as well as all the catalogues that had been constructed over the years, computer equipment, microfilm and photo labs, and administrative documents, were all burned.

45 Riedlmayer Andras, Erasing the Past: The Destruction of Libraries and Archives in Bosnia-Herzegovina, *Middle East Studies Association Bulletin*, Vol. 29, No. 1, July 1995, pp. 7-11.

46 The National Library was destroyed in the fire, along with 80 per cent of its contents. Some three million books went up in flames, along with hundreds of original documents from the Ottoman Empire and the Austro-Hungarian monarchy. The artefacts are a testimony to Bosnia's centuries-old history and its identity as a multicultural society. The destruction of the National Library at the beginning of the Bosnian War was a symbol of one of the conflict's central objectives - crushing the cultural identity of an entire society. A new word was created to describe the tragedy "Culturcide". Samir

On November 9, 1993, after relentless shelling, the elegant structure disintegrated and fell into the Neretva River. A jewel of Ottoman architecture, Stari Most (Old Bridge) was built in 1566 by a pupil of the great architect Sinan at the order of Sultan Suleiman the Magnificent. A 17th-century explorer described it as a 'rainbow arch', 'thrown from rock to rock as high as the sky'. Stari Most was a defining element of Mostar's identity as an urban landscape, and its annihilation made it even more meaningful. The ruined bridge came to symbolise the senseless destruction of heritage in the modern world. The Old Bridge did not just provide a passage across the river, it was the 'friendship bridge' that linked the city's diverse inhabitants – Bosnians, Croats, Serbs, Muslims, Jews, and Orthodox Christians.[47]

Old Mostar Bridge: Whether a legitimate military target

The destruction of the Old Mostar Bridge during the 1993 war is a special case. The war at the time pitted the HVO Croat forces against Bosnian (ABiH) soldiers in the town of Mostar. The bridge allowed the latter to bring arms supplies and to bring food and medicines to besieged Muslim civilians on the west bank. The issue became debatable, whether the Old Bridge was a legitimate military target for the HVO forces.

In 2013, the Trial Chamber of the International Criminal Tribunal for the former Yugoslavia (ICTY)[48] considered that it was a legitimate military

Huseinovic and Zoran Arbutina, Out of Ashes, August 25, 2012, available at: https://www.dw.com/en/burned-library-symbolizes-multiethnic-sarajevo/a-16192965.

47 The project to rebuild the Old Bridge and restore its surroundings was launched by UNESCO in July 1998 as a partnership between UNESCO, the World Bank, and the city of Mostar. The reconstruction of the bridge under the auspices of UNESCO represents a landmark event in heritage protection. The joint appeal by UNESCO, the World Bank and Mostar authorities was answered by five donor countries – Croatia, France, Italy, the Netherlands, and Turkey – as well as the Council of Europe Development Bank. While the World Bank handled the financial organization and the city of Mostar disbursement of funds, UNESCO was mainly responsible for the technical and scientific coordination. It has set a precedent in peacebuilding processes and shows that our shared heritage can be a basis for social cohesion, inclusion, and citizenship.

48 The International Criminal Tribunal for the Former Yugoslavia (ICTY) was established by the Security Council vide Resolution 827(1003) which dealt with war crimes that took place during the conflicts in the former Yugoslavia in the 1990s. The Tribunal was the first court to undertake the prosecution and adjudication of the gravest international crimes since the post-World War II Nuremberg and Tokyo trials. The ICTY was provided with a mandate and authority to persecute persons responsible for serious violations of international humanitarian law committed in the territory of former Yugoslavia since 1991, specifically grave breaches of the Geneva Conventions

objective. In its judgment, the Court stated that the Old Bridge was indeed a military target, but added that its destruction was disproportionate to the military gains achieved. It was therefore an illegal act, a war crime, and a crime against humanity, being an underlying act of persecution on political, racial, and religious grounds as a crime against humanity and unlawful infliction of terror on civilians as a violation of the laws and customs of war.[49]

The 2013 ICTY judgment concluded that the destruction of the Old Mostar Bridge was a war crime and a crime against humanity because the destruction of the Old Bridge was accompanied by a "will to terrorise" the civilians who were now completely under siege. In 2017, the Appeals Court, in its judgement reversed the conclusion of the 2013 decision, stating that because the bridge was a military target its destruction was legal, producing "a definite military advantage". Therefore, the Court said, its destruction could not be considered "wanton destruction not justified by military necessity." [50]

The Serbs believed that if there were no mosques, there would be no Muslims and by destroying the mosques, the Muslims would lose a motive to return to their villages. The removal of the Bosnian Muslims population from Croat-held areas was a key aim of the attack. In rural areas or on

of 1949, violations of customs or laws of war, genocide, and crimes against humanity. During its mandate, which lasted from 1993-2017, it irreversibly changed the landscape of international humanitarian law, provided victims with an opportunity to voice the horrors they witnessed and experienced, and proved that those suspected of bearing the greatest responsibility for atrocities committed during armed conflicts can be held accountable. It examined more than 4,650 witnesses and a total of 161 individuals were indicted by the Court. Walasek Helen, "Cultural Heritage, the Search for Justice and Human Rights," in Walasek Helen (ed), 2017, *Bosnia and the Destruction of Cultural Heritage*, London: Routledge, pp. 310-311.

49 The 2013 judgement (paragraph 1294-1366), however, takes the different elements into account in reaching this conclusion. It points to the historic and symbolic value of the bridge, recognizing while "the Old Bridge was essential to the ABiH for the combat activities of its units on the front line, for evacuations and for sending troops, provisions and material and that it was used for this purpose." But the Trial Chamber also recognized that the Old Bridge was also "essential for supplies to the inhabitants of the Muslim enclave on the right bank of the Neretva" river.

50 This point of view was vigorously contested in a dissenting opinion by Judge Fausto Pocar. He expressed surprise that his colleagues on the Appeals Court had ignored the 1954 Convention on the protection of cultural property, which stipulates in Article 4, para 2 that there can only be a waiver for the destruction of cultural heritage "in cases where military necessity imperatively requires such a waiver", with military necessity being defined by the absence of alternative to the destruction.

urban fringes, ruins of destroyed structures were often left to crumble, the stones lying in heaps where they had fallen. But in town and village centres there was usually active intervention. Ruins of religious places were bulldozed, debris trucked away and sites levelled so not a single trace of the structures could be seen. The levelled sites went on to be used as parking lots, markets or locations for garbage dumpsters or were left as empty, often rubbish-strewn spaces.[51] The particular targeting of minarets and their removal from the landscape was noted as "a kind of architectural equivalent to the removal of the population, and visible proof that the Muslims had left".[52] By the end of the war, with one exception, not a single minaret on a functioning mosque was left intact on territories occupied by Bosnian Serb forces.[53] The ethnic cleansing took place accompanied by the vast devastation of religious and cultural property.[54]

The war in Bosnia was held under the gaze of the global public. The international community was deeply involved in the war from the very beginning and thousands of external actors were present in the country. This includes UN peacekeepers and observers, humanitarian aid workers, journalists, and other members of the media. The destruction of cultural heritage was a determining factor in former Yugoslavia's wars in the 1990s. Cultural cleansing often went alongside ethnic cleansing, seeking to wipe out the links that unite communities around their culture. The deliberate and widespread destruction of cultural heritage in Bosnia and Croatia led to considerable activities in the international arena. The Statute of the

51 The remains of the Ferhadija Mosque were dumped at a municipal landfill site along with the remains of the historic Arnaudija Mosque, or thrown into a nearby reservoir, while fragments of the Aladza were discovered by a team from the Federation Commission on Missing Persons excavating a mass grave site in Foca in 2000. Rubble from the eighteenth-century Savska Mosque in Brcko, a mosque which was completely obliterated by its destroyers, its foundations were dug up, covering the mass grave of local Muslims murdered during ethnic cleansing.

52 Colin Kaiser, Report on Destruction of Cultural Property 09-Jul-02, Krajisnik Case, Case No. IT-00-39, 2002, p. 4.

53 Marija Arnautovic, "Bosnia: The Village Where Hate Never Triumphed," *Institute for War and Peace Reporting*, TRI Issue 642, April 10, 2010.

54 The ethnic cleansing campaign of the Bosnian war featured forced mass expulsion, mass killing, mass rape, internment in concentration camps, torture, and intentional destruction of religious and cultural property of the expelled population. There were two explicit aims in this destruction: (i) to eliminate any evidence of the expelled population's historic evidence on the territory, and (ii) by removal of these markers of community identity, to discourage those who survived ethnic cleansing from ever returning. Walasek Helen (ed), 2017, *Bosnia and the Destruction of Cultural Heritage*, London: Routledge, pp. 5-6.

International Criminal Tribunal for the Former Yugoslavia (ICTY) of 1993 was an important addition to international criminal law of the destruction of cultural property. More than fifteen ICTY judgments sanction the destroyers of cultural heritage, such as those who ordered bombing causing the fire that destroyed the Sarajevo library, burning 90% of the manuscripts, or the old town of Dubrovnik.

Kosovo (1999-2004)

During the conflict of 1999, as well as its immediate aftermath and again during the March 2004 riots, Kosovo's cultural heritage of both Albanian and Serbian communities suffered extensive damage due mostly to deliberate aggression. The nature of the destruction of cultural property showed that it was not merely collateral damage but was intended to eradicate the historical presence as well as the contemporary lives of the target community.

The Republic of Kosovo is situated in the heart of the Balkans, bordered by Albania, Macedonia, Montenegro, and Serbia. It covers an area of about 10,000 square km, and is populated by nearly two million people: 93% Albanians, and 7% Serbs, Turks, Bosnians, and other ethnic groups. Albanian and Serbian are the two key languages. Most of the population is either Islamic or Catholic; the Serb community is Orthodox. The territory possesses a multicultural historical environment, with evidence of settlement since long before it became successively part of the Roman, Byzantine and Ottoman Empires. In the early 20th century, it was under the dominion of the kingdoms of Serbia, Slovenia, and Croatia. After the Second World War, Kosovo became a province in the Federal Republic of Yugoslavia and enjoyed a certain degree of autonomy from 1974 to 1989. The Yugoslav Republic began to break up during the early 1990s with Slovenia, Croatia and Bosnia breaking away from the state; Kosovo then became part of Serbia.

During the conflict, historic monuments in Kosovo were systematically targeted due to their high visibility and association with national identity.[55] From the spring of 1998 until the summer of 1999, Kosovo was exposed to dramatic armed conflict and ethnic cleansing. About a million Kosovo Albanians were driven from their homes and thousands were killed. Their houses and traditional cultural heritage monuments and sites

55 Defreese Michelle, Kosovo: Cultural Heritage in Conflict, *Journal of Conflict Archaeology*, Vol. 5, No. 1, June 2009, pp. 257-270.

were looted and destroyed. In all, eighteen months of the Yugoslav Serb counterinsurgency campaign between 1998 and 1999 within Kosovo resulted in 225 or a third out of a total of 600 mosques being damaged, vandalised, or destroyed.[56] Some Islamic architecture was damaged within the context of the fighting.

Mosques and other Islamic buildings; however, in certain urban neighbourhoods and villages became the only targets of violence against architecture, while in other locations every mosque and all Islamic buildings became targeted. Often after an attack on a village and the fleeing of the population from villages, towns and cities, attacks on mosques, other Islamic buildings and architecture were undertaken and widespread by the Yugoslav Serb army. Attacks at times entailed the toppling of a mosque minaret, having minaret tops shot off, explosive devices placed in a minaret or within a mosque, bulldozing of mosques, fires started in a mosque, artillery aimed at a minaret and walls riddled with bullets. The vandalisation of mosques also occurred, anti-Albanian and anti-Islamic vandalism, the graffitiing of facades with images and text and in certain examples, anti-Albanian and pro-Serbian graffiti was inscribed on the walls of a mosque. During the war, 65 (a third of a total of 183) Kosovo public libraries were fully destroyed resulting in the combined loss of 900,588 volumes. The Haddam Suleiman Aga library, founded in 1595 in Jakobe, was burned down by Yugoslav Serb troops resulting in the loss of 1,300 rare books and 200 manuscripts written in Albanian in Arabic script-Aljamiado.[57]

The 1998/99 conflict-affected not only the built heritage but also Kosovo's Museum collections and archives. On the eve of hostilities in late 1998, more than 1200 of the most valuable items from the collections of the National Museum of Kosovo in Pristine and from regional museums in Prizren and Mitrovica were taken to Belgrade on the pretext of an exhibition at the National Museum from 1998 to 1999. The damage and destruction of cultural heritage sites did not end when the conflict ended in June 1999.

During an outbreak of ethnic riots between March 17 and 19, 2004, additional cultural heritage was damaged. ethnic Albanian mobs attacked Serbian homes, churches, and schools throughout Kosovo. The attacks

56 Herscher Andrew and Riedlmayer Andras, Monument and crime: The destruction of historic architecture in Kosovo, *Grey Room*, Vol. **1** (1), 2000, pp. 108–122.

57 Riedlmayer Andras J., Crimes of War, Crimes of Peace: Destruction of Libraries during and after the Balkan Wars of the 1990s, *Library Trends*, Vol. 56, Issue 1, 2007, pp. 107-132; Under Orders: War Crimes in Kosovo, Human Rights Watch, 2001.

took place under the watch of 20,000 KFOR NATO-led troops, the United Nations Mission in Kosovo (UNMIK), the local Kosovo Police Service (KPS) and the Kosovo Protection Force (KZK). The violence left 19 dead, 250 homes looted and burned, as well as churches, monasteries, and several graveyards heavily damaged, looted, burned, or destroyed.[58] In the town of Prizern, many medieval buildings were badly harmed and damaged. The Church of Bogorodica Ljeviska, Holy Mother of God completed in 1307 was burned from the inside. The monastery of Holy Archangels which contained the tomb of King Dusan, from the 14th century was burned and looted in the presence of German KFOR soldiers. Near Prizern, in Zivinjane, the Church of Holy Sunday was dynamited.[59] Many believe that the destruction of Kosovo's non-Serb architectural heritage was a planned and methodical element of ethnic cleansing.

This priceless heritage is still endangered by a variety of factors, which include a limited understanding of the value of cultural heritage; a shortage of experience in heritage management and planning; the prevalence of illegal construction and the inability of the authorities to enforce regulations to protect historic monuments and sites; lack of proper inventory and information systems; and lack of public awareness and education. More than two decades after the armed conflict, many cultural heritage monuments, and sites in urban and rural areas, including historic mosques and traditional residential architecture, remain beyond adequate care, technical assessment, or restoration. Historic centres and archaeological sites are left to the mercy of time and the destructive interventions of developers.

Afghanistan: A Wilful Destruction of Buddhas of Bamiyan (2001)

Bamiyan means "the place of shining light." The central valley of Bamiyan is located at 2,500 meters and is watered by two rivers flowing down from sources in the Kuh-e Baba: The Kakrak River to the east and the Foladi River to the west. The principal archaeological sites are in the long east-west central valley of Bamiyan and the Kakrak and Foladi river valleys.[60] Bamiyan

58 Branko Bjelajac and Felix Corley, Kosovo: Nobody charged for destruction of Orthodox churches and monasteries, Forum 18 News Service, May 6, 2004.

59 Serbenco Eduard, The Protection of Cultural Property and Post-Conflict Kosovo, *Revue Quebecoise de droit International*, Vol. 18-2, 2005, pp. 91-125.

60 Margottini Claudio (ed.), 2009, *After the Destruction of Giant Buddha Statues in Bamiyan (Afghanistan) in 2001: A UNESCO's Emergency Activity for the Recovering*

was a religious site from the 2nd century with the belief of Buddhist time with conquering of Muslims under the AI- Mahdi. The colossal standing Buddha statues were an impressive 55 metres and 38 metres tall, which were carved into two richly decorated niches in the Bamiyan Cliffs. Numerous caves surrounded the Buddha cave, and the surface was decorated with the painting. Most cave shows appear with elaborate centres for philosophy, split the culture for art and Gandhara culture. The two Buddha statues had survived the rise and fall of empires for nearly fourteen hundred years along the ancient 'Silk Road.'[61] The niches were surrounded by a honeycomb of some 750 manmade caves, many of which exhibited elaborate frescoes and sculptures. The carbon dates to the Buddha of Bamiyan in 591-644 CE in the western Buddha. The Eastern Buddha in 544-595 CE. Chinese monk and traveller Hsuan Tsang, who visited the site in 634 AD reported that it was a thriving centre of Buddhism and described in detail the ceremonies and rituals he witnessed there.

Following the September 11, 2001 attacks in the United States, the US Special Forces invaded Afghanistan, with the support of northern rebel groups overthrew the Taliban government. The Taliban formed during the 1980s as a religious movement aiming to restore the Islamic traditions of their country. However, their ambition soon became political. Gradually, under the pretence of bringing order in the years after the Soviet invasion, Taliban militia groups gained control of the government of Afghanistan. In doing so, they began imposing laws that altered people's lifestyles to accommodate the government's interpretation of Islamic principles. These changes included restrictions on the public conduct of women, monitoring of media and the annihilation of artworks that were judged to be in opposition to the Taliban ideology.

In 1999, the UN did not recognise the Taliban but rather imposed severe trade sanctions which were further strengthened in 2000. On January 26, 2001, Mullah Omar issued a decree:

---

and Rehabilitation of Cliff and Niches, Italy: Springer, pp. 293, at p. vii.

61 The Buddha was not a mere representation of flourishing Buddhism in the valley of Bamiyan but also a symbol of protection for all the merchants and travellers who were travelling these roads. It was a symbol of wealth and prosperity, and law and justice, for anyone who could lay eyes on that magnificent mountain. It was a symbol of familiarity for any traveller as it would translate as a symbol of identity. Nabi Aisha, Crossroad of Culture: A Contested Space of Culture and Cultural Terrorism - Bamiyan, Afghanistan, *International Journal of Arts and Social Science*, Vol. 5, Issue 11, November 2022, p. 9.

> Given the fatwa (religious edict) of prominent Afghan scholars and the verdict of the Afghanistan Supreme Court, it has been decided to break down all statutes/ idols in different parts of the country. This is because these idols have been gods of infidels, who worshipped them, and these are respected now and perhaps may be turned into gods again. The real God is only Allah, and all other false gods should be removed.

This public announcement of the destruction of non-Islamic statutes, including Bamiyan Buddhas, led to an immense international protest. UNESCO sent an appeal to the Taliban via the Islamabad office in Pakistan and issued international press releases and interviews calling for the suspension of the edict to destroy Buddha statues. Various appeals by prominent authorities including offers to buy the statutes went in vain. Buddha statues were dynamited by the Taliban on March 11, 2001, in front of the heritage community. Later the destruction was put on the internet by journalists who filmed the destruction in situ. In addition, the Kabul Museum was looted and Buddhist and other art objects were destroyed. A few days later, the Taliban invited journalists to take photographs of the giant empty niches that were circulated the world.[62]

The intentional destruction of cultural heritage conducted by the Taliban government was justified as a necessary step towards the cultural and religious purification of the nation. Although the destruction of heritage and the plundering of artefacts has taken place since antiquity, the destruction of the two Buddhas of Bamiyan represented an important turning point for the international community. This abominable act of destruction was part of a widespread Taliban-led campaign of destruction of important cultural relics, a phenomenon often referred to as iconoclasm.[63] The term iconoclasm encompasses intentional destruction or resistance against images and artwork in general. It is an aggressive act against concepts and value structure behind an object. To a greater extent, it comes with a carefully planned announcement and attention-seeking orchestration that must be considered as an independent means of communication, with a view of achieving higher political goals. Therefore, the Taliban incident at

62 Falser Michael, The Bamiyan Buddhas, Performative Iconoclasm and the "Image of Heritage," in Tomaszewski A. and Giometti S. (ed), The Image of Heritage, March 6-8, 2009, Florence, Italy, pp. 157-169.

63 Kanchana Wangkeo, Monumental Challenges: The Lawfulness of Destroying Cultural Heritage During Peacetime, *Yale Journal of International Law*, Vol, 28, 2003, p. 183; defining iconoclasm as the "destruction of icons due to the belief that the images are imbued with an unacceptable symbolic significance".

Bamiyan cannot be reduced to primitive vandalism, rather it is the first large-scale live act of performative iconoclasm.[64]

A deliberate act of destruction by the Taliban was motivated by an extremist ideology that aimed to destroy culture, identity and history, the loss of the Buddhas revealed how the destruction of heritage could be used as a weapon against local populations. By destroying the huge Buddha statues that had been watching over the Bamiyan Valley for 1,500 years, the Taliban have committed crimes against humanity. They have destroyed not only part of Afghanistan's historical legacy but also exceptional evidence of the meeting of several civilisations and heritage that belonged to the whole human race. Apart from these Buddhas being a huge loss, what has just been done is unprecedented. For the first time, a central authority in a state has usurped the right to destroy part of our common heritage.

UNESCO Declaration concerning the Intentional Destruction of Cultural Heritage

Immediately after the collapse of the Taliban regime, UNESCO responded quickly to the challenge of rehabilitating Afghanistan's endangered cultural heritage which, in some instances, had suffered irreversible damage and loss. Since 2002, an international project, funded by the UNESCO Japan Funds-in Trust for Preservation of the World Cultural Heritage and coordinated by UNESCO, has been operating in Bamiyan.

On March 12, 2001, UNESCO condemned the Taliban's destruction of the Buddhas of Bamiyan which has been confirmed by UNESCO Special Envoy. The UNESCO Director-General (DG) in a press release stated that in destroying the Buddhas of Bamiyan, the Taliban have committed:

> ".... a crime against culture. It is abominable to witness the cold and calculated destruction of cultural properties which were the heritage of the Afghan people, and, indeed, of the whole of humanity. The Buddhas of Bamiyan were not inscribed on the World Heritage List but deserved to be and their destruction represents a true cultural crime. This crime against culture was committed while people throughout the world raised their voices to prevent it. The Taliban heeded neither the unprecedented scope of international mobilisation nor the advice against their decision, spontaneously issued by the highest religious

64 Falser Michael, The Bamiyan Buddhas, Performative Iconoclasm and the "Image of Heritage," in Tomaszewski A. and Giometti S. (ed), The Image of Heritage, March 6-8, 2009, Florence, Italy, pp. 157-169.

> authorities of Islam. The loss is irreversible. Everything possible must be done to stop further destruction. … I hope that it will not provide fanatics elsewhere with an excuse for acts of destruction targeting Moslem cultural properties. The senseless violence few should not be met with further acts of violence, which would be equally intolerable."

At its 31st session in 2001, immediately after the wilful destruction of the Buddhas of Bamiyan by the Taliban government of Afghanistan, the General Conference of UNESCO adopted a resolution entitled 'Acts constituting a crime against the common heritage of humanity'.[65] To maximise the protection of the cultural heritage of humanity, and in particular, against destructive acts, the resolution called on all Member States of UNESCO and all other states of the world to become Parties to the 1954 Hague Convention and its two Protocols and other related conventions.[66] The General Conference reiterated the fundamental principles included in these instruments to prevent the destruction of cultural heritage including looting and illicit excavations, and invited the DG UNESCO to formulate a Draft Declaration concerning the Intentional Destruction of Cultural Heritage. This resulted in the UNESCO Declaration concerning the Intentional Destruction of Cultural Heritage, adopted by the General Conference in 2003 at its thirty-second session.

The General Conference recalled the principles of all UNESCO's conventions, recommendations, declarations, and charters for the protection of cultural heritage, as well as Articles 8(2)(b)(ix) and 8(2)(e)(iv) of the Rome Statute of the ICC, and Article 3(d) of the Statute of the International Criminal Tribunal for the former Yugoslavia, related to the intentional destruction of cultural heritage. The General Conference recalled the tragic destruction of the Buddhas of Bamiyan that affected the international community as a whole; and expressed serious concern about the growing number of acts of intentional destruction of cultural heritage. It resolved that states should take all appropriate measures to prevent, avoid, stop, and suppress acts of intentional destruction of cultural

65 General Conference 31st Session, 31 C/4612 September 2001.

66 This includes the 1970 UNESCO Convention on the Means of Prohibiting and Preventing the Illicit Import, Export and Transfer of Ownership of Cultural Property, the 1995 UNIDROIT Convention on Stolen or Illicitly Exported Cultural Objects, and the 1972 UNESCO Convention on the World Cultural and Natural Heritage to maximize the protection of the cultural heritage of humanity, and against destructive acts.

heritage, wherever such heritage is located. Some of the recommendations of the General Conference were as follows:[67]

> **State responsibility**: A State that intentionally destroys or intentionally fails to take appropriate measures to prohibit, prevent, stop, and punish any intentional destruction of cultural heritage of great importance for humanity, whether it is inscribed on a list maintained by UNESCO or another international organisation, bears the responsibility for such destruction, to the extent provided for by international law.
>
> **Individual criminal responsibility**: States should take all appropriate measures, by international law, to establish jurisdiction over, and provide effective criminal sanctions against, those persons who commit, or order to be committed, acts of intentional destruction of cultural heritage of great importance for humanity, whether it is inscribed on a list maintained by UNESCO or another international organisation.
>
> **Human rights and international humanitarian law**: In applying this Declaration: States recognise the need to respect international rules related to the criminalisation of gross violations of human rights and international humanitarian law when intentional destruction of cultural heritage is linked to those violations.
>
> **Public awareness**: States should take all appropriate measures to ensure the widest possible dissemination of this Declaration to the public and to target groups, inter alia, by organising public awareness-raising campaigns.

The Resolution urged that the state parties should adopt the appropriate legislative, administrative, educational, and technical measures, within the framework of their economic resources, to protect cultural heritage and should revise them periodically to adapt them to the evolution of national and international cultural heritage protection standards.

In 2007 the World Heritage Committee gave four corrective measures which would eventually lead to the removal of Bamiyan from the List of World Heritage in Danger. These include site security by the State party, the long-

67 The General Conference of the United Nations Educational, Scientific and Cultural Organization (UNESCO) meeting in Paris at its thirty-second session in 2003. UNESCO Declaration Concerning the Intentional Destruction of Cultural Heritage. General Conference, 32nd session, Paris 2003 32C/25 date July 17, 2003.

term stability of the Buddha niches, the conservation of the archaeological remains and the formation of a master plan for the management of the Bamiyan. On the 90th anniversary of the diplomatic relations between Japan and Afghanistan, the government of Japan announced USD 3.8 million in support for the cause of prevention and protection of the site in Bamiyan. UNESCO has been working towards the goal of preserving the site while trying to evaluate all the possibilities for its future. The future of the Bamiyan Buddhas is in flux in which there is no one possible way, an ideal solution, of achieving it. The measures that UNESCO has taken along with the Afghan government reflect the complexity of the situation.[68]

UNESCO as a self-proclaimed guardian of the 'heritage of humanity' may have to reconsider its role in globalised power relations in the world. If we consider that the protection of the world's cultural property encompasses all of humanity, we should first protect its regional stakeholders. According to Falser (2009), in the case of Bamiyan that was and still is not the case: in 2001, the local population was massacred by the Taliban without any global protest and today, when Western scientists are back to rebuild Bamiyan as UNESCO World Heritage, ground realities have remained unchanged.[69] In recent years, the caves surrounding the Buddhas – with wall paintings by the monks – were defiled and defaced by the soldiers of the various factions in Afghanistan. Though the country's civil war ended with the Taliban takeover, the Islamic State group has carried out attacks on the Taliban and there is an anti-Taliban insurgency in some areas. In May 2024, three Afghan nationals and three Spanish tourists were killed in the central Afghanistan city of Bamiyan, besides seven others were injured, while walking through a bazaar in the mountainous city.[70]

Syria (2011 onwards)

In March 2011 Syria's government, led by President Bashar al-Assad, faced an unprecedented challenge to its authority when pro-democracy protests erupted throughout the country. Protesters demanded an end to the

68 Nabi Aisha, Crossroad of Culture: A Contested Space of Culture and Cultural Terrorism - Bamiyan, Afghanistan, *International Journal of Arts and Social Science*, Vol. 5, Issue 11, November 2022, p. 9.

69 Falser Michael, The Bamiyan Buddhas, Performative Iconoclasm and the "Image of Heritage," in Tomaszewski A. and Giometti S. (ed), The Image of Heritage, March 6-8, 2009, Florence, Italy, pp. 157-169.

70 Mackintosh Thomas, Three Spanish tourists killed in central Afghanistan gun attack, BBC News, May 18, 2024.

authoritarian practices of the Assad regime, in place since Assad's father became president in 1971.[71] The Syrian government used violence to suppress demonstrations, making extensive use of police, military, and paramilitary forces.[72] After months of crackdown by the government's security apparatus, various armed rebel groups such as the Free Syrian Army began forming across the country, marking the beginning of the Syrian insurgency. Opposition militias began to form in 2011, and by mid-2012 the conflict had expanded into a full-fledged civil war. As the protests increased in strength and size, the regime responded with heavier force.

The conflict, which began as protests President Assad's regime, quickly escalated into a full-scale war between the Syrian government, which was backed by Russia and Iran. Anti-government rebel groups were backed by the US and a rotating number of US allies, including France, the UK, Italy, Saudi Arabia, Turkey, Jordan, and the United Arab Emirates (UAE). It is over 14 years since the conflict in Syria began; has killed more than 350,000 [73] people and caused the displacement of half the Syrian population.[74]

Syrian President Assad now controls about two-thirds of Syria's territory and has achieved normalcy with several Arab states, as well

71 When Assad succeeded his father in 2000, he came to the presidency with a reputation as a modernizer and a reformer. The hopes that were raised by Assad's presidency went largely unfulfilled. Assad revived the authoritarian tactics of his late father's administration, including pervasive censorship and surveillance and brutal violence against suspected opponents of the regime. Assad also oversaw significant liberalization of Syria's state-dominated economy, but those changes mostly served to enrich a network of crony capitalists with ties to the regime. The environmental crisis also played a role in Syria's uprising. Between 2006 and 2010, Syria experienced the worst drought in the country's modern history. Hundreds of thousands of farming families were reduced to poverty, causing a mass migration of rural people to urban shantytowns.

72 Available at: https://www.britannica.com/event/Syrian-Civil-War.

73 In June 2021, the Syrian Observatory for Human Rights (SOHR) said the total number of those killed from March 2011 to June 2021 could be as high as 606,000, including 495,000 documented by the organisation. The total includes civilians, rebels, government and terrorist fighters, and others.

74 In addition to the bloodshed, more than half of Syria's pre-war population of 22 million have had to flee their homes. Some 6.8 million are internally displaced, with more than two million living in tented camps with limited access to basic services. Another 6 million are refugees or asylum-seekers abroad. Neighbouring Egypt, Lebanon, Iraq, Jordan, and Turkey, which are hosting 5.7 million of them, have struggled to cope with one of the largest refugee exoduses in recent history. However, this number does not include the 0.4–1.1 million unregistered refugees. The problems arising from refugees also have other consequences for the hosting countries.

as reinstatement in the Arab League, bringing him out of isolation. His military, along with Russian air support, continues to fight Hayat Tahrir al-Sham (HTS), a coalition of Islamist militant groups in northwest Syria. The Kurdish-dominated Syrian Defence Forces (SDF), which controls most of northeastern Syria, regularly clashes with Arab tribes that accuse the group of discrimination. Turkey and its proxies also control areas along the northern border. Factionalised fighting has made space for the self-proclaimed Islamic State to maintain a presence and launch attacks. The US has nearly 900 military personnel in Syria to undertake counter-terrorism operations.[75] Additionally, Israel regularly strikes Iranian and Syrian military positions in Syria and has increased attacks, including attacking the Damascus and Aleppo airports, since Hamas's October attack on Israel.

Syria's cultural heritage is rich and complex, dating back millennia. Home to a succession of empires, Syria claims some of the earliest cities in human history, if not the earliest. Numerous Bronze Age civilisations left their successive marks, including the Babylonians, the Assyrians, and the Hittites, to name but a few. They in turn were replaced by the Greeks, the Sassanians, the Persians, the Romans, and the Arabs, many of whom chose Syrian cities as their capitals. The European Crusaders came and left some of the most impressive castles known, and the Ottoman Empire also made its mark. All these cultures co-existed and conflicted, forming something new and special found nowhere else in the world. Today Syria has six UNESCO World Heritage Sites: Damascus, Aleppo, Palmyra, Bosra, the Crack des Chevaliers and Saladin's Castle, and the Ancient Villages of Northern Syria. These sites alone represent at least two thousand years of history.

Today, three campaigns drive the conflict: coalition efforts to defeat the self-proclaimed Islamic State (IS), violence between the Syrian government and opposition forces, and military operations against Syrian Kurds by Turkish forces.[76] The continued destruction, looting, and trafficking of cultural

75 US troops in Syria are officially part of an 80-nation American-led Defeat Islamic State Coalition headquartered in Iraq. They operate legally under the 2001 Congressional Authorization for Use of Force Resolution. The US President Trump did not withdraw all US servicepeople from eastern Syria as he had intended, during his presidency the United States reduced its troops there from about 2,000 to 900. Aftandilian Gregory, US Troops to stay in Syria and Iraq but perhaps Not for Long, February 22, 2024, available at: https://arabcenterdc.org/resource/us-troops-to-stay-in-syria-and-iraq-but-perhaps-not-for-long/.

76 Conflict in Syria, The Centre for Preventive Action, February 13, 2024. Available at: https://www.cfr.org/global-conflict-tracker/conflict/conflict-syria.

property, especially during times of political instability and armed conflict in Syria has been a matter of concern for the international community.

Because of the continuing threats, all six Syrian World Heritage properties were inscribed on the List of World Heritage in Danger, at the 37th session of the World Heritage Committee, held in Cambodia in June 2013. Much of Syria's rich cultural heritage has likewise been destroyed. Damage inflicted on the physical infrastructure of Syria, including its monuments and historical and heritage places, has been immense, due to the direct impact of war and the loss of control by the authorities over the country's vast archaeological and cultural heritage. Direct damage was caused to many historical monuments and sites when they were used by armies and militias for shelter or as military outposts to control the surrounding areas.[77] All six of the country's UNESCO World Heritage sites have been damaged significantly, with IS militants deliberately blowing up parts of the ancient city of Palmyra. Three types of destruction have occurred in Syria: destruction of archaeological sites by fighting; looting and pillaging at sites; and thefts from museums. Thefts have been carried out by highly professional thieves who have come and seized specific pieces. Particularly vulnerable to the fighting have been citadels and castles, which were often built on high grounds so that soldiers in ancient times could spot the approach of their enemy. Rebels periodically claim sites, such as the famous Crusaders' castle, and the Krak des Chevaliers. Then the Syrian army fights to get it back, almost inevitably damaging the ancient walls, roofs, and carvings.[78]

The most significant heritage losses involved the Great Mosque of Aleppo (Umayyad Mosque)[79] during the Civil War. [80] The mosque was extensively

77 Bandarin Francesco, "The Destruction of Aleppo: The Impact of the Syrian War on a World Heritage City," in Cuno, James, and Thomas G. Weiss, (eds.), 2022, *Cultural Heritage and Mass Atrocities*, Los Angeles: Getty Publications, pp. 186-201.

78 Alissa J. Rubin, Syria's Past Is Being Lost in War, *The New York Times*, March 14, 2014.

79 The Great Mosque of Aleppo (Umayyad Mosque) is the largest and one of the oldest mosques in the walled old city of Aleppo, a UNESCO World Heritage site in Syria. It was built in the 8th century, and reconstructed during the 11th and 14th centuries. The mosque is purportedly home to the remains of Zechariah, the father of John the Baptist. The minaret of the mosque, 45 m in height, was the oldest surviving part of the monument dating back to 1090.

80 The so-called Battle of Aleppo, one of the longest and most deadly conflicts since World War II, raged for five years, from 2012 to the end of 2016, and involved a range of actors, both on the Syrian government's side (the Syrian army, Hezbollah, other Shiite militias, Iranian government forces, and later the Russian army) and on that of

damaged by fire and armed conflicts during the Syrian civil war. The fighting between rebels and the Syrian regime left the mosque burned, scarred by bullets, trashed, and stained with soot. Antique furnishings and intricately sculpted colonnades have been charred, valuable Islamic relics ransacked and ancient artefacts – including a box purported to contain a strand of the Prophet Muhammad's hair – looted. The minaret was finally brought down by heavy fighting and shelling in April 2013. Bashar al-Assad's regime and anti-government activists traded blame for the attack. The fallen structural material of the minaret remains scattered inside the courtyard and exposed to further looting and shelling attempts. A 2018 report by UNITAR and UNESCO documented damage at the end of 2016 to more than 33,500 structures in Aleppo.[81]

The Syrian city of Palmyra, [82] was captured by Daesh in May 2015. Within a few months of capture, Daesh began a campaign of attacks against cultural property to systematically erase its history. Ancient monuments in the Valley of the Tombs were destroyed in August 2015. The Temple of Baalshamin was dynamited and levelled on 24 August. Days later, the Temple of Bel,[83] one of Palmyra's primary sites and among the most important remaining

the opposition (the Free Syrian Army, the Aleppo Military Council, IS, and the Syrian Islamic Front). Kurdish militias such as the People's Protection Units (YPG), other US-backed groups, and the Turkish army were also involved. Many of these groups were loosely organized, with frequent movements of fighters from one to another. The war in Aleppo took place over several phases, with different degrees of destruction and impact on a civilian population that paid a very high price, affected directly by aerial bombing, shelling, snipers, and mine explosions. Bandarin Francesco, "The Destruction of Aleppo: The Impact of the Syrian War on a World Heritage City," in Cuno, James, and Thomas G. Weiss, (eds.), 2022, *Cultural Heritage and Mass Atrocities*, Los Angeles: Getty Publications, pp. 186-201.

81 UNESCO and UNITAR, Five Years of Conflict. For a comprehensive analysis of damage to Syrian cities; REACH and UNITAR, Syrian Cities Damage Atlas: Thematic Assessment of Satellite Identified Damage, Chatelaine, Switzerland: REACH, March 2019; Also see: UN-Habitat, City Profile, Aleppo: Multi-Sector Assessment, Damascus: UN-Habitat, May 2014.

82 Known as the Pearl of the Desert, Palmyra – which means the City of Palms – lies 210 km northeast of Damascus. Before the Syrian conflict erupted in 2011, more than 150,000 tourists visited Palmyra every year.

83 The Temple of Bel at Palmyra has been the most important site and the most important temple in the Middle East alongside Baalbek in Lebanon. Before the arrival of Christianity in the second century, Palmyra worshipped the Semitic god, Bel, along with the sun god Yarhibol and the lunar god Aglibol. Construction on the temple began in 32 BC and ended in the second century. It later served as a church and a mosque.

ancient religious monuments in West Asia was reduced to rubble. Finally, the ancient Roman Triumphal Arch was destroyed in October 2015.[84]

The reports of illegal excavations in different archaeological sites, and reports of apparently planned and intentional destructions of symbolic monuments have also caused serious concerns. The destruction within the Ancient City of Aleppo, which hosts a very rich urban heritage, including mosques, shrines, and public places such as the *souk* and the *khans*. Some of the city's urban heritage has been severely affected, and some have almost vanished in the conflict. Monuments and sites are almost impossible to be properly protected under the threat of the raging civil war, when rebel and regime forces set up bases in almost every significant site, including the historic ones. Since culture can only be protected in peacetime, it is important to preserve credible and truthful information about the monument (such as its original building material) to be able to safeguard its genuine cultural and historical value.

Looting and Pillage of Cultural Property[85]

When IS was at the height of its power, it had access to numerous archaeological sites and museums. Portrayed as propaganda for its intolerant religious ideology, IS engaged in the systematic and widespread destruction of ancient sites and museums.[86] Since 2011, the country's cultural heritage has been subject to widespread destruction, looting and trafficking. The IS and others have seized upon instability in the country to destroy and steal cultural property, including historical monuments,

84 Brammertz Serge, Kevin C. Hughes, Alison Kipp and William B. Tomljanovich, Attacks against Cultural Heritage as a Weapon of War: Prosecutions at the ICTY, *Journal of International Criminal Justice*, Vol. 14, No. 5, December 2016, pp. 1143-1174.

85 Destruction of cultural property entails intentional or unintentional bombing and damage to sites and objects. Looting involves the illegal removal of undocumented objects from a site or structure not already excavated. According to the Archaeological Institute of America, while excavating, archaeologists study changes in the soil and measure and document the locations of artefacts and the context in which they are found. When looters dig for artefacts, they destroy this context, leading to a loss of knowledge, according to some art market experts. According to State officials, the demand for cultural artefacts has resulted in the destruction of archaeological sites and the loss of the context surrounding them; this context contains information essential to understanding the development of cultures. Cultural Property: Protection of Iraqi and Syrian Antiquities, Report to Congressional Requesters, August 2016, p. 56.

86 For IS, destroying such heritage is thus a part of their duty. Roberts Dr David, Why IS militants destroy ancient sites, *BBC News*, September 1, 2015.

mosaics, and other ancient art and antiquities. The most extensive and systematic looting of cultural property has happened in areas controlled by the IS, which has engaged in these activities to finance its military and terrorist operations. The protection of Syrian cultural heritage has since become a matter of international concern due to its connection with terrorism and transnational organised crime.

The United Nations expressed concern that the destruction and looting of such property in Syria has reached unprecedented levels and constitutes the worst cultural heritage crisis since World War II. In 2014, Irina Bokova, the Director-General of UNESCO, deplored that archaeological sites are being systematically looted and the illicit trafficking of cultural objects has reached unprecedented levels.[87] The looting and trafficking of Syrian cultural property have become a matter of international concern for three main reasons: (i) the proceeds of the illicit antiquities trade have financed IS' brutal military operations in Syria (and also Iraq), which is why they have been dubbed 'blood antiquities'; (ii) the traffic involves transnational organised crime and the financing of terrorism, and (iii) cultural heritage is increasingly considered as 'heritage of mankind' and thus as deserving of the protection of the international community as a whole. The UN believes that this is being done on an industrial scale, adding tens of millions of dollars to IS' wider war economy.[88] In 2015, the UN Security Council passed a resolution calling on countries to prohibit the trade in illegally removed cultural materials from Syria and Iraq.[89]

87 Statement by UN Secretary-General Ban Ki-moon, UNESCO Director-General Irina Bokova and UN and League of Arab States Joint Special Representative to Syria Lakhdar Brahimi: 'The destruction of Syria's cultural heritage must stop,' dated March 12, 2014.

88 Satellite images show that many historic sites in Syria are being ransacked almost daily. In the area surrounding the ancient ruins of Apamea (a famous World Heritage Site), near Hama, looters dug more than 15,000 pits in one year. How much has been stolen is impossible to tell because objects illegally removed from the ground are not documented. It could be decades before anybody even finds out they exist. O'Brien Jane, IS looting provokes call for global response, BBC News, Washington, April 17, 2015.

89 Condemning the destruction of cultural heritage in Iraq and Syria, particularly by ISIL and the Al-Nusrah Front, Security decided that all Member States should take steps, in cooperation with Interpol, the United Nations Educational, Scientific and Cultural Organization (UNESCO) and other international organizations, to prevent the trade in items of cultural, scientific, and religious importance illegally removed from either country during periods of conflict. Security Council Resolution 2199 (2015), SC/11775, February 12, 2015.

The Traffic in Blood Antiquities

The structure of the traffic in blood antiquities has been characterised as a network of loosely connected interchangeable participants, like other trafficking networks. Three levels of actors play a role in this fluid network: looter, trafficker, and buyer. The first stage of the trade consists of stealing or looting artefacts from museums, and religious shrines and through illegal excavations in the source country. Many different actors have participated in the looting of antiquities in Syria, including Hezbollah, al-Nusrah, most non-state actors involved in the conflict and even al-Assad's forces and local villagers. IS established a Ministry for Natural Resources (Diwan al-Rikaz) which enforced a strict licensing system prohibiting anyone from excavating archaeological sites without a stamped permit. Excavation licenses were granted in exchange for around 60 per cent of the proceeds. Additionally, 20 to 50 per cent taxes were levied on the sale of looted antiquities by private traffickers in its territory.

Once the artefacts are looted in the source country, the next stage in the illicit trade is smuggling and trafficking. In most cases, looted antiquities cross multiple borders before they are sold for high profits in market countries--mainly Western countries and the Gulf. The transfer through transit countries occurs at the hands of a network of traffickers, who exploit differences in legal regimes and the weaknesses of certain legal systems to their benefit. The buyer is the third and final actor in the traffic in blood antiquities. Buyers include private collectors and museums in wealthy countries. As antiquities are generally sold at very high prices, it is ultimately their demand that drives the trade. Unlike the traffic in drugs or arms, buyers acquire antiquities primarily in legitimate sales. The Archaeological Institute of America estimates that as many as 90 per cent of Greco-Roman antiquities in collections may be looted. buyers frequently purchase antiquities even when they know that the artefacts are looted.[90]

Internal armed conflict has destroyed Syria's economic, social, and cultural structures. The country that existed in 2011 is hardly recognisable today, except for a few areas that have been preserved from destruction.[91] In the summer of 2015, eighty-two-years-old Professor Khaled al-Asaad, the head of archaeology at Palmyra, Syria for more than four decades, was

90 Terlinden Marie, 'Blood Antiquities': Funding the Islamic State with Art, Institute for International Law, Working Paper No. 236, March 2023, p. 62.

91 Bandarin Francesco, "The Destruction of Aleppo: The Impact of the Syrian War on a World Heritage City," in Cuno, James, and Thomas G. Weiss, (eds.), 2022, *Cultural Heritage and Mass Atrocities*, Los Angeles: Getty Publications, pp. 186-201.

brutally beheaded by Islamic State militants, as he reportedly refused to tell the location of hidden artefacts. Reportedly Asaad's beheaded body was tied to a pole on a street in the city.[92] As the violations, abuses, and crimes continue into the 13th year in Syria, a UN Commission of Inquiry concludes: "The warring parties' attempts to resolve the conflict militarily have enabled the violation or abuse of nearly every core human right. Parties to the conflict have cumulatively committed almost every crime against humanity listed in the Rome Statute, and nearly every war crime applicable in a non-international armed conflict.[93]

Ukraine (2022 onwards)

The ongoing war between Russia and Ukraine, which started on February 24, 2022, has had a disastrous impact on civilian life and inflicted significant harm on civilians and civilian property including cultural property.[94] The armed conflict has resulted in the damage or destruction of hundreds of cultural buildings and objects in Ukraine, including museums, theatres, monuments, statues, places of worship, cemeteries, historical buildings, libraries, archives, schools and universities, and local cultural centres.[95] The Ukraine's Ministry of Culture and Information Policy has documented almost 3,000 cases of damage to cultural heritage as of January 2024.[96]

92 Beheaded Syrian scholar refused to lead Isis to hidden Palmyra antiquities, *The Guardian*, August 18, 2015.

93 Statement by Paulo S. Pinheiro, Chair of the Independent International Commission of Inquiry on the Syrian Arab Republic, UN Syria Commission of Inquiry: Those responsible for atrocities during 12 years of violence must be brought to justice, UN Human Rights Office of the High Commissioner, March 17, 2023.

94 According to the UN, the vast majority of civilian casualties in the war have resulted from the use of explosive weapons in populated areas. As of February 22, 2024, the Office of the United Nations High Commissioner for Human Rights (OHCHR) had recorded 30,457 civilian casualties, including 10,582 deaths, since the beginning of the war. Two-Year Update: Protection of Civilians: Impact of Hostilities on Civilians since February 24, 2022, UN Office of the High Commissioner for Human Rights (OHCHR), February 22, 2024.

95 Gerntholtz Liesl, PEN America and PEN Ukraine, Ukrainian Culture Under Attack: Erasure of Ukrainian Culture in Russia's War Against Ukraine, December 02, 2022, Available at: https://pen.org/report/ukrainian-culture-under-attack/.

96 The Ministry documented the damage or destruction of 902 "cultural heritage sites," including architectural landmarks, historical sites, and urban planning and monumental art sites, and the damage or destruction of 1,938 "objects of cultural infrastructure," including creative hubs, libraries, educational institutions, theatres, and museums. "Due to Russian Aggression in Ukraine, 902 Cultural Heritage Sites Have Been Affected," Ministry of Culture and Information Policy of Ukraine, February

PEN America and PEN Ukraine's new report, *Ukrainian Culture Under Attack: Erasure of Ukrainian Culture in Russia's War Against Ukraine* makes clear that culture is not collateral damage in the war against Ukraine: it is a target, a central pillar of Russian President Vladimir Putin's justification for the war. Putin has repeatedly claimed that Ukrainian culture and language simply do not exist. By targeting art museums, music halls, libraries, theatres, and historical sites, he attempts to make it so. Russia's actions, which included damaging important cultural buildings and undermining the teaching of Ukrainians in those territories, now serve as a blueprint for their cultural erasure efforts in areas they have invaded and occupied since the full-scale war against Ukraine began on February 24, 2022. They have been supplemented by the physical destruction of cultural infrastructure on a massive scale.

As of May 22, 2024, UNESCO reported verifying damage to 375 cultural sites based on its preliminary assessments. This includes 137 religious sites, 172 buildings of historical and/or artistic interest, 31 museums, 20 monuments, 14 libraries, and 1 archive.[97] Given the widespread impact of the use of explosive weapons in populated areas, it is likely responsible for a significant portion of the cultural heritage damage in such areas.[98]

Reportedly, Russian, and separatist forces have appropriated and looted museums in the territories they illegally occupy. In the southern city of Melitopol in April 2022, Russian soldiers oversaw the removal of at least 198 rare gold artefacts as well as silver coins and other precious objects from the Melitopol Museum of Local History. The gold objects date back to the fourth century B.C. and the Scythian empire. Soldiers also kidnapped museum workers. The Russian-appointed de facto museum stated that the authorities do not regard the treasures as part of the Ukrainian cultural legacy, but that they "are of great cultural value for the entire former Soviet

---

8, 2024, https://mcip.gov.ua/en/news/due-to-russian-aggression-in-ukraine-902-cultural-heritage-siteshave-been-affected/ (accessed February 25, 2024); "1938 Cultural Infrastructure Objects Have Suffered Damage or Destruction due to Russian Aggression," Ministry of Culture and Information Policy of Ukraine, February 6, 2024, available at: https://mcip.gov.ua/en/news/1938-cultural-infrastructure-objects-have-suffered-damage-or-destruction-due-to-russianaggression/.

97 Damaged cultural sites in Ukraine verified by UNESCO, May 27, 2024. Available at: https://www.unesco.org/en/articles/damaged-cultural-sites-ukraine-verified-unesco.

98 According to UNESCO, the total cost of destruction to Ukrainian cultural property was US $3.5 billion. Destroying Cultural Heritage: Explosive Weapons' Effects in Armed Conflict and Measures to Strengthen Protection, Human Rights Watch, 2024, p. 86.

Union." In late April, Ukrainian officials reported that Russian forces stole and moved more than 2,000 unique exhibit items from museums across southern Ukraine, as well as works by the 19th-century Mariupol native Arkhip Kuindzhi and the painter Ivan Aivazovsky who lived in Crimea for much of his life, as well as a unique handwritten Torah scroll, and the Gospel of 1811 made by the Venetian printing house for the Greeks of Mariupol. Between October 31 and November 3, 2022, the Oleksiy Shovkunenko Kherson Art Museum was looted by armed men dressed in civilian clothing. Russian occupying forces and Russian collaborators carried out "everything they saw, everything they could reach." The museum's collection includes more than 10,000 pieces of art. The Albin Havdzynskyi Picture Gallery, located in the temporarily occupied city of Nova Kakhovka in the Kherson region, was robbed by occupying Russian forces after the "evacuation of the population" was announced due to a possible counter-offensive by the Ukrainian army.[99]

Russian bombardments and other attacks have destroyed and damaged hundreds of places where Ukrainians enjoy and experience culture, sites small and large, local, and national, from community cultural houses to fine art museums. Some of these attacks were deliberate, targeted attacks, such as on Mariupol's Academic Regional Drama Theatre, which was sheltering hundreds of civilians, including children, when Russian aircraft dropped two bombs on it in March 2022. In the Kyiv region, in the first days of the Russian assault, a Russian missile struck the Ivankiv Historical and Local History Museum, setting it on fire, the only building in the village to be struck during that time.[100]

Russian forces have also repeatedly and indiscriminately attacked densely populated areas using explosive weapons. These attacks have caused widespread death and injury, as well as massive destruction and damage to civilian infrastructure, including cultural heritage sites. The damage and destruction cannot be seen as simply incidental, the magnitude of the destruction suggests a deliberate campaign to destroy civilian infrastructure as well as cultural objects. Several significant local museums, such as the Ivankiv Local History Museum[101] and the National Literary and Memorial

99 Gerntholtz Liesl, Ukraine Culture under Attack: Erasure of Ukrainian Culture in Russia's War Against Ukraine, PEN/Barbey Freedom to Write Centre, 2022, p. 56.

100 Destroying Cultural Heritage: Explosive Weapons' Effects in Armed Conflict and Measures to Strengthen Protection, Human Rights Watch, 2024, p. 86.

101 Fires resulting from the Russian shelling of Ivankiv, a town north of Kyiv, burned and destroyed the local history and art museum on the second and third day of Russia's

Museum of Hryhorii Skovoroda has been completely damaged. In March 2022, explosive weapons also damaged several architectural and historic landmarks near Freedom Square, Kharkiv. A Russian attack severely damaged a 19th-century Odesa's Transfiguration Cathedral (also known as the Spaso-Preobrazhensky Cathedral) on July 23, 2023.[102]

The bombings of churches, libraries, and residences have destroyed major areas of Ukraine. As with the Nazis' pilfering of paintings, bronze sculptures, and art in the last few years of World War II, in the first months after the invasion, the Russian army looted museums, stole art, and destroyed churches with missiles and tank shells.[103] Reports have also surfaced of the systematic plunder of Ukrainian museums by Russian forces, which is a war crime.[104]

The ferocity of the ongoing Russian-Ukraine war is threatening to erase the cities and cultural history of the Ukrainian people. Also in danger are monuments that are part of the World Heritage of Humanity, such as the Cathedral of St. Sophia in Kyiv, the medieval old town of Lwow, and the Potemkin Stairs in Odesa.[105] Given that the conflict is still ongoing, the damage will continue to increase. The 1954 Convention for the

full-scale invasion. The Ivankiv Local History Museum houses art and artefacts of local and national heritage. It held the works of the well-known 20th-century Ukrainian folk artist Maria Prymachenko, who had been a resident of Ivankiv. The destruction of the museum and some of its collections demonstrates the vulnerability of movable cultural heritage to the use of explosive weapons in populated areas.

102 Odesa's Transfiguration Cathedral is relatively new, but its history has given it national importance. It originally dates to 1808 and was enlarged as the city grew. The cathedral came to have a central role in the life of Odesa. For example, it provided shelter to residents during the British bombing of Odesa in the Crimean War in 1854 and housed significant icons over the years. The style of the Transfiguration Cathedral is emblematic of Ukraine's art historical traditions.

103 Russian military forces looted the Kherson Regional Museum as well as another museum, cathedral, and national archive in Kherson during an eight-month occupation of the city in 2022. Kuijt Ian, Shydlovskyi P. and Donaruma W., Spotlighting War's Cultural Destruction in Ukraine, April 9, 2024. Available at: https://www.sapiens.org/archaeology/ukraine-cultural-heritage-war-destruction/.

104 As reported 341 cultural sites—including 26 religious structures, 150 buildings of historical or artistic importance, and 31 museums—across Ukraine have been damaged. Additionally, more than 15,000 pieces of Ukrainian fine art and artefacts have been reported as missing. Solomon Tessa, UNESCO Reports 341 Cultural Sites in Ukraine Damaged, Puts Recovery Costs at $9 B. ART news, February 15, 2024.

105 Botti F. and Bianchi C., Cultural Heritage and Religious Phenomenon Between Urbicide and Cancel Culture: The Other Side of The Russian–Ukrainian Conflict, *Religions*, Vol. 14(4), 2023, pp. 535-555.

Protection of Cultural Property in the Event of Armed Conflict and the 1999 Second Protocol have not been successful in Ukraine. Any damage to cultural heritage is a common loss for humanity. The war in Ukraine not only harms Ukrainian cultural heritage but also the cultural heritage of the world.[106]According to Botti & Bianchi (2023), there is a religious dimension to the Russia-Ukraine dispute. The Russians aim to destroy the symbolic places of Ukrainian religious identity (urbicide) to eliminate the spiritual unity between Russian and Ukrainian people. Ukrainians, on the other hand, attempt to erase Russian presence and common religious and cultural roots by destroying worship buildings related to the Moscow Patriarchate tradition.[107]

Gaza (2023 onwards)

On October 7, 2023, the Palestinian Hamas[108] breaking the shackles of decades old siege, launched an unprecedented assault on Israel. According to reports, more than 1200 Israelis were killed, and more than 250 soldiers and civilians, foreign nationals, including women and children, were taken from Israeli communities to Gaza as hostages.[109] In response to the assault, on the next day Israel's security cabinet declared war on Hamas. Israel started "Operation Iron Swords" to dismantle the Hamas military and administrative capabilities.[110] The Israeli operation is continuing to date,

106 Kocak Bilgin Yasemin and Hazarhun Eda, The Cultural Heritage Impact of The Russia-Ukrainian War, *Tourism Academic Journal*, Vol. 10(2), 2023, pp. 307-321.

107 Botti F. and Bianchi C., Cultural Heritage and Religious Phenomenon Between Urbicide and Cancel Culture: The Other Side of The Russian–Ukrainian Conflict, *Religions*, Vol. 14(4), 2023, pp. 535-555.

108 The Palestinian group Hamas is officially designated a terrorist organisation by the governments of Israel, the United States, and the United Kingdom. Hamas spokesperson Mohammed Deif, the commander-in-chief of the Hamas' military wing said the attack against Israel was in response to the continued Israeli crimes against the Palestinian people and violations at the Al-Aqsa Mosque.

109 Sexual violence remains prevalent during the current conflicts. Hamas is accused of kidnapping, raping, and sexually assaulting Israeli women during the October 7 attack. It has been difficult finding rape survivors, while many victims are killed by their attackers, and survivors and witnesses are not able to come forward due to the impact. In addition, Israeli children were indiscriminately victims of violence.

110 On October 28, 2023, the Israeli Defence Forces (IDF) commenced a ground offensive in Gaza. The Israeli Government said it aims to "destroy Hamas' governing and military capabilities and to bring the hostages home."

more than 36,000 Palestinians have been reported killed and about 80,000 injured across Gaza and Israel.[111]

The relatively small region of the Gaza Strip, located within the State of Palestine, is characterised by a diverse array of historical heritage and the fertility of its soil. It is renowned for agriculture, particularly citrus farming, and boasts a coastal view along the Mediterranean Sea, which has also made it known for fishing and trade. Gaza City holds immense strategic importance due to its geographic location between two contrasting regions. To the south is the arid coastal plain of Palestine, characterised by sandy dunes and poor vegetation, while to the north lies a temperate region with fertile soil, abundant rainfall, and rich vegetation. Gaza has been historically referred to as a crucial gateway between Asia and Africa. The prestigious status of Gaza is further corroborated by the numerous Pharaonic artefacts found in the city and its vicinity. Notable discoveries include figurines, jewellery, gold necklaces, ivory and marble statues, copper and marble vessels, and tools. Gaza Strip is home to a significant and valuable number of historical and heritage sites that date back to different historical periods.

Cultural and historical heritage stands as a significant component of the cultural identity of the Palestinian people. The city of Gaza is rich with numerous archaeological sites and buildings that hold cultural, religious, and historical significance, reflecting the history and civilisation of the Palestinian people and embodying the culture, customs, and traditions of the various populations that have inhabited this region over time. These sites vary, including mosques, churches, and baths. Unfortunately, the recent war has directly and indirectly affected many of these archaeological sites, destroying a significant portion of the cultural heritage in the Gaza Strip.[112] The total architectural heritage in Gaza Governorate amounts to 195 sites, representing 60% of the overall architectural heritage in the Gaza Strip.

The cultural heritage in the Gaza Strip has been subjected to direct and indirect damage and losses due to the recent war, which began on October

111 Zanotti Jim and Sharp Jeremy M., Israel, and Hamas Conflict in Brief: Overview, U.S. Policy, and Options for Congress, Congressional Research Service Report (USA), June 3, 2024, pp. 16. There are allegations that Hamas disinformation about the number of civilian casualties in Gaza is being taken at face value and cited by US officials. Tobin Yoni, U.S. Officials Should Stop Using Hamas's Casualty Figures, The Jewish Institute for National Security of America, March 6, 2024.

112 Al-Barsh Ahmed, Report on the Impact of the Recent War in 2023 on the Cultural Heritage in Gaza Strip – Palestine, Heritage for Peace, November 7, 2023, p. 43.

7, 2023, and continues to date without interruption. Various forms of targeting affected archaeological sites, buildings, and facilities. Some were destroyed, some were partially damaged, and others suffered severe harm. More than 100 Gaza ancient cultural or archaeological sites have been damaged or destroyed by Israeli attacks.[113] The casualties include the 13th Century Great Omari Mosque, the 12th Century Greek Orthodox Church of Saint Porphyrius, a Roman cemetery in northern Gaza excavated only last year, and Gaza's main public library and central archives were ravaged. Also, memorials to prominent Palestinian figures have been bulldozed.[114] The destruction of ancient Palestinian heritage demonstrates the threat the conflict poses not just to Palestinian lives but to Palestinian culture and identity.

Through blast and fragmentation effects as well as secondary fires, bombing and shelling can directly damage buildings of architectural, historic, or religious significance. For example, in December 2023, the use of explosive weapons by Israeli forces toppled part of the minaret, crumbled the roof, and left pockmarks on the walls of the Great Omari Mosque, which was originally built in the 7th century and is the oldest in Gaza.[115] Fragments of an explosive weapon and the debris dispersed by its detonation also directly affect cultural heritage. They can scar building facades and surface decorations and shatter-stained glass windows. If they

113 Reliefweb, a United Nations Office for the Coordination of Human Affairs (OCHA) affiliate, estimates that 66 mosques in Gaza have been destroyed since October 7, an act that is a total violation of the rules of war. In total, Reliefweb estimates that 146 places of worship have been "partially damaged." The research was conducted by Euro-Med Human Rights Monitor which is documenting the war's toll on Gaza. In a separate report, Heritage for Peace, a Spanish NGO, claimed that 104 cultural heritage sites in Gaza have been either destroyed or damaged. Daniel Roche, Reports by the United Nations, and Heritage for Peace reveal many destroyed or damaged cultural heritage sites in Gaza, December 14, 2023.

114 Some of the archaeological sites that have been damaged/ destroyed in Gaza because of the ongoing armed conflict include: Jabaliya Byzantine Church, Perferius Orthodox Church, Omari Mosque (Jabaliya), Balakhiyah Site (Anthedon) in Gaza, Sheikh Shaaban Mosque, and Al-Zafar Dmari Mosque (Shuja'iya), Maqam Khaleel Al-Rahman (Abasan), Maqam Al-Khidr (Deir Al-Balah), and Centre for Manuscripts and Ancient Documents. Al-Barsh Ahmed, Report on the Impact of the Recent War in 2023 on the Cultural Heritage in Gaza Strip – Palestine, Heritage for Peace, November 7, 2023, p. 43.

115 Daniel Estrin, Israeli Strike Leaves Gaza's Oldest Mosque in Ruins, NPR, December 9, 2023; Stephanie Mulder, Gaza's Oldest Mosque, destroyed in an Airstrike, Was Once a Temple to the Philistine and Roman Gods, a Byzantine and Catholic Church, and Had Engravings of Jewish Ritual Objects.

penetrate the windows of a place of worship, museum, or archives, they can damage interior walls or objects within, such as paintings, sculptures, tapestries, or books.

While explosive weapons are not incendiary weapons, they frequently start devastating fires. The presence of flammable materials, such as wood, paper, or fabric, can quickly spread flames. Wood structures or wood roofs of masonry buildings are especially threatened. The contents of archives and libraries place them at heightened risk. The physical threat to cultural heritage caused using explosive weapons does not end at the time of the attack. Structural damage caused by an initial attack can weaken walls or foundations and lead to the complete collapse of a building later.[116]

Reportedly over 60 percent of Gaza's total building stock has been destroyed or damaged; over 52,000 housing units have been destroyed and 253,000 have been partially damaged. Not all the destruction to Gaza's heritage stems from direct military attacks. The water and sewage crisis caused by the war is also affecting coastal archaeology. The United Nations Office for the Coordination of Humanitarian Affairs (OCHA) reported in mid-November that fuel shortages had shut down sewage pumping stations and raw sewage was flowing into the streets in some areas. Sewage has reportedly also been spilling into the Mediterranean and the Wadi Gaza coastal wetlands, which extend from east Gaza to the coast, where it discharges to the sea. Water pollution poses a substantial threat to the preservation of underwater archaeology. The death toll from the current conflict has passed 36,000, but one of the less-talked-about aspects of Israel's bombardment is the destruction of cultural heritage: documents, monuments, and artefacts.[117]

Both Israel and Palestine have ratified the 1954 Hague Convention for the Protection of Cultural Property in the Event of Armed Conflict, although Israel has not signed the 1999 Second Protocol. This multilateral treaty stipulates that signatory states shall respect cultural property in their territories and the territories of the other parties by refraining from "any act of hostility" against such property, or from any actions that "expose it to destruction or damage in the event of armed conflict."

116 Destroying Cultural Heritage: Explosive Weapons' Effects in Armed Conflict and Measures to Strengthen Protection, Human Rights Watch, 2024, p. 92.

117 Karen Attiah, Destroying Gaza's cultural heritage is a crime against humanity, *The Washington Post*, December 01, 2023.

Legal Framework for the Protection of Cultural Property

The effectiveness of the international system of protection for cultural heritage during conflict is put into question by destruction during the armed conflict---whether international or non-international. As seen in the cases discussed in this chapter, the armed conflicts have caused extensive damage to the world heritage and archaeological sites of global significance. In the post-World War II period, the United Nations system has developed tools to address situations of this nature. Today, cultural property is protected under a broad legal framework made up of international humanitarian law (IHL),[118] international treaties on transnational law enforcement, human rights law, and binding UN Security Council resolutions. The main tools for cultural heritage protection are the 1954 Hague Convention for the Protection of Cultural Property in the Event of Armed Conflict, and its two protocols of 1954 and 1999. The body of law governing the protection of cultural property is discussed in the next Section.

118 International humanitarian law (IHL) is the body of international law that regulates the conduct of armed conflict and seeks to limit its effects, protecting people who are not part of the hostilities and binds those involved in a conflict to respect the cultural property and promote its protection. The violation of this core obligation constitutes a war crime, and, under certain circumstances, its destruction may even amount to crimes against humanity. Cunliffe Emma, Nibal Muhesen and Marina Lostal, The Destruction of Cultural Property in the Syrian Conflict: Legal Implications and Obligations, *International Journal of Cultural Property*, Vol. 23, No. 1, 2016, pp. 1– 31.

Section II

Evolution of Legal Framework

Chapter 3

Genesis of Laws for Protection of Cultural Property

The killing of human beings and the destruction of property, including cultural and religious ones, have long been unfortunate outcomes of war and occurred for centuries. Humanity has struggled against war and has made great efforts to reduce its most destructive effects, of which the loss of cultural property constitutes a negligible part. We have no statistics about how many works of art and heritage belonging to all mankind were destroyed in the past few centuries. No data is available to show as to how many works of literature and art were destroyed when at the end of the 12th Century, Invader Bakhtiyar Khilji demolished the Monastery and burned the valuable library at Nalanda University in India.[1]It scarcely needs recalling that these belonged to a heritage shared by all mankind. More than 800 years later, on June 24, 2014, after ISIS leader Abu Bakr al-Baghdadi declared the formation of an Islamic Caliphate stretching from northern Syria into Iraq, ISIS militants, who had taken control of the city of Mosul in Iraq, methodically laid explosives in and around the famed

1 More than 500 years before Oxford University was founded, India's Nalanda University was home to nine million books and attracted 10,000 students from around the world. Founded in 427 CE, Nalanda is considered the world's first residential university, a sort of medieval Ivy League institution home to nine million books that attracted 10,000 students from across Eastern and Central Asia. They gathered here to learn medicine, logic, mathematics, and Buddhist principles. In the 1190s, the university was destroyed by a marauding troop of invaders led by Turko-Afghan military general Bakhtiyar Khilji, who sought to extinguish the Buddhist centre of knowledge during his conquest of northern and eastern India. The campus was so vast that the fire set on by the attackers is said to have burned for three months. The archaeological remains of Nalanda are now a UNESCO World Heritage site. Mukherjee Sugato, Nalanda: The university that changed the world, *BBC: Places that Changed the World*, February 23, 2023, available at: https://www.bbc.com/travel/article/20230222-nalanda-the-university-that-changed-the-world.

shrine and mosque of the Prophet Younis and blew up the ancient site. The shrine was built on an archaeological site dating back to the eighth century BC and was renovated in the 1990s under Saddam Hussein.[2] It was a popular destination for Muslim and Christian pilgrims from around the world. No military necessity ought to warrant their destruction of a place of learning or mosque, just as there can be no justification for attacking and killing the civilian population.

The concept of international law of war law goes back to ancient history and exists in every culture, religion, and tradition. An essential component of the law of war has been a division between rules that protected certain groups of persons and those that protected property not related to war, including cultural property.[3] Thus, sometimes during the latter half of the nineteenth century, states began to codify rules to limit the detrimental effects of warfare on the cultural property. However, the law has not kept pace with societal expectations or the changing nature of warfare. Professor Nahlik (1976), an eminent specialist in the protection of cultural property, described the relationships between the protection of individuals and cultural and historical property in the following words: "The human individual is mortal and generations follow one upon the other. It is nevertheless possible for every generation; however, fleeting its existence, to leave here an immortal trace of its genius, embodied in a work of art here, a historical monument or cultural property. We should never forget the relationship between what is fleeting and what, alone, can endow people and their works with perennial qualities."[4]

2 The destruction, which reduced the shrine and Iraq's oldest mosque to a mound of rubble, was captured on video and subsequently posted online. Arimastu Louise Arimatsu and Mohbuba Choudhury, Protecting Cultural Property in Non-International Armed Conflicts: Syria and Iraq, *International Law Studies*, Vol. 91, 2015, pp. 641-696.

3 It is sometimes argued that rules belonging to the former group are far more important than those of the latter. This assertion may be true about objects which have merely a material or financial value. If destroyed they can generally be replaced, sometimes, to the benefit of the apparent loser, who may receive more up-to-date equipment or machinery than that destroyed. But there is no possibility of replacement concerning most of those objects which qualify as cultural property. Their value often consists in their very uniqueness, which makes them irreplaceable. Nahlik Stanislaw E., International Law and the Protection of Cultural Property in Armed Conflicts, *Hastings Law Journal*, Vol. 27, 1976, pp. 1070.

4 Nahlik Stanislaw E., International Law and the Protection of Cultural Property in Armed Conflicts, *Hastings Law Journal*, Vol. 27, 1976, pp. 1069-1087.

The treatment of property in the conquered territory in ancient times in India was based on the principles of benevolence and justice. Ordinarily, the conqueror has only the right of the usufruct of immovable property, and he was to spare religious institutions and works of fine arts. As regards permanent structures in conquered countries, the conqueror was not to demolish the forts and gateways.[5] According to Bandyopadhyay (1920), "With regard to enemy property, the evidence of the Greek writers conclusively proves that wholesale destruction or ravaging of the enemy's property was not the general practice in ancient Indian warfare."[6] However, Greece and Rome followed inhuman practices in ancient warfare. In ancient Greece, towns taken by the storm were liable to destruction, the men of military age were killed, while the other citizens were reduced to slavery and general plunder followed. Roman practice was less barbarous but the sacking of dwelling houses, the seizure of corn and other provisions, the setting fire of most property, and the destruction of the rest all was right and fair by the laws of war.[7] According to Toman Jiri (1996), respect for religious property and places was linked to their sacred nature and not to the artistic value of the temples and the property inside them.[8]

Jurist Hugo Grotius, in his 1625 treatise on the laws of war, has urged belligerents not to turn into 'enemies of mankind' by destroying objects of cultural value. Grotius cites the impassioned plea of a Roman general, Belisarius, to the king of the Goths in the 6th century AD, to refrain from destroying Rome, pointing out that 'to ruin or destroy it, would be injurious to Mankind of all Ages; to rob our Ancestors of the Memory of their just Praise; and future Ages the Pleasure of so glorious a Sight. ... If you be Conqueror, then by destroying the city, you destroy not what is another is, but your own; and by preserving it, you will enjoy the most beautiful Possessions in the World. On the other side, if you should be vanquished, preserving the City of Rome will be a great Argument to incline your Conqueror to shew Mercy to you, but if it be destroyed your Affairs will be lost beyond any Hopes of Mercy.[9]

5 Viswanatha S.V., (1925), *International Law in Ancient India*, Bombay: Longman, Greens and Co, p. 182-183.

6 Bandyopadhyay Pramathanath, 1920, *International Law and Custom in Ancient India*, Calcutta University Press, p. 128.

7 Bandyopadhyay Pramathanath, 1920, *International Law and Custom in Ancient India*, Calcutta University Press, p. 130.

8 Toman Jiri, 1996, *The Protection of Cultural Property in the Event of Armed Conflict, Commentary on 1954 Convention*, Ashgate, UNESCO, p. 4.

9 Hugo Grotius, 1625, *The Rights of War and Peace* Book III, Chapter 12, para. 2, fn. 11.

The Lieber Code

The roots of positive international law come from a concept of war developed in the nineteenth century. The laws were written by the states to regulate interstate wars and to protect the rights of soldiers and the destruction of property. The First modern laws of war came in the form of the Lieber Code. On April 24, 1863, US President Abraham Lincoln issued "General Orders No. 100: Instructions for the Government of the Armies of the United States in the Field," commonly known as the "Lieber Code" after its main author Francis Lieber. The Lieber Code set out rules of conduct during hostilities for Union soldiers throughout the US Civil War.[10] It had a certain influence on the law concerning cultural property.

Article 34 of the Lieber Code specifies that as a rule, the property belonging to churches, hospitals, or other establishments of an exclusively charitable nature, to establishments of education, or foundations for the promotion of knowledge, whether public schools, universities, academies of learning or observatories, museums of the fine arts, or a scientific character should not be considered public property;[11] but it may be taxed or used when the public service requires it. According to Article 35, classical works of art, libraries, scientific collections, or precious instruments, such as astronomical telescopes, as well as hospitals, must be secured against all avoidable injury, even when they are contained in fortified places whilst besieged or bombarded. Article 36 states: "If such works of art, libraries, collections, or instruments belonging to a hostile nation or government, can be removed without injury, the ruler of the conquering state or nation may order them to be seized and removed for the benefit of the said nation. The ultimate ownership is to be settled by the ensuing treaty of peace. In no case shall they be sold or given away, if captured by the armies of the United States, nor shall they ever be privately appropriated, or wantonly

10 The Lieber Code was a major step forward in making war less hellish, with its specific provisions banning any kind of slavery, insisting on equal treatment for all soldiers without regard to their race, prohibiting the destruction of cultural properties (like libraries), proscribing the needless taking or destruction of private property, and providing specific provisions for the humane treatment of prisoners. Finkelman Paul, Francis Lieber and the Modern Law of War, *The University of Chicago Law Review*, Vol. 80, 2013, pp. 2071-2132.

11 Article 31 of the Lieber Code provides: "A victorious army appropriates all public money, seizes all public movable property until further direction by its government, and sequesters for its benefit or of that of its government all the revenues of real property belonging to the hostile government or nation. The title to such real property remains in abeyance during military occupation, and until the conquest is made complete."

destroyed or injured." Article 37 of the Code affirmed that "the United States acknowledges and protects, in hostile countries occupied by them, religion and morality; strictly private property; the persons of the inhabitants, especially those of women: and the sacredness of domestic relations. Offences to the contrary shall be rigorously punished." Accordingly, Article 44 of the Lieber Code provides: "All robbery, all pillage or sacking, even after taking a place by main force ... are prohibited under the penalty of death, or such other severe punishment as may seem adequate for the gravity of the offence."

The Lieber code also had an impact on the development of military law in other countries, particularly on the service regulations for the field armies of France, Germany, Great Britain, Italy, Japan, Russia, and Spain. The Franco-Prussian War (1870-71) also roused public opinion, particularly when the cathedral and library in Strasbourg were destroyed.

The Hague Conventions of 1899 and 1907

After negotiations of the 1868 Declaration of St. Petersburg,[12] the Tsar of Russia convened a Diplomatic Conference at Brussels in July 1874 with the broader objective of deliberating on the draft of "an international agreement respecting the laws and customs of war." The Final Protocol of the Brussels Conference 1874 and the attached Brussels Declaration (Project of an International Declaration concerning the Laws and Customs of War) of August 27, 1874 mark an important step in the creation of a new body of law to limit the effects of war. It regulated the methods and means of combat and paved the way for an official codification, which was accomplished at the two peace conferences convened at The Hague in 1899 and 1907.

The second Convention concerning the Laws and Customs of War on Land, July 29, 1899, and the fourth Convention with Other Powers Respecting the Laws and Customs of War on Land, October 18, 1907, were both concerned with the laws and customs of land warfare and are both pertinent to the protection of cultural objects in warfare.[13] Annexed to both conventions were the Regulations on the Laws and Customs of War

12 The 1868 Declaration of St. Petersburg prohibited the use of explosive or fulminating projectiles weighing less than 400 gm in war.

13 The two international peace conferences held in 1899 and 1907 played a particularly important role in the development of the protection of cultural property in times of war. This was especially true of Conventions Nos IV and IX of 1907. The protection of cultural property is covered by these Conventions first by provisions relating to the

on Land, which have formed until now the most important basis for the law of armed conflict in force among all states. Provisions bearing on the protection of cultural property appear in two different chapters of the 1907 Regulations: section two, on hostilities, and section three, on occupation of enemy territory.[14] The former contained in Article 23, forbids among other things, the destruction or seizure of the enemy's property unless it is "imperatively demanded by the necessities of war." Other provisions of the same chapter contained under Article 25, deal with bombardments. As originally formulated in 1899, it forbade the bombing of undefended towns or villages.

At the 1907 conference, some delegates moved to include in this article a list of those means of assailing such towns or villages which should be considered forbidden. The French military delegate; however, argued that given the rapid progress in the technology of war, no means should be mentioned and that the prohibition in question should extend to all bombings to protect humanity against such means as might be invented in the future. This motion was accepted and Article 25, which is one of the most important in the whole law of war states:[15]

> The attack or bombardment, by whatever means, of towns, villages, dwellings, or buildings which are undefended is prohibited.

Article 27, paragraph 1, states that in the case of a bombardment which is not prohibited (one launched against a town which is defended), every possible effort shall be made to spare buildings dedicated to religion, art, science, or charitable purposes, provided they are not being used at the time for military purposes. The second paragraph of the same article asks the besieged to indicate all edifices or places of this kind "by some particular or visible signs" which, however, are not described.[16]

---

protection of civilian property in general (especially by Articles 23(g), 25, 28 and 47 of the Hague Regulations) as well as by special provisions concerning cultural property.

14 The Regulations Respecting the Laws and Customs of War on Land, October 18, 1907.

15 Hague Convention (IV) Respecting the Laws and Customs of War on Land and Its Annex: Regulations Concerning the Laws and Customs of War on Land, 1907. Article 1 of the Convention provides that the Contracting Powers shall issue instructions to their armed land forces which shall conform with the Regulations respecting the laws and customs of war on land, annexed to the present Convention. Annexed to the Convention were "The regulations Respecting the Laws and Customs of War on Land."

16 Article 27, second paragraph states, "It is the duty of the besieged to indicate the presence of such buildings or places by distinctive and visible signs, which shall be notified to the enemy beforehand."

The above omission was corrected in the Ninth Convention, concerning bombardment by naval forces, signed at The Hague on the same day, October 18, 1907. According to Article 5 of the Ninth Convention:[17]

> In bombardments by naval forces, all the necessary measures must be taken by the commander to spare as far as possible sacred edifices, buildings used for artistic, scientific, or charitable purposes, historic monuments, hospitals, and places where the sick or wounded are collected, on the understanding that they are not used at the same time for military purposes.
>
> It is the duty of the inhabitants to indicate such monuments, edifices, or places by visible signs, which shall consist of large, stiff rectangular panels divided diagonally into two coloured triangular portions, the upper portion black, the lower portion white.

Section three of the Regulations appended to the Fourth Convention of 1907, which establishes the rights and duties of the occupying authorities, requires them to reestablish public order and safety and to respect, in principle, the laws in force in the occupied country. The section further forbids any kind of pillage under Article 47 and defines those categories of public property under Article 53, which may be requisitioned, for strictly military uses.[18] As far as immovable public property is concerned, Article 55 of the regulations specifically states:

> The occupying State shall be regarded only as administrator and usufructuary of public buildings, real estate, forests, and agricultural estates belonging to the hostile State, and situated in the occupied country. It must safeguard the capital of these properties, and administer them in accordance with the rules of usufruct.

The above provisions have only an indirect bearing on cultural property. However, the following provision contained under Article 56, the last in the regulations of 1907, is the most significant:

17 Convention (IX) concerning Bombardment by Naval Forces in Time of War, The Hague, October 18, 1907.

18 Article 53 states: An army of occupation can only take possession of cash, funds, and realizable securities which are strictly the property of the State, depots of arms, means of transport, stores, and supplies, and, generally, all movable property belonging to the State which may be used for military operations. All appliances, whether on land, at sea, or in the air, adapted for the transmission of news, or the transport of persons or things, exclusive of cases governed by naval law, depots of arms, and, generally, all kinds of munitions of war, may be seized, even if they belong to private individuals, but must be restored and compensation fixed when peace is made.

> The property of municipalities, that of institutions dedicated to religion, charity and education, the arts, and sciences, even when State property, shall be treated as private property.
>
> All seizure of, destruction or wilful damage done to institutions of this character, historic monuments, works of art and science, is forbidden and should be made the subject of legal proceedings.

The above provisions, if interpreted and applied in good faith, afford adequate protection to nearly every kind of cultural property against the imminent dangers occasioned by war.[19]

Martens Clause

The 'Martens Clause' was based upon and took its name from a declaration read by Professor von Martens, the Russian delegate at the Hague Peace Conferences in 1899.[20] The Martens Clause has formed a part of the laws of armed conflict since its first appearance in the preamble to the 1899 Hague Convention with respect to the laws and customs of war on land. The Preamble to the 1899 Hague Convention II[21], states:

> Until a more complete code of the laws of war is issued, the High Contracting Parties think it right to declare that in cases not included in the Regulations adopted by them, populations and belligerents remain under the protection and empire of the principles of international law, as they result from the usages established between civilised nations, from the laws of humanity and the requirements of the public conscience.

19 Nahlik Stanislaw E., International Law and the Protection of Cultural Property in Armed Conflicts, *The Hastings Law Journal*, Vol. 27, 1976, pp. 1069-1087.

20 The Martens Clause was originally devised to cope with a disagreement between the parties to the Conference regarding the status of resistance movements in occupied territory, i.e., the 'status of civilians who took up arms against an occupying force.' Large military powers argued that they should be treated as *francs-tiers* (free shooters) and subject to execution, while smaller states contended that they should be treated as lawful combatants. The Clause was originally formulated to resolve this dispute; however, it subsequently reappeared in various other treaties regulating armed conflicts.

21 The Hague Convention (II) with Respect to the Laws and Customs of War on Land and its annex: Regulations concerning the Laws and Customs of War on Land. The Hague, 29 July 1899.

The Clause appears in a slightly modified form in the 1907 Hague Conventions:[22]

> Until a more complete code of the laws of war has been issued, the High Contracting Parties deem it expedient to declare that, in cases not included in the Regulations adopted by them, the inhabitants and the belligerents remain under the protection and the rule of the principles of the law of nations, as they result from the usages established among civilised peoples, from the laws of humanity, and the dictates of the public conscience.

The Martens Clause has served as fundamental guidance in the interpretation of international customary law or treaty law. The Martens Clause has become a central principle of contemporary international military and humanitarian law and continues to play a key role in ensuring the ongoing humanisation of warfare. Its humanistic essence and purpose stem from the fact that it regulates military situations occurring in the course of hostilities between conflicting parties that are not covered by existing international and national legal standards.[23] The Martens clause and another provision of the Regulations appended to the Fourth Convention stating that the right of belligerents to adopt means of injuring the enemy is not unlimited, constitute a sufficient barrier against any unwarranted actions on the part of belligerents. According to Nahlik (1976), Article 25 of the 1907 Hague Regulations, especially if linked with the Martens

22 The Hague Convention (IV) respecting the Laws and Customs of War on Land and its annex: Regulations concerning the Laws and Customs of War on Land. The Hague, 18 October 1907: Preamble paragraph 8.

23 In December 1868, Fyodor F. Martens (1845–1909), a Russian, submitted his master's thesis "On the Law of Private Property in Time of War," to the Law Faculty. He successfully defended this thesis on October 5, 1869, and was awarded a master's degree in international law by the Faculty Council. The thesis presented by Martens was such a serious study, both in terms of its relevance and its scholarly depth, that it was published as a separate book by the decision of the university's Faculty of Law. Martens firmly opposed the prevailing concepts of the day regarding the dominance of might over right. Such ideas, he believed, were unworthy of human beings and pernicious for international relations. Martens was a humanist, and he laid out a logical basis for his humanist international legal views. Martens' work On the Law of Private Property in Time of War was the first specific Russian academic study dedicated to the problems of international military and humanitarian law. Ivanenko Vitaliy, the origins, causes and enduring significance of the Martens Clause: A view from Russia, *International Review of the Red Cross*, No. 920-921, November 2022, pp. 1708-1724.

clause, does provide for adequate protection of cultural property against any attack by aircraft as well.[24]

The Hague Rules of Air Warfare

The First World War showed that aircraft could be used not only for reconnaissance but also more effectively as weapons to attack areas, especially the enemy's residential and industrial areas far behind the front, otherwise inaccessible to land or naval forces. Article 25 of the above-mentioned Hague Regulations on land warfare, which had previously been regarded as adequate, became ineffective in the cases of the use of aircraft. Article 25 thus lost its significance.

The victorious powers soon realised that this situation was untenable in the long run. Therefore, when the President of the United States invited the governments of Great Britain, France, Italy, and Japan to a disarmament conference in Washington in August 1921, the law of air warfare and its further development were on the agenda.[25] Draft treaties were put forward by both the British and the Americans. However, the many new weapons that had appeared during the recent war made negotiations at the Conference more difficult than expected. When it became clear that the Conference was not going to deal with rules for air warfare, it adopted a resolution, on February 4, 1922, to set up an international commission of jurists to address the matter. The Commission met from December 11, 1922, to February 12, 1923, in The Hague. It was made clear from the very beginning that the Commission had not been set up to adopt an international treaty but only to clarify the questions raised; the Commission's findings could then be used by the States as the basis for a treaty. The Commission adopted the text of the Hague Rules of Air Warfare on February 19, 1923. It contained 62 articles divided into 10 sections.

The articles which could relate to the protection of cultural property are as follows:

Article 24: Military objectives

1. Aerial bombardment is legitimate only when directed at a military objective an object of which the destruction or

24 Nahlik Stanislaw E., International Law and the Protection of Cultural Property in Armed Conflicts, *The Hastings Law Journal*, Vol. 27, 1976, pp. 1069-1087.

25 Hanke Heinz Marcus, the 1923 Hague Rules of Air Warfare: A contribution to the development of international law protecting civilians from air attack, *International Review of the Red Cross*, No. 292, March 1993, pp. 11-44.

injury would constitute a distinct military advantage to the belligerent.

2. Such bombardment is legitimate only when directed exclusively at the following objectives: military forces; military works; military establishments or depots; factories constituting important and well-known centres engaged in the manufacture of arms, ammunition, or distinctively military supplies; lines of communication or transportation used for military purposes.
3. The bombardment of cities, towns, villages, dwellings, or buildings not in the immediate neighbourhood of the operations of land forces is prohibited. In cases where the objectives specified in paragraph (2) are so situated, that they cannot be bombarded without the indiscriminate bombardment[26] of the civilian population, the aircraft must abstain from bombardment.
4. In the immediate neighbourhood of the operations of land forces, the bombardment of cities, towns, villages, dwellings, or buildings is legitimate if there exists a reasonable presumption that the military concentration is sufficiently important to justify such bombardment, having regard to the danger thus caused to the civilian population.
5. A belligerent state is liable to pay compensation for injuries to a person or property caused by the violation by any of its officers or forces of the provisions of this article.

Article 25: Protected Objects

In bombardment by aircraft, all necessary steps must be taken by the commander to spare as far as possible buildings dedicated to public worship, art, science, or charitable purposes, historic monuments, hospital ships, hospitals, and other places where the sick and wounded are collected, provided such buildings, objects and places are not at the time used for military purposes. Such

26 The text offers no precise definition of the term "indiscriminate." Though this word soon found its way into the vocabulary of the law of war, it was formally defined only later in the 1977 Protocol in addition to the Geneva Conventions (Article 51, paras. 4 and 5). For lack of a firm definition, the word "indiscriminate" was frequently misinterpreted. For the same reason, it has often been criticized as unrealistic, especially in connection with the words at the end of the sentence in which it appears: ".... the aircraft must abstain from bombardment."

buildings, objects and places must by day be indicated by marks visible to aircraft. The use of marks to indicate other buildings, objects, or places than those specified above is to be deemed an act of perfidy. The marks used as aforesaid shall be in the case of buildings protected under the Geneva Convention the red cross on a white ground, and in the case of other protected buildings, a large rectangular panel divided diagonally into two pointed triangular portions, one black and the other white.

A belligerent who desires to secure by night the protection for the hospitals and other privileged buildings above mentioned must take the necessary measures to render the special signs referred to sufficiently visible.[27]

Article 26: Historical Monuments

The following special rules are adopted for the purpose of enabling states to obtain more efficient protection for important historic monuments situated within their territory, if they are willing to refrain from the use of such monuments and a surrounding zone for military purposes, and to accept a special regime for their inspection.

1. A state shall be entitled, if it sees fit, to establish a zone of protection around such monuments situated in its territory. Such zones shall in time of war enjoy immunity from bombardment.
2. The monuments around which a zone is to be established shall be notified to other Powers in peacetime through the diplomatic channel: the notification shall also indicate the limits of the zones. The notification may not be withdrawn in time of war.
3. The zone of protection may include, in addition to the area occupied by the monument or group of monuments, an outer zone, not exceeding 500 metres in width, measured from the circumference of the said area.

27 The provision in Article 25 of the Air Warfare Rules protecting cultural objects and hospitals followed the rules applicable to land and naval warfare (Article 27 of the Hague Regulations governing land warfare; Article 5 of the Hague Convention No. IX) and adapted them to the conditions of air warfare.

4. Marks clearly visible from aircraft either by day or by night will be employed for the purpose of ensuring the identification by belligerent airmen of the limits of the zones.
5. The marks on the monuments themselves will be those defined in Article 25. The marks employed for indicating the surrounding zones will be fixed by each state adopting the provisions of this article, and will be notified to other Powers at the same time as the monuments and zones are notified.
6. Any abusive use of the marks indicating the zones referred to in paragraph 5 will be regarded as an act of perfidy.
7. A state adopting the provisions of this article must abstain from using the monument and the surrounding zone for military purposes, or for the benefit in any way whatsoever of its military organisation, or from committing within such a monument or zone any act with a military purpose in view.
8. An inspection committee consisting of three neutral representatives accredited to the state adopting the provisions of this article, or their delegates, shall be appointed for the purpose of ensuring that no violation is committed of the provisions of para 7. One of the members of the committee of inspection shall be the representative (or his delegate) of the state to which has been entrusted the interests of the opposing belligerent.

The Hague Rules of Air Warfare in many ways represented a new departure, especially as regards aerial bombardment. Experience in the First World War had already shown that aircraft could operate far beyond the area in which opposing ground troops met face to face. The Allies had visualised aircraft as a very promising weapon. France had refused to sign the Hague Rules on Air Warfare because it considered the existing rules for land and naval warfare as sufficient to cover air warfare as well. The Anglo-Americans were already so geared to air warfare that they could not accept restrictions on it. The Netherlands and Japan — States which at that time had no air forces to speak of — advocated the adoption of the tightest possible restrictions. the Netherlands and Japanese delegations wanted aerial bombardment in the rear to be generally prohibited. They called for an absolute prohibition on the aerial bombardment of cities and towns behind the front, regardless of what they contained. Due to these differing opinions, the Air Warfare Rules never got beyond the draft stage. However, the Hague Rules of Aerial Warfare played a decisive part in the emergence of binding customary international law in the pre-war period. Their semi-official status and their clear and practical approach, in comparison to other texts, to regulating aerial bombardment ensured that they were extensively used both as a basis for the study of international law and in actual political practice.[28]

The Treaty on the Protection of Artistic and Scientific Institutions and Historic Monuments

In 1929, Russian painter and philosopher Nicholas Roerich[29] and Paris University international law and political science professor George Chklaver drafted an international treaty dedicated to the protection of cultural values. The intent was to create a neutral status for cultural property, paralleling the medical one previously established by the Red Cross. Roerich simultaneously proposed a distinctive emblem to identify objects protected under the treaty; a "banner of peace." The banner follows the colour scheme of the Red Cross flag to provide a distinctive and highly recognisable emblem. The draft treaty accompanied by an appeal from Roerich to governments and peoples of all countries was published in 1930. Committees supporting Roerich's proposed treaty were established in Paris, France and Bruges, Belgium, and an International Union of the Roerich Pact was founded in Bruges in 1931.

Annual international conferences promoting the treaty gained momentum and in 1933, thirty-five countries recommended governments of all nations sign the Pact. Also in 1933, the Committee of the Pan-American Union passed a resolution recommending the governments of American countries join the "Roerich Pact" or "Washington Pact." The US acted first and signed on in 1934. On April 15, 1935, representatives of 21 South, Central, and North American countries signed "The Treaty on the Protection of Artistic and Scientific Institutions and Historic Monuments."

According to Article 1, the Roerich Pact applies during peacetime and war to historic monuments, museums, and scientific, artistic, educational, and cultural institutions. No mention is made of movable cultural

28 Hanke Heinz Marcus, the 1923 Hague Rules of Air Warfare: A contribution to the development of international law protecting civilians from air attack, *International Review of the Red Cross*, No. 292, March 1993, pp. 11-44.

29 As early as the Russo-Japanese War of 1904, Nikolai Roerich, designer of the popular 'Enemy of mankind' poster decrying German destruction of cultural sites in the First World War had given thought to the creation of a comprehensive system for the international protection of monuments during hostilities. O'Keefe Roger, 2006, *The Protection of Cultural Property in Armed Conflict*, Cambridge University Press, p. 51.

property, which is protected only insofar as it is housed in a museum or other protected institution. Article 1 also lays down the Pact's essential obligations. Protected property is to be considered 'neutral' and is to be 'respected and protected' by belligerents.[30] Parties undertake in Article 2 to adopt legislation necessary to ensure protection and respect. Article 3 of the Pact states that to identify the monuments and institutions mentioned in Article 1, use may be made of a distinctive flag (red circle with a triple red sphere in the circle on a white background) in accordance with the model attached to this Treaty.

Article 4 obliges Parties to send to the Pan-American Union (now the General Secretariat of the Organization of American States) a list of the monuments and institutions 'for which they desire the protection agreed to', and obliges the Pan-American Union to send all the Parties copies of these lists and to inform them of changes to them. Article 5 states that the monuments, museums, and institutions cease to enjoy the privileges of respect and protection if used for military purposes, but military use is the sole ground on which a belligerent may withdraw these privileges: military necessity as such is no justification. The Pact establishes a dual system for identifying the monuments, museums and institutions covered by its provisions.

The Pact having eight articles is still in force for its 10 States Parties: Brazil, Chile, Colombia, Cuba, Dominican Republic, El Salvador, Guatemala, Mexico, the USA, and Venezuela. It recognises that the defence of cultural property is more important than their use or destruction for military purposes and that their protection has precedence over military necessity.

After the Second World War had begun, the diplomatic conference scheduled to adopt the Preliminary Draft International Convention for the Protection of Historic Buildings and Works of Art in Times of War was prevented from taking place. Instead, the International Museums Office (OIM) drafted a Declaration on the Protection of Cultural Property during Armed Conflict, a statement of principles, ten articles in length, based on the draft convention but without its compliance regime. It was designed to form the basis of bilateral agreements between the belligerents. The attempt

30 The Treaty on the Protection of Artistic and Scientific Institutions and Historic Monuments, 1935, Article 1: The historic monuments, museums, scientific, artistic, educational, and cultural institutions shall be considered as neutral and as such respected and protected by belligerents. The same respect and protection shall be due to the personnel of the institutions mentioned above. The same respect and protection shall be accorded to the historic monuments, museums, scientific, artistic, educational, and cultural institutions in time of peace as well as in war.

to secure agreement on ad hoc declaration remained unsuccessful due to the German invasion of the Netherlands, Belgium, and France in 1940.[31] Due to the insufficiency of the law on bombardment from air and land, cultural property was extensively damaged during the war. However, there were many genuine efforts on both sides to preserve and protect cultural heritage during the Second World War.

Special Protective Measures

The Allies also adopted special measures for the protection of cultural property during hostilities and belligerent occupation. Before the Allied invasion of Sicily in mid-1943, President Roosevelt authorised the establishment of the American Commission for the Protection and Salvage of Artistic and Historic Monuments in Europe. It was headed by US Supreme Court Justice Owen Roberts and known as the 'Roberts Commission'. The word 'Europe' in the formal name was replaced by 'War Areas' when the scheme was extended to Asia. One of the Commission's tasks was to work with the appropriate branch of the US military, museum officials and art historians to protect works of cultural value, so far as it was consistent with military necessity. A special section was formed, under the auspices of the War Department, within the School of Military Government at Charlottesville, to train certain officers in the Specialist Branch of the service so that they could be attached to the staffs of the US military to advise the commanding officers of such troops as to the location of and the care to be given to the various artistic and historic objects in occupied territory.

In November 1943, the Monuments, Fine Arts and Archives (MFA&A) section was established at Headquarters, Chief of Staff, Supreme Allied Command (COSSAC).[32] The officers of MFA&A accompanied or followed American forces in the war zones in Italy, France, and Germany. The

31 O'Keefe Roger, 2006, The Protection of Cultural Property in Armed Conflict, Cambridge University Press, p. 61.

32 In November 1943, when the Civil Affairs Section of Monuments, Fine Arts, and Archives was established at Headquarters COSSAC, the duties of the section were: (i) Record and assess war damage suffered by historic monuments before our occupation; take or advise the steps necessary to prevent further deterioration; supervise and pass estimates for repairs; (ii) Prevent damage by troops; affix notices, close buildings or procure guards; check billeting; interest the troops by lectures or otherwise; and investigate charges of wanton damage brought against the Allied troops and report proved cases; (iii) Prevent the looting, sale or removal of objects of art; and (iv) Establish the fact of looting by enemy troops. Available at: https://history.army.mil/books/wwii/civaff/ch31.htm.

MFA&A officers rendered services concerning works of art, cathedrals, and other cultural monuments, both immovable and movable in Europe, so that their destruction, if consistent with military operations, could be avoided. By December 1943, MFA&A officers had drawn up plans for the rapid protection of historic buildings on the fall of Rome. In Florence and the shattered towns of Normandy, the officers of MFA&A restrained sappers who were keen to bulldoze and clear damaged architecture. The British government had also set up a Monuments, Fine Arts and Archives branch to perform the same function as its American counterpart, under an Archaeological Advisor to the Director of Civil Affairs.

The US military directives placed strict restrictions on the use of monuments for military purposes. No buildings listed in the sections 'Works of Art' in the respective zone handbooks issued by the Political Warfare Executive were to be used for military purposes 'without the explicit permission of the Allied Commander-in-Chief or the General Officer Commanding-in-Chief'. Commanders were also authorised to close and place out of bounds to troops any buildings listed in the zone handbooks that they deemed necessary, a measure to be enforced by guards if required. A supplementary list of historical buildings of secondary importance was also prepared. These were permitted to be used for military purposes when it was deemed necessary, although commanders were reminded that 'buildings containing art collections, scientific objects, or those which when used would offend the religious susceptibilities of the people' ought not to be occupied when alternative accommodation was available.[33]

After World War II, international organisations recognised the need to create conventions or laws to help protect cultural sites and materials in conflict zones, so that the devastating destruction would not happen again. The United Nations Educational, Scientific and Cultural Organization (UNESCO) was created in 1945 in response to the destruction of cultural heritage during World War II. UNESCO is an organisation focused on preserving cultural heritage around the world. The goal of the organisation is to assist countries that need to preserve their educational and cultural resources. The next chapter will cover the development and provisions of the first international treaty for the protection of cultural Property in the time of armed conflict.

33 Directive to Commander-in-Chief of United States Forces of Occupation Regarding the Military Government of Germany, Available at: https://avalon.law.yale.edu/wwii/ger02.asp.

Chapter 4

The 1954 Hague Convention and Protocol

Introduction

WWII witnessed an unprecedented level of destruction of property during military operations that resulted in the doom of whole historic cities, and many wonders of European culture have shown the need for a new system of protection.[1] The pre-war idea of drafting a comprehensive convention dealing specifically with the protection of cultural property in the event of war was revived on the initiative of the Italian government, under the auspices of the United Nations Educational, Scientific and Cultural Organization (UNESCO). After several years of preparatory work, a diplomatic conference was convened at The Hague in April 1954, and after four weeks of extensive discussion, the conference established the ultimate texts for adoption on May 14, 1954; which entered into force on August 7, 1956.[2] The instruments signed at the conference were:

- Final Act of the Conference;
- Convention for the Protection of Cultural Property in the Event of Armed Conflict (with Regulations for the Execution of the Convention for the Protection of Cultural Property in the Event of Armed Conflict annexed thereto);
- Protocol for Protection of Cultural Property in the Event of Armed Conflict; and
- Resolutions Adopted by the Conference.

1 Ryska Ivan, Military Necessity and Cultural Protection in Laws of War: Historical Overview, *International and Comparative Law Review*, Vol. 21, No. 2, 2021, pp. 187-211.

2 The Convention for the Protection of Cultural Property in the Event of Armed Conflict, 1954, has been ratified by 135 states so far.

The conference's resolution expressed the hope that the provisions of the convention would be observed in military actions undertaken under the auspices of the United Nations. The 1954 Convention applies to armed conflicts of all possible kinds, regardless of the parties and the nature of their conflict.

The Preamble

The Preamble to the 1954 Hague Convention contains two main ideas: it first reminds us of the experience of the Second World War, during which cultural property suffered grave damage, and then points out that, with the development of the technique of warfare, cultural property is increasingly threatened with destruction. The second paragraph of the Preamble refers to the cultural heritage of all mankind and stresses the contribution of each person to the formation of that heritage. This paragraph is also based on the Constitution of UNESCO which states that, among the purposes of the Organization, is to maintain, increase and diffuse knowledge 'By assuring the conservation and protection of the world's inheritance of books, works of art and monuments of history and science, and recommending to the nations concerned the necessary international conventions.' The third paragraph stresses the importance of the preservation of the cultural heritage for all peoples of the world and the need to ensure that it receives international protection. The fourth paragraph refers to the principles concerning the protection of cultural property during armed conflict, as established in The Hague Conventions of 1899 and 1907. The final paragraph of the Preamble signifies that the importance of all the possible steps to protect cultural property outweighs any other consideration.

A broad definition is given of cultural property; on the other hand, the extent of actual protection is relatively narrow. The choice of protected property is left to the discretion of the States on whose territory the cultural property is situated. Chapter II of the Convention (articles 8 to 11) adopts a different approach. Cultural property is defined here in a restrictive sense which also enables the level of material protection to be increased. The threshold of protection is high: the definition of property relates only to a limited range of cultural property in the form of movable and immovable items of 'very great importance.'[3]

3 Toman Jiri, 1996, *The Protection of Cultural Property in the Event of Armed Conflict, Commentary on 1954 Convention*, Ashgate, UNESCO, p. 97.

Definition

The 1954 Convention having 40 articles is divided into eight chapters. Article 1 of the Convention defines cultural property as:

A. Movable or immovable property of great importance to the cultural heritage of every people, such as:

- Monuments of architecture, art, or history, whether religious or secular;
- Archaeological sites, groups of buildings which are of historical or artistic interest;
- Works of art;[4]
- Manuscripts, books, and other objects of artistic, historical, or archaeological interest;
- Scientific collections and important collections of books or archives;
- Reproductions of the above property;[5]

B. Buildings[6] whose main and effective purpose is to preserve or exhibit movable cultural property, such as:

---

4 Works of art were defined broadly to include the decorative and graphic arts. The terms also covered exhibitions of works of art, galleries, art museums and all productions of a period or country in the arts. Toman Jiri, 2009, *Cultural Property in War: Improvement in Protection, Commentary on the 1999 Second Protocol to the Hague Convention*, UNESCO, p. 51

5 This protection is accorded to important collections of books without their necessarily having to be of artistic, historical, or archaeological interest. Any important library is thus protected, probably in the spirit of protecting human knowledge. Archives, as a living memory containing documents offering irrefutable evidence of the past, are also protected. As the concept of archives varies widely from country to country, the clearer concept of 'collections - of documents or objects - of scientific interest', which includes historical archives and the major libraries, was preferred. The aim was to cover also any other collection of documents or objects of scientific interest. Toman Jiri, 2009, *Cultural Property in War: Improvement in Protection, Commentary on the 1999 Second Protocol to the Hague Convention*, UNESCO, p. 52.

6 Such buildings are protected not because of their historical value but because of their purpose and their content. Toman Jiri, 2009, *Cultural Property in War: Improvement in Protection, Commentary on the 1999 Second Protocol to the Hague Convention*, UNESCO, pp. 53-54.

- Museums;
- Large libraries;
- Depositories of archives;
- Refuges intended to shelter other cultural property in the event of armed conflict;

C. Centres containing a large amount of cultural property as defined in subparagraphs A and B above, will be known as "centres containing monuments."[7] This property is cultural property irrespective of its origin or ownership.

This broad definition has the flexibility to include new forms of cultural property that were of unseen importance or were unimagined in 1954, for example, film archives and digital archives and information. It can also include underwater cultural property. However, according to Boylan, Article 1 of the Convention provides a very simple basic definition of cultural property.[8]

The definition in Article 1 of the Convention refers to 'importance' and not to the value of cultural property. Certain objects, although of limited value, may be important for the national culture while others, even though of great value, can be replaced and are therefore less important. The concept of 'importance' enables the national authorities to draw up a list of properties to be protected. Such a list should not be too extensive because, if protection is made too broad and thus lowers the threshold at which an object is considered important, the material possibility of protection will also be reduced. The enemy army must not be confronted with a multiplicity of buildings marked with the distinctive emblem of the Convention. In such a situation, while conducting military operations, the enemy army may resort to the clause of military necessity and will not be able to make its decisions considering the importance of that property.[9]

The other definition that is sometimes used to define cultural property is the definition in the 1972 Convention Concerning the Protection of the World

7 The term 'centres' comprises a group of historical or artistic monuments situated in the same vicinity, such as the districts of certain cities or even entire cities.

8 Boylan P. J., Review of the Convention for the Protection of Cultural Property in the Event of Armed Conflict, UNESCO, 1993, p. 232.

9 Toman Jiri, 2009, *Cultural Property in War: Improvement in Protection, Commentary on the 1999 Second Protocol to the Hague Convention*, UNESCO, p. 50.

Culture and Natural Heritage (the World Heritage Convention), which relates to heritage considered to have "outstanding universal value".[10] The 1970 UNESCO Convention on the Means of Prohibiting and Preventing the Illicit Import, Export and Transfer of Ownership of Cultural Property, relates to movable cultural property and uses different definitions.[11] For IHL, "cultural property" must be understood as a specific legal concept, which differs from that of "cultural heritage." The latter, which exists in a variety of international standard-setting instruments, is generally intended to be broader in scope than the notion of cultural property, as it also encompasses all the intangible aspects of cultural life. In contrast, while there is no agreed definition of cultural property under international law,

10 The term "cultural property" has been superseded by the concept of "cultural heritage," which was originally developed with the 1972 Convention Concerning the Protection of the World Cultural and Natural Heritage (WHC). Accordingly, the term "cultural heritage" is today used in legal parlance to embrace any manifestation of artistic and creative processes having a public or private dimension. As such, cultural heritage conveys an understanding that is broader than that of "cultural property" (or "cultural objects" or "cultural goods") used to indicate tangible movable assets. In addition, the term "cultural heritage" emphasizes that the values inherent in cultural heritage expressions—which are given to them by the individual or the people who created them, or for whom they were created, or whose identity and history they share—must be transmitted from one generation to the next with the duty to preserve. Renold Marc-Andre and Chechi Alessandro, "International Human Rights Law and Cultural Heritage," in Cuno James and Thomas G. Weiss (ed), 2022, *Cultural Heritage and Mass Atrocities*, Los Angeles: Getty Publications, pp. 396-410.

11 Under Article 1 of the 1970 Convention, the term "cultural property" means property which, on religious or secular grounds, is specifically designated by each State as being of importance for archaeology, prehistory, history, literature, art or science and which belongs to the following categories: (a) Rare collections and specimens of fauna, flora, minerals and anatomy, and objects of palaeontological interest; (b) property relating to history, including the history of science and technology and military and social history, to the life of national leaders, thinkers, scientists and artist and to events of national importance; (c) products of archaeological excavations (including regular and clandestine) or of archaeological discoveries; (d) elements of artistic or historical monuments or archaeological sites which have been dismembered; (e) antiquities more than one hundred years old, such as inscriptions, coins and engraved seals; (f) objects of ethnological interest; (g) property of artistic interest, such as (i) pictures, paintings and drawings produced entirely by hand on any support and in any material (excluding industrial designs and manufactured articles decorated by hand); (ii) original works of statuary art and sculpture in any material; (iii) original engravings, prints and lithographs; (iv) original artistic assemblages and montages in any material; (h) rare manuscripts and incunabula, old books, documents and publications of special interest (historical, artistic, scientific, literary, etc.) singly or in collections; (i) postage, revenue and similar stamps, singly or in collections; (j) archives, including sound, photographic and cinematographic archives; and (k) articles of furniture more than one hundred years old and old musical instruments.

one common feature of the definitions provided in IHL treaties is the fact that the notion of protected cultural property is limited to material objects. IHL provides a comprehensive set of rules when it comes to protecting cultural property from the effects of armed conflict. Not only does it restrict the behaviour of the warring parties during hostilities, but also purports to prepare for the protection of valuable cultural property in peacetime.

The drafters of the 1954 Hague Convention tried to provide a concrete definition to guarantee a higher degree of protection for cultural property. The term 'cultural property' as defined in Article 1, is only applicable to the 1954 Hague Convention and its two protocols, and not to subsequent UNESCO standards relating to cultural property. After 1954, UNESCO adopted two more conventions in 1970 and 1972. They use significantly different definitions. The former referred to movable objects including natural heritage such as "rare collections and specimens of fauna, flora, minerals and anatomy, and objects of paleontological interest." The 1972 Convention referred only to immovable cultural heritage but again extended the scope of the definition by including landscapes. Between 1956 and 1980, UNESCO adopted nine recommendations, all with a different definition of cultural property. The Statutes of the ICTY in Article 3(d) did not use the term cultural property, but refers to "institutions dedicated to religion, charity and education, the arts and sciences, historic monuments and works of art and science." Therefore, a more consistent definition of cultural property is necessary as vague definitions can lead to omission.[12]

Article 2 of the Convention states, "For the present Convention, the protection of cultural property shall comprise the safeguarding of and respect for such property." Article 2 sets out a general and comprehensive definition of protection and comprises two separate aspects: safeguarding and respect. The term 'safeguarding' consists of all the positive measures which are designed to ensure the best possible material conditions for the protection of cultural property; the term 'respect for such property' on the other hand has a negative connotation. It represents an obligation not to commit several prohibited acts. Respect, therefore, implies a requirement to refrain from certain acts, such as placing cultural property in peril or causing damage to it. This general provision has been further clarified in Articles 3 and 4 of the Convention.

12 Auwera Sigrid Van der, International Law and the Protection of Cultural Property in the Event of Armed Conflict: Actual Problems and Challenges, *The Journal of Arts Management, Law and Society*, Vol. 43, 2013, pp. 175-190.

Article 3 states that the state parties shall adopt appropriate measures in times of peace for the safeguarding of cultural property situated within their own territory against the foreseeable effects of an armed conflict. Article 4, expresses recognition of the principle of respect as one which already exists in international conventions and in customary law and represents a dictate of the universal conscience. Paragraph 1 of Article 4 states the following:

> The High Contracting Parties undertake to respect cultural property situated within their own territory as well as within the territory of other High Contracting Parties by refraining from any use of the property and its immediate surroundings or of the appliances in use for its protection for purposes which are likely to expose it to destruction or damage in the event of armed conflict, and by refraining from any act of hostility directed against such property.

Article 4, paragraph 2, however, enables the Parties to waive the obligations mentioned in paragraph 1 in cases where military necessity imperatively requires this. Military necessity is considered as one of the most elusive concepts of international humanitarian law (IHL). The term 'military necessity' has not been defined, but has been inserted into the framework for the protection of cultural property during armed conflicts as an exception to the basic duty of respect for cultural property enshrined in Article 4 of the 1954 Hague Convention.

The notion of 'respect for cultural property' also includes a requirement to prohibit, prevent and, if necessary, put a stop to any form of theft, pillage or misappropriation of cultural property and any acts of vandalism directed against it. However, this limitation under Article 4, paragraph 3 cannot be waived, not even for reasons of imperative military necessity. The Contracting Parties undertake to refrain from requisitioning movable cultural property situated in the territory of another High Contracting Party.[13] The state parties, vide Article 4, para 4, of the Convention undertake to refrain from any act directed by way of reprisals against cultural property. This ban is absolute with no exception whatsoever. Pursuant to paragraph

13 The application of this provision posed a problem during the Suez Conflict in 1956 when Egypt requisitioned the French Institute of Oriental Archaeology in Cairo. The prohibition of requisitioning should also apply to property existing on the territory of a High Contracting Party but belonging to the nationals of another High Contracting Party, as in the case of the collections of the historical or scientific institutes in Athens, Cairo, Paris, and Rome. The same guarantee should also apply with respect to movable cultural property made available on loan for an exhibition. Toman Jiri, 1996, *The Protection of Cultural Property in the Event of Armed Conflict, Commentary on 1954 Convention*, Ashgate, UNESCO, p. 71.

5, the state parties cannot evade the obligations incumbent upon them under Article 4, in respect of another state party by reason of the fact that the latter has not applied the measures of safeguard referred to in Article 3.[14]

Military Necessity

While there is no doubt that destruction is an inevitable consequence of every war, the idea that the destruction of cultural works could be avoided started emerging in the second half of the 19th century. In an earlier attempt, Emer de Vattel (1839) introduced the concept of military necessity and the protection of cultural property in a war. Vattel recognises the special status of cultural property and states that the "edifices which do honour to human society" such as temples, tombs, public buildings, and all works of remarkable beauty. They do not contribute to increasing the enemy's strength and there is no advantage achieved by destroying them.[15]

The Lieber Code, as discussed in the last chapter, was the first formal set of rules laid down by a state as to how both its own armies and that of its enemies should be treated. Article 14 of the Code states, "Military necessity, as understood by modern civilised nations, consists in the necessity of those measures which are indispensable for securing the ends of the war, and which are lawful according to the modern law and usages of war." The term "lawful according to the modern law and usages of war," has been further clarified in Articles 15 and 16 of the Code. Article 15 provides several examples of measures applicable against the enemy and its property, which are legitimate to achieve the aims of a conflict. Article 16 clarifies the limiting role of military necessity in *jus in bello*, declaring:

> Military necessity does not admit of cruelty---that is, the infliction of suffering for the sake of suffering or for revenge, nor of maiming or wounding except in fight, nor of torture to extort confessions. It does not admit of the use of poison in any war, nor of the wanton

14 This paragraph refers to a situation in which, by reason of internal circumstances or because a conflict broke out shortly after the adoption of the Convention, the organization of the safeguard of cultural property in a particular country has not been completed. The opponent cannot use that fact as a pretext to refrain from according to the cultural property of this country the respect which he has undertaken to ensure, save of course in the event of imperative military necessity. Toman Jiri, 1996, *The Protection of Cultural Property in the Event of Armed Conflict, Commentary on 1954 Convention*, Ashgate, UNESCO, p. 72.

15 Vattel Emmerich de, 1839, *Law of Nations or the Principles of Natural Law*, Philadelphia: T. & J. W. Johnson, Law Booksellers, p. 366-368.

devastation of a district. It admits of deception but disclaims acts of perfidy; and, in general, military necessity does not include any act of hostility which makes the return to peace unnecessarily difficult.

The Lieber Code also contains rules establishing the legal status of cultural property during armed conflict. It states that: "Classical works of art, libraries, scientific collections, or precious instruments, such as astronomical telescopes, as well as hospitals, must be secured against all avoidable injury, even when they are contained in fortified places whilst besieged or bombarded."[16] However, the Lieber Code does not always protect cultural property. Article 15 of the Lieber Code generally allows "all destruction of property" in case it is inevitable so cultural property is not excluded. There were various instances in the Civil War when the US military failed to observe the principle of military necessity.

The evolving use of military necessity was a justification by Germany for the development of the maxim *Kriegsraison geht vor Kriegsmanier* (the necessities of war take precedence over the rules of war) before WW I, under which military necessity outweighed any rule of humanitarian law.[17] The application of the Kriegsraison doctrine leads to a vacuum in armed conflicts where legal limitations find no application and the achievement of military objectives has absolute priority. The doctrine thus created a climate in warfare, where the inviolability of the laws of war and the protection of individuals was not significant. This doctrine is also incompatible with the principle of the law of war embodied in Article 22 of the Hague Regulations according to which the belligerents do not have an unlimited choice as to the means that they may deploy to harm the enemy. The Kriegsraison doctrine was rejected by modern IHL as inconsistent and too permissive.[18]

Post World War II, the International Military Tribunal (IMT) at Nuremberg introduced a new understanding of the military necessity principle in the Hostages Case. The IMT held that military necessity permits a belligerent, subject to the laws of war, to apply any amount and kind of force to compel the complete submission of the enemy with the least possible expenditure

16 Article 34, The 1863 Lieber Instructions for the Administration of the Armies (United States).

17 Forrest Craig J.S., The Doctrine of Military Necessity and the Protection of Cultural Property During Armed Conflict, *California Western International Law Journal*, Vol. 37, No. 2, Spring 2007, p. 186.

18 Kolitsch Finn-Valentin, Resurrection of Kriegsraison? The Military Necessity Principle and the Essence of International Humanitarian, Unpublished Master thesis, Lund University, 2022, p. 76.

of time, life, and money. The IMT highlighted that the destruction of property to be lawful must be imperatively demanded by the necessities of war. Destruction as an end is a violation of international law. There must be some reasonable connection between the destruction of property and the overcoming of the enemy forces. [19]

The 1949 Geneva Conventions do not address issues of cultural property and the concept of military necessity. The Fourth Geneva Convention relating to the protection of civilians prohibits the destruction of property belonging to private persons by occupying power except for cases when it is required by military necessity. The provision may indirectly cover cultural property as well but in a real sense, it does not recognise the special nature of cultural property.[20]

The destruction of cultural property during armed conflict can appear because of different actions. For instance, it can be directly targeted during military operations, or the destruction can emerge as mere collateral damage, or it can be also damaged or destroyed during the conflict outside military operations for various reasons. All those three modalities are, however, related to the doctrine of military necessity. The doctrine of necessity underlies both *jus ad bellum* and *jus in bello.*[21] Modern application of the principle of necessity is restricted to the use of force in self-defence or by the collective security system established under Chapter VII of the United Nations Charter and aims to maintain international peace and security. The military necessity principle in the modern day is

19 *United States of America v. Wilhelm List and others*, Hostages Case, February 19, 1948. The accused were charged with committing War Crimes: Atrocities or offences against persons or property constituting violations of the laws or customs of war, including but not limited to, murder, ill-treatment, or deportation to slave labour or for any other purpose, of civilian population from occupied territory, murder or ill-treatment of prisoners of war or persons on the seas, killing of hostages, plunder of public or private property, wanton destruction of cities, towns or villages, or devastation not justified by military necessity.

20 Article 53 of the Geneva Convention (IV) relative to the Protection of Civilian Persons in Time of War of August 12, 1949, provides: "Any destruction by the Occupying Power of real or personal property belonging individually or collectively to private persons, or the State, or to other public authorities, or social or cooperative organizations, is prohibited, except where such destruction is rendered necessary by military operations."

21 *Jus ad bellum* refers to the legal norms which restrict the circumstances in which states can resort to the use of force, while *jus in bello* refers to the placing of limits on how hostilities are conducted (i.e., the means and methods of warfare) when restraints on the use of force fail.

widely recognised as a limiting legal principle of IHL that is also included in international customary law. Military necessity is the only exception to the general rule of protection of cultural property. The concept of military necessity was used to justify the degrading treatment of detainees in US offshore prisons at Guantánamo Bay after 9/ 11.

In military parlance, 'military necessity' is commonly identified with the desirability of a certain military result rather than an extraordinary circumstance or emergency. At present, military necessity is defined in terms of the general principle of restraint in warfare, to emphasise its prohibitive effect on the use of force. Whatever may be viewed as necessary is not always permissible in an armed conflict, but everything permissible must also be necessary. The principle of military necessity involves both a consideration of military aims, and a 'genuine necessity requirement.'[22] The principle of military necessity in general can be defined with reference to the definition of the military objective in Article 52 of the 1977 Additional Protocol I as "those objects which by their nature, location, purpose or use make an effective contribution to military action and whose total or partial destruction, capture or neutralisation, in the circumstances ruling at the time, offers a definite military advantage." In an armed conflict, military necessity can only justify violations which are made in pursuit of a lawful and legitimate aim and are the only way to secure it. In particular, the assertion commonly found in various military manuals, whereby the principle of military necessity allows for the volume of force necessary to achieve the goal, i.e. the total submission of the enemy, ought to be reconsidered.[23] Despite the frequent use and broad acknowledgement of the military necessity principle in IHL, it remains undefined in law.[24]

The responsibility for safeguarding and preserving measures for the protection of cultural property rests with the national authorities, who accordingly must take the necessary action even if their territory is occupied. Article 5 of the Convention, however, demands close cooperation between the Occupying Power and the national authorities. The first paragraph

22 Geiss, R., "Military necessity: A fundamental "principle" fallen into oblivion," in Ruiz Fabri, H., Wolfrum, R. and Gogolin, J. (eds.) 2010, *Select Proceedings of the European Society of International Law*, Hart Publishing, pp. 554-568.

23 Drazewska Berenika, 2022, *Military Necessity in International Cultural Heritage Law*, Leiden: Brill Nijhoff, p. 99

24 Kolitsch Finn-Valentin, Resurrection of Kriegsraison? The Military Necessity Principle and the Essence of International Humanitarian, Unpublished Master thesis, Lund University, 2022, p. 29.

of Article 5 stipulates that the Occupying Power shall, as far as possible, support the national authorities in their efforts to safeguard cultural property. Paragraph 2 of Article 5 makes provision for situations in which the national authorities are unable to take the necessary urgent action to preserve damaged cultural property. It will then be the responsibility of the occupying Power to act itself.[25]

Distinctive Marking

The distinctive marking of cultural property is not compulsory and is not a condition for the respect of cultural property. The absence of a distinctive marking which permits the identification of such property might lessen the responsibility of the adverse party in the event of bombardment since the act of destruction might be excused on the grounds of ignorance of the presence of cultural property. Article 6 of the Convention, which appears in the section concerning general protection, refers to Article 16 of the Convention and the distinctive emblem described therein.

The 1954 Convention created a distinctive emblem known as the blue shield – a shield, pointed below, per saltire blue and white – to facilitate the recognition of cultural property by parties in armed conflict.[26] The distinctive emblem of the Convention is used in three different forms: (i) Blue shield emblem used alone, (ii) Blue shield emblem repeated three times in a triangular formation (one shield below, and (iii) Blue shield emblem outlined by a detached external red band.

General Protection

The blue shield emblem may be used alone to mark cultural property under general protection, or to indicate personnel engaged in its protection or overseeing the Convention's implementation. When used alone, the distinctive emblem indicates the general level of protection afforded under international law to all objects, structures and sites qualifying as cultural

25 The careful wording of the second paragraph seems to have been a response to several practices manifest in WW II: (i) the reluctance of some Occupying Powers, usually for logistical reasons, to intervene to shore up monuments damaged in the course of hostilities; (ii) the overexuberance and insensitivity of some engineering corps when charged with clearing encumbering 'debris' and structurally unsound 'ruins'; and (iii) the deliberate modification contrary to national traditions of certain cultural property in German-occupied territory on the pretext of restoration. O'Keefe Roger, 2006, *The Protection of Cultural Property in Armed Conflict*, Cambridge University Press, p. 137.

26 Articles 16 and 17, The Convention for the Protection of Cultural Property in the Event of Armed Conflict, 1954.

property. Affixing the blue shield emblem on cultural property is not mandatory but it may prevent unintended damage and deter unlawful targeting of cultural property during an armed conflict. However, the decision to mark cultural property must be carefully assessed as an explicit indication of cultural value may transform it into a target. The practice of using the blue shield emblem is not uniform. The size, position, and even number of emblems affixed on a single property may vary. The authorisation to use such emblems in some States lies with national governments; some States have delegated this authority to local governments.

Special Protection

The blue shield emblem repeated three times in a triangular formation (one shield below) may be used to mark immovable cultural property, refuges to store moveable cultural property, or certain transports for cultural property that are under special protection. A limited number of refuges for sheltering movable cultural property, centres containing monuments, and immovable cultural property "of very great importance" may be placed under special protection under the 1954 Hague Convention. Special protection is granted by entry on the International Register of Cultural Property under Special Protection. The States Parties undertake to ensure the immunity of such cultural property under special protection by refraining from any act of hostility directed against it, and from any use of such property or its surroundings for military purposes. This immunity may only be waived in exceptional cases of unavoidable military necessity by the officer commanding a force the equivalent of a division in size or larger. The distinctive marking of cultural property under special protection has practical importance for parties in conflict. Therefore, the use of the blue shield emblem repeated three times in a triangular formation on such property is mandatory during armed conflict. When affixed, such distinctive markings should be visible from the ground at regular intervals, clearly indicating the perimeter of a centre containing monuments, and at the entrance to other locations under special protection.

A transport exclusively engaged in the transfer of cultural property may be granted special protection to ensure the safe movement of cultural property. In this case, the blue shield emblem repeated three times in a triangular formation shall be placed on the transport vehicles to be visible in daylight from the air as well as from the ground. Like immovable cultural property under special protection, the States Parties undertake to ensure the immunity of the transport by refraining from any act of hostility directed against it.

Enhanced Protection

The blue shield emblem outlined by a detached external red band is the distinctive emblem for cultural property under enhanced protection, a mechanism established by the 1999 Second Protocol to provide immunity and protection to a limited amount of cultural property of the "greatest importance to humanity." The 1999 Second Protocol itself does not contain any provision on a distinctive marking of cultural property under enhanced protection. The distinctive marking was developed by the Committee for the Protection of Cultural Property in the Event of Armed Conflict and endorsed by the 6th Meeting of the Parties to the 1999 Second Protocol in 2015, and modalities for use are detailed in the Guidelines for Implementation of the Protocol. The distinctive emblem for cultural property under enhanced protection is intended to ensure the recognition and identification of cultural property under enhanced protection. Particularly during armed conflicts, its use can ensure the effectiveness of the provisions of the 1999 Second Protocol, promoting the immunity of such property. The marking of cultural property under enhanced protection with the distinctive emblem is not mandatory, but it can be an effective measure to ensure better protection. The decision to place a distinctive emblem on a cultural property under enhanced protection, and the extent of its visibility, is determined by the concerned State authorities.

The blue shield emblem may also be used to indicate people with allocated duties overseeing the implementation of the 1954 Hague Convention or personnel engaged in the protection of cultural property, whether military or civilian. They may wear an armlet bearing the blue shield emblem, issued by the competent national authorities. To indicate their authority, such people should carry a special identity card bearing the emblem. The card should mention at least their surname and first name, date of birth, title or rank, and the function of the holder. The card should also display a photograph of the holder, his/her signature, or fingerprints (or both), and should bear an embossed stamp of the competent authorities. The holder(s) may not, without a legitimate reason, be deprived of this card or of the right to wear the armlet. The card's precise appearance is a matter for each State.

The authorisation, placement, and degree of visibility of the distinctive emblem is up to the competent authorities of each state. However, it should be displayed without alterations or embellishments, and accompanied by the authorisation of the state party. The emblem may be displayed on flags or armlets; it may be painted on an object or represented in any other appropriate form. Each state adopts its own rules and practice on the authorisation of the use of the distinctive markings, without prejudice to its international obligations. UNESCO may provide technical advice on the effective use of the Blue Shield emblem.[27]

Military Measures

Article 7 of the 1954 Convention relates to military measures which must be observed to foster in the members of the armed forces a spirit of respect for the culture and cultural property of all peoples.[28] The Hague Convention refers only to military measures and entrusts their implementation to the military authorities. The state parties are required to give precise instructions to the military authorities for the respect and protection of cultural property. Paragraph 2 of Article 7 provides for the preparation and establishment in peacetime of the services or specialist personnel within the armed forces whose purpose will be to secure respect for cultural property and to cooperate with the civilian authorities responsible for safeguarding it. To take the appropriate measures and to get the troops to respect cultured property, the commanding officers of military establishments need advisers who will give them an expert opinion on the subject. Article 82 of the 1977 Additional Protocol I provide that the Parties to the conflict in time of armed conflict shall ensure that legal advisers are available to advise the military commanders at the appropriate level on the application of the Geneva Conventions and Additional Protocol I. To implement IHL applicable in the event of armed conflicts, several states have emphasised a military manual as a training tool. These manuals contain the provisions on the protection of cultural property.[29] This is a critical provision because

27 Distinctive Marking of Cultural Property: Rules and Practices, UNESCO / Blue Shield International, 2021, p. 16.

28 Article 7 of the 1954 Convention follows the provisions contained in the Fourth Hague Convention of 1907 and the Geneva Conventions of 1949. Article 1 of the Hague Convention states that the Contracting Powers shall give instructions in conformity with the Regulations of their land forces. The Geneva Conventions (Articles 47/48/127/144 of the respective Convention) provide that the study of these conventions shall form an integral part of military, and if possible, of civil instruction programmes so that the principles may become known to the entire population; to the armed fighting forces, the medical personnel, and the chaplains.

29 A few examples are The US Department of Defence Law of War Manual (June 2015, updated July 2023) chapter V, para 5.18. pp. 301-320; The British Joint Service Manual

the armed forces will be ultimately responsible for executing the provisions of the Convention, and is related to the obligation to disseminate the Convention laid down in Article 25.[30] Military authorities must also address the issue of cultural looting and destruction within the framework of the more general law of war.

Regime of Special Protection

Chapter II of the Convention (Articles 8 to 11) establishes a regime of 'special protection' applicable above and beyond the general protection provided for in Chapter I. These provisions are designed to provide a higher standard of protection in respect of a narrower range of property, which relates specifically to the obligation to refrain from using cultural property and its surroundings for military purposes. All the obligations applicable to movables and immovables which come within the definition of cultural property under Article 1 are equally applicable to property which additionally qualifies for special protection under Article 8. Article 8, first paragraph, defines the property to which special protection is granted. This definition is in three parts: the first defines the property as such, the second points out that only cultural property of very great importance may benefit from special protection, and the third part lays down two conditions which preclude special protection if they are not met. There are three categories of property to which special protection is to be given: (i) a limited number of refuges intended to shelter movable cultural property in the event of armed conflict;[31] (ii) centres containing monuments; and (iii) other immovable cultural property of very great importance.

---

of the Law of Armed Conflict (JSP 383, 2004 Edition), pp. 14-15 and 70-73; Australian Defence Doctrine Publication 06.4—Law of Armed Conflict (2006), pp. 5.45-5.47. The German Joint Service Regulation 15/2, Law of Armed Conflict Manual published in May 2013, contains Chapter 9 on the Protection of Cultural Property.

30 Article 25 of the Convention provides: The High Contracting Parties undertake, in time of peace as in time of armed conflict, to disseminate the text of the present Convention and the Regulations for its execution as widely as possible in their respective countries. They undertake to include the study thereof in their programmes of military and, if possible, civilian training, so that its principles are made known to the whole population, especially the armed forces and personnel engaged in the protection of cultural property.

31 These shelters should be specially built to protect the property against bombardment and fire or dryness and dampness. The number of refuges is not fixed precisely, but it is preferable not to increase their number unduly as this would merely heighten the difficulty of providing protection. The number of refuges will depend on the size of the territory, the quantity of property to be protected and on transport problems, fire risks, etc.

These three categories of property 'of very great importance' may be placed under special protection, but only if the two following conditions are fulfilled and respected. First, the protected property must be situated at an adequate distance[32] from any large industrial center or any important military objective constituting a vulnerable point, such as, for example, an aerodrome, broadcasting station, establishment engaged in work of national defence, a port or railway station of relative importance or a main line of communication. Second, the protected property must not be used for military purposes.[33] Article 8, paragraph 2 states that a refuge for movable cultural property may also be placed under special protection, whatever its location, if it is so constructed that, in all probability, it will not be damaged by bombs. The guarding of cultural property mentioned in paragraph 1 above by armed custodians specially empowered to do so or their presence in the vicinity of such cultural property shall not be deemed to be used for military purposes.[34]

Under Article 8, paragraph 5, if any cultural property mentioned in Paragraph 1 is situated near an important objective, it may be placed under special protection if the High Contracting Party asking for that protection undertakes, in the event of armed conflict, to make no use of the objective and particularly, in the case of a port, railway station or aerodrome, to divert all traffic therefrom. In that event, such diversion should be prepared in a time of peace.[35]

32 The text of the 1954 Convention does not clarify the notion of 'adequate distance'. It must be interpreted in the light of the specific situation and there is no general criterion to state exactly what distance is involved. The notion of an 'adequate distance' must therefore be assessed on a case-by-case basis. Considering the evolution of military weapons technology, the definition of the distance which can be considered "adequate" concerning military objectives (those enumerated in Article 8) may give rise to problems.

33 Article 8, paragraph 3 clarifies, "A centre containing monuments shall be deemed to be used for military purposes whenever it is used for the movement of military personnel or material, even in transit. The same shall apply whenever activities directly connected with military operations, the stationing of military personnel, or the production of war material are carried on within the centre."

34 Article 8, paragraph 4, The Convention for the Protection of Cultural Property in the Event of Armed Conflict, 1954.

35 In contrast to Article 8(1)(a), Article 8(5) makes no mention of large industrial centres, the reference being only to important military objectives, and it is unclear whether cultural property situated near such centres may also benefit from an undertaking made in accordance with the provision. the only state to have made a peacetime undertaking in accordance with article 8(5) has been Italy and about cultural property

The special protection is granted to cultural property of the highest importance by its entry in the International Register. Entry in this Register is, therefore the decisive consideration as it marks the start of special protection.[36] According to O'Keefe (2006), this has two corollaries: (i) eligible cultural property does not enjoy special protection unless and until it is entered in the Register, and (ii) the entry of cultural property in the Register is conclusive proof of its grant of special protection.[37]

Under Article 12(2) of the Regulations, the duty to maintain the Register is vested in the Director-General of UNESCO, who is obliged to furnish copies of it to the Parties and the UN Secretary-General. It is the Director-General who, by Article 15(1) of the Regulations, is mandated to enter eligible cultural property in the Register; which could be made only in accordance with the provisions of the Convention and its Regulations.[38] Article 14(1) of the Regulation grants the right to object to the registration of given cultural property within four months of the date on which the Director-General sent the Party its copy of the application. The valid reasons for objection could be that it is not a cultural property as defined in Article 1 of the Convention or that it does not comply with the conditions laid down in Article 8 of the Convention.

Immunity under Special Protection

Article 9 of the Convention deals with the immunity of cultural property under special protection. Accordingly, the Parties undertake 'to ensure the immunity of cultural property under special protection by refraining, from

situated in the Vatican City, a separate state. O'Keefe Roger, 2006, *The Protection of Cultural Property in Armed Conflict*, Cambridge University Press, p. 150.

36 Article 8(6), The Convention for the Protection of Cultural Property in the Event of Armed Conflict, 1954.

37 O'Keefe Roger, 2006, *The Protection of Cultural Property in Armed Conflict*, Cambridge University Press, p. 152.

38 Chapter II of the Regulations for the Execution of the Convention spells out the procedure for the entry of cultural property in the Register. In accordance with article 13(1) of the Regulations, it is up to the Party in whose territory the relevant refuge, centre containing monuments or other immovable cultural property is situated to submit to the Director-General of UNESCO an application for its entry in the Register. Article 13(2) specifies, however, that the Occupying Power is competent to make such an application in the event of belligerent occupation. Copies of applications, which Article 13(1) stipulates must contain a description of the location of the property in question and certification of its compliance with the provisions of Article 8 of the Convention, are to be sent by the Director-General to all the Parties, under Article 13(3).

the time of entry in the International Register, from any act of hostility directed against such property and, except for the cases provided for in paragraph 5 of Article 8, from any use of such property or its surroundings for military purposes'.[39] Article 9 needs to be read in conjunction with Article 11, which deals with the withdrawal of the immunity enjoyed by cultural property under special protection. Paragraph 2 of Article 11 provides that, aside from the cases provided for in paragraph 1, 'immunity shall be withdrawn from cultural property under special protection only in exceptional cases of unavoidable military necessity, and only for such time as that necessity continues'. In addition, the second sentence of Article 11(2) specifies that such necessity can be established 'only by the officer commanding a force the equivalent of a division in size or larger'. The final sentence adds that, whenever circumstances permit, the opposing Party is to be notified a reasonable time in advance of the decision to withdraw immunity. Paragraph 1 of Article 11 provides that if one of the Parties 'commits, in respect of any item of cultural property under special protection, a violation of the obligations under Article 9, the opposing Party shall, so long as this violation persists, be released from the obligation to ensure the immunity of the property concerned'. Article 11(3) states that the Party withdrawing immunity shall inform the Commissioner-General for Cultural Property as soon as possible in writing, stating the reasons.

Identification and Control

Article 10 of the Convention provides that, during an armed conflict, cultural property under special protection is to be marked with a distinctive emblem, as discussed above. The emblem is repeated three times in the case of such property, in accordance with Article 17(1)(a) of the Convention. Article 17(4), applicable to both special and general protection, further requires that the display of the emblem on immovable cultural property be accompanied by an authorisation duly dated and signed by the Party's competent authority. As Article 10 itself makes clear, and in contradistinction to general protection, the use of the distinctive emblem to identify cultural property under special protection is mandatory during armed conflict. According to Article 10, cultural property under

39 The term 'act of hostility' in Article 9 has the same meaning as it does in Article 4(1), extending beyond attacks to encompass demolitions. As for the second aspect of immunity, Article 4(1) speaks of any use of the property, of its immediate surroundings or the appliances in use for its protection 'for purposes which are likely to expose it to destruction or damage in the event of armed conflict', article 9 prohibits any use of the property or its surroundings 'for military purposes'. O'Keefe Roger, 2006, *The Protection of Cultural Property in Armed Conflict*, Cambridge University Press, p. 157.

special protection 'shall be open to international control as provided for in the Regulations for the Execution of the Convention'.

Transport of Cultural Property

The 1863 Lieber Code, discussed in the previous chapter, had provisions relating to the transport of cultural property. Article 36 provided: "If such works of art, libraries, collections, or instruments belonging to a hostile nation or government, can be removed without injury, the ruler of the conquering State or nation may order them to be seized and removed for the benefit of the said nation. The ultimate ownership is to be settled by the ensuing treaty of peace. In no case shall they be sold or given away if captured by the armies of the United States, not shall they ever be privately appropriated or wantonly destroyed or injured."

The transportation of cultural property is governed by Articles 12 to 14 of the 1954 Hague Convention. The Convention makes provision for two types of transport. The first, as specified in Article 12 of the Convention, is governed by conditions which provide that the opposing Party is informed of all relevant details some time in advance of the transfer and international supervision ensured. In this case, transport enjoys the same immunity as that afforded to cultural property under special protection. Thus, the Parties must refrain from any act of hostility directed against them, and that both they and the movable cultural property they are transporting are immune from seizure, placing in prize or capture. The transport used must display the distinctive emblem repeated three times. The conditions governing this kind of transport are set out in the Regulations for the Execution of the Convention.[40]

The second type of transport, as specified in Article 13 of the Convention, covers situations in which it proves impossible to take the steps envisaged in Article 12 and where, for that reason, complete immunity cannot be provided. Article 13 was designed at the outset to provide for evacuation to

40 Article 17 of the Regulations provides that the Party wishing to obtain immunity for the transport of cultural property must address a request and requisite details to the Commissioner-General for Cultural Property. If the Commissioner-General is satisfied that the transfer of the property to the proposed location is justified, he should appoint a suitable number of inspectors to verify that only the cultural property listed in the request is transferred and to accompany the property to its destination. Article 18 of the Regulations dealing with supplementary provision for the transport of cultural property abroad, provides that if cultural property remains in the territory of another state, that state 'shall be its depositary and shall extend to it as great a measure of care as that which it bestows upon its cultural property of comparable importance'.

refuges at the opening of hostilities. It also applied in the case of transport not planned in peacetime but necessitated, during a conflict, by unforeseen circumstances requiring immediate action.[41] Both types of transport may, under certain conditions, be entitled to the protection of the distinctive emblem. In both cases, the property is protected against seizure,[42] placing it in prize or capture. Therefore, both cultural property and the means of transport enjoy immunity. However, the right to visit and search are not curtailed.[43]

Article 15 of the 1954 Hague Convention contains a provision concerning the personnel, civilian or military, engaged in the protection of cultural property. It provides, "personnel engaged in the protection of cultural property shall, in the interests of such property, be respected and, if they fall into the hands of the opposing Party, shall be allowed to continue to carry out their duties whenever the cultural property for which they are responsible." Article 15, therefore, refers only to respect for personnel. Under Article 17 of the Convention, personnel assigned to the protection of cultural property may use the distinctive emblem as a means of identification. Under Article 21 of the Regulations for the Execution of the Convention, such persons may (optionally) wear an armlet bearing the distinctive emblem, issued, and stamped by the competent authorities. They also carry a special identity card bearing the same emblem of which they may not be deprived without legitimate reasons.

41 In all cases where, for various reasons, the transfer cannot be notified in advance or placed under international control - and cannot therefore be effected according to the requirement set out in Article 12 and the Regulations for the Execution of the Convention; Article 13 provides for a minimum of protection: the High Contracting Parties shall take "so far as possible the necessary precautions to avoid acts of hostility directed against the transport described in paragraph 1 of the present article and displaying the distinctive emblem." For these cases, the 1954 Convention requires that transport display the emblem. Toman Jiri, 1996, *The Protection of Cultural Property in the Event of Armed Conflict, Commentary on 1954 Convention*, Ashgate, UNESCO, pp. 166-167.

42 In law, seizure is defined as a procedure whereby movable or immovable property is placed in the hands of the judicial or administrative authority in the private or public interest. Seizure also occurs in Articles 23(g), 53 and 54 of the 1907 Hague Regulations respecting the Laws and Customs of War on Land.

43 Article 14, The Convention for the Protection of Cultural Property in the Event of Armed Conflict, 1954.

Non-International Armed Conflict

In the event of a non-international armed conflict occurring within the territory of one of the state parties, each party to the conflict remains bound by the provisions of the 1954 Convention which relates to respect for cultural property. The parties to the conflict shall endeavour to bring into force, using special agreements, all, or part of the other provisions of the 1954 Convention and UNESCO may offer its services to the parties to the conflict. The application of these provisions shall not affect the legal status of the parties to the conflict.[44]

Dissemination

The provision of the 1954 Convention applies both in times of peace and in times of war. The state parties under Article 25 are responsible for the dissemination of the provisions of the Convention and its Regulations for execution as widely as possible in their respective countries. They undertake to include the provisions of the Convention and Regulations in the curriculum of the armed forces, especially those engaged in the protection of cultural property in the military and, if possible, amongst the civilian population. Within the armed forces, the main effort of instruction should be directed to the officers who are in the majority and go into action in an armed conflict. They should be the first to receive instructions. The inclusion of the study of the Convention in civilian training programmes is, however, qualified by the words 'if possible'. Similar provisions are contained in Article 47/48/127/144 common to the four Geneva Conventions of 1949. Most of the States which have signed and ratified the 1954 Convention have included it in the training programmes of military academies. A few have included the provisions of the Convention and Regulations in their Military Manuals.

The US Law of War Manual (2015) issued by the Department of Defence contains elaborate provisions regarding the protection of cultural property in armed conflict. It states,

> Certain types of property receive additional protection as cultural property. Cultural property, the areas immediately surrounding it, and appliances in use for its protection should be safeguarded and respected. Some obligations with respect to cultural property apply

44 Article 19, The Convention for the Protection of Cultural Property in the Event of Armed Conflict, 1954. This article is based on Article 3 common to all four Geneva Conventions of 1949.

during non-international armed conflict. There are also obligations with respect to cultural property during occupation and peacetime. Certain treaty obligations with respect to cultural property may only apply on the territory of Parties to the 1954 Hague Cultural Property Convention, but the United States has previously identified some of these obligations as customary international law. The defence personnel, therefore, in the absence of contrary guidance by competent authority, should act as if they were legally bound by the rules for the protection of cultural property in the 1954 Hague Cultural Property Convention during hostilities even when conducting operations in the territory of a State that is not a Party to the 1954 Hague Cultural Property Convention.[45]

Further, "Acts of hostility may be directed against cultural property, its immediate surroundings, or appliances in use for its protection when military necessity imperatively requires such acts. The requirement that military necessity imperatively requires such acts should not be confused with convenience or be used to cloak slackness or indifference to the preservation of cultural property. This waiver of obligations concerning cultural property is analogous to the requirement that enemy property may only be seized if imperatively required by the necessities of war. For example, if cultural property is being used by an opposing force for military purposes, then military necessity generally would imperatively require its seizure or destruction."[46]

Role of UNESCO

The state parties under Article 23 may call upon the United Nations Educational, Scientific and Cultural Organization (UNESCO) for technical assistance in organising the protection of their cultural property, or in connection with any other problem arising out of the application of the Convention or the Regulations for its Execution. The Organization is mandated to accord such assistance within the limits fixed by its programme and by its resources. UNESCO is also authorised to make, on its initiative, proposals on this matter to the state parties.[47] UNESCO's

45 The US Department of Defence Law of War Manual (June 2015, updated July 2023) chapter V, para 5.18. pp. 301-320.

46 The US Department of Defence Law of War Manual (June 2015, updated July 2023) chapter V, para 5.18.5.1, pp. 301-320.

47 Technical assistance by the states has been taken from UNESCO on various occasions. At the request of the Egyptian (and Israeli) authorities for technical assistance

general mandate under Article 1 (3) of its Constitution also provided a useful means by which to urge respect for cultural property during the war in Bosnia-Herzegovina.[48]

UNESCO is an intergovernmental organisation composed of states that form part of the international community. Its powers and competence are established, by the decision of the member states, in its Constitution. UNESCO's role in the protection of cultural property in the event of armed conflict is not based exclusively on the 1954 Hague Convention but has its origin in the Organization's Constitution, which gives UNESCO a general mandate "to maintain, increase and diffuse knowledge: by assuring the conservation and protection of the world's inheritance of books, works of art and monuments of history and science, and recommending to the nations concerned the necessary international conventions."

To carry out this mandate in peacetime, UNESCO has adopted numerous recommendations and conventions, in particular, the Convention on the Means of Prohibiting and Preventing the Illicit Import, Export and Transfer of Ownership of Cultural Property, adopted by the General Conference at its session in Paris on 14 November 1970, and the Convention concerning the Protection of the World Cultural and Natural Heritage, approved by the General Conference at its seventeenth session in Paris on 16 November 1972.

In giving UNESCO this mandate, the States thereby recognised that the protection of cultural property was no longer an internal affair but a question of concern to the whole of humanity and the international community in general. Moreover, under this same mandate, the international community

in preserving the monastery of St Catherine in the wake of the Sinai War in 1956, UNESCO sent an expert to ascertain that this monument and the valuable collections housed in it were in a satisfactory state of preservation after the military operations in the region. In response to Cambodia's request in June 1970 for technical assistance in organising the protection of its cultural property in the face of North Vietnamese and Viet Cong attacks, the Director-General dispatched an expert to assess the situation and to make recommendations accordingly, followed by a team of technical experts with special equipment to facilitate the packing and storage of movable cultural property at the Angkor Conservancy and the National Museum in Phnom Penh. In June 1982, the Lebanese authorities requested that the Director-General send a personal representative to the archaeological site at Tyre in southern Lebanon. UNESCO has provided technical and financial support for the restoration of the Museum of Islamic Art and its holdings in Egypt after it was destroyed because of the terrorist operation in 2014.

48 O'Keefe Roger, 2006, *The Protection of Cultural Property in Armed Conflict*, Cambridge University Press, p. 186.

also gave UNESCO the right to take cultural initiatives, such as formulating recommendations, adopting international conventions, offering its services, making proposals, and giving advice, not only in situations of armed conflict but also in other exceptional situations, such as internal strife, natural disasters, and so on. Without that right, UNESCO would certainly not be able to carry out this mandate.

As UNESCO celebrates 70 years of the Hague Convention, experience has shown that the organisation can fulfil its mission and that the action it has taken to protect cultural property is credible. UNESCO stands on the frontline of international cooperation in close coordination with sister agencies of the UN System and shares knowledge, data, and expertise to strengthen global coordination in the field of protection of cultural property in the face of current global challenges.

The First Protocol

During the Second World War, the systematic removal of artworks and antiquities by Nazi Germany from the countries occupied by it and the subsequent entry of many of these pieces into the market (where they were purchased by private collectors and public institutions alike) motivated the drafters of the 1954 Convention to address the question of the exportation and importation of cultural property from occupied territory. Given the difficulties of several governments in adopting provisions on the restitution of property from occupied territories, it was decided to separate them from the Convention and to adopt them in the form of a separate Protocol. The Protocol to the Convention for the Protection of Cultural Property in the Event of Armed Conflict (now called the First Protocol), was adopted and came into force on August 7, 1956, the same time as the Convention. It has been ratified by 112 states.

The purpose of the First Protocol is to prevent the exportation of cultural property and to provide for the restitution of illegally exported objects. The Protocol regulates the protection of cultural property of cultural property, as defined in Article 1 of the Convention, during occupation through the following:

- Prohibition of all exportations from the occupied territory and the requirement of its return to the territory of the State from which the property was exported;[49]

49 The Protocol does not say how the state party is to prevent exportation, the measures to be taken being left to its judgment and discretion. The 1970 Convention is much

- ➢ Prohibition of retention of cultural property. When the occupation ends, the State must return the cultural object to the formerly occupied authorities;
- ➢ Prohibition of the sale of cultural property. If the cultural property is sold, the purchaser is entitled to fair compensation to be paid by the occupying power.[50]

The state parties, under Article 2 of the Protocol, are obliged to take into custody cultural property imported into its territory either directly or indirectly from any occupied territory. This action shall either be taken automatically upon the importation of the property or, failing this, at the request of the authorities of that territory. At the close of hostilities, the state party is to return, to the competent authorities of the territory previously occupied, cultural property which is in its territory, if such property has been exported in contravention of the principle laid down in the Protocol. Such property shall never be retained as war reparations. The state party whose obligation it was to prevent the exportation of cultural property from the territory occupied by it, shall pay an indemnity to the holders in good faith of any cultural property which has to be returned.[51] Article 5 of the Protocol provides that cultural property coming from the territory of a state party and deposited by it in the territory of another state party to protect such property against the dangers of an armed conflict, shall be returned by the latter, at the end of hostilities, to the competent authorities of the territory from which it came. This obligation is independent of the Convention's regime for the transport of cultural property abroad under

---

more precise on this issue. see Articles 6 and 7 of the 1970 Convention.

50 The obligation imposed on an Occupying Power goes beyond ensuring that its occupation authorities or military forces do not export cultural property from the territory: paragraph 1 encompasses a duty to prevent private parties from doing so. Nor is the obligation limited to exportation contrary to local law; rather, paragraph 1 obliges a belligerent occupant to prevent all exportation of cultural property. O'Keefe Roger, 2006, *The Protection of Cultural Property in Armed Conflict*, Cambridge University Press, p. 198.

51 The state party whose obligation it was to prevent the exportation of cultural property from the territory occupied by it shall pay an indemnity to the holders in good faith of any cultural property which has to be returned in accordance with Article 3 of the Protocol. This obligation thus constitutes a sort of sanction, a consequence of failure to fulfil the requirements of the first paragraph of the Protocol. Toman Jiri, 1996, *The Protection of Cultural Property in the Event of Armed Conflict, Commentary on 1954 Convention*, Ashgate, UNESCO, p. 346.

special protection, which contains an analogous obligation of return in Article 18 of the Regulations.

Protected Cultural Property in the 1977 Additional Protocols

The Diplomatic Conference on the Reaffirmation and Development of International Humanitarian Law Applicable in Armed Conflicts adopted two new instruments in Geneva in 1977: the Optional Protocol I and Optional Protocol II, supplementing the 1949 Geneva Conventions. Additional Protocol I (AP I), deals with international armed conflicts, and Additional Protocol II (AP II) deals with non-international armed conflict. Both Protocols contain brief provisions relating specifically to cultural property, which prohibit attacks against it, prohibit its use in support of the military effort and, in the case of international armed conflict, prohibit making it the object of reprisals. Articles 48, and 50–53 of AP I are a significant advance in the protection of cultural property. They provide that only military objectives may be attacked. They also define military objects and civilian objects, address proportionality, and prohibit reprisals against cultural property.

The basic rule of protection and distinction is contained in Article 48 of AP I. It is the foundation on which codification of the laws and customs of war rests. It provides, "In order to ensure respect for and protection of the civilian population and civilian objects, the Parties to the conflict shall at all times distinguish between the civilian population and combatants and between civilian objects and military objectives and accordingly shall direct their operations[52] only against military objectives." Article 52 of AP I deal with the general protection of civilian objects. It states that civilian objects shall not be the object of attack or reprisals. Civilian objects are all objects which are not military objectives. Attacks shall be limited strictly to military objectives. The military objectives are limited to those objects which by their nature, location, purpose, or use make an effective contribution to military action and whose total or partial destruction, capture or neutralisation, in the circumstances ruling at the time, offers a definite military advantage. In case of doubt, whether an object which is normally dedicated to civilian purposes, such as a place of worship, a

52 The word "operations" should be understood in the context of the whole section I of Part IV of the AP I; it refers to military operations during which violence is used, and not to ideological, political, or religious campaigns. Sandoz Y, et.al., 1987, *Commentary on the Additional Protocols of 8 June 1977*, Geneva: ICRC, p. 600.

house or other dwelling or a school, is being used to make an effective contribution to military action, it shall be presumed not to be so used.

Article 53(a) forbids acts of hostility directed against the historic monuments, works of art or places of worship which constitute the cultural or spiritual heritage of peoples. Article 53(b) and (c) prohibit the use of such objects in support of the military effort or to make such objects the object of reprisals. The protection laid down in this article is accorded "without prejudice" to the provisions of other relevant international instruments, which include the 1954 Convention and other relevant international instruments. As in the 1954 Hague Convention, not all places of worship are protected; those having "only a local renown or sanctity which does not extend to the whole nation" are outside the protection of both the Convention and the Protocol. Unlike the 1954 Convention, there is no provision for waiver of protection in Article 53, and no provision for derogation for reason of military necessity.[53] However, if the enemy makes improper use of the protected cultural object, it loses its protection.

Article 85 of AP I relate to the repression of breaches and grave breaches of the Protocol. AP I, lists grave breaches of the Protocol. Article 85(4) states that the following shall be regarded as a grave breach when committed wilfully and in violation of the Geneva Convention or AP I: Making the recognised historic monuments, works of art or places of worship which constitute the cultural or spiritual heritage of peoples and to which special protection has been given by special arrangement within the framework of a competent international organisation, the object of attack, causing as a result extensive destruction to it. Further, the said object has been attacked, where there is no evidence of the violation by the adverse Party of Article 53(b) of AP I and when such historic monuments, works of art and places of worship are not located in the immediate proximity of military objectives.

To constitute a grave breach, an attack on a protected object must be committed wilfully, the object must not have been used in the military effort, the object must not have been located near a military objective, and the attack must cause extensive destruction of the object.[54] Additionally, the object must have been given special protection within the framework

53 Black's Law Dictionary states that military necessity is a principle of warfare allowing enough coercive force, subject to the laws of war, to achieve a desired end, if the force used is not more than is called for by the situation. Garner Bryan A., *Black's Law Dictionary*, Tenth Edition, Thomson Reuters, p. 1143.

54 Sandoz Y, et.al., 1987, *Commentary on the Additional Protocols of 8 June 1977*, Geneva: ICRC, pp. 1002-03.

of a competent international organisation.[55] In Article 85.4 of AP I, also there is no provision for waiver of protection or derogation for reason of military necessity.

The prohibition on attacks against cultural property is supported by mandatory precautions in attacks deriving from Article 57, para 2 of AP I and customary international law.[56] It states, "Those who plan or decide upon an attack (the parties to the conflict) shall take all feasible precautions in the choice of means and methods of attack to avoid and in any event minimising, incidental damage to civilian objects (cultural property)." Further, they shall, "Refrain from deciding to launch any attack which may be expected to cause incidental damage to civilian objects, ...which would be excessive about the concrete and direct military advantage anticipated." [57] An attack shall be cancelled or suspended if it becomes apparent that the objective is not a military one or is subject to special protection or that the attack may be expected to cause incidental damage to civilian objects, ..., which would be excessive about the concrete and direct military advantage anticipated."[58]

AP II, dealing with non-international armed conflict provides a measure for the safeguard of cultural property; however, Article 16, repeats verbatim the substantive wording of Article 53 of AP I.[59] The object and purpose of Article 53 AP I and Article 16 AP II was to restate the fundamental obligation of respect laid down in the 1954 Cultural Property Convention. The terms 'historic monuments' and 'works of art' in Article 53 AP I and Article 16 AP II should be seen as shorthand for the full range of

55 The UNESCO Convention Concerning the Protection of World Cultural and Natural Heritage, 1972.

56 Where a state is not party to one or other treaty regulating the protection of cultural property in armed conflict, it remains bound by obligations imposed by the customary international law of armed conflict—that is, by what might loosely be called 'unwritten' rules of international law, developed over time through the maintenance among states of a general practice accepted as law. As it relates to cultural property, the content of this customary international law of armed conflict mirrors the rules largely embodied in treaty form in the 1954 Hague Convention and its two Protocols.

57 Article 57, para 2, a (ii) and (iii) of 1977 Additional Protocol I.

58 Article 57, para 2(b) of 1977 Additional Protocol I.

59 Solis Gary D., 2016, The Law of Armed Conflict: International Humanitarian Law, Cambridge: Cambridge University Press, p. 721.

immovable and movable cultural property referred to in Article 1 of the 1954 Convention.[60]

Conclusion

The 1954 Hague Convention for the Protection of Cultural Property in the Event of Armed Conflict was adopted in 1954 in the wake of the large-scale destruction of cultural heritage carried out during the Second World War. The Hague Convention of 1954 and its Protocol is often referred to, as the first multilateral treaty to focus exclusively on the protection of cultural heritage during hostilities. The 1954 Hague Convention considers all buildings used for religious, scientific, artistic, and charitable purposes, all historical buildings, and every work of art to be a cultural property. The Convention seeks to protect the cultural property of member nations, and effectively establishes a body of internationally recognised cultural property. The Convention divides cultural property into two classes. The first type of cultural property is entitled to the standard protections afforded in prior treaties. A very narrow second class of cultural property, however, is afforded greater protection. Specially protected property is designated by member states and entered into an International Register of Cultural Property.

Since the passage of the 1954 Hague Convention, several other treaties have enhanced the protections afforded cultural property and emphasised the international and human rights foundations of cultural property. In 1966, the United Nations General Assembly adopted the International Covenant on Economic, Social and Cultural Rights. Although the Covenant does not explicitly mention cultural property, it recognises "cultural rights" as intimately tied to human rights. Approaching cultural rights from a different angle, the 1970 Convention on the Means of Prohibiting and Preventing the Illicit Import, Export, and Transfer of Ownership of Cultural Property stems from the flow of stolen goods onto the international art and antiquities market. The Convention requires member states not only to identify and control the export of cultural property but also to prevent the import of illegally obtained goods.

Several armed conflicts that erupted in the 1990s, particularly those in former Yugoslavia, revealed certain gaps in the implementation of the Hague Convention. Due to this reason, the UNESCO Secretariat, along

60 Fleck Dieter (ed.), 2021, *The Handbook of International Humanitarian Law*, Oxford: Oxford University Press, pp. 481-482.

with several interested states, initiated the review of the 1954 Convention in 1991. The result of this was the elaboration and subsequent adoption of the Second Protocol to the Hague Convention at the March 1999 Hague Diplomatic Conference. The Second Protocol of 1999 advances several essential legal, military, and technical aspects of cultural heritage protection and is discussed in the next chapter.

Chapter 5

The 1999 Second Protocol

Introduction

International law concerning the protection of cultural property[1] in the event of armed conflict has continued to develop after the 1954 Hague Convention. The inadequacies of the 1954 Convention were first observed during the 1980 Iran-Iraq War, which wrought considerable destruction to the cultural heritage of Iran. Iraq's invasion and occupation of Kuwait in August 1990 was accompanied by the plunder of Kuwaiti cultural institutions. The 1991 Gulf War and its aftermath shattered the cultural heritage of Iraq. During the 1990s wars in the former Yugoslavia, hundreds of religious and cultural sites were systematically destroyed to eradicate the culture of targeted groups in given areas.

In the twenty-sixth session of the UNESCO General Conference held during October-November 1991, it was noted that the international system to safeguard the world's cultural heritage during armed conflict was inadequate.[2] In his report to the 1992 Executive Board, the Director-General indicated that the 1954 Hague Convention no longer met current requirements, citing slow ratification and unsatisfactory geographical distribution, the small number of entries in the International Register of

1 Cultural property is unique if there is no other comparable cultural property that is of the same cultural significance. The unique character may be deduced from a variety of indicative criteria including age; history; community; representativity; location; size and dimension; shape and design; purity and authenticity in style; integrity; context; artistic craftsmanship; aesthetic value; and scientific value.

2 The UNESCO General Conference, at its 26th Session in 1991, reaffirmed its conviction 'that the preservation of the world cultural and natural heritage is of the utmost importance to all humankind' and called 'on all States to increase their effort [in that area] to achieve better implementation of existing instruments and to reinforce UNESCO's action.' Resolution 26C/3.9, adopted on 6 November 1991.

Cultural Property under Special Protection, cumbersome procedures, a lack of attention to the current state of 'military science', complex procedures for the appointment of Commissioners-General, and weak UNESCO assistance. Three possible courses of action were proposed: (i) review of the 1954 Convention, (ii) adoption of a protocol, and (iii) the undertaking of practical measures. Following an eight-year review of the Hague Convention, initiated by the Secretariat of UNESCO and several interested States, the March 1999 Hague Diplomatic Conference adopted the Second Protocol to the 1954 Hague Convention.[3] It entered into force on March 9, 2004, and has been ratified by 88 states. The Second Protocol is additional and supplementary to the 1954 Hague Convention as indicated in Article 2 of the Protocol. The Hague Convention remains the principal and basic text, and no State can become party to the Second Protocol without already being party to the Hague Convention.[4] The Protocol significantly strengthens the protection of cultural property in times of war. Enhanced protection, a new category of protection for cultural property of national, regional, and universal value and particular importance to humankind has been created. The Second Protocol also specifies the sanctions to be imposed for severe violations concerning cultural property and defines the conditions in which individual criminal responsibility shall apply. It also establishes a twelve-member Intergovernmental Committee to oversee the implementation of the Second Protocol and de facto the Convention. In terms of its scope of application, the Second Protocol applies to both international and non-international armed conflicts, without distinction.[5]

3 During the expert and High Contracting Parties meetings, the review process for the Hague Convention was discussed. Four different possible options were considered: (1) Amending the 1954 Hague Convention; however, any amendments would have required unanimous adoption by all States party to the Convention. Article 39 of the Convention provides the details of such a procedure. Since this was for all practical purposes impossible, this option was abandoned. (2) Adopting a new, separate convention. Such a procedure would have required long and substantial negotiations and have had the disadvantage of creating two separate systems, potentially creating more problems rather than resolving existing ones. This option was not mentioned during the review process, hence rejected. (3) Adopting a protocol aimed at revising the 1954 Convention. Several delegations strongly advocated this option, but because unanimity would again have been required, it was rejected by most delegations. (4) Adopting a new additional protocol, which would in no way amend the 1954 Convention but would supplement it and apply only to the States that ratified it. Toman Jiri, 2009, *Cultural Property in War: Improvement in Protection, Commentary on the 1999 Second Protocol to the Hague Convention*, UNESCO, p. 37.

4 Article 41, para. 1 of the 1999 Second Protocol.

5 O'Keefe Roger, 2006, *The Protection of Cultural Property in Armed Conflict*, Cambridge University Press, p. 241.

Preamble

The Second Protocol to the 1954 Hague Convention, represents a major step forward in the protection of cultural property under international humanitarian law. A short preamble to the Protocol reaffirms the importance of the provisions of the 1954 Hague Convention and asserts the necessity to supplement the provisions through measures to reinforce their implementation. It stresses the need for enhanced protection of cultural property in armed conflict more efficiently. The Preamble affirms that the rules of customary international law will continue to govern questions not regulated by the provisions of the Second Protocol.

Definitions

Article 1 of the Second Protocol defines different expressions used in the Protocol. The term "military objective" means an object which by its nature, location, purpose, or use makes an effective contribution to military action and whose total or partial destruction, capture or neutralisation, in the circumstances ruling at the time, offers a definite military advantage.[6] The term "illicit" means under compulsion or otherwise in violation of the applicable rules of the domestic law of the occupied territory or international law.[7]

Relationship to the 1954 Convention

The relationship between the Second Protocol and the 1954 Convention is stipulated in Article 2, which states that the Protocol 'supplements the Convention in relations between the Parties'.[8] The word "supplements'" in Article 2 signifies that the Protocol does not affect the rights and obligations of the States parties to the Convention. Parties to both the Convention and the Protocol are bound by both, to the extent that their provisions are compatible, in their mutual relations, and Parties to the Convention alone remain bound in their mutual relations only by the Convention, its provisions unaffected. For the States, party to both Convention and

6 Article 1(f), the 1999 Second Protocol. It is based on the definition in Article 52, paragraph 2 of the 1977 Additional Protocol I to the Geneva Conventions.

7 Article 1(g), the 1999 Second Protocol.

8 'Party' is defined in article 1(a) to mean a State Party to the Second Protocol, and articles 40 to 42, cross-referenced with article 1(d), reflect that States Parties to the Second Protocol must also be High Contracting Parties to the Convention.

Protocol and a party to the Convention alone, they are bound in their mutual relations by the Convention alone.[9]

Article 4(b), in a partial exception to the general rule laid down in Article 2, makes special provision for the relationship between chapter 3 of the Protocol, embodying the new special protection for cultural property known as "enhanced protection", and chapter II of the 1954 Convention dealing with special protection. Article 4(b) states that the application of the provisions of chapter 3 of the Protocol is without prejudice to the application of the provisions of chapter II of the Convention, 'save that, as between Parties to the Protocol where cultural property has been granted both special protection and enhanced protection, only the provisions of enhanced protection shall apply.' Article. 4(b) further provides that the rule between Parties to the Protocol also applies between a Party to the Protocol and a state which 'accepts and applies' the Protocol by Article 3(2).[10]

Scope of Application

The Second Protocol applies equally to both international and non-international armed conflicts. Article 3(1) provides that, in addition to the provisions which are to apply in times of peace, the Second Protocol is to apply in the situations referred to in Article 18, paragraphs 1 and 2 of the Convention, namely in the event of declared war or any other armed conflict arising between two or more States parties, even if the state of war is not recognised by one of them, and in all cases of partial or total occupation of the territory of a State party, even if the occupation meets with no armed resistance. Article 3(1) further states that the Protocol shall apply in the situations referred to in Article 22(1) of the Protocol. In turn, Article 22(1) provides that the Protocol shall apply in the event of armed conflict not of an international character occurring within the territory of one of the States Parties.

9 O'Keefe Roger, 2006, *The Protection of Cultural Property in Armed Conflict*, Cambridge University Press, p. 243.

10 In other words, the rest of the Protocol supplements the Convention in relations between the Parties, the regime of enhanced protection under the Protocol replaces the regime of special protection under the Convention between Parties to both Protocol and Convention, but only in cases where the cultural property in question has been granted both special and enhanced protection. Where both states are Parties to the Protocol but the cultural property in question has been granted only special protection by the provisions of article 8 of the Convention, the obligations laid down in chapter II (specifically, articles 9 to 11) of the Convention continue to govern their conduct in respect of that property. O'Keefe Roger, 2006, *The Protection of Cultural Property in Armed Conflict*, Cambridge University Press, p. 243-244.

In a provision lifted directly from Article 3(1) of Additional Protocol II, Article 22(3) of Protocol, which is like Article 3(1) of 1977 APII, provides that nothing in the Second Protocol 'shall be invoked to affect the sovereignty of a State or the responsibility of the government, by all legitimate means, to maintain or re-establish law and order in the State or to defend the national unity and territorial integrity of the State'. Article 22(4) provides that nothing in the Protocol shall prejudice the primary jurisdiction of a Party in whose territory an armed conflict not of an international character occurs over the violations outlined in Article 15. Finally, Article 22(6) makes it clear that the application of the Second Protocol to non-international armed conflicts does not affect the legal status of the parties to the conflict. Article 3, paragraph 2, states, "When one of the parties to an armed conflict is not bound by this Protocol, the Parties to this Protocol shall remain bound by it in their mutual relations. They shall furthermore be bound by this Protocol about a state party to the conflict which is not bound by it if the latter accepts the provisions of this Protocol and so long as it applies them." The acceptance must be in the form of a declaration accompanied by an effective application.[11]

The Safeguarding of Cultural Property in Times of Peace

Chapter 2 of the Second Protocol deals with general provisions regarding protection and supplements chapter I of the 1954 Convention. Article 5 of the Second Protocol gives additional impetus to Article 3 of the Convention. It provides that preparatory measures should be taken in times of peace for the safeguarding of cultural property against the foreseeable effects of an armed conflict pursuant to Article 3 of the Convention. Such non-exhaustive measures include the preparation of inventories, the planning of emergency measures for protection against fire or structural collapse, the preparation for the removal of cultural property or the provision for adequate in situ protection of such property, and the designation of competent authorities responsible for the safeguarding of cultural property. The provision is designed to function as a concise set of operational guidelines for the implementation of the obligation already imposed by Article 3 of the Convention. Given the expenditure and expertise needed to implement Article 5, the fund for the Protection of Cultural Property in the Event of Armed Conflict shall be established pursuant to Article 29

11 Toman Jiri, 2009, *Cultural Property in War: Improvement in Protection, Commentary on the 1999 Second Protocol to the Hague Convention*, UNESCO, p. 67.

of the Second Protocol.[12] The 'Fund' is to be used to provide financial or other assistance in support of preparatory or other measures to be taken in peacetime in accordance with Article 5. A state party may also call on UNESCO for technical assistance in organising preparatory action to safeguard cultural property, by Article 33(1), and Article 33(2) encourages Parties to provide technical assistance either bilaterally or multilaterally.

In practice, the measures listed in Article 5 are not only valuable guidance for States on how to implement Article 5 but are regularly referred to as a yardstick by the Committee established under Article 24 of the Second Protocol when considering requests for enhanced protection. States requesting enhanced protection for cultural property must show, inter alia, how they fulfil the safeguarding measures listed in Article 5 about the property concerned.

Respect for Cultural Property

Article 6 of the Second Protocol on respect for cultural property, is a supplementary provision, related to Article 4 of the Convention. Article 6(a) deals with the waiver of the obligation to refrain from acts of hostility directed against cultural property. It states that a waiver based on imperative military necessity under Article 4(2) of the Convention may be invoked to direct an act of hostility against cultural property only when, and for as long as, two cumulative conditions are met: (i) when and for as long as the cultural property in question 'has, by its function, been made into a

12 A Fund is established under Article 29 of the Second Protocol to provide financial or other assistance to support preparatory or other measures to be taken in peacetime in accordance with Articles 5, 10(b) and 30. It will be in the form of financial or other assistance about emergency, provisional or other measures to be taken to protect cultural property during periods of armed conflict or of immediate recovery after the end of hostilities. The Fund shall constitute a trust fund, in conformity with the provisions of the financial regulations of UNESCO. Disbursements from the Fund shall be used only for such purposes as the Committee shall decide in accordance with the guidelines as defined in Article 23 para 3(c). The Committee may accept contributions to be used only for a certain programme or project, provided that the Committee shall have decided on the implementation of such programme or project. The resources of the Fund shall consist of (a) Voluntary contributions made by the Parties; (b) Contributions, gifts or bequests made by other States; UNESCO or other organizations of the United Nations; other NGOs/ INGOs; and public or private bodies or individuals; (c) Interest accruing on the Fund; (d) Funds raised by collections and receipts from events organized for the benefit of the Fund; and (e) All other resources authorized by the guidelines applicable to the Fund.

military objective';[13] and (ii) when and for as long as there is 'no feasible alternative available to obtain a similar military advantage to that offered by directing an act of hostility against that objective'. Military objectives have been defined under Article 1(f) of the Second Protocol.[14] Article 6(d) of the Second Protocol adds a procedural obligation, providing that, in the event of an attack based on a decision taken by Article 6(a), "an effective advance warning shall be given whenever circumstances enable." The word 'effective' implies both that the warning is successfully transmitted and received and that it is given long enough in advance to enable the opposing party either to cease its use of the cultural property or, to enable the opposing party to come to some other arrangement to obviate an attack on the property.[15]

Article 6(b) of the Second Protocol states that a waiver based on imperative military necessity according to Article 4 (2) of the Convention may be invoked to use cultural property for purposes which are likely to expose it to destruction or damage only when, and for as long as, "no choice is possible between such use of the cultural property and another feasible method for obtaining a similar military advantage." Article 6(c) of the Second Protocol stipulates that the decision to invoke military necessity shall only be taken by an officer commanding a force the equivalent of a battalion in size or larger, or a force smaller in size where circumstances do not permit otherwise. The lack of a universally accepted definition of military necessity leaves room for a loose interpretation of this provision and even its abuse.[16]

An example of the Second Protocol's waiver of enhanced protection that would allow the destruction of cultural property could be an old and

13 By article 6(a)(i), military necessity may be invoked to justify an act of hostility against cultural property only when that property has been made into a military objective necessarily implies that military necessity may never be invoked to justify demolishing such property, since it is only attacks which depend on whether an object is a military objective. O'Keefe Roger, 2006, *The Protection of Cultural Property in Armed Conflict*, Cambridge University Press, p. 255.

14 The term "military objective" means an object which by its nature, location, purpose, or use makes an effective contribution to military action and whose total or partial destruction, capture or neutralisation, in the circumstances ruling at the time, offers a definite military advantage. Article 1(f), the 1999 Second Protocol.

15 O'Keefe Roger, 2006, *The Protection of Cultural Property in Armed Conflict*, Cambridge University Press, p. 256.

16 Hladik Jan, Protection of Cultural Property: Legal Aspects, *International Law Studies*, Vol. 80, pp. 319-329.

historic bridge that is the sole river crossing for an approaching military force. Despite its being recognised as a cultural object, if it is used to block an enemy crossing and there is no alternate crossing site within a feasible distance, it is being used for military purposes, it loses its protection and it may be attacked.[17]

Precautions in Attack

Article 7 of the Second Protocol dealing with precautions in attack imposes four distinct but related obligations.[18] Article 7(a) requires each Party to the conflict to do everything feasible to verify that the objectives to be attacked are not cultural property protected under Article 4 of the Convention. Article 7(b) obliges Parties to the conflict to take all feasible precautions in the choice of means and methods of attack 'to avoid, and in any event to minimise, incidental damage to cultural property protected under Article 4 of the Convention'. Article 7(c) compels Parties to the conflict to 'refrain from deciding to launch any attack which may be expected to cause incidental damage to cultural property protected under Article 4 of the Convention which would be excessive about the concrete and direct military advantage anticipated'. Article 7(d) obliges Parties to the conflict to cancel or suspend an attack in two circumstances: (i) if it becomes apparent that the objective of the attack is cultural property protected under Article 4 of the Convention; and (ii) if it becomes apparent that the attack may be expected to cause incidental damage to cultural property protected under article 4 of the Convention which would be excessive about the concrete and direct military advantage anticipated.

Precautions against the effects of hostilities

The Second Protocol imposes additional obligations to take precautions against the effects of hostilities. Article 8(a), stipulates that the Parties to the conflict shall, to the maximum extent feasible, remove movable cultural property from the vicinity of military objectives or provide for adequate in situ protection. Article 8(b) states that they shall avoid locating military objectives near cultural property.[19] The use of the term 'parties to

17 Solis Gary D., 2016, *The Law of Armed Conflict: International Humanitarian Law*, Cambridge: Cambridge University Press, p. 719.

18 Article 7 of the Second Protocol is based on Article 57 of 1977 Additional Protocol I.

19 Article 8 of the Second Protocol is modelled on Article 58(a) and (b) of 1977 Additional Protocol I.

the conflict' indicates that the obligations it imposes arise only after the outbreak of hostilities.

Protection of Cultural Property in Occupied Territory

An Occupying Power is obliged to prohibit and prevent the illicit transfer of ownership of antiquities, works of art, buildings, archaeological sites, and monuments. Article 9 of the Protocol, like Article 4(3) of the Convention, obliges Parties to prohibit and prevent illicit activities not only when committed by their forces and occupation authorities but also when committed by private persons. The term 'illicit' is defined in Article 1(g) of the Second Protocol to mean 'under compulsion or otherwise in violation of the applicable rules of the domestic law of the occupied territory or international law'.[20]

Article 9 of the Second Protocol supplements Articles 4 and 5 of the 1954 Convention and partly replaces the First Protocol to the 1954 Convention. The wording of Article 9 pursues the aim of ensuring the highest possible standard of protection for cultural property in the occupied territory while, at the same time, not losing sight of the practicability of these provisions, in situations of long-term occupation. Article 9 applies between States parties to the Second Protocol only and only in relation to territory occupied by another State Party. Article 9 paragraph 1 obliges the occupying power to prohibit and prevent any illicit export, other removal, or transfer of ownership of cultural property, any archaeological excavation, save where this is strictly required to safeguard, record, or preserve cultural property, or, any alteration to, or change of use of, cultural property which is intended

20 The applicable rules of international law for article 1(g) comprise, first, the relevant rules of the law of international armed conflict applicable during the belligerent occupation, namely the customary prohibitions on the misappropriation and seizure of private property and of the publicly owned cultural property reflected in articles 46 and 56 respectively of the Hague Rules, as well as the customary ban on pillage recognised in article 47 of the Hague Rules and in article 33 of the Fourth Geneva Convention; the prohibition on any form of theft, pillage or misappropriation of cultural property implicit in article 4(3) of the 1954 Hague Convention, to which Parties to the Second Protocol are perforce also Parties. Where the relevant Parties are also Parties to the First Protocol to the Convention, article 1 of that Protocol, which obliges each Party to prevent the export of cultural property from territory occupied by it. In addition, where the Occupying Power is also a Party to the Convention on the Means of Prohibiting the Illicit Import, Export and Transfer of Ownership of Cultural Property, article 11 provides that the 'export and transfer of ownership of cultural property under compulsion arising directly or indirectly from the occupation of a country by a foreign power shall be regarded as illicit. O'Keefe Roger, 2006, *The Protection of Cultural Property in Armed Conflict*, Cambridge University Press, p. 261.

to conceal or destroy cultural, historical, or scientific evidence. Article 9 paragraph 2 stipulates that any archaeological excavation of, alteration to, or change of use of, cultural property in occupied territory shall, unless circumstances do not permit, be carried out in close cooperation with the competent national authorities of the occupied territory.

Enhanced Protection

Enhanced protection, unlike special protection and inclusion on the World Heritage List, is available for immovable and movable cultural property alike. The procedure by which enhanced protection is granted is designed to be more objective and transparent and is contained in Chapter 3 (Articles 10-14) of the Second Protocol. The conditions of eligibility for enhanced protection as laid down in Article 10 of the Protocol provides that cultural property may be placed under enhanced protection if it meets the following three conditions: (i) it is the cultural heritage of the greatest importance for humanity;[21] (ii) it is protected by adequate domestic legal and administrative measures recognising its exceptional cultural and historic value and ensuring the highest level of protection; and (iii) it is not used for military purposes or to shield military sites and a declaration has been made by the Party which has control over the cultural property, confirming that it will not be so this way. Cultural property under enhanced protection continues to enjoy the benefit of the general provisions regarding protection laid down in the 1954 Convention and the Protocol, except to the extent that the provisions of Chapter 3 are more specific.[22] Article 10 contains no requirement that cultural property under enhanced protection be situated an adequate distance[23] from the nearest military objective.

21 Article 10(a)'s requirement that the cultural property in question constitute 'cultural heritage of the greatest importance to humanity' is stricter than the requirement in Article 8 of the Convention, which speaks of 'very great importance'.

22 Thus, cultural property under enhanced protection is protected not just by Article 12 of the Protocol, as defined by Article 13, but also by Articles 3, 4(3), 4(4), 4(5) and 5 of the Convention and by articles 5, 7, 8 and 9 of the Protocol. It also means that it is protected by article 4(1) of the Convention to the extent that the expression 'act of hostility' used in that provision is more compendious than the term 'attack' used in articles 12 and 13 of the Protocol. O'Keefe Roger, 2006, *The Protection of Cultural Property in Armed Conflict*, Cambridge University Press, p. 264.

23 The term "adequate distance" is not defined by the Convention and is therefore left to the discretion of each state party to the Convention. Hladik Jan, Protection of Cultural Property: Legal Aspects, *International Law Studies*, Vol. 80, p. 325.

Granting of Enhanced Protection

The procedure for the granting of enhanced protection is regulated by Article 11 of the Second Protocol. This provision is linked to articles 25 to 27 of the Second Protocol, under an Intergovernmental Committee for the Protection of Cultural Property in the Event of Armed Conflict is established, The Committee, consisting of 12 members, has two main functions: (i) to grant, suspend or cancel enhanced protection for cultural property and to establish, maintain and promote the List of Cultural Property under Enhanced Protection; and (ii) to promote the identification of cultural property under enhanced protection.[24]

For granting enhanced protection each Party to the Second Protocol should submit to the Committee a list of cultural property for which it intends to request the granting of enhanced protection.[25] The State Party which has jurisdiction or control over the cultural property may request that it be included in the List to be established by Article 27 1(b). This request shall include all necessary information related to the criteria mentioned in Article 10. The Committee may invite a Party to request that cultural property be included in the List.[26] Article 11(2)'s reference to 'control' implies that an Occupying Power is authorised to request the inclusion of cultural property located in the territory it occupies. Article 11(s) authorises other Parties, the International Committee of the Blue

24 The Committee is the intergovernmental executive body entitled by the Second Protocol to perform, in co-operation with the Director-General, the following functions: (i) to develop Guidelines for the implementation of the Second Protocol; (ii) to grant, suspend or cancel enhanced protection for cultural property and to establish, maintain and promote the List; (iii) to monitor and supervise the implementation of the Second Protocol and to promote the identification of cultural property under enhanced protection; (iv) to consider and comment on reports of the Parties, to seek clarifications as required, and to prepare its report on the implementation of the Second Protocol for the Meeting of the Parties; (v) to receive and consider requests for international assistance from Parties as provided by the Second Protocol; (vi) to determine the use of the Fund; and, (vii) to execute other functions assigned to it by the Meeting of the Parties. Guidelines for the Implementation of the 1999 Second Protocol to the Hague Convention of 1954 for the Protection of Cultural Property in the Event of Armed Conflict; Endorsed by the third Meeting of the Parties to the Second Protocol to the Hague Convention of 1954 for the Protection of Cultural Property in the Event of Armed Conflict, UNESCO Headquarters, November 24, 2009, para 19.

25 Article 11(1), the 1999 Second Protocol.

26 Article 11(2), the 1999 Second Protocol. The List referred to is the International List of Cultural Property under Enhanced Protection as defined under Article 1(h) of the Second Protocol.

Shield and other INGOs with 'relevant expertise' to recommend specific cultural property to the Committee. In such cases, the Committee may decide to invite a Party to request inclusion of that cultural property in the List.[27] Article 11(4) clarifies: "Neither the request for inclusion of cultural property situated in a territory, sovereignty, or jurisdiction over which is claimed by more than one State, nor its inclusion, shall in any way prejudice the rights of the parties to the dispute.

By Article 11(5), the Committee is to inform all the Parties of the receipt of a request for inclusion in the List. The Parties may submit representations regarding such a request to the Committee within 60 days. These representations shall be made only based on the criteria mentioned in Article 10. They shall be specific and related to facts. The Committee shall consider the representations, providing the Party requesting inclusion with a reasonable opportunity to respond before taking the decision. When such representations are before the Committee, decisions for inclusion in the List shall be taken, notwithstanding Article 26, by most four-fifths of its members present and voting. Article 11(6) states that, when deciding upon a request, the Committee should ask for the advice of the government and NGOs, as well as of individual experts. Article 11(7) makes it clear that decisions to grant or deny enhanced protection may be made only based on the criteria in Article 10.

Article 11(8) provides for an extraordinary procedure. In exceptional cases, when the Committee has concluded that the Party requesting inclusion of cultural property in the List cannot fulfil the criteria of Article 10 (b), it may decide to grant enhanced protection, provided that the requesting Party submits a request for international assistance under Article 32.[28] Another exceptional measure in the event of armed conflict is contained in Article 11(9). It provides that on the outbreak of hostilities, a Party involved in the conflict may, on an emergency basis, communicate to the Committee a request for enhanced protection for cultural property under

27 Article 11(3), the 1999 Second Protocol.

28 Article 11(8), the 1999 Second Protocol. In other words, a Party's lack of the technical or financial expertise to put in place adequate domestic legal and administrative measures recognising the exceptional cultural value of the cultural property in question and ensuring the highest level of protection for it is not necessarily a bar to the inclusion of that property on the List. However, the Party in question may ask for assistance from the Committee under Article 32(1). O'Keefe Roger, 2006, *The Protection of Cultural Property in Armed Conflict*, Cambridge University Press, p. 271.

its jurisdiction or control. The Committee is bound to transmit any such request to 'all the Parties to the conflict' and is to consider representations from the Parties concerned on an expedited basis. It is required to take its decision as soon as possible and must do so by most four-fifths of its members present and voting. The Committee may grant provisional enhanced protection pending the outcome of the regular procedure for the granting of enhanced protection, provided that the provisions of Article 10 (a) and (c) are met. Enhanced protection shall be granted to cultural property by the Committee from the moment of its entry into the List, and the Director-General is required to send to the Secretary-General of the UN and to all Parties notification of any decision of the Committee to include cultural property on the List.[29]

Immunity of Cultural Property and Its Loss

Articles 12 and 13 of the Second Protocol provide the basic rule as to the immunity of cultural property under enhanced protection, the latter the circumstances in which this immunity is lost. Article 12 provides that the Parties to the conflict shall ensure the immunity of cultural property under enhanced protection by refraining from making such property the object of attack or from any use of the property or its immediate surroundings in 'support of military action.'[30]

Article 13(1) specifies the two circumstances in which cultural property under enhanced protection can lose such protection: (a) if such protection is suspended or cancelled by Article 14; or (b) if, and for as long as, the property has, by its use, become a military objective.[31] Article 14(1) states that, where cultural property no longer meets any one of the three criteria specified in Article 10, the Committee may suspend its enhanced

29 Article 11(10) and (11), the 1999 Second Protocol.

30 The concept of 'military action', referring to military operations, is more restrictive than the notion of 'the military effort', which is a very broad concept, encompassing all military activities connected with the conduct of war, with the result that the protection granted by article 12 against military use, is possibly narrower than that provided by articles 53 and 16 of the 1977 Additional Protocols I and II respectively. O'Keefe Roger, 2006, *The Protection of Cultural Property in Armed Conflict*, Cambridge University Press, p. 272.

31 In brief, cultural property loses its enhanced protection under any of the three conditions: (i) the enhanced protection is suspended by the Committee; (ii) the enhanced protection is cancelled by the Committee; or (iii) the cultural property has become, by its use, a military objective.

protection status or cancel that status[32] by removing that cultural property from the List. Under Article 14(2), the Committee may further suspend cultural property's enhanced protection in the event of a serious violation of Article 12 arising from its use in support of military action, and may exceptionally cancel enhanced protection by removing cultural property from the List in cases where such violations are continuous. The suspension is a provisional measure which does not result in a permanent loss of the enhanced protection but in an interruption of the protection when the criteria for granting it are no longer met. When the criteria are met again, the Committee will decide whether to resume the enhanced protection. Before taking such a decision, the Committee shall allow the Parties to make their views known.[33]

Article 13(2), specifies three cumulative conditions when a cultural property becomes a military object of attack as mentioned in Article 13(1)(b): (i) the attack is the only feasible means of terminating the use of the property; (ii) all feasible precautions are taken in the choice of means and methods of attack, to terminate such use and avoid, or in any event minimising, damage to the cultural property; and (iii) unless circumstances do not permit, due to requirements of immediate self-defence, the attack is ordered at the highest operational level of command.[34] Effective warning must be issued to the opposing forces requiring the termination of the use of the referred property, and reasonable time must be given to the opposing forces to redress the situation.[35]

---

32 Cancellation is a definitive measure. It leads to the permanent loss of the enhanced protection. The Committee may cancel enhanced protection under two conditions: (i) the cultural property no longer meets any of the criteria laid down in Article 10; or, (ii) there is a continuous and serious violation of Article 12 about cultural property under enhanced protection arising from its use in support of military action. Since cancellation is a definitive measure, the Committee may only cancel the enhanced protection if the criteria laid down in Article 10, which are no longer met, cannot be fulfilled later. The Committee may exceptionally cancel the enhanced protection if the cultural property is continuously used in support of military action. The condition of "continuity" is met if the use exceeds six months and if there is no evidence that such use will end. Guidelines for the Implementation of the 1999 Second Protocol to the Hague Convention of 1954 for the Protection of Cultural Property in the Event of Armed Conflict; Endorsed by the third Meeting of the Parties to the Second Protocol to the Hague Convention of 1954 for the Protection of Cultural Property in the Event of Armed Conflict, UNESCO Headquarters, November 24, 2009, para 86-88.

33 Article 14(4), the 1999 Second Protocol.

34 The highest operational level of command means the highest level of military command.

35 Article 13(2)(c)(ii) and (iii), the 1999 Second Protocol.

Criminal Responsibility

The states party to the Second Protocol must ensure that the following are offences under domestic law:[36]

1. Making cultural property under enhanced protection the object of attack;
2. Using cultural property under enhanced protection or its immediate surroundings in support of military action;
3. Extensive destruction or appropriation of protected cultural property;[37]
4. Making protected cultural property the object of attack; and
5. Theft, pillage, or misappropriation of, or acts of vandalism directed against protected cultural property.

These five offences within the meaning of the Second Protocol, are known collectively as serious violations of the Protocol. The first two acts mentioned above relate solely to cultural property under enhanced protection. Each Party must ensure that it adopts such measures as may be necessary to establish offences outlined in Article 15(1) as criminal offences under its domestic law punishable by appropriate penalties.[38] Three of the five violations are grave breaches of either the Geneva Conventions or Additional Protocol I; the other two are war crimes under the Rome Statute of the International Criminal Court.[39]

36 Article 15, the 1999 Second Protocol.

37 Negligently inflicting incidental damage to cultural property covered by Article 15(1)(c) is not a serious violation of the Protocol. The requirement that, for it to amount to a war crime, incidental damage to cultural property must be 'extensive. O'Keefe Roger, 2006, *The Protection of Cultural Property in Armed Conflict*, Cambridge University Press, p. 279.

38 France has modified its Criminal Procedure Law in 2018 by adding a new law on military planning. Article 689-14 specifies: "… any person who usually resides on the territory of the Republic and is guilty of the offence of attacks against the cultural property specified in points (a) to (c) of Article 15, paragraph 1 of the 1999 Second Protocol may be prosecuted and sentenced under the conditions specified in Article 689-1. The prosecution of any such offences may only be performed at the request of the public ministry." According to Article 689-1, this involves any persons who are guilty outside of the Republic of one of the offences listed in these Articles.

39 Solis Gary D., 2016, *The Law of Armed Conflict: International Humanitarian Law*, Cambridge: Cambridge University Press, p. 719.

The second sentence of Article 15(2) states that when adopting the measures required by the first sentence of the provision, Parties are to comply with 'general principles of law and international law, including the rules extending individual criminal responsibility to persons other than those who directly commit the act'. International law also embodies criminal responsibility where; to facilitate the commission of an offence, a person aids, abets, or otherwise assists in its commission or attempted commission, including providing the means for its commission.[40] Further, international law under Article 28 of the Rome Statute, also recognises secondary criminal responsibility in the form of command and superior responsibility.

The State Party must take necessary legislative measures to establish its jurisdiction over offences included in Article 15 in the following cases: (i) when such an offence is committed in the territory of that State; (ii) when the alleged offender is a national of that State; and (iii) in the case of offences outlined in Article 15 (a) to (c), when the alleged offender is present in its territory.[41] Article 16(2)(a) provides, "Concerning the exercise of jurisdiction and without prejudice to Article 28 of the Convention, the Second Protocol does not preclude the incurring of individual criminal responsibility or the exercise of jurisdiction under national and international law that may be applicable, or affect the exercise of jurisdiction under customary international law." Article 16(2), provides that, "except in so far as a State which is not Party to this Protocol may accept and apply its provisions in accordance with Article 3(2), members of the armed forces and nationals of a State which is not Party to this Protocol, except for those nationals serving in the armed forces of a State which is Party to this Protocol, do not incur individual criminal responsibility by this Protocol, nor does this Protocol impose an obligation to establish jurisdiction over such persons or to extradite them."

Under Article 17(1) of the Second Protocol, the Party in whose territory the alleged offender, who has committed serious violations embodied in Article 15(1) (a) to (c), is found to be present, the Party if does not extradite that person, it must submit the case to its competent authorities for prosecution, without undue delay. The proceedings for the prosecution must be held in accordance with its domestic law or if applicable, the relevant rules of international law. This obligation on the Parties is if they do not extradite the suspect, they must submit the case to their prosecuting

40 Article 25(3)(c), The Rome Statute of International Criminal Court.

41 Article 16(1), the 1999 Second Protocol.

authorities for prosecution. Article 17(2) embodies fundamental procedural safeguards for alleged offenders. It stipulates that any person against whom proceedings are being carried out in connection with the Convention or the Second Protocol shall be guaranteed fair treatment and a fair trial in accordance with domestic law and international law at all stages of the proceedings. In any case, these guarantees shall not be less favourable to such person than those provided by international law. These guarantees are not restricted to prosecution but also apply to extradition proceedings.[42]

The offences included in Article 15 (1) (a) to (c) are extraditable in any extradition treaty existing between any of the Parties before the entry into force of this Protocol. Article 18 of the Second Protocol contains several technical provisions relevant to extradition. Article 19 deals with mutual legal assistance. The state parties are to afford one another the greatest measure of assistance in connection with investigations or criminal or extradition proceedings brought in respect of the offences stated in Article 15, including assistance in obtaining evidence necessary for the proceedings. Article 20 clarifies that for extradition, offences under Article 15 (a) to (c), shall not be regarded as political offences. A request for extradition or mutual legal assistance based on such offences may not be refused on the sole ground that it concerns a political offence an offence connected with a political offence or an offence inspired by political motives.

Other Violations

According to Article 21, the State Party shall adopt necessary legislative, administrative or disciplinary measures to suppress the following acts when committed intentionally: (i) any use of cultural property in violation of the 1954 Convention or Second Protocol; and (ii) any illicit export, other removal, or transfer of ownership of cultural property from occupied territory in violation of the 1954 Convention or Second Protocol. This obligation laid down in Article 21 is declared to be without prejudice to Article 28 of the Convention.

Non-International Armed Conflict

The protection of cultural property in non-international armed conflicts is governed by Article 22 of the Second Protocol. The Protocol shall not apply to situations of internal disturbances and tensions, such as riots, isolated and sporadic acts of violence and other acts of a similar nature. The Second

42 O'Keefe Roger, 2006, *The Protection of Cultural Property in Armed Conflict*, Cambridge University Press, p. 286.

Protocol shall not prejudice the primary jurisdiction of a Party in whose territory a non-international armed conflict occurs over the violations stated in Article 15. UNESCO may offer its services to the parties to the conflict.

National Implementation and Dissemination

The 1999 Second Protocol includes numerous provisions requiring state parties to put in place measures to strengthen the protection of cultural property in peacetime, as well as in the event of armed conflicts. These include, among others, preparatory measures – the preparation of inventories; the planning of emergency measures for protection against fire or structural collapse; the preparation for the removal of movable cultural property or the provision for adequate in situ protection of such property, and the designation of competent authorities responsible for the safeguarding of cultural property against the foreseeable effects of an armed conflict, legislative measures related to the individual criminal responsibility and jurisdiction, as well as capacity-building initiatives to improve the implementation of the 1954 Hague Convention and its Protocols.

The state parties are to disseminate the contents of the Second Protocol as widely as possible, both in times of peace and in times of armed conflict. The military or civilian authorities who, in times of armed conflict, may assume responsibilities concerning the application of the Protocol, must be fully acquainted with the text of the Protocol. In particular, the state parties must take following actions: (i) incorporate guidelines and instructions on the protection of cultural property in their military regulations; (ii) develop and implement, in cooperation with UNESCO and relevant governmental and non-governmental organisations, peacetime training and educational programmes; (iii) communicate to one another, through the Director-General, information on the laws, administrative provisions and measures taken by them; (iv) communicate to one another through the Director-General, the laws and administrative provisions which they may adopt to ensure the application of this Protocol.[43] A Party may call upon UNESCO for technical assistance in organising the protection of its cultural property, such as preparatory action to safeguard cultural property, preventive and organisational measures for emergencies and compilation of national

43 Article 30, the 1999 Second Protocol.

inventories of cultural property, or in connection with any other problem arising out of the application of the Second Protocol.[44]

The Blue Shield

The 1999 Hague Convention Second Protocol identifies the Blue Shield as an advisory body to UNESCO on the protection of cultural property. Created in 1996, the Blue Shield is an international NGO working to protect cultural property in the event of armed conflict and natural disaster. Its work is focused primarily on the 1954 Hague Convention and its Protocols but sits within the wider context of UN Security Council Resolutions and UNESCO's strategic agenda. The Blue Shield sits at the intersection of the heritage community and the armed forces, bringing the expertise of one to support and enrich the decision making of the other.[45] The Blue Shield believes strongly that our work will be more effective if adequate preparations for conflicts and disasters are made in peacetime. The key areas in which the Blue Shield operates are:

- Preparation and training for those preventing, mitigating, or responding to tangible and intangible cultural heritage damage during conflict and disasters;
- Protection of tangible and intangible cultural property during armed conflict (according to the principles of the 1954 Hague Convention for the Protection of Cultural Property in the Event of Armed Conflict);
- Offering support and assistance after conflict when armed forces may still be deployed;
- Situations that do not meet the criteria for an official armed conflict, but where heritage destruction may still be occurring;
- Environmental disasters (whether natural or man-made), as many of the organisations involved in reacting to natural and human-

44 Article 33, the 1999 Second Protocol.

45 The Blue Shield, a voluntary organisation has nearly 30 national committees, overseen by the Blue Shield International Board (BSI), and has divided its work into six areas of activity: policy development; proactive protection and risk preparedness; education, training, and capacity building; supporting emergency response and armed conflict activity; post-disaster recovery and long-term support; underpinned by coordination, all aimed at the protection of Cultural Property. For more details see: https://theblueshield.org/.

made environmental disasters are the same as those involved in armed conflict;

- Prevention of the illicit trafficking that follows the increased looting seen during and after armed conflicts and disasters, as emergency situations often create the conditions that allow increased looting, and illicit trafficking of objects: the Blue Shield also works in partnership with organisations like ICOM to stop illicit trafficking of cultural property.

Conclusion

The 1999 Second Protocol, in addition to the provisions which are to be implemented in time of peace, applies: (i) In the event of declared war or of any other armed conflict which may arise between two or more of the Parties, even if the state of war is not recognised by one or more of them; (ii) To all cases of partial or total occupation of the territory of a Party, even if the said occupation meets with no armed resistance; and (iii) In the event of an armed conflict not of an international character, occurring within the territory of one of the Parties. The Second Protocol creates a new category of protection, "Enhanced Protection," which in addition to the basic Convention's "special protection" and supplements the Convention by reinforcing the provisions related to the safeguarding of and respect for cultural property in the event of armed conflict. The Second Protocol represents a considerable advance on the level of protection in the Convention in the following respects: (i) it provides for conditions in which the notion of "military necessity" may be applied, thus preventing possible extensive interpretations or abuses; (ii) it creates a new category of enhanced protection for cultural heritage of the greatest importance for humanity which is protected by relevant national legislation and is not used for military purposes; and (iii) it elaborates sanctions for serious violations against cultural property and defines conditions when individual criminal responsibility is applicable. In addition, a further important advance is the establishment of a twelve-member Intergovernmental Committee, which will have functions related to the implementation of the Second Protocol.

The Second Protocol took an important step in addressing the difficulties posed by the "military necessity" doctrine. The adoption of the Second Protocol undoubtedly enhanced the legal framework governing the protection of cultural property. Notwithstanding, certain challenges persist and new challenges have emerged. Unfortunately, in the last 25 years since the adoption of the Second Protocol, we have witnessed many examples of use that exposed cultural property to attacks and consequently destruction and damage, for instance, during the battles in the town of Iraq, Syria, Mali, Ukraine, and Palestine where historic monuments were used in support of military action, thereby rendering them military objects. It, therefore, remains a serious concern. The 1977 Second Protocol has been ratified by 88 states so far. India has neither signed nor ratified the Second Protocol.

Chapter 6

Protection of Cultural Property under International Criminal Law

The Rome Statute of the International Criminal Court (ICC), adopted in July 1998, heralded a new era in the fight against the most serious crimes of concern to the international community. The preamble of the Rome Statute establishes the purpose of the ICC. It states: "Affirming that the most serious crimes of concern to the international community as a whole must not go unpunished and … to put an end to impunity for the perpetrators of these crimes … for the sake of present and future generations, … to guarantee lasting respect for and the enforcement of international justice." The Rome Statute is unique in many ways. It has created a permanent tribunal, the ICC, to deal with all crimes of serious concern to the international community. The ICC's jurisdiction and mandate are not limited to specific events in specific places, or to any specified time-frame. Its powers and functions include holding individuals accountable and subjecting the accused to investigation, arrest, detention, prosecution and if found guilty, incarceration. The Rome Statute creates obligations on the part of the State parties to provide the means to enforce these powers.

The ICC was founded on the recognition "that all peoples are united by common bonds, their cultures pieced together in a shared heritage and concern", and "that this delicate mosaic may be shattered at any time." The Rome Statute confers upon the Court jurisdiction over crimes against or affecting cultural heritage, complementing international law governing the protection of cultural heritage and associated human rights.[1] The concern

1 See The 1977 Additional Protocol I, article 53; the 1977 Additional Protocol II, article 6; the 1954 Convention for the Protection of Cultural Property in the Event of Armed Conflict with Regulations for the Execution of the Convention, Article 4; and the 1999 Second Protocol to the Hague Convention of 1954, article 15.

for the protection of cultural heritage expressed in these international instruments has proven well founded: crimes against and affecting cultural heritage are a pervasive feature of the atrocities within the jurisdiction of the ICC.

The ICC has jurisdiction to prosecute four categories under international law: (i) genocide, or the intent to destroy in whole or in part a national, ethnic, racial, or religious group; (ii) crimes against humanity, or violations committed as part of large-scale attacks against civilian populations, including murder, rape, imprisonment, slavery, and torture; (iii) war crimes, or grave breaches of the laws of war, which include the Geneva Conventions' prohibitions on torture, the use of child soldiers, and attacks on civilian targets, such as hospitals or historical monuments which are not military objectives; and (iv) crimes of aggression, or the use or threat of armed force by a state against the territorial integrity, sovereignty, or political independence of another state, or violations of the UN Charter.[2] These crimes are of recent origin and their recognition and subsequent development are closely associated with the human rights movements after World War II. Additionally, these crimes must be committed by the nationals of a State Party to the Rome Statute, committed in the territory of a State Party to the Rome Statute, or committed in the territory of a State not party to the Rome Statute that has accepted the ICC's jurisdiction. [3]

The two provisions of the ICC that are most directly applicable to attacks on cultural heritage are the war crimes set out in articles 8(2)(b)(ix) and 8(2)(e)(iv), which apply to international and non-international armed conflicts respectively. Among other objects, they proscribe intentionally directing attacks in armed conflict against certain types of buildings and monuments which fall within the (broader) definition of "cultural

2 Rome Statute of the International Criminal Court, 1998, Article 5-8.

3 Individual criminal responsibility for the deliberate destruction of cultural property in the event of armed conflicts has long been recognized under international law. From the 1907 Hague Regulations to the 1977 Additional Protocols to the Geneva Conventions, the 1954 Hague Convention as well as the Statutes of both the International Criminal Tribunal for the former Yugoslavia (ICTY), unjustified endangering or destruction of cultural property in time of armed conflict has been recognized as a serious violation of international humanitarian law and has now acquired the status of a customary norm. The 1999 Second Protocol represents the most comprehensive international instrument in this field, to this list of legal instruments to deter and impose sanctions on crimes against cultural property, has been substantial. Not only has it further clarified those acts which constitute serious violations requiring a criminal sanction if committed intentionally, but it has also strengthened the way States can arrive at effective national enforcement.

property." However, since "cultural property" itself only touches on the tangible aspects of human culture, these provisions still reflect only part of the protection which may be afforded by the crimes in the Rome Statute to cultural heritage. Indeed, attacks against or affecting cultural heritage may constitute or relate to numerous other crimes under the Statute. The term "cultural heritage" thus more properly reflects the rich corpus of human achievement that the Statute and international law seek to protect.

The Trial of Mr Ahmad Al Faqi Mahdi

On December 17, 2015, Mr. Ahmad Al Faqi Al Mahdi was charged by the ICC [ICC-01/12-01/15] for the intentional direction of attacks against ten buildings of a religious and historical character in Timbuktu, Mali, between June 30, 2012 and July 11, 2012. The case against Ahmad Al Faqi Al Mahdi before the ICC is the first, and the only one that has revolved exclusively around the war crime of intentionally directing attacks against religious and historic buildings under Article 8(2)(e)(iv) of the Rome Statute. This case is discussed in greater detail as follows.

The Accused

Ahmad Al Faqi Al Mahdi, also known as Abou Tourab, was a member of the radical Islamic group Ansar Eddine, a Malian armed jihadist group linked to al-Qaeda in the Islamic Maghreb (AQIM). Al Mahdi served as head of the Islamic Police in Timbuktu (Mali) and was one of the four commanders of Ansar Eddine during its brutal occupation of Timbuktu in 2012.[4] A Tuareg armed rebellion erupted in the north of Mali in January 2012, when the so-called National Liberation Movement of Azawad launched an offensive. Other Islamist groups present in the geographic area, including Ansar Eddine, quickly joined the offensive. Various hostilities took place during this time, most in flagrant violation of international humanitarian law (IHL).

4 Mali is, after Niger, the largest country in West Africa. Divided into ten regions; the five regions of the north, Gao, Kidal, Timbuktu, Menaka and Taodudeni represent two-thirds of the surface of the country but only ten per cent of its approximately 18 million inhabitants. The country currently ranks 177 out of 186 on the 2014 Human Development Index. Factors affecting the environmental, economic, social, and political context include limited economic growth and a highly undiversified economy, limited mainly to agriculture (75% of the population) and extractive industries, vulnerability to commodity price fluctuations, high population growth rates, and impact of climate change, among others.

Several northern cities were captured by the rebelling groups from early April 2012 until January 2013, when French and Malian troops intervened to suppress the rebellion. Between June 2012 and July 2012, Timbuktu came under the control of Ansar Eddine and another Islamist group. During this time, Al Mahdi worked closely with the leaders of all the armed groups in the area, and, according to the allegations asserted against Al Mahdi, played an active role in the occupation of Timbuktu.[5]

The ICC indicted Al Mahdi on several charges of war crimes, specifically intentional attacks against ten religious and historic buildings and monuments. Article 8.2(e)(iv) of the Rome Statute of the ICC provides that war crimes include "intentionally directing attacks against buildings dedicated to religion, education, art, science or charitable purposes, historic monuments, hospitals and places where the sick and wounded are collected, provided they are not military objectives." Article 8.2(e)(iv) constitutes lex specials to other provisions proscribing the destruction of civilian property. According to the Elements of Crime, five conditions must be met, for an individual to be held accountable for the destruction of cultural property in an armed conflict. To prove the crime charged, it must be proven that:

1. The perpetrator directed an attack.
2. The object of the attack was one or more buildings dedicated to religion, education, art, science or charitable purposes, historic monuments, hospitals, or places where the sick and wounded are collected, which were not military objectives.
3. The perpetrator intended such buildings or buildings dedicated to religion, education, art, science or charitable purposes, historic monuments, hospitals, or places where the sick and wounded are collected, which were not military objectives, to be the object of the attack.
4. The conduct took place in the context of and was associated with an armed conflict, not of an international character.
5. The perpetrator was aware of factual circumstances that established the existence of an armed conflict.[6]

5 Stereo Milena, Individual Criminal Responsibility for the Destruction of Religious and Historic Buildings: The Al Mahdi Case, *Case Western Reserve Journal of International Law*, Vol. 63, 2017, pp. 63-73.

6 The Rome Statute, Elements of Crimes, Article 8(2)(e)(iv).

Article 8.2(e)(iv) criminalizes the act of directing a specific kind of attack irrespective of whether the buildings in question are destroyed. All the buildings which Al Mahdi was charged with attacking had been under UNESCO protection, and most had been listed as World Heritage sites.

Facts of the Case

In January 2012, a non-international armed conflict took place in the territory of Mali. In the context of and about that conflict, armed violence took place and led to different armed groups taking control of the north of the country. In early April 2012, following the retreat of Malian armed forces, the groups Ansar Dine and Al-Qaeda in the Islamic Maghreb (AQIM) took control of Timbuktu. From then until January 2013, Ansar Dine and AQIM imposed their religious and political edicts on the territory of Timbuktu and its people. They did so through a local government, which included an Islamic tribunal, an Islamic police force, a media commission and a morality brigade called the *Hesbah*. Mr Al Mahdi was viewed as an expert on matters of religion and was consulted in this capacity, including by the Islamic tribunal. Mr Al Mahdi was very active in aspects of the Ansar Dine and AQIM administration. He led the *Hesbah* from its creation in April 2012 until September 2012 and wrote a document on its role and objectives.

In late June 2012, the leader of Ansar Dine – Iyad Ag Ghaly – decided to destroy the mausoleums, in consultation with two prominent AQIM members – Abdallah Al Chinguetti and Yahia Abou Al Hamman. Mr Al Mahdi was also consulted by the governor of Timbuktu, Abou Zeid, before this decision was made and expressed his opinion that all Islamic jurists agree on the prohibition of any construction over a tomb, but recommended not destroying the mausoleums to maintain relations between the population and the occupying groups. Nevertheless, Ag Ghaly instructed to proceed to Abou Zeid, who in turn transmitted it to Mr Al Mahdi in his capacity as the chief of the *Hesbah*. Despite his initial reservations, Mr Al Mahdi agreed to conduct the attack without hesitation on receipt of the instruction. Mr Al Mahdi wrote a sermon dedicated to the destruction of the mausoleums, which was read at the Friday prayer at the launch of the attack. He determined the sequence in which the buildings were to be attacked. Al Mahdi also communicated news of the destruction of these sites to journalists. During one such press interview during the attack, Mr Al Mahdi said the following:

> I do not know the truth about those saints. We just know that fools [...] come and take sand from those places to get blessed [...]. That is why we consider this campaign as an effort that is exerted in collaboration with the imams [...] We only paid attention to the buildings constructed above the graves in the cemetery and the tombs that are annexed to the mosques from the outside. [...] As for demolishing these buildings, [...] we think that we have already introduced this matter gradually, as we have spent four months explaining to the people what is right and what is wrong, and now is the time for implementation.[7]

The attack itself was carried out between around June 30, 2012 and July 11, 2012. Ten of the most important and well-known sites in Timbuktu were attacked and destroyed by Mr Al Mahdi and other individuals. All these sites were dedicated to religion and historic monuments and were not military objectives.

Referral of the Case

The Malian government itself referred the situation in Mali to the ICC in 2012. The Office of the Prosecutor (OTP) then opened an official investigation into alleged crimes committed in Mali in January 2013, and in February 2013, the Malian government and the ICC signed a cooperation agreement in accordance with Section IX of the Rome Statute. Al Mahdi was detained in a prison in Niger. On September 18, 2015, the ICC Pre-Trial Chamber I issued an arrest warrant against Al Mahdi and sent representatives to meet with Niger government officials. On September 26, 2015, he was transferred to the ICC detention facility at The Hague by authorities of the government of Niger.[8]

On March 24, 2016, charges against Al Mahdi, consisting of war crimes constituted by attacks against religious and cultural sites, were confirmed by Pre-Trial Chamber I. In addition to the ICC's charges against Al Mahdi, human rights groups accused Al Mahdi of other crimes, and have encouraged the OTP to consider credible allegations of Al Mahdi's

7 See case details at ICC website: No. ICC-01/12-01/15, Date: September 27, 2016.

8 On September 18, 2015, the Single Judge of Pre-Trial Chamber I issued a warrant for Mr Ahmad Al Faqi Al Mahdi's arrest. Mr Al Mahdi was transferred to The Hague on September 26, 2015, and his first appearance took place on September 30, 2015. On December 17, 2015, the Office of the Prosecutor ('Prosecution') filed its document containing the charge. It contained a single charge alleging that Mr Al Mahdi is responsible for the war crime of attacking protected objects under Article 8.2(e)(iv) of the Statute.

involvement in crimes committed against civilians, including rape, sexual slavery, and forced marriage. Al Mahdi indicated that he would plead guilty on March 1, 2016; his trial opened on August 22 and concluded within a single week. The court sentenced Al Mahdi on September 27, 2016.

Background

Ahmad Al Faqi Al Mahdi was a member of Ansar Dine, a movement associated with AQIM, and had worked closely with the leaders of the two-armed groups in the context of the structures and institutions they established. Until September 2012, he was the head of the *Hesbah* (a body set up in April 2012 to uphold virtue and prevent vice). He was also associated with the work of the Islamic tribunal of Timbuktu and was involved in executing its decisions. The warrant of arrest against him was issued by ICC Pre-Trial Chamber I on September 18, 2015 and he was surrendered to the ICC on September 26, 2015.

Al Mahdi's role

The ICC Trial Chamber found that Mr Al Mahdi knew that he exercised joint control over the attack and was fully implicated in its execution. He was the head of the *Hesbah*, one of four primary institutions established by Ansar Dine and AQIM upon occupying Timbuktu. He had overall responsibility for the execution phase of the attack, supervising the execution of the operations, using the *Hesba*'s members and determining the sequence in which the buildings would be destroyed, making the necessary logistical arrangements, and justifying the attack to the broader world through media interviews. Al Mahdi supervised the destruction, collected, brought, and distributed the necessary tools, personally participated in the destruction of at least five sites and justified the attack before the media. As the head of the *Hesbah* and an expert on religious matters, he played a key role in the destruction. He also was present at all the attack sites, giving instructions and moral support, and he participated in the attack that led to the destruction of at least five sites.

Admission of guilt

On August 22, 2016, at the opening of the trial, Mr Al Mahdi admitted guilty to the war crime consisting of attacking 10 historic and religious monuments in Timbuktu, Mali, between around June 30, 2012 and July 11, 2012. In its Judgment, the Chamber was satisfied that the Accused understands the nature and consequences of the admission of guilt and that his admission was voluntarily made after sufficient consultation with defence counsel and is supported by the facts of the case.

The Trial Chamber thought that an admission of guilt is undoubtedly a mitigating circumstance and gives it substantial weight. In this regard, the Chamber noted that the admission was made early, fully and appears to be genuine, led by the real desire to take responsibility for the acts he committed and showing honest repentance. This admission of guilt undoubtedly contributed to the rapid resolution of this case, thus saving the Court's time and resources and relieving witnesses and victims of what can be a stressful burden of giving evidence in Court. Moreover, this admission may also further peace and reconciliation in Northern Mali by alleviating the victims' moral suffering through acknowledgement of the significance of the destruction.[9]

Sentence

To determine the nine-year sentence, the Chamber took into consideration the gravity of the crime, Mr Al Mahdi's culpable conduct and his circumstances. The Chamber also noted that even if inherently grave, crimes against property are generally of less gravity than crimes against persons. The Chamber also considered that the targeted buildings were not only religious but had also symbolic and emotional value for the inhabitants of Timbuktu. The mausoleums of saints and mosques of Timbuktu were an integral part of the religious life of its inhabitants and constituted a common heritage for the community. They reflected their commitment to Islam and played a psychological role to the extent of being perceived as protecting the people of Timbuktu. Furthermore, all the sites but one were UNESCO World Heritage sites. As such, the attacks on them appear to be of gravity as their destruction affects not only the direct victims of the crimes but also people throughout Mali and the international community.

The Chamber considered five mitigating circumstances, namely:

1. Mr Al Mahdi's admission of guilt, and the fact he showed honest repentance and provided a detailed account of his acts. The Chamber noted that his admission of guilt may also further peace and reconciliation in Northern Mali by alleviating the victims' moral suffering through acknowledgement of the significance of the destruction;

9 Para 100, ICC decision in case No. ICC-01/12-01/15, Dated: September 27, 2016.

2. Mr Al Mahdi's cooperation with the Prosecution despite potential security implications for his family in Mali, and the fact that he took responsibility for his actions as early as the first day of his interviews with the Prosecution, which enabled the parties to reach an agreement sufficiently early in the proceedings;
3. Mr Al Mahdi's remorse and the empathy he expressed with the victims, including his call on people not to become involved in similar conduct and his offer to reimburse the cost of a door at the Sidi Yahia Mosque. Mr Al Mahdi has expressed his 'deep regret and great pain' and insisted that the remorse he was feeling was for the damage caused to his family, his community in Timbuktu, his country, and the international community;
4. Mr Al Mahdi's initial reluctance to commit the crime and the steps he took to limit the damage caused by advising against the use of bulldozers to attack the buildings so as not to damage the graves next to the mausoleums and making sure the attackers showed respect for the constructions next to the mausoleum while carrying out the attack; and
5. Even if of limited importance, Mr Al Mahdi's good behaviour in detention.

To sufficiently and adequately reflect the moral and economic harm suffered by the victims of the case and fulfil the objectives of sentencing, the Chamber imposed a sentence that it deemed proportionate to the gravity of the crime and the individual circumstances and culpability of Mr Al Mahdi.

Judgement

On September 27, 2016, Trial Chamber VIII of the International Criminal Court (ICC)[10] delivered its judgment in the case of *The Prosecutor v. Ahmad Al Faqi Al Mahdi.* The Chamber unanimously found Mr Al Mahdi guilty beyond reasonable doubt as a co-perpetrator of the war crime consisting of intentionally directing attacks against religious and historic buildings in Timbuktu, Mali, in June and July 2012. The Chamber sentenced Mr Al Mahdi to nine years' imprisonment. The time he has spent in detention since his arrest upon the ICC warrant issued on September 18 2015 was

10 ICC Trial Chamber VIII is composed of Judge Raul C. Pangalangan (Presiding Judge), Judge Antoine Kesia-Mbe Mindua and Judge Bertram Schmitt.

to be deducted from the sentence. In an open session, the Presiding Judge read a summary of the judgment and sentence.

Reparation Order

On August 17, 2017, Trial Chamber VIII of ICC issued a Reparations Order in the case of The Prosecutor v. Ahmad Al Faqi Al Mahdi, concluding that Mr Al Mahdi is liable for Euros 2.7 million in expenses for individual and collective reparations for the community of Timbuktu for intentionally directing attacks against religious and historic buildings in that city. Noting that Mr Al Mahdi is indigent, the Chamber encouraged the Trust Funds for Victims (TFV) to complement the reparations award and directed the TFV to submit a draft implementation plan. The Chamber considered the observations of the ICC Prosecutor, the Defence, the Legal Representatives of Victims (LRV) representing the 139 reparations applicants, the TFV, the ICC Registry, four appointed experts and amici curiae, including UNESCO. The Chamber recalled the reparations principles established by the ICC Appeals Chamber's decision in the Lubanga case, including the non-discrimination principle. Trial Chamber VIII also stressed that reparations in the present case are designed – to the extent achievable – to relieve the suffering caused by the serious crime committed enable victims to recover their dignity and deter future violations. Reparations may assist in promoting reconciliation between the victims of the crime, the affected communities, and the convicted person.

The Chamber highlighted the importance of cultural heritage and stressed that, because of their purpose and symbolism, most cultural property and cultural heritage are unique and of sentimental value. Their destruction thus carries a message of terror and helplessness; destroys part of humanity's shared memory and collective consciousness, and renders humanity unable to transmit its values and knowledge to future generations. The Chamber ordered reparations for three categories of harm: damage to the attacked historic and religious buildings, consequential economic loss, and moral harm. Reparations are to be collected for the rehabilitation of the sites and for the community of Timbuktu to address the financial loss and economic harm as well as the emotional distress suffered because of the attack. It may also include symbolic measures – such as a memorial, commemoration, or forgiveness ceremony – to give public recognition of the moral harm suffered by the Timbuktu community and those within it.

The Chamber also ordered individual reparations for those whose livelihoods exclusively depended upon the attacked buildings and those whose ancestors' burial sites were damaged in the attack. The limited number of individual reparations ordered should be prioritised during the implementation. The Chamber concluded that it considered Mr Al Mahdi's apology to be genuine, categorical, and empathetic. As a symbolic measure to ensure that victims have access to Mr Al Mahdi's apology, the Chamber orders the Registry to produce an excerpt of the video of Mr Al Mahdi's apology and post it on the Court's website. In addition, the Chamber ordered one symbolic euro to be received by the Malian State and UNESCO given the specific nature of the case. The Chamber assessed Mr Al Mahdi's liability for these reparations at 2.7 million Euros. Noting Mr Al Mahdi's indigence, the Chamber encourages the TFVs to complement any individual or collective reparations to the extent possible.

There are apparently, three challenges the Al Mahdi reparations posed, namely: (i) whether 'unborn children' should be included in the pool of victims resulting from the destruction given that cultural heritage law is premised on the idea that cultural heritage should be preserved for the benefit of future generations; (ii) what place women ought to occupy in the implementation of reparations despite the customary practices of side-lining them; and (iii) the decision of whether to memorialize or not to memorialize events surrounding the crime of destruction of cultural heritage. The Al Mahdi reparations order had identified 'those whose ancestors' burial sites were damaged in the attack (such as the descendants of the Saints) as one of the categories of victims entitled to compensation. However, it did not specify a cut-off date of birth for such descendants to be included in the pool of victims. Laws for the protection of cultural heritage exist precisely based on the premise that cultural sites belong to humankind and ought to be preserved for their transmission to future generations. The question thus arises: considering that this case only involved the loss of cultural heritage, should the concept of direct descendants of the Saints be extended to unborn generations of those families? [11]

Big Success for the ICC or Improper Use of Resources?

While some have applauded the ICC prosecution of Al Mahdi as a victory for the institution and as a groundbreaking legal precedent, others have criticized the court's decision to go after a relatively little-known defendant, for a relatively insignificant crime. These arguments are as follows.

11 Lostal Marina, Implementing Reparations in the Al Mahdi Case: A Story of Monumental Challenges in Timbuktu, *Journal of International Criminal Justice*, Vol. 19, 2021, pp. 831–854.

Victory for the ICC: The ICC has been perceived as an inefficient institution, as cases against other alleged criminals have languished.[12] However, the trial of Al-Mahdi was short and efficient. The ICC has a small budget, and completing an efficient trial without expending many resources represents an important legal accomplishment for the ICC to pursue other cases and alleged criminals.[13] Since the beginning of the case, Al-Mahdi promised to cooperate with the ICC. He is the first-ever defendant in the ICC to plead guilty. This conveys a message that the ICC is efficient and capable of arresting individuals and completing trials within a reasonable period. Al-Mahdi's surrender to the ICC was accomplished through the cooperation of both Niger and Mali, two African states. This cooperation may help the ICC to counter criticism of bias against the African continent and the perception that African states are somehow against the institution.[14] Al Mahdi's conviction also enhances the image of the ICC as an institution prosecuting crimes that shock the conscience of mankind, such as the destruction of UNESCO sites. This case marks the first time that the destruction of cultural sites has been prosecuted as a war crime at the ICC.

Improper Use of Resources: Many scholars have criticized the Al Mahdi case as stretching the limits of the ICC to a breaking point because the case fails to respect two core principles of the ICC: gravity and

12 Sudanese President Omar al-Bashir has been free since becoming the first person charged by the ICC for genocide. Joseph Kony, the notorious leader of the Lord's Resistance Army, continues to wreak havoc in Central Africa, 10 years after being indicted. The trials of Kenyan President Uhuru Kenyatta and Deputy President William Ruto collapsed because of a lethal combination of shoddy case construction by ICC prosecutors and Kenyan political interference.

13 The ICC's annual budget for 2023 stands at roughly $185 million—the vast majority of which comes from member states. Contributions are determined by the same method the United Nations uses to assess dues, which roughly correspond to the size of each member's economy. In 2020, the largest contributions [PDF] came from Japan, Germany, France, and the United Kingdom. Some countries, notably Brazil and Venezuela, have run up millions of dollars in overdue payments. The UN General Assembly can approve additional funding for cases referred to the court by the Security Council. Some governments and transnational organizations also offer voluntary contributions. Some analysts have criticized the ICC as too expensive. Others counter that the court's cost-effectiveness cannot be based solely on the number of cases it tries or convictions it secures.

14 Since its inception, the ICC has faced criticism from many parties and has been unable to gain the membership of major powers, including the United States, India, China, and Russia. The ICC has indicted more than forty individuals, most from African countries Two African countries have withdrawn from the jurisdiction of the ICC, and many African governments complain that its prosecutions have singled out Africa.

complementarity.[15] The ICC was established to exercise its jurisdiction over persons for the most serious crimes of international concern. Article 17(1)(d) of the Rome Statute provides that a case is inadmissible before the ICC if the case is not of sufficient gravity to justify further action by the court. The Prosecutor has stated, in the context of the Al Mahdi case, that "attacks against religious buildings are so grave that they warrant action by the international community.," In today's context, it is difficult to say that the destruction of buildings should qualify as one of the most serious crimes of international concern. Al Mahdi was selected for prosecution for pragmatic reasons, which had little to do with the gravity principle.[16] Al Mahdi's alleged crimes were not very serious and it remains questionable whether the war crime of destruction of cultural property is grave enough to warrant prosecution in the ICC.[17]

In addition, the Al Mahdi prosecution does not satisfy the principle of complementarity. Al Mahdi had already been indicted on terrorism charges in Niger before the ICC issued its arrest warrant. When Niger was informed that the ICC wanted to prosecute Al Mahdi, the authorities transferred Al Mahdi and relinquished jurisdiction over the case. Niger never stated that it was unwilling or unable to prosecute Al Mahdi, and the ICC authorities themselves never bothered with the complementarity issue. It appears that the ICC's decision to prosecute al Mahdi was contrary to the complementarity principle.

The Prosecutor's decision to charge Al Mahdi with a war crime for his actions in the conflict was somewhat surprising. The case of Al Mahdi is somewhat unlike those that usually come before the ICC, which represent some of the most heinous acts committed by mankind—genocide, crimes against humanity, crimes of aggression, and war crimes. Often, these acts involve the slaughter of innocent civilians, the horrific treatment of

15 Eva Vogelvang and Sylvain Clerc, The Al Mahdi Case: Stretching the Principles of the ICC to a Breaking Point? *Justice Hub*, August 29, 2016.

16 Stereo Milena, Individual Criminal Responsibility for the Destruction of Religious and Historic Buildings: The Al Mahdi Case, *Case Western Reserve Journal of International Law*, Vol. 63, 2017, p. 71.

17 Although the destruction of cultural and religious buildings may constitute an attack on humanity, as recent ISIS-perpetrated attacks on the cultural heritage of Syria may demonstrate, this does not automatically lead to the conclusion that the ICC should prosecute the perpetrators. The gravity threshold imposes a limitation on the court: considering its limited resources, the court should focus on the prosecution of those most responsible for serious crimes. It may be argued that Al Mahdi's alleged crimes are not grave enough.

enemy combatants, the use and forced recruitment of child soldiers, mass campaigns of sexual violence, and other atrocities committed against people.[18]

According to William Schabas (2017), the so-called claims of "landmark," "historic judgment," and "breakthrough" by a few were not true and a closer look at the Rome Statute suggests that Al Mahdi did not commit the crime for which he was convicted.[19] Al Mahdi admitted responsibility for acts relating to the destruction of several mausoleums and the door of a mosque in Timbuktu, Mali, buildings that had been traditionally used by the local population as part of their religious observance. In 2012, when civil war erupted in Mali, the government abandoned the northern provinces and religious extremists associated with Ansar Dine seized control of Timbuktu. The Prosecutor of the International Criminal Court observed that "the Ansar Dine leadership can control and govern parts of the territory through local councils established in towns that fell under its control. In addition, the group reportedly set up a specialized police force in Timbuktu to enforce the Sharia law."[20] As an eminent religious personality who had joined the rebels, Al Mahdi delivered a sermon condemning worship at the mausoleums. Subsequently, the rebel administration ordered that the mausoleums be destroyed. Al Mahdi, who presided over a morality tribunal known as the Hisbah, played a crucial role in implementing the decision to destroy the buildings or structures in question, which at the time were classified by UNESCO as "world heritage."

Al Mahdi pleaded guilty to Article 8(2)(e)(iv), which applies to non-international armed conflict. That the structures targeted by Al Mahdi were "buildings dedicated to religion" or that they were "historic monuments" does not seem to be seriously disputed. It was precisely because of their religious significance, something that did not suit the beliefs of the regime with which Al Mahdi was associated, that they were destroyed. They did not constitute a "military objective." Although civil war continued in the country, Timbuktu seems to have been securely in the hands of the rebels at the time and would remain so until the first months of the following year.

18 Jayaraman Shiva, The Destruction of Cultural Property at the International Criminal Court: *The Prosecutor v. Al Mahdi*, International Immersion Programme Papers, 2017, p. 18.

19 Schabas William, Al Mahdi Has Been Convicted of a Crime He Did Not Commit, Case W. Res. J. Int'l L., Vol. 49, 2017, pp. 75-102.

20 Office of the Prosecutor, Situation in Mali, Art. 53(1), Report, January 16, 2013, para. 82.

Indeed, based on the record before the Court it does not seem that there was any activity that could be called "military" or "combat" at the time the structures were destroyed. For this reason, it is not at all evident that the implementation of the administrative decision to destroy the structures carried out "with a variety of tools, including pickaxes and iron bars,"[21] constituted an "attack" as the term is used in Article 8 of the Rome Statute. And if it was not an "attack" as the term is meant in article 8(2)(e)(iv), then Al Mahdi did not commit the offence.

Article 22(2) of the Rome Statutes provides: The definition of a crime shall be strictly construed and shall not be extended by analogy. In case of ambiguity, the definition shall be interpreted in favour of the person being investigated, prosecuted or convicted." According to Schabas, in this respect, the ICC may differ from other international criminal tribunals that have been set up temporarily and were more liberal.[22] Al Mahdi is the first accused person to be tried for "attacks" on cultural property. declaring that article 8(2)(e)(iv) has not previously been applied by the Court, the Trial Chamber said it would proceed to interpret this crime and its elements. It did not cite any case law to support its conclusions. That "attacks" is to be interpreted concerning Article 49(1) of the 1977 Additional Protocol I. The concept of attack as defined in this provision refers to the use of armed force to carry out a military operation during an armed conflict. It refers to any combat action, thus offensive acts and defensive acts or counterattacks. Thus, for this definition, it does not matter whether the acts are committed by an aggressor or by the party acting in self-defence. Al Mahdi was responsible for a disgraceful act of destruction but he was not involved in an "attack" as this term is used in Article 8(2)(e) of the Rome Statute. Indeed, there was no "attack" on the buildings and structures of Timbuktu, as the word "attack" is meant in Article 8(2)(e) of the Rome Statute. While some scholars of cultural heritage law and supporters of the ICC have celebrated the Al Mahdi prosecution for enhancing the visibility of cultural heritage and broadcasting the seriousness of crimes against it, the ICC's decision in this case may be of limited value as a precedent.[23]

21 Al Mahdi (ICC-01/12-01/15), Decision on the confirmation of charges against Ahmad Al Faqi Al Mahdi, March 24, 2015, para. 37.

22 Schabas William, Al Mahdi Has Been Convicted of a Crime He Did Not Commit, *Case W. Res. J. Int'l L.*, Vol. 49, 2017, p. 77.

23 Recent Cases, International Criminal Law—Rome Statute—ICC imposes a first sentence for War Crime of Attacking Cultural Heritage, *Harvard Law Review*, Vol. 130, 2017, pp. 1978-1986.

Conclusion

On September 27, 2016, the ICC sentenced Ahmad Al Faqi Al Mahdi to nine years in prison. This is the first time in the Court's history, that a defendant was charged with committing a war crime for destroying a protected object or site of cultural importance in a non-international armed conflict, violating Article 8(2)(e)(iv) of the Rome Statute. Al Mahdi was alleged to have attacked several UNESCO World Heritage Sites in Timbuktu, including several shrines and mausoleums, within the context of a non-international armed conflict in Northern Mali. Willful destruction of cultural property is a serious crime of international concern. This was the first case before the ICC where a defendant pled guilty and received a reduced prison sentence. The Al Mahdi case is in line to end impunity for the most serious crimes of international concern. This is an interesting development in the field of international criminal law. The conviction of Al Mahdi shows that the ICC and international community will hold future perpetrators of such acts accountable and will certainly prosecute similar attacks on cultural property.

Section III

Protection of Cultural Property

Chapter 7

Role of the Armed Forces

Throughout history, cultural sites and objects have been destroyed intentionally during an armed conflict to gain military advantage. Damage to cultural property can also be caused accidentally or as collateral damage from an attack by the armed forces. International humanitarian law (IHL) prohibits the wilful destruction of cultural property in armed conflict. It obliges combatants to respect and protect cultural property. Therefore, it is paramount that every military officer at the lowest level in the field is aware of his obligations while encountering cultural property during operations. The intentional destruction, damage, or misappropriation of cultural property in armed conflict can result in prosecution for war crimes and reparations.[1] In 1998, the United Nations Compensation Commission awarded close to USD 19,000,000 to an individual Kuwaiti collector for the destruction and pillage by invading and occupying Iraqi forces of his collections of Islamic art and rare books, which Iraq was compelled by the Security Council to pay.

The Role of Military Commander

Military preparedness and the preservation of life and well-being require an understanding of the role of cultural heritage in warfare. Military

1 Culpable individuals include not just those who physically destroy, damage, or misappropriate the property but also those who in some other way participate intentionally in its destruction, damage, or misappropriation. It also includes military commanders who fail, intentionally or simply negligently, to take all necessary and reasonable measures within their power to prevent or repress such crimes or to submit them to the competent authorities for investigation and, where appropriate, prosecution. In 2016, the International Criminal Court sentenced Ahmad Al Faqi Al Mahdi to nine years' imprisonment for committing a war crime consisting of intentionally directing attacks against religious and historic buildings in Timbuktu, Mali, in June and July 2012.

commanders at all levels bear operational responsibility for ensuring that military forces abide by the rules of IHL and adopt best practices for the protection of cultural property in armed conflict. The responsibilities of commanders are legal as well as operational. They are reflected in the military law of a commander's state and are punishable under that law in the event of the commander's failure. They are also enshrined in international law. Military commanders can be held criminally responsible under international law for war crimes, crimes against humanity, and other international crimes committed because of their failure to exercise control properly over forces under their command.[2]

In 2006, while serving in Afghanistan, a special forces officer briefed the commander of Combined Forces Command–Afghanistan, about a night raid that his unit was going to conduct. Although the Commander did not have operational control of the mission, other units coordinated with him. The special forces unit wanted to capture a Taliban bombmaker responsible for the death of at least two members of their team. When the military located the bombmaker in a village, the unit prepared for a midnight attack. The Commander disagreed with this approach, contending that the operation would traumatise the village by raiding at midnight, having loud Blackhawk helicopters circling overhead, and disrespecting the culture by violating women's privacy rules during the search. Even if the bombmaker was captured, the Commander contended that the exact threat would be replicated in a month, so he suggested apprehending him on the road and not in a village. That context is one of protecting cultural heritage while engaged in military operations. Protecting cultural heritage sites has crucial strategic implications due to the symbolic and economic interconnections between cultural sites, artefacts, and populations. These inextricable links

2 Command responsibility imposes both forward-looking and backwards-looking obligations upon a commander to promote compliance with the law of war by his subordinates. *Ex-ante*, a commander must prevent war crimes by his subordinates. *Ex-post*, a commander must punish war crimes committed by his subordinates. A commander's failure to uphold either his duty to prevent or duty to punish may give rise to his responsibility for war crimes. Bantekas Ilias, Contemporary Law of Superior Responsibility, *American Journal of International Law*, Vol. 93, Issue 3, July 1999, pp. 573-595; Also see: Article 86 and 87 to 1977 Additional Protocol I, and Article 28 to the Rome Statute of the International Criminal Court, 1998. In Article 87, reference to 'commanders' encompassed persons in command "at the highest level to leaders with only a few men under their command." This consistent irrelevance of rank in attributing superior responsibility indicates that the international law-making institutions look to actual and effective control, rather than formality.

can incite populations to participate in actions against military forces when cultural sites are harmed.[3]

Today, ever-widening access to digital communications and social media increases the risk that even seemingly minor and unintended harm to cultural heritage can quickly rouse local, regional, and international reactions. Therefore, military commanders at all levels must have a clear understanding of the laws and practices for safeguarding cultural heritage during military operations. Although IHL defines cultural property and delineates what armed forces may lawfully target, military commanders also need to be mindful of the broader definition of cultural heritage, the symbolism and economic value of cultural artefacts, and the disconnect between perception and legality. For example, in certain circumstances, a mosque may legally be targeted, yet its damage or destruction can evoke reactions that have strategic consequences. Additionally, while an external military force might not be involved in damaging cultural heritage, during conflict it may be perceived by the host nation as required to protect cultural sites from attack. The UM military has been blamed for their failure to take steps to prevent the looting of the National Museum of Iraq in Baghdad.[4]

Military Manual/ Dissemination

Article 7(1) of the 1954 Hague Convention requires state parties to introduce into their military regulations or instructions the necessary provisions to ensure observance of the Convention. It equally requires them to foster in the members of their armed forces a spirit of respect for the culture and cultural property of all peoples'. Article 25 of the Convention states that the State parties must disseminate the text of the 1954 Convention and the Regulations for its execution as widely as possible in their respective countries. The States must include the study of the Convention in their programmes of military and, if possible, civilian training, so that its principles are made known to the whole population, especially the armed forces and personnel engaged in the protection of cultural property. This is a peace-time obligation.

3 Beitler Ruth Margolies and Dexter W. Dugan, "Practicing the Art of War While Protecting Cultural Heritage: A Military Perspective," in Cuno James and Thomas G. Weiss (ed), 2022, *Cultural Heritage and Mass Atrocities*, Los Angeles: Getty Publications, pp. 500-516.

4 The United States Army ignored warnings from its civilian advisers that could have stopped the looting of priceless artefacts in Baghdad. Martin Paul and Ed Vulliamy, US army was told to protect the looted museum, *The Guardian*, April 20, 2003.

The 1999 Second Protocol in Article 30 provides that the States must adopt appropriate means to strengthen appreciation and respect for cultural property by their entire population. The States parties are to disseminate the Protocol as widely as possible, both in times of peace and in times of armed conflict. The military or civilian authorities who, in times of armed conflict, assume responsibilities concerning the application of the Protocol, must be fully acquainted with its text. The states parties have an obligation to (i) incorporate guidelines and instructions on the protection of cultural property in their military regulations; (ii) develop and implement, in cooperation with UNESCO and relevant governmental and non-governmental organisations, peacetime training and educational programmes; (iii) communicate to one another, through the Director-General, information on the laws, administrative provisions and measures undertaken by them; and (iv) communicate to one another, as soon as possible, through the Director-General, the laws and administrative provisions which they have adopted to ensure the application of this Protocol.

Military Manual

The military manual serves as a practical guide to the armed forces. It contains legal obligations contained in IHL treaties including the provisions relating to the protection of cultural property.[5] It lists the responsibilities of the states and individuals with suggestions as to best military practice at the different levels of command and during the different phases of military operations, whether by land, sea, or air. The importance to military forces of the protection of cultural property in armed conflict is abstract, strategic, and legal. In abstract terms, cultural property forms a vital part of the cultural identity of individuals, communities, peoples, and all humanity. Its preservation is essential to human well-being and flourishing. In strategic terms, the protection of cultural property in armed conflict is imperative.

5 Of particular importance in terms of provisions necessary for the observance of the 1954 Hague Convention, the 1999 Second Protocol and other rules of IHL for the protection of cultural property in armed conflict is the promulgation within military forces and the inculcation by commanders into their subordinates of 'rules of engagement' (ROE). ROE provide authorization for and imposes restrictions on, among other things, the use of armed force, the positioning and posture of forces, and the employment of specific capabilities. Best practice dictates that competent military authorities issue and implement ROE specifically designed to protect cultural property, both immovable and movable, whenever their military forces are deployed on operations. O'Keefe Roger, Peron Camille, Musayev Tofig, and Ferrari Gianluca, 2016, Protection of Cultural Property: Military Manual, UNESCO, p.18.

Avoidable destruction, damage and looting of cultural property by military forces endangers mission success. Taking due care to spare cultural property from destruction, damage and all forms of misappropriation can win hearts and minds. In legal terms, a state may be held responsible [6] for its failure to protect cultural property and may also be compelled to make reparation to another state or person for its destruction, damage, or misappropriation.[7]

The integration of cultural property considerations into targeting decisions is both an international legal obligation and a practical necessity.[8] The armed forces must have a written manual because in the event of an armed conflict, their forces must comply with a set of obligations and they need to be trained on these obligations in advance. This would be possible only if there was an appropriate structure in place. The necessity of a Manual is envisaged in Article 1 of the 1899 Hague Convention II, concerning the laws and customs of war on land. The Convention makes it obligatory for a State Party to issue instructions which shall conform with the regulations attached to the 1954 Convention. The use of the word 'instructions' speaks of a direct commitment by the State Parties to act in a manner consistent with their treaty obligations, providing elaboration and explanation. The 1949 Geneva Conventions necessitate the preparation of a law of war manual. According to the terms of Articles 48, 49, 128 and 145, which are common to the four Geneva Conventions of 1949, the State Parties must communicate to one another the official translations of the treaties and the

6 Culpable individuals include not just those who physically destroy, damage, or misappropriate the property but also those who in some other way participate intentionally in its destruction, damage, or misappropriation. It includes military commanders who fail, intentionally or simply negligently, to take all necessary and reasonable measures within their power to prevent or repress such crimes or to submit them to the competent authorities for investigation and, where appropriate, prosecution.

7 O'Keefe Roger, Peron Camille, Musayev Tofig, and Ferrari Gianluca, 2016, *Protection of Cultural Property: Military Manual*, UNESCO, p. 91.

8 Parties to the conflict must do everything feasible to verify that the objectives to be attacked are not cultural property. In legal terms, it involves two distinct questions. First, military decision-makers must assess whether the specific cultural property may itself be attacked. Secondly, military decision-makers must assess whether any attack on an otherwise lawful military objective, such as a military installation, may be expected to cause incidental damage to nearby cultural property that would be excessive about the concrete and direct military advantage anticipated from neutralising the objective. Both rules are backed up by further rules about the execution of attacks. O'Keefe Roger, Peron Camille, Musayev Tofig, and Ferrari Gianluca, 2016, *Protection of Cultural Property: Military Manual*, UNESCO, p. 26.

laws and regulations they have adopted to ensure their implementation. The term' laws and regulations' should be understood in the broadest sense. It covers all legal instruments issued both by the executives and the legislative powers that have any bearing on the implementation of the treaties in question. The word 'implementation' covers all measures that must be taken — both wartime and peacetime — to ensure the rules of the law of war are fully respected.

The 1954 Convention and its 1999 Second Protocol does not require that a separate military manual be prepared by the States parties for the protection of cultural property. A military manual on laws of war could also contain provisions relating to the protection and other obligations relating to cultural property. Signatories to the 1954 Hague Convention on the Protection of Cultural Property must introduce in peacetime into their military regulations or instructions such provisions as may ensure observance of the Convention, and to foster in the members of their armed forces a spirit of respect for the culture and cultural property of all peoples. Under the Convention, the States are required to position specialist personnel within the armed forces to foster respect for cultural property and to cooperate with the civilian authorities responsible for safeguarding it.

A manual on laws of war serves four important purposes. First, it reaffirms the commitment of the highest authorities of the armed forces or the government to respecting the law of war in general, *i.e.*, of all sources including treaty law, customary law, and general principles, as well as accepted state practices. Second, it provides the information necessary for training armed forces personnel and others who need to be familiar with relevant aspects of the law of war. Third, it serves as an example or a model for other states and their armed forces which have not yet adopted such a manual. Lastly, a manual advises members of the armed forces and civilians, who are involved in a decision-making process on issues relating to armed conflict, both during the preparation of military operations or during such operations.[9]

9 In 2006, the Supreme Court of Israel, in a case of the legality of targeted killings of Palestinian militants by the Israel Defence Forces, specifically cited military manuals from the UK, France, the Netherlands, Australia, Italy, Canada, Germany and New Zealand, in addition to the US's Air Force Manual as evidence for the customary nature of the prohibition of attacking civilians unless they were taking a direct part in hostilities.

The military manual on laws of war will not create new laws. It will restate or interpret the rules that already exist in the treaties which the State has ratified. A large number of states have manuals on the law of war for the effective functioning of their armed forces. The following is a brief description of provisions relating to the protection of cultural property contained in such manuals issued by a few States:

Argentina

Argentina's Law of War Manual (1989) defines cultural property by Article 1 of the 1954 Hague Convention for the Protection of Cultural Property. The Manual provides that in the event of bombardment, assault or siege, all necessary precautions shall be adopted, as far as possible, to respect buildings devoted to worship, the arts, the sciences, and charity, as well as historic monuments, provided such buildings and monuments, which must display special, visible signs, are not used for military purposes. The manual further states, concerning combat operations: "The destruction of enemy property shall be permissible as far as required by military operations and subject to the limitations imposed by the requirement of respect for artistic, scientific and historical property." Concerning non-international armed conflicts in particular, the Manual states: "Cultural objects and places of worship which constitute the cultural or spiritual heritage of peoples enjoy special protection; they may not be attacked."

Australia

Australian Manual: Law of Armed Conflict (2006)[10] states that the 1954 Convention on Cultural Property places an obligation on defenders and attackers by requiring nations to refrain from the uses of cultural property that would expose such property to danger in armed conflict and to refrain from acts of hostility against cultural property. The Manual follows the definition of cultural property as contained in the 1954 Convention. It provides that the historic monuments, places of worship and works of art, which constitute the cultural and spiritual heritage of peoples, are protected from acts of hostility. These objects must not be used in support of any military effort or be the subject of reprisals. It states that the buildings devoted to religion, the arts, or charitable purposes; historic monuments; and other religious, cultural, or charitable facilities should not be attacked, provided they are not used for military purposes. It is the responsibility

10 Law of Armed Conflict: Executive Series ADDP 06.4, Australian Defence Headquarters, May 111, 2006.

of the local population to ensure that such buildings are marked with a distinctive emblem. Further, enemy vessels engaged in transporting cultural property under special protection are exempted from attack. Improper use of the protective emblem of cultural property is also prohibited. Booby traps should not be attached to or associated with historic monuments, works of art or places of worship which constitute the cultural or spiritual heritage of people.

The Australian Manual also states that in the context of siege warfare, buildings devoted to religion, art, and science should not be made the specific subject of attack unless they are being used for military purposes, subject to warning requirements. The besieged population should indicate by visible signs the buildings or places to be protected and should notify the attacking force of these signs.

Australian Military Manual: Analysis

The multiplication of legal regimes concerning the protection of cultural property in armed conflict has made the task of understanding and dissemination extremely complicated. This is because each of these legal instruments provides a slightly different conception of "cultural property" and a different regime of protection. For instance, take the issue as covered under the Australian Defence Force Manual.[11] The Manual in Para 9.27 and 9.28 deals with cultural objects and cultural property as follows:

> Cultural objects: The Law of Armed Conflict (LOAC) provides for the specific protection of cultural objects and places of worship, which supplements the general protection given to civilian objects. Buildings dedicated to religion, science or charitable purposes, and historic monuments, are given immunity from attack as far as possible, so long as they are not being used for military purposes. Such places are to be marked with distinctive and visible signs, which must be notified to the other party.
>
> Cultural property: Cultural property is also protected. Cultural property includes movable and immovable objects of great importance to the cultural heritage of people, whether their state is involved in the conflict or not, such as historical monuments, archaeological sites, books, manuscripts or scientific papers and the buildings or other

11 Law of armed Conflict, ADDP 06.4, Commonwealth of Australia 2006, p. 242.

> places in which such objects are housed.[12] Obligations are placed upon all parties to respect cultural property by not exposing it to destruction or damage in the event of armed conflict and by refraining from any act of hostility directed against such property. These obligations may be waived where military necessity requires such waiver, as in the case where the object is used for military purposes.
>
> Para 9.29 of the Manual further states, "Historic monuments, places of worship and works of art, which constitute the cultural and spiritual heritage of peoples, are protected from acts of hostility. These objects must not be used in support of any military effort or be the subject of reprisals.

The Australian Manual provides three different sets of instructions, one for each of its respective categories:

(a) Para 9.2 of the Manual states that cultural, religious, and historic buildings and items have special protection and as far as possible have immunity from attack;

(b) Para 5.45 states that buildings devoted to religion, the arts, or charitable purposes; historic monuments; and other religious, cultural, or charitable facilities should not be attacked, provided they are not used for military purposes; and

(c) Para 9.46 states that cultural property is generally protected. This includes but is not limited to, all buildings, locations, manuscripts, objects, works of art, archives, archaeological sites, historical documents, and book collections which have any cultural significance.

It thus creates confusion as to what extent the "cultural objects" in the first part are different from the "buildings devoted to arts" in the second, or from the "historic documents, manuscripts, and works of art" in the last. According to Yostal (2013), there is a complex web of overlapping and confusion on the terms: "cultural property" and "protection" in the Australian Manual. Despite the availability of many international legal documents, none of them have been able to provide a specific regime for

12 The term cultural property has been defined in the Australian Manual as, "Movable and immovable objects of sufficient artistic or religious importance to constitute the heritage of all people, including that which has been renovated or restored. Cultural property includes historical monuments, archaeological sites, books, manuscripts or scientific papers and the buildings or other places in which such objects are housed." The Australian Defence Force Manual, Appendix.

the protection of cultural property in armed conflict.[13] This legal void is at odds with the urgent need for a clear mandate to counter the belligerent practices that deliberately target world heritage sites.[14] Similarly, Security Council Resolution 2139 of 2014, called on all parties to the Syrian conflict to save Syria's 'rich societal mosaic' and cultural heritage, and take appropriate steps to ensure the protection of Syria's World Heritage Sites."[15] Thus, to date, international law has been unable to provide a distinct regime for the protection of cultural heritage in times of armed conflict.

Brazil

Brazil is a party to all the main instruments in IHL, including the four Geneva Conventions and their Additional Protocols. Brazil's International Law of Armed Conflicts Manual (2011),[16] under the heading "Protection of Cultural Property," states: "For protection under the international law of armed conflict, cultural property refers to any movable or immovable property of great importance to the cultural heritage of every people, such as buildings or groups of buildings of outstanding architecture, artistic, historical or religious monuments, archaeological sites, works of art, manuscripts, books and other objects of historical or archaeological interest, as well as scientific collections and important collections of books

13 Lostal Marina, 2017, *International Cultural Heritage Law in Armed Conflict: Case-Studies of Syria, Libya, Mali, the Invasion of Iraq, and the Buddhas of Bamiyan*, Cambridge: Cambridge University Press, p. 4.

14 For instance, world cultural heritage is defined by the 1972 World Heritage Convention as comprising monuments, buildings, and sites of outstanding value. The 1954 Hague Convention provides a specific regime of protection for property of great value. The 1999 Second Protocol supplements the 1954 Convention by creating an enhanced protection regime for cultural heritage of the greatest importance to humanity, a category whose defining features appear very similar to those of World Heritage Sites. It aims to ensure full and effective protection of specifically designated cultural property during international or non-international armed conflicts. However, to date, only 29 properties are listed as cultural property under enhanced protection whereas the World Heritage List contains 1,199. In September/ December 2023, one property in Palestine and 25 properties in Ukraine were put under the category of Cultural Property under Provisional Enhanced Protection. For more information see: https://whc.unesco.org/en/list/.

15 Security Council Resolution 2139 dated February 22, 2014, S/RES/2139 (2014) para 8 states, "Calling on all parties to immediately end all violence which has led to human suffering in Syria, save Syria's rich societal mosaic and cultural heritage, and take appropriate steps to ensure the protection of Syria's World Heritage Sites."

16 Brazil Manual MD34-M-03, 1st Edition, 2011, Ministry of Defence, Joint Chiefs of Staff of the Armed Forces, Head of Preparation and Deployment, approved by Legislative Order No. 1,069/MD of 5 May 2011.

or archives or reproductions of the property defined above." Further, buildings whose main and effective purpose is to preserve or exhibit the cultural property defined above, such as museums, large libraries and depositories of archives, and refuges intended to shelter this property in the event of armed conflict, must be protected. Based on the principles of the LOAC, cultural objects may not be regarded as military targets. Vessels engaged in transporting cultural property under special protection enjoy immunity from attack.

Canada

According to Canada's Law of Armed Conflict (LOAC) Manual (1999),[17] the following actions are prohibited: to commit any acts of hostility directed against the historic monuments, works of art or places of worship which constitute the cultural or spiritual heritage of peoples. The Manual provides that care must be taken to avoid locating military personnel and material in or near protected cultural objects and places of worship. Cultural objects and places of worship should be marked with the international sign [of the blue shield]. However, the absence of such a sign does not deprive such objects of protection. Further, not all cultural objects and places of worship are protected as cultural or religious property by the LOAC. Only those cultural objects and places of worship which constitute the "cultural or spiritual heritage of peoples" are protected. Therefore, a small village church may not be protected by the cultural protection provisions of the LOAC, but a major cathedral (e.g., the Vatican) is likely entitled to protection. However, the fact that an object is not a cultural object does not mean that it is not a "civilian object". It would be entitled to protection under that status.

Cultural objects and places of worship being used by the adverse party in support of its military effort may become legitimate targets. The Manual provides, "Whether you attack cultural objects and places of worship which have become legitimate targets will depend on your mission. If so, the principle of proportionality is particularly important, as the location or object should not be damaged any more than what the mission requires. Where possible, the opposing force should be warned to stop using a cultural object or place of worship for military purposes before an attack is launched."

17 Canada, *The Law of Armed Conflict at the Operational and Tactical Level*, Office of the Judge Advocate General, 1999, p. 4-7, para 63–70; see also para 6-4, and 39.

The Manual defines it as a grave breach of the 1977 Additional Protocol I: "Attacks against clearly-recognised historic monuments, works of art or places of worship which constitute the cultural or spiritual heritage of peoples, where there is no evidence of prior use of such objects in support of the adverse party's military effort and where such places are not located in the immediate proximity of legitimate targets."[18] Concerning non-international armed conflicts in particular, the manual states: "It is forbidden to commit any hostile acts directed against historic monuments, works of art or places of worship which constitute the cultural or spiritual heritage of peoples."[19]

Rule 9 of Canada's Code of Conduct (2001) provides that as a rule, buildings or property dedicated to cultural or religious purposes may not be attacked. Every attempt should be made to avoid unnecessary desecration or destruction of cultural objects and places of worship. Cultural and religious property should not be targeted. If cultural or religious property is used for a military purpose, it loses its protection. Thus, care must be taken to avoid locating military personnel and material in or near these locations. If the opposing force is using a religious or cultural site for military purposes it becomes a legitimate target. Whether you attack this legitimate target will depend on your mission. If so, the principle of proportionality is particularly important as the location or object should not be damaged any more than what the mission requires. The tactical method selected for the attack should not place Canadian Force (CF) personnel under undue risk yet should cause the least possible damage to the church. Where possible, the opposing force must be warned to stop using a cultural or religious site for a military purpose before an attack.[20] Canada's Code of Conduct for CF Personnel, issued by the Office of the Judge Advocate General (2005) provides additional measures for the protection of cultural property.

---

18 Canada, *The Law of Armed Conflict at the Operational and Tactical Level*, Office of the Judge Advocate General, 1999, p. 16-3, and p. 16-4.

19 Canada, *The Law of Armed Conflict at the Operational and Tactical Level*, Office of the Judge Advocate General, 1999, p. 17-5.

20 Canada, *Code of Conduct for CF Personnel*, Office of the Judge Advocate General, 4 June 2001, Rule 9, pp. 1–5.

Croatia

According to Croatia's LOAC Compendium (1991),[21] acts of hostility against cultural objects are prohibited. However, cultural objects under general protection lose their immunity in cases of imperative military necessity. The existence of such necessity must be established by the local commander. The Compendium further qualifies "unlawful attacks on cultural objects" as war crimes. Croatia's Commanders' Manual (1992) states: states that specifically protected objects may not be attacked. The immunity of a marked cultural object may be withdrawn in case of imperative military necessity. In attack, the immunity of a marked cultural object shall only be withdrawn when the fulfilment of the mission so requires. The warning shall give time for safeguard measures and information on the withdrawal of immunity. Marked cultural objects whose immunity has been withdrawn shall still be respected to the extent the fulfilment of the mission permits.[22]

Denmark

The Military Manual on International Law Relevant to Danish Armed Forces in International Operations (2016), makes provisions for the protection of cultural property in the event of armed conflict. Para 5.6 of the Manual states that cultural property belongs to the category of civilian objects which, in cases of doubt, must be presumed to have civilian status. Cultural property enjoys basic protection against attack. The Manual explains three levels of protection in addition to the usual protection from attack afforded civilian objects: extended protection, special protection, and enhanced protection. Under para 6.21 of the Manual, Danish armed forces undertake to refrain from any use of cultural property and its immediate surroundings for purposes which are likely to expose it to destruction or damage. The Manual provides that the decision to invoke imperative military necessity must, at a minimum, be made by a Danish battalion commander/Commander MTAA team or – if circumstances do not permit otherwise – be assessed by a commanding officer at the highest possible inferior rank. This may be the case, for instance, when communication with the TOC or Combined Air Operations Centre (CAOC) is not possible in a situation that requires immediate action.

21 Croatia, *Compendium "Law of Armed Conflicts,"* Republic of Croatia, Ministry of Defence, 1991, p. 10, and 56; Croatia, Basic Rules of the Law of Armed Conflicts – Commanders' Manual, Republic of Croatia, Ministry of Defence, 1992, pp. 13–14, 55 and 69.

22 International Committee of the Red Cross database, available at: https://ihl-databases.icrc.org/zh/customary-ihl/v2/rule38#b156fcd1-c375-4273-8573-685fa427d476.

France

France's LOAC Manual (2001) restates the definition of cultural property set out in Article 1 of the 1954 Hague Convention for the Protection of Cultural Property. The Manual adds: "The protection enjoyed by such property may be lifted only if military necessity so demands or if such property is used for military purposes by the enemy. Only a commander of a division or larger unit has the authority to lift the immunity. This measure must be notified to the adverse party sufficient time in advance."

France's LOAC Teaching Note (2000) states that "the law of armed conflict grants specific protection to certain specially marked installations and zones", including certain works and installations containing dangerous forces. The Teaching Note further states: "In general, cultural property (religious building, place of worship, monument, museum, important work of art …) is protected. Its immunity may be lifted only in case of imperative military necessity and according to an order received from a higher authority. In such a case, warning must be given to allow the civilian population to seek refuge or to evacuate the combat area. The means of combat must be proportionate to limit, as much as possible, damage to such cultural property."

Germany

Germany's Law of Armed Conflict Manual (2013)[23] deals with the protection of cultural property under Chapter 9. The manual refers to the 1954 Hague Convention and its Protocols of 1954 and 1999. It states that cultural property must be respected by all Parties to a conflict; cultural property may be neither directly nor indirectly used in support of military efforts. Parties to a conflict must refrain from any act of hostility directed against cultural property.[24] Specific provisions for the protection of cultural property are contained in Para 906 to 914. The provisions for special protection are contained under para 915 to 923 and enhanced protection under para 924 to 928. The protection of cultural property also extends to periods of occupation. This means that a Party occupying a territory must undertake to prohibit, prevent and, if necessary, put a stop to any form of theft, pillage, seizure, or other misappropriation of, and any acts of vandalism directed against cultural property. In addition, the provision

23 Joint Service Regulation (Zeva) 15/2, Federal Ministry of Defence, Berlin, May 1, 2013.

24 Para 904, Joint Service Regulation (ZDv) 15/2, Federal Ministry of Defence, Berlin, May 1, 2013.

relating to the transport of cultural property and its distinctive marking is based on the 1954 Hague Convention and its Protocols.[25]

Israel

Israel's Manual on the Rules of Warfare (2006) makes provision for the protection of shrines and cultural property in armed conflict as follows: "These are the structures devoted to religion, beliefs or knowledge and constitute part of the spiritual or cultural heritage of a people. It is possible to claim, nevertheless, that these structures affect the military morale of the opposing side, but they are not considered legitimate targets. The provision imposing the duty to spare such structures as far as possible during hostilities first appeared in the Hague Rules. Following the massive destruction of cultural property during World War II (ancient bridges, cathedrals), the 1954 Hague Convention was formulated for the protection of cultural property. The soldiers of the Israel Defence Force (IDF) are compelled to act everywhere according to this Convention by the General Staff Order 33.1033. This clearly shows that attacks are forbidden on mosques or churches which are not perceived as posing a threat to our forces.[26]

Italy

Italy's IHL Manual (1991) states: "Cultural property and places of worship are entitled to protection in all circumstances provided they are not illicitly used for military purposes." The LOAC Elementary Rules Manual (1991) states that the specifically protected objects may not be attacked. The immunity of a marked cultural object may be withdrawn in case of imperative military necessity. In attack, the immunity of a marked cultural object shall only be withdrawn when the fulfilment of the mission so requires. The warning shall give time for safeguard measures and information on the withdrawal of immunity. Marked cultural objects whose immunity has been withdrawn shall still be respected to the extent the fulfilment of the mission permits. The manual qualifies indiscriminate attacks against cultural property as a war crime. Further, If the protective emblem appears three times, the Cultural Object is subject to special

25 Para 929 to 947, Joint Service Regulation (ZDv) 15/2, Federal Ministry of Defence, Berlin, May 1, 2013.

26 Israel, *Rules of Warfare on the Battlefield*, Military Advocate-General's Corps Command, IDF School of Military Law, Second Edition, 2006, pp. 24–25.

protection. In this case, the order to violate the protective emblem can be given by a Commanding Officer no lower in rank than Major-General.[27]

Netherlands

The Military Manual (2005) of the Netherlands states: "The belligerents must, in particular, spare monuments, works of art, scientific collections, museums etc." In its chapter on behaviour in battle, the manual states that hostile acts against such property must be avoided. Further, exceptions to the respect for cultural property may be allowed only on specific conditions. An attack may be directed at cultural property only in a case of unavoidable military necessity if that cultural property, by its function, has changed into a military objective and there is no practical alternative means of obtaining equal military advantage. In a case of unavoidable military necessity, cultural property may be used for military purposes only if no practical and feasible alternative approach exists to such military use. Whether imperative military necessity exists may be determined only by the commanding officer of a unit of battalion size or higher rank. If no other option exists in the circumstances, a commanding officer of lower rank may also take such a decision. In the case of an attack on cultural property as defined above, it must be possible in some way to give a suitable warning.[28]

The parties to an armed conflict must ensure the immunity of cultural property that has been placed under enhanced protection, by refraining from any use of such property as objectives of attack or any use of the property or its direct environs in support of military action. Cultural property under enhanced protection can only forfeit such protection in most exceptional circumstances. Decisions on this may only be taken at the highest level of operational command. In its chapter on non-international armed conflict, the manual states: Hostile actions (deliberate attacks) against historic monuments, works of art and places where religious services are held are prohibited, if they do not constitute military objectives.

New Zealand

The 2021 New Zealand's Manual of Armed Forces Law, Vol. 4, Law of Armed Conflict (DM 69), chapter 14, section 8 deals with the protection

27 International Committee of the Red Cross database, available at: https://ihl-databases.icrc.org/zh/customary-ihl/v2/rule38#b156fcd1-c375-4273-8573-685fa427d476.

28 International Committee of the Red Cross database, available at: https://ihl-databases.icrc.org/zh/customary-ihl/v2/rule38#b156fcd1-c375-4273-8573-685fa427d476.

of cultural property in armed conflict. The Manual defines cultural property as movable and immovable property which constitutes the cultural or spiritual heritage of peoples or is of great importance to the cultural heritage of every people. The term includes cultural property under 'enhanced protection'. According to Manual para 14.8.2, Places of worship means buildings dedicated to religion, sacred edifices and all other places of worship or spiritual significance, regardless of religion, for example, cathedrals, churches, mosques, temples, and shrines. The term is not limited to large or imposing buildings. Places of great religious significance may be simple in appearance and may include natural features as well as artificial structures. Where places of worship are of great cultural significance, the rules relating to cultural property apply. Further, property protected under the Hague Cultural Property Convention is to be marked with a distinctive emblem. Failure to display the symbol(s) does not deprive cultural property of its protection if it is known to be such by the attacking force. The members of the New Zealand Defence Forces (NZDF) are not to misuse the emblems relating to the protection of cultural property.

Members of the NZDF are to respect and protect cultural property and are not to: (i) attack, damage or destroy cultural property; (ii) use cultural property and its immediate surroundings in support of military action or in a manner likely to expose it to damage or destruction; (iii) make the cultural property the object of reprisals; (iv) requisition, steal, vandalise, mark or 'tag' cultural property; (v) booby-trap cultural property; or (vi) attack, seize, take in prize or capture cultural property that is being transported.[29] Members of the NZDF are not to conduct reprisals against cultural property and places of worship. Further, the NZDF commanders do not have the authority to order reprisals of their initiative. Members of the NZDF are not to conduct reprisals against any person or object unless expressly ordered by CDF on the authority of the Minister of Defence. If faced with breaches of LOAC by the opposing force, the commander of a New Zealand force is to bring the matter to the attention of CDF without delay.[30] New Zealand has also passed the Cultural Property (Protection in Armed Conflict) Act 2012.

29 Para 14.8.10, 2021, New Zealand's Manual of Armed Forces Law, Vol. 4, Law of Armed Conflict.

30 Para 17.10.4 and 5, Para 14.8.10, 2021, New Zealand's Manual of Armed Forces Law, Vol. 4, Law of Armed Conflict.

Russian Federation

The Russian Federation's Regulations on the Application of IHL (2001) states: "The prohibited methods of warfare include … destroying cultural property, historic monuments, places of worship and other objects of the cultural or spiritual heritage of peoples, as well as using them to achieve success in combat operations."[31] The Regulations further states: "Cultural property enjoying special protection includes cultural property entered into the International Register of Cultural Property under Special Protection. From the time of entry in the Register, the parties to a conflict shall refrain from any act of hostility directed against this property, as well as from any use of such property or its surroundings for military purposes."

About internal armed conflict, the Regulations states: "It is prohibited to commit any acts of hostility directed against cultural property." [32] The Russian Federation's Military Manual (1990) states that "the bombardment by military aircraft or vessels of historic monuments [and] churches … which are undefended and not used for military purposes" and "the destruction of cultural property, historical monuments, places of worship, and other buildings which represent the cultural or spiritual heritage of a people" are prohibited methods of warfare.[33]

Spain

Spain's LOAC Manual (2007) defines cultural property by Article 1 of the 1954 Hague Convention for the Protection of Cultural Property. About its protection from attack, the manual states: "The immunity granted to cultural property under general protection may be waived only in cases where military necessity imperatively requires such a waiver." However, military necessity is subject to the condition that the waiver may only be invoked when and for as long as there is no feasible alternative. The decision

31 Russian Federation, *Regulations on the Application of International Humanitarian Law by the Armed Forces of the Russian Federation*, Ministry of Defence of the Russian Federation, Moscow, 8 August 2001, para. 85. Russian Federation, *Regulations on the Application of International Humanitarian Law by the Armed Forces of the Russian Federation*, Ministry of Defence of the Russian Federation, Moscow, 8 August 2001, para 7.

32 Russian Federation, *Regulations on the Application of International Humanitarian Law by the Armed Forces of the Russian Federation*, Ministry of Defence of the Russian Federation, Moscow, 8 August 2001, para 1.

33 Russian Federation, *Instructions on the Application of the Rules of International Humanitarian Law by the Armed Forces of the USSR*, Appendix to Order of the USSR Defence Minister No. 75, 1990, para 5(n) and (s).

to withdraw immunity from cultural property under special protection can only be taken at the division commander level or higher "in exceptional cases of unavoidable military necessity." The manual further states: "Acts of hostility must not be directed against monuments, works of art or places of worship which constitute the cultural and spiritual heritage of peoples. They must not be attacked, destroyed, or damaged." The manual also states that it is prohibited to attack personnel engaged in the protection of cultural property: As far as is consistent with the interests of security, such personnel must be respected and, if they fall into the hands of the opposing party, allowed to continue to carry out their duties.[34]

Ukraine

Ukraine's IHL Manual (2004) states that personnel responsible for the defence and protection of cultural property are "protected under international humanitarian law" and that directing attacks against such persons or "clearly identifiable cultural property" constitutes "a serious violation of international humanitarian law".[35] The Manual follows the definition of cultural property contained under Article 1 of the 1954 Hague Convention. The Ukraine's manual defines the personnel engaged in the protection of cultural property as persons charged with the task of protecting cultural property. Such personnel are authorised to possess personal small arms for self-defence. The manual further states: "Cultural property of exceptional importance is guaranteed special protection. The number of such objects is limited and they are included in the International Register of Cultural Property under Special Protection.

The Manual prohibits the destruction of cultural property, historical sites, places of religion, and objects, constituting the cultural or spiritual heritage of the people; it is also prohibited to use such objects to succeed in warfare. The manual also states that during the conduct of hostilities, under exceptional circumstances, the commander (commanding officer) may designate: (i) the direction of the main attack (primary effort) that includes objects protected under international humanitarian law; and (ii) withdrawal of immunity of cultural property in case of its use by the enemy and fire damage to the enemy positioned at the objects protected by the laws of war. The decision to withdraw protection from cultural property

34 International Committee of the Red Cross database, available at: https://ihl-databases.icrc.org/zh/customary-ihl/v2/rule38#b156fcd1-c375-4273-8573-685fa427d476.

35 Ukraine, *Manual on the Application of IHL Rules*, Ministry of Defence, 11 September 2004, para 1.2.33 and 1.8.5.

that enjoys special status shall be made by a commander at least of the level of brigade commander (or of an equal level). In case of military necessity, withdrawal of immunity of cultural property shall be limited in time and concern the least important parts thereof.[36]

United Kingdom

The UK has recently taken a few steps, though very late, relating to the protection of cultural property during armed conflict. In 2017, it ratified the 1954 Hague Convention on the Protection of Cultural Property in the Event of Armed Conflict and its Protocol of 1954 and 1999. It has also passed the Cultural Property (Armed Conflict) Act. In addition, the UK has announced the creation of a new, Reserve Cultural Property Protection (CCP) Unit.[37]

The British Law of Armed Conflict Manual (2004) prohibits any acts of hostility directed against the historic monuments, works of art or places of worship which constitute the cultural or spiritual heritage of peoples.[38] In general, all civilian objects are protected. However, the protection of cultural property and places of worship is given special emphasis in the law of armed conflict, both in respect of protection from attack and in respect of discouraging their use for military purposes, so that the need to attack such property does not arise. Because of its wording, the prohibition … only applies to very important cultural properties of international stature. According to the Manual, property loses its protection if it is used for military purposes.

Making recognised cultural property the object of an attack can amount to a grave breach of the 1977 Additional Protocol I if the property has not been used for military purposes and it is not in the immediate proximity of

36 Ukraine, *Manual on the Application of IHL Rules*, Ministry of Defence, 11 September 2004, §§ 2.2.4 and 2.3.1.3; see also para 2.51.

37 The Cultural Property Protection Unit is a reserve unit set up in 2017 following the British Government's formal ratification of the 1954 Hague Convention for the Protection of Cultural Property in the Event of Armed Conflict. The first commander of the cross-service unit was Lieutenant-Colonel Tim Purbrick of The Royal Lancers. The unit is tasked with advising on the safeguarding of artworks and cultural heritage sites in war zones.

38 United Kingdom, *The Manual of the Law of Armed Conflict*, Ministry of Defence, 1 July 2004, Para 5.25,

a military objective. In its chapter on air operations, the manual states that "cultural objects are specially protected".[39]

The British Manual states that the 1954 Hague Convention and its 1999 Second Protocol also applies to non-international armed conflicts. It is prohibited to commit any act of hostilities against cultural property, so long as it is not being used for military purposes. Intentionally directing attacks against buildings dedicated to religion, education, art, science, or charitable purposes, and historic monuments, provided they are not military objectives, is a war crime.[40]

The United States

The United States participated actively in the negotiation and drafting of the 1954 Hague Cultural Property Convention and was one of the first to sign it. However, the US ratified the 1954 Hague Cultural Property Convention in March 2009. It has not ratified the Protocols to the 1954 Convention. The Department of Defence (DoD) Law of War Manual (June 2015, Updated 2023) serves as the authoritative statement on the law of war. The Manual describes the rights, duties, and liabilities of personnel engaged in duties related to the protection of cultural property. It also addresses the protection of cultural property during hostilities, including provisions of the Convention as well as the protection of cultural property in non-international armed conflict.[41]

The Law of War Manual, Para 5.18 defines cultural property in the language of Article 1 of the 1954 Hague Convention. It states that certain types

39 United Kingdom, *The Manual of the Law of Armed Conflict*, Ministry of Defence, 1 July 2004, para 12.26.

40 United Kingdom, *The Manual of the Law of Armed Conflict*, Ministry of Defence, 1 July 2004, para 15.18–15.18.3; see also para 15.52 (on situations in which Additional Protocol II is applicable).

41 A variety of other publications and guidance issued by US Department of Defence components for their personnel also include references to the Convention and its requirements related to the protection of cultural property, where appropriate. For example: The Law of Air, Space, and Cyber Operations (2020), issued by the Judge Advocate General of the U.S. Air Force; Operational Law Handbook, issued by the Judge Advocate General's Legal Centre and School, U.S. Army, Charlottesville, Virginia, 2020; Department of the Army Field Manual (FM) 6-27 / Marine Corps Tactical Publication (MCTP) 11-10C, The Commander's Handbook on the Law of Land Warfare (2019); Navy Warfare Publication (NWP) 1-14M, MCTP 11-10B, Commandant Publication (COMDTPUB) P5800.7A, The Commander's Handbook on the Law of Naval Operations, 2017; Department of the Army, Graphic Training Aid (GTA) 41-01-002, Civil Affairs Arts, Monuments, And Archives Guide, 2015.

of property receive additional protection as cultural property. Cultural property, the areas immediately surrounding it, and appliances in use for its protection should be safeguarded and respected. Some obligations concerning cultural property apply during non-international armed conflict. There are also obligations concerning cultural property during occupation and peacetime. Certain treaty obligations concerning cultural property may only apply on the territory of Parties to the 1954 Hague Convention, but the US has previously identified some of these obligations as customary international law. The US defence personnel, therefore, in the absence of contrary guidance by competent authority, should act as if they were legally bound by the rules for the protection of cultural property in the 1954 Hague Convention during hostilities even when conducting operations in the territory of a State that is not a Party to the 1954 Hague Cultural Property Convention.

The Manual states that during armed conflict, different classes of persons may be engaged in duties related to the protection of cultural property. These classes of persons may include: specialist personnel in the armed forces, armed custodians specially empowered to guard cultural property, as well as persons who are engaged in duties of control by the Regulations for the Execution of the 1954 Hague Convention. So far as consistent with the interests of security, such personnel should be respected and permitted to carry out their duties for the protection of cultural property. No special agreement may be concluded that would diminish the protection afforded by the 1954 Hague Cultural Property Convention to the personnel engaged in the protection of cultural property.[42]

According to the Manual, the protecting Power shall appoint delegates to perform certain functions in the protection of cultural property. The delegates of the Protecting Powers shall take note of violations of the 1954 Hague Convention, investigate, with the approval of the Party to which they are accredited, the circumstances in which they have occurred, make representations locally to secure their cessation, and, if necessary, notify the Commissioner-General of such violations. They shall keep the Commissioner-General informed of their activities.[43]

According to Manual para 5.18.3, no use should be made of cultural property, its immediate surroundings, or appliances in use for its protection,

42 The Department of Defence (DoD) Law of War Manual (June 2015, Updated 2023), Para 4.14, at p. 138.

43 The Department of Defence (DoD) Law of War Manual (June 2015, Updated 2023), Para 4.14.2.3, p. 140

for purposes that are likely to expose it to destruction or damage in the event of armed conflict. However, such use is permissible when military necessity imperatively requires such use. Uses that would be likely to expose cultural property to destruction or damage in the event of armed conflict would include: (i) using the cultural property for military purposes; (ii) placing military objectives near cultural property; or (iii) using the cultural property in such a way that an adversary would likely regard it as a military objective. For example, such uses would include billeting military personnel in buildings that constitute cultural property, or placing artillery, mortars, or anti-air systems on the grounds of cultural property. In addition, it is prohibited to deliberately use the threat of potential harm to cultural property to shield military objectives from attack, or otherwise to shield, favour, or impede military operations. There is no waiver of this obligation in cases of imperative military necessity.

The US Military Manual, para 5.18.6.1 dictates that military commanders must take reasonable measures to prevent or stop any form of theft, pillage, or misappropriation of, and any acts of vandalism directed against cultural property. This obligation may also be viewed as part of the obligation to take feasible precautions to reduce the risk of harm to cultural property. What efforts would be reasonable would depend on a variety of factors, such as the availability of forces, the commander's mission, and enemy threats. What efforts would be reasonable would also depend on the information available to the commander at the time. The failure of a State to fulfil its obligations in peacetime to safeguard cultural property during armed conflict does not relieve other States of their obligation to respect cultural property.

Military Doctrines: NATO

In recent years, cultural property protection has been increasingly put forward in NATO's military doctrine as a tactical and operational objective across all three of its core tasks of deterrence and defence, crisis prevention and management, and cooperative security. NATO's 2018 Military Concept on the Protection of Civilians stresses the importance of understanding and interacting with the human environment, including local culture and history, to ensure operational effectiveness. Based on NATO's Protection of Civilians policy, a Bi-Strategic Command Directive on "Implementing Cultural Property Protection in NATO Operations and Missions" was subsequently developed in 2019. It holds that cultural property protection considerations are crucial to NATO's continuous strategic awareness and sets forward guidelines for NATO's command structure to integrate them into all phases of military operations and missions.

NATO Allies have also been instrumental in enhancing cultural heritage protection in conflict at the national level. Allies have taken measures to integrate the protection of cultural heritage international rules, norms, and principles into their national legislation. For instance, Canada's Cultural Property Export and Import Act of 1985 seeks to ensure the preservation of the country's cultural heritage and prevent the illicit traffic of cultural objects (Government of Canada, 2022). Since 2005, it is also an offence under the country's Criminal Code for Canadians to damage, destroy or illicitly export protected cultural property situated outside of Canada, whether in peacetime or during conflict. Similarly, France adopted the Law on Freedom of Creation, Architecture and Heritage in 2016 to enhance the protection of cultural heritage situated on its territory. The law also gives France the possibility to offer temporary shelter to cultural heritage at risk due to armed conflict abroad, upon the request of the concerned State or the UN Security Council. In addition, the Allies have made efforts to integrate cultural protection principles into their national military doctrine and practice. They have taken steps to build relevant capacity within their national armed forces by setting up specialised units and providing relevant training to support operational readiness.

Training

Article 25 of the 1954 Hague Convention and Article 30(3)(b) of its 1999 Second Protocol oblige states parties to provide their armed forces with peacetime training and other education in the protection of cultural property in armed conflict. The States follow different practices in imparting training and education to their armed forces in the protection of cultural property in armed conflict. For instance, Austria has issued a Directive for the Military Protection of Cultural Property and the Military Safeguarding of Cultural Heritage (December 2009); Belgium has a course on protected places and property for advisors on the law of armed conflict (May 2011); El Salvador, follows its instruction manual on the protection of cultural property in the event of armed conflict (November 2000). Italy has issued its Directive on the Protection of Cultural Property in the Event of Armed Conflict (2012), and France follows its Handbook on the Protection of Cultural Property in the Event of Armed Conflict (2015). The US, besides training, has also produced a pocket guide for its military personnel on heritage preservation. UNESCO has developed a range of training materials for military and associated personnel on the protection of cultural property in both armed conflict and stabilisation missions. Military personnel tasked with securing the protection of cultural property in armed conflict can be found today in the armed forces of a variety of states.[44]

UNESCO Training Programme: Understanding the ramifications of protecting cultural heritage necessitates critical education and training in cultural awareness. To this end, UNESCO has developed an online training programme for the military, police, and law enforcement officials. This course has been developed to support the implementation of rules governing the protection of cultural property, which aim to protect cultural property in armed conflict and prevent it from being destructed, pillaged, looted, or illicitly trafficked. The course is likely to provide a better understanding of the international legal framework for the protection of cultural heritage in armed conflict, as well as good practices in the application of the law. Although broadly applicable to military operations and activities, the course has been made with UN peacekeeping operations in mind. It describes some real-life situations from earlier missions in conflict areas and touches on relevant topics, such as gender and civil-military cooperation.[45]

There are many reasons why conflict actors, both state and non-state, train their sights on cultural heritage. Attacks on both tangible (buildings, monuments, and artefacts) and intangible (practices, customs, and knowledge) heritage are not only forms of propaganda by deed, but serve to deny people their very identities – their sense of self.[46] International

44 O'Keefe Roger, Peron Camille, Musayev Tofig and Ferrari Gianluca, 2016, Protection of Cultural Property: Military Manual, UNESCO, pp. 19-22.

45 This course is composed of five lessons. The first lesson explains the overall importance of protecting cultural property in the course of military operations and the set of international rules that have been put in place to this end. In lesson two, cultural property is defined, and the identification of cultural property in the field is discussed. Lesson three focuses on engagement with cultural property in the course of operations, when it may come under attack or fall victim to collateral damage. In the fourth lesson, the obligation to protect cultural property under the force's control is discussed. Lastly, the fifth lesson takes a look at the indispensable cooperation with civil authorities, heritage institutions, and experts. Protection of Cultural Property: Online Course for the Military, Police and Law Enforcement, UNESCO and the Peace Operations Training Institute, UNESCO, 2020, p. 60.

46 This loss is particularly egregious as cultural heritage is central to a person's sense of belonging and attachment to place. It anchors, orientates, and locates a person, a people, in time and space. In short, this destruction disrupts and dislocates, often

Humanitarian Law, including The Hague Convention for the Protection of Cultural Property in the Event of Armed Conflict (1954), to which 133 state parties are currently signatories, require states to ensure heritage is not damaged or misappropriated in war. Many states are conscious of their obligations and are acting to build relevant capabilities.

The US Army hosts a cultural protection programme at Fort Drum, in New York, where pre-deployment trainings are regularly organised, while the Netherlands have a long-standing Cultural Affairs and Information (CAI) Section within its armed forces which provides instructions on cultural heritage during all military pre-deployment training programmes. The US Army has also set up a Heritage and Preservation Officer Programme while the British armed forces have established a Property Protection Unit. Italy is one of the countries with the richest historical and cultural heritage in the world. Italy partnered with UNESCO in 2016 to create the "Blue Helmets of Culture" Task Force, a rapidly deployable unit composed of personnel from the Carabinieri Command for the Protection of Cultural Property and experts from the Ministry of Culture who can be sent to protect cultural property at risk anywhere in the world.[47] The Columbian Institute ICANH also issued guidelines for the military in 2009 which specified appropriate behaviour for the army towards the protection of cultural property.[48]

leaving victims psychologically adrift and emotionally hopeless. Clack Timothy, Cultural Heritage on the Frontline: the destruction of peoples and identities in war, University of Oxford, Expert Opinion, October 4, 2022.

47 The Carabinieri Command for the Protection of Cultural Heritage (Carabinieri TPC) is the first police specialized department created with the sole aim of combating the illicit traffic of Cultural Property. The command is functionally placed under Italy's Minister of Culture. The Commander of the TPC is one of the direct aides to the Minister, although not formally subordinate. Despite its peculiar organization and objectives, the TPC is a police department and, therefore, basically executes police tasks and plays a role regarding the safety and protection of the national cultural heritage, through the prevention and repression of the multiple interrelated criminal activities. It carries out preventive measures and direct interventions, but only about crimes involving cultural property. Spadari Luigi, CARABINIERI TPC, since 1969 in defence of our cultural heritage, Centre of Excellence for Stability Police Units, 2021.

48 In 2009, the Columbian Instituto Colombiano de Antropología Historia issued guidelines in this regard. Vargas Catalina Bateman, "The effects of conflict on the archaeological park of Ciudad Perdida (Lost City) in Colombia," in Lambert Simon and Cynthia Rockwell (ed.), Protecting Cultural Heritage in Times of Conflict, ICCROM, 2010, pp. 6-10. Under these guidelines, the troops must: (i) Understand and apply the legislation on protection of cultural heritage; (ii) Respect and observe the recommendations of the ICANH authorities; (iii) Abstain from displaying weapons or other combat elements to visitors (for photo or video purposes); (iv) Abstain

Issues in India

India, throughout its 5,000 years of history has developed its own rules of warfare. These rules were founded in ancient India on the principle of humanity. In the *Vedic* period, as society began to stabilise and became more politically and socially organised, the *Vedas*, the *Sastras* and the epics of *Ramayan* and *Mahabharat* started prescribing the laws and customs of war. The ancient Hindu text acknowledged the distinction between military objects, which could be the targets of attack; and non-military objects, which could not. Warfare, as a rule, was confined to combatants, cities or towns were not allowed to be ravaged during war, even while the armed forces were marching through them. [49] According to *Agnipurana* the concept of just war ordained the parties to leave the temples and other places of worship as well as the fruit and flower garden unmolested. *Manu* holds that the victorious king should worship in the temples, honour the priests, and proclaim peoples' safety in the conquered country. *Kautilya's Arthashastra* (400 BC) for the military was founded on the principle of humanity and the destruction of cities or towns during war was prohibited.[50] The *Mahabharata* and the laws of *Manu* also contain provisions that forbid the use of certain weapons and regulate the protection of enemy property.

India has the world's largest volunteer military. The armed forces have fought four major wars and since the last four decades, its army has been actively engaged in internal armed conflicts. It has also taken proactive action in neutralising non-state actors across the international borders. India is one of the biggest contributors of the forces for the UN Peacekeeping

---

from throwing trash, extracting flora or fauna and archaeological or ethnological material, and damaging the park's archaeological and natural heritage; (v) Inform their superior in rank or the park staff about any fortuitous archaeological find; (vi) Abstain from hunting, cutting wood and building fires; (vii) Separate the solid wastes and dispose of biodegradable materials in the places indicated; and take other kinds of trash (plastics, cardboard, paper, cans), down to town; (viii) Define a place away from the archaeological structures and visitor paths to place the encampment; (ix) Define a secure and adequate place for cooking to avoid forest fires; and (x) Execute the programmes of sanitation, management and preservation of ecosystems included in the armed forces' process of environmental management, designed to prevent and minimize the impact on the environment due to their institutional mission.

49 M. K. Sinha, Hinduism and international humanitarian law, *International Review of the Red Cross*, Vol. 87, No. 858, June 2005, pp.284-285.

50 Kautilya's Arthashastra proves that the ancient Hindus knew the composition of many kinds of asphyxiating gases, but Kautilya disallows their indiscriminate use even in the most stubborn siege warfare. Bandhopadhyay Pramathanath, 1920, *International Law and Custom in Ancient India*, Calcutta: University Press, p. 148.

Missions. However, to date, no written manual on the law of war specifies the duties and obligations of the members of the armed forces engaged in various armed conflicts. India is one of the countries with the richest historical and cultural heritage in the world. There is an urgent need to come up with an authoritative restatement of the law governing the armed conflicts including India's obligations under the 1954 Hague Convention and its Protocol. Military manuals need not reflect only the most basic level of treaty compliance. As policy guides, manuals must also represent larger international and national ideals. Indeed, the manuals do implicitly recognise the 1954 Hague Convention. However, it would be preferable if the manuals did not just recognise the Convention, but also incorporated significant elements of the Convention into Indian military policy. For the manual to stay relevant for the armed forces personnel, the government must review the manual, and update it at regular intervals say, every five years. This is important for the manual to keep serving its purpose, to disseminate IHL, and ensure IHL compliance.

Today, both domestic and international law play an increasingly important part in the activities of the armed forces. The law of war is a part of the world's military heritage and the members of the armed forces are bound to obey it. There need not be any conflict between the law of war and military doctrines that form the basis for effective combat operations. To prevent violations, the law must become an integral part of operations. The conduct of military operations is governed by international law, including the law of war, applicable international human rights law, and the UN Charter. States and individuals are obliged to comply with the law of war. All States are obliged to train their forces to comply with the law of war and with other provisions of international law that impact military operations. Civilians and military personnel responsible for implementing the law of war should be informed about the applicable rules. The national military manuals serve two main functions: they are an instrument for disseminating the laws of war and for expressing that a nation understands its legal obligations. Even wars have rules, and those rules must be disseminated. There is no requirement for a separate manual on the protection of cultural property, these provisions could be part of the national military manual on the law of war.

Chapter 8

Emerging Issues in the Protection of Cultural Property

One of the by-products of armed conflict is the destruction of cultural property, which could be intentional or unintentional. Cultural property often ravaged during such conflict includes works of art, religious sites, ancient monuments and historical documents.[1] A plethora of modern examples indicate that conflict-related destruction and looting of cultural property continue even now.[2] In this chapter, a few additional issues relating to the protection of cultural property during armed conflict are discussed. These include the impact of explosive weapons on cultural property; nuclear disarmament and the protection of cultural property; protection of cultural property in UN peacekeeping operations; the impact of social

1 The plunder of art has been the aim of war for centuries, or at least a direct corollary of any armed conflict or intervention. The collections of Western museums were formed, in part, with the archaeological and historical spoils from military campaigns, including from the Indian region. Norms have greatly changed, however, and plunder is no longer an acceptable practice. Losson Pierre, Does the International Trafficking of Cultural Heritage Fuel Military Conflicts? *Studies in Conflict and Terrorism*, Vol. 40, No. 6, 2017, pp. 484-495.

2 In the event of armed conflict, cultural property can be endangered in various ways. The damage can be unintentional, when cultural property is demolished during an attack on a military target (collateral damage), for example, or when cultural property is neglected. The archaeologists leave countries at war and sites are consequently left unprotected. Museums are temporarily closed and conservation efforts on monuments are halted. The maintenance of cultural property is no longer a priority. Regretfully, the threat to cultural property can also be intentional. In some cases, the destruction of cultural property can become an aim in itself. In identity-bound conflicts, the warring parties can destroy the symbolic goods of the "other" to underscore their historic claims to the territory. Auwera Sigrid Van der, International Law and the Protection of Cultural Property in the Event of Armed Conflict: Actual Problems and Challenges, *The Journal of Arts Management, Law, and Security*, Vol. 43, 2013, pp. 175-190.

media; the destruction of cultural property as a weapon of war; and the protection of cultural property versus combatants lives in armed conflict.

The Use of Explosive Weapons

In recent armed conflicts in Gaza, Myanmar, Sudan, Syria, Ukraine, Yemen, and elsewhere, the use of explosive weapons has killed and injured thousands of civilians and caused long-term harm to cultural property. When used in populated areas, explosive weapons kill and injure civilians and destroy civilian objects. The explosive weapons also cause serious harm to cultural heritage.[3] According to Explosive Weapons Monitor, explosive weapons have caused harm to civilians and their infrastructure in at least 75 countries and territories in 2023.[4] In early May 2022, Russian forces fired a munition that struck a museum complex, including the final home of the 18th-century Ukrainian philosopher and poet Hryhorii Skovoroda. The attack sparked a fire that raged for nearly nine hours. By the time the blaze was extinguished, almost all that remained were scorched walls and a pockmarked statue of the national figure.[5]

According to the UN, the vast majority of civilian casualties in the Russian-Ukraine War have resulted from the use of explosive weapons in

3 Technologically, there are many types of explosive weapons, including bombs, artillery shells, grenades, missiles, landmines and improvised explosive devices, which are activated by the detonation of a highly explosive substance. Types of weapons that are particularly problematic include indirect fire weapons, such as artillery, rockets and mortars, weapons that fire in salvos, such as multi-launch rocket systems, large air-dropped bombs and surface-to-surface ballistic missiles. Such systems variously involve munitions with a large destructive radius, weapons with inaccurate delivery systems or weapon systems that deliver multiple munitions over a wide area. The use of explosive weapons may have a devastating impact, in particular those with wide-area impacts, in populated areas having a concentration of civilians and/or civilian objects. Many of these weapons were originally designed for use in open battlefields and are inherently indiscriminate when used in populated areas. Their use may result in increased civilian casualties and property damage as well. When living spaces are severely restricted due to high levels of explosive ordnance, contamination continues to kill and injure years after the fighting has stopped and hamper reconstruction efforts. United Nations Office for Disarmament Affairs, available at: https://disarmament.unoda.org/convarms/explosive-weapons/.

4 Explosive Weapon Monitor Report 2023, April 2024, pp. 66. Available at: https://www.explosiveweaponsmonitor.org/sites/default/files/downloads/EWM_Annual%20Report_2023_0.pdf.

5 Docherty Bonnie, Explosive Weapons Pose Threats to Cultural Heritage: States Have a Tool to Protect It, Jus Security, June 4, 2024, available at: https://www.justsecurity.org/96357/explosive-weapons-cultural-heritage/.

populated areas. The war has also had a significant impact on Ukraine's cultural heritage.[6] As of January 2024, Ukraine's Ministry of Culture and Information Policy had documented almost 3,000 cases of damage to cultural heritage. As of mid-March 2024, UNESCO has verified damage to 346 cultural properties based on its preliminary assessments.[7] Given the widespread impact of the use of explosive weapons in populated areas, it is likely responsible for a significant portion of the cultural heritage damage in such areas.

According to Human Rights Watch,[8] impact of explosive weapons can have a direct as well as direct impact on cultural heritage. The blast produced by detonations on or near cultural heritage can bend and break the structural elements of a building, even concrete and steel, leading to the collapse of part or all of an entire edifice. Explosive weapons use is particularly harmful to cultural heritage because sites are often old or made of more vulnerable materials, such as unreinforced masonry, clay, stone, or wood. Fragments of an explosive weapon and the debris dispersed by its detonation also directly affect cultural heritage. They can scar building facades and surface decorations and shatter glass windows. If they penetrate the windows of a place of worship, museum, or archives, they can damage interior walls or objects within, such as paintings, sculptures, tapestries, or books. While explosive weapons are not incendiary weapons, they frequently start devastating fires. The presence of flammable materials, such as wood, paper, or fabric, can quickly spread flames. In December 2023, the use of explosive weapons by Israeli forces toppled part of the minaret, crumbled the roof, and left pockmarks on the walls of the Great Omari Mosque, which was originally built in the 7th century and is the oldest in Gaza.

As regards, the indirect effects of explosive weapons on cultural heritage, structural damage caused by an initial attack can weaken walls or foundations and lead to the complete collapse of a building at a later date. Holes in the roof or walls or loss of windows leave cultural heritage sites

6 As reported, the Russians have begun using the FAB-3000 super-powerful glide bombs. These high-explosive bombs carry nearly 1,500 kg of explosive and have tremendous power, potentially causing severe concussions to people tens of meters from the explosion's epicentre. Tom Watling, Has Russia just dropped a deadly new 3,000kg glide bomb in Ukraine? *Independent*, June 21, 2024.

7 Damaged Cultural Sites in Ukraine Verified by UNESCO, UNESCO, updated March 18, 2024, Available at: https://www.unesco.org/en/articles/damaged-cultural-sites-ukraine-verified-unesco?hub=66116.

8 Destroying Cultural Heritage: Explosive Weapons' Effects in Armed Conflict and Measures to Strengthen Protection, Human Rights Watch, April 2024, p. 87.

open to exposure and speed up the decay of a building, its collections, and interior decorations. Damage to internet infrastructure can lead to the loss of digital databases of cultural heritage, such as collections of scanned manuscripts, that are not backed up. Explosive weapons may thus destroy both the original and digital versions of manuscripts, artworks, buildings, or monuments, making it harder to recover any losses. Loss of infrastructure due to attacks with explosive weapons indirectly affects cultural heritage because it can shut down climate control and security systems, endangering art, artefacts, and archives. In Iraq, flooding from water pipes hit by missiles damaged buildings containing items of cultural heritage. [9] Loss of cultural property can also affect local economies, as some structures or sites can be a source of direct revenue for the civilian population, and even contribute to the wider economy. Civilians face the direct consequences of explosive weapons' impacts on cultural heritage. People who live or seek shelter in cultural heritage sites may be killed or injured during an attack. In protracted armed conflicts, the direct and indirect effects on essential services and cultural heritage accumulate with the multiple and repeated use of heavy explosive weapons and make the recovery difficult very costly and time-consuming.[10]

The Human Rights Watch Report (2024) states that at least 15 of the hundreds of people sheltering in the Donetsk Academic Regional Drama Theatre in Mariupol, Ukraine, died during a Russian airstrike on March 16, 2022. Civilians also experience indirect effects from cultural heritage destruction. They may lose their livelihoods or even their homes when explosive weapons strike cultural heritage sites. In Yemen, damage to such sites in Taizz hurt the tourist industry, and residents of the Old City of Sanaa were forcibly displaced when their homes were destroyed. Harm to cultural heritage may also result in a loss of history. The bombing of Old Sanaa, for example, damaged both a World Heritage Site and buildings that people have lived in continuously since the 11th century.[11]

9 Damage to nearby civilian infrastructure can also indirectly affect cultural heritage by unleashing damaging materials. For instance, during the US military's 2003 invasion of Iraq, even missiles that "struck targets cleanly" damaged nearby water pipes, "flooding adjacent buildings containing cultural heritage." Beitler Ruth Margolies and Dexter W. Dugan, "Practicing the Art of War While Protecting Cultural Heritage: A Military Perspective," in Cuno James and Thomas G. Weiss, 2022, Cultural Heritage and Mass Atrocities, Los Angeles: Getty Publications, pp. 500-516.

10 *Explosive Weapons with Wide Area Effects: A Deadly Choice in Populated Areas*, ICRC, Geneva, January 2022, pp 150.

11 Destroying Cultural Heritage: Explosive Weapons' Effects in Armed Conflict and Measures to Strengthen Protection, Human Rights Watch, April 2024, pp. 87; Docherty

There is no dispute that any use of explosive weapons in populated areas must comply with the rules of IHL. However, there are divergent views on whether these rules sufficiently regulate the use of such weapons, or whether there is a need to clarify their interpretation or to develop new standards or rules. Based on the effects of explosive weapons in populated areas being witnessed today, there are serious questions regarding how the parties using such weapons are interpreting and applying IHL. The divergent practice of militaries, and contrasting views among experts and in the case law of international criminal tribunals regarding what is or is not legally acceptable, may point to ambiguities in IHL and the need for states to clarify their interpretation of the relevant IHL rules or to develop clearer standards to effectively protect civilians."[12]

The International Committee of the Red Cross has recommended that political authorities of the states and the parties to armed conflict must take the following preventive measures:[13]

- Ensure that the protection of civilians is explicitly identified as a strategic objective at the highest level before military operations and that the armed forces integrate it into all military orders.
- Ensure that the military authorities develop specific military doctrine or adapt existing doctrine to address the humanitarian concerns and the operational challenges posed by the conduct of hostilities in populated areas, including urban warfare.
- Mandate doing everything possible to keep hostilities in populated areas to a minimum, including by moving them outside populated areas or moving the population outside areas of hostilities, and other measures to prevent or mitigate civilian harm.

Bonnie, Explosive Weapons Pose Threats to Cultural Heritage: States Have a Tool to Protect It, *Jus Security*, June 4, 2024, available at: https://www.justsecurity.org/96357/explosive-weapons-cultural-heritage/.

12 International Humanitarian Law and the Challenges of Contemporary Armed Conflicts, Report prepared for the 32nd International Conference of the Red Cross and Red Crescent, Geneva, 2015 (ICRC Challenges Report 2015), p. 51; International Humanitarian Law and the Challenges of Contemporary Armed Conflicts, Report prepared for the 33rd International Conference of the Red Cross and Red Crescent, Geneva, 2019 (ICRC Challenges Report 2019), p. 14.

13 *Explosive Weapons with Wide Area Effects: A Deadly Choice in Populated Areas*, ICRC, Geneva, January 2022, p 150.

- Review, amend, adapt or update existing policies or develop new policies to mitigate the risk to civilians posed by the use of explosive weapons with a wide impact area in populated areas.

The humanitarian consequences of the use of heavy explosive weapons in urban and other populated areas are well documented in recent and ongoing armed conflicts in many parts of the world. Their devastating direct and indirect effects are largely the result of a deadly combination: the weapons' technical characteristics and consequent wide impact area, which may extend beyond the targeted military objective. Consequently, heavy explosive weapons are inappropriate for use in populated areas, as such use entails a high risk of affecting civilians and civilian objects including cultural heritage. Restrictions and limitations on the use of heavy explosive weapons in urban and other populated areas would contribute to a reduction in civilian casualties. However, the reality on the ground dictates that much attention needs to be given while planning and carrying out operations in populated areas.

Nuclear Weapons and Protection of Cultural Property

At the beginning of 2024, nine states—the US, the Russian Federation, the UK, France, China, India, Pakistan, the Democratic People's Republic of Korea (North Korea) and Israel—together possess approximately 12,121 nuclear weapons, which 9,585 are considered to be potentially operationally available.[14] A single thermonuclear weapon can have the destructive power of a million times the largest conventional weapon.[15] The detonation of a nuclear weapon produces a blast wave, a thermal wave, instantaneous radiation, a radioactive fall-out and an electromagnetic pulse. If several

14 Kristensen Hans M. and Matt Korda, "World Nuclear Forces," *SIPRI Yearbook 2024: Armaments, Disarmament and International Security*, SIPRI 2024, pp. 271-367.

15 Nuclear weapons that release a large portion of their energy in fusion reactions are called thermonuclear weapons or, more popularly, hydrogen (H) bombs. The dominant fusion reactions are between isotopes of hydrogen-deuterium and tritium. The fusion reaction cannot be triggered by a conventional charge alone. To get hydrogen isotopes to fuse in sufficient quantities rapidly enough to produce an explosion requires very high temperatures, like those in the interior of the sun. Therefore, thermonuclear weapons use a fission component with plutonium-239 or uranium-235 to trigger the fusion reaction. The main radioactive contaminants from thermonuclear weapons come from the fission triggers and any uranium-238, uranium-235, or plutonium-239 close enough to the fusion portion of the weapon to be split by neutrons from the fusion reaction. In the case of a 1-megaton H-bomb, the fission trigger contributes only about 3 per cent of the radioactive contamination; the rest comes from the uranium-238 tamper.

powerful weapons are used at the same time, global environmental disturbance and climatic changes may take place. Radiation exposure—including fallout from nuclear tests—causes acute and long-term illnesses that are often deadly, as well as genetic and inter-generational health effects. The effects of nuclear weapon detonation will have serious prolonged effects on human beings and their surrounding environment. The entire global economy would be severely impacted.[16] It will also result in the destruction and the irreversible loss of cultural heritage.

The Japanese cities of Hiroshima and Nagasaki were destroyed in 1945 by the only two nuclear explosions detonated in conflict. One of the persons, who witnessed the damage caused by the nuclear weapon states, "When I walked out onto the bridge and looked over toward Hiroshima Castle, toppled to earth and flattened, a great wave of emotion swept over me. Grief and the ability to think, reviving periodically, made my heart ache... Hiroshima, too, had its history, and it saddened me to march forward over the corpse of its past."[17]

Nuclear weapons have not been used in conflict since 1945. However, nuclear weapons tests by the US at Bikini Atoll in the Marshall Islands affected the geology and environment so deeply that it is now considered a UNESCO World Heritage Site in itself, 'bearing witness to the consequences of the nuclear tests on the civil populations of Bikini and the Marshall Islands, in terms of population displacement and public health.[18]

16 Khera Kishore Kumar and Jha U. C., 2022, *Nuclear Weapons: Untangling the Societal Enigma*, New Delhi: Vij Books, p. 229.

17 Ota Yoko, "City of Corpses", in Minear Richard H. (edited & translated), 1990, *Hiroshima: Three Witnesses*, Princeton University Press, pp. 416. Yoko also says: 'The fact that the castle had been demolished so utterly told me something. Even supposing a new city was to be built on this land, there would be no rebuilding of the castle.

18 The US selected Bikini Atoll in the Marshall archipelago in the Pacific Ocean for testing its nuclear weapons. After the displacement of the local inhabitants, 23 nuclear tests were carried out from 1946 to 1958. The cumulative force of the tests in all of the Marshall Islands was equivalent to 7,000 times that of the Hiroshima bomb. In the Marshall Islands, people relocated from their homes and communities during the tests at Bikini Atoll have been unable to return due to 'near-irreversible environmental contamination' and thus the destruction of the Marshall Islands' cultural heritage. Their tangible cultural heritage has been lost for generations along with the natural environment. The site has not undergone any substantial reconstruction; human presence there has remained very limited because of the radionuclides produced by the explosions. UNESCO: Bikini Atoll Nuclear Test Site, available at: https://whc.unesco.org/en/list/1339/.

A good amount of cultural heritage is situated in regions widely considered at high risk of a nuclear conflict: East Asia, South Asia, and between Russia and the US. There is also a constant threat to the likely use of nuclear weapons in the ongoing armed conflicts. Russia is the largest nuclear weapon state in the world. According to its nuclear doctrine Russia does not advocate first use of nuclear weapons, but neither does it rule out first use in response to a conventional attack that threatens the existence of the state. Russia has continued to make threats regarding the use of nuclear weapons in the context of Western support for Ukraine. In May 2024 Russia carried out tactical nuclear weapon drills close to the Ukrainian border. Israel does not publicly acknowledge possessing nuclear weapons. However, it is believed that Israel is also modernising its nuclear arsenal and appears to be upgrading its plutonium production reactor site at Dimona. There is a growing concern that North Korea might intend to use these weapons very early in a conflict. According to Dan Smith, SIPRI Director, "There are numerous sources of instability—political rivalries, economic inequalities, ecological disruption, an accelerating nuclear arms race. We are now in one of the most dangerous periods in human history."[19] Along with areas containing critical infrastructure industries, heavily populated cities are likely targets for strategic nuclear weapons. In the event of a nuclear exchange between one or more states possessing nuclear weapons, considerable cultural heritage is likely to be destroyed.

Cities targeted as part of nuclear-war strategies contain cultural monuments, architecture, museums, galleries, libraries, archives and other sites that would be lost in a nuclear exchange. Similarly, military bases outside urban centres would also be targeted, resulting in varying degrees of damage to cultural heritage and antiquities. The impact of this destruction on future generations would be immeasurable. States possessing nuclear weapons are not the only countries whose heritage is at risk of destruction. Countries hosting nuclear weapons would also be at a serious risk. They could also be targeted with nuclear weapons in a conflict. Furthermore, the transportation of nuclear weapons at sea also endangers the heritage of countries whose waters are transited.

Given the difficulties associated with restoring or recovering heritage damaged by conventional weapons, several factors will have to be considered when restoring heritage caught in a nuclear blast. For instance, it would be difficult to quantify exactly what has been lost. Archaeological

19 Role of nuclear weapons grows as geopolitical relations deteriorate, SIPRI June 17, 2024.

sites, both above ground and underwater, or sites such as caves and the seabed, could be lost before they are yet to be documented. The mass migration of the population in the aftermath of a nuclear attack would also contribute to the decline of cultural knowledge, artefacts, traditions, languages and religions.

A nuclear conflict between two or more states would cause unprecedented destruction to cultural and natural heritage. The impact will be faced by both, the nuclear as well as non-nuclear weapon states. The nine states possessing nuclear weapons are home to 215 UNESCO World Heritage Sites. Non-nuclear-weapon countries that host nuclear weapons contain 127 World Heritage Sites within their territory, and dozens more are found in states that are members of nuclear alliances that would also be put at risk in a nuclear exchange. Thus, the nuclear weapon states have special liabilities and responsibilities in terms of risk assessments for their human impact, including for the protection of cultural heritage. These states must consider the risks posed to cultural heritage and the mitigation strategies they use in their nuclear weapons doctrines and policies. The need to protect cultural heritage should be considered an integral part of the case to prohibit and eliminate nuclear weapons.[20]

UN Peacekeeping Operations and Cultural Property

In the Preamble to its Charter, the UN placed the maintenance of peace among nations as its primary reason for existence. The Security Council, while acting on behalf of the UN, has been conferred with the responsibility of maintaining international peace and security. The Charter of the UN provides that it shall not intervene in the domestic jurisdiction of any state, except in enforcement measures taken under Chapter VII. Peacekeeping operations have traditionally been associated with Chapter VI of the UN Charter dealing with the 'Pacific Settlement of Disputes'. However, the Security Council need not refer to a specific chapter of the Charter when passing a resolution authorising the deployment of a peacekeeping operation and has never invoked Chapter VI. In recent years, the Security Council has adopted the practice of invoking Chapter VII of the Charter when authorising the deployment of peacekeeping operations in volatile post-conflict settings where the State is unable to maintain security and

20 Aghlani Sasan, Patricia Lewis and Beyza Unal, Nuclear Disarmament and the Protection of Cultural Heritage, Chatham House, International Security Department, October 2017, p. 14.

public order. The UN does not have its military force and depends on contributions from Member States.

In the past, international peacekeepers have witnessed attacks on cultural heritage by the states engaged in armed conflict. In 1948, the UN Security Council mandated the UN Truce Supervision Organization (UNTSO) to observe the armistice that ended the first Arab–Israeli war. The armistice line ran through Jerusalem, where Jordanian forces held the Old City and holy sites. Both sides were responsible for damage to historical buildings. The Jordanians used synagogues in the Jewish quarter of the Old City as stables, while Israeli troops used churches on the front line as barracks. In 1954, new fighting erupted in Jerusalem, and while UNTSO observers tried to mediate cease-fires, Arab officials accused the Israelis of bombarding religious sites. The Lebanese permanent representative to the UN in New York complained to the Security Council that shells had hit the Old City's medieval citadel and Armenian monastery, and fallen close to the Church of the Holy Sepulchres.[21] With just a handful of military observers on the spot, UNTSO had neither the mandate nor the resources to focus on cultural heritage issues. But things have changed and the peacekeeping forces have grown in size and ambition.[22] In the past 75 years, more than 2 million uniformed and civilian UN Peacekeepers have worked to save and change lives in the world's most fragile political and security situations. Today, there are over 63,500 military peacekeepers contributed by national armies from across the globe.[23]

The protection of cultural property during peace operations under Chapters VI and VII of the UN Charter has been generally ignored. The model agreement between the UN and member States contributing personnel and equipment to peacekeeping operations was drafted in 1991. It includes a standard clause which states that the peacekeeping operations shall observe and respect the principles and spirit of general international conventions applicable to the conduct of military personnel. These international conventions include the four Geneva Conventions of 1949,

21 UN Security Council Letter Dated July 5, 1954, from the Alternate Representative of Lebanon on the Security Council Addressed to the President of the Security Council, UN Doc. S/3264, July 7, 1954.

22 Gowan Richard, "Peace Operations and the Protection of Cultural Heritage," in Cuno James, and Thomas G. Weiss, (eds.), 2022, *Cultural Heritage and Mass Atrocities*, Los Angeles: Getty Publications, pp. 517-530.

23 By the end of April 2024, there were a total of 63, 579 individuals (troops, police units, and experts) deployed in UN missions all over the world. Available at: https://peacekeeping.un.org/sites/default/files/00-front_page_msr_april.pdf.

the Additional Protocols of 1977 and the 1954 Hague Convention on the Protection of Cultural Property. In addition, Section 6.6 of the 1999 UN Secretary-General bulletin, applicable to UN peacekeepers, states:

> The United Nations force is prohibited from attacking monuments of art, architecture or history, archaeological sites, works of art, places of worship and museums and libraries which constitute the cultural or spiritual heritage of peoples. In its area of operation, the United Nations force shall not use such cultural property or their immediate surroundings for purposes which might expose them to destruction or damage. Theft, pillage, misappropriation and any act of vandalism directed against cultural property is strictly prohibited.[24]

Article 4 of the 1954 Hague Convention provides that the High Contracting Parties must prohibit, prevent and, if necessary, put a stop to any form of theft, pillage or misappropriation of, and any acts of vandalism directed against cultural property. They must also refrain from any act directed by way of reprisals against cultural property. This provision of the Convention shows that the forces bound by IHL, like the UN peacekeepers, must protect cultural property from destruction, theft, pillage or misappropriation. The UN peacekeepers, though not bound by the international treaties relating to IHL or the protection of cultural properties, remain subject to the principles and rules of the UN. Peacekeepers must be legally responsible for the protection of cultural property and it should be defined in the Status of Force Agreements (SOFA).

On March 24, 2017, the Security Council unanimously adopted Resolution 2347, dealing exclusively with the destruction and trafficking of cultural heritage by terrorist groups and in situations of armed conflict.[25] Paragraph 17 of the Resolution called upon the states to prevent and counter trafficking of cultural property illegally appropriated and exported in the context of armed conflicts, notably by terrorist groups. Para19 of the resolution, referring to the decision of the International Criminal Court in Mali, provided:

> …… the mandate of United Nations peacekeeping operations, when specifically mandated by the Security Council and by their rules of

24 Secretary-General's Bulletin, Observance by United Nations forces of international humanitarian law, ST/SGB/1999/13 dated August 9, 1999.

25 Maintenance of international peace and security: destruction and trafficking of cultural heritage by terrorist groups and in situations of armed conflict, UN, S/RES/2347 dated March 24, 2017.

> engagement, may encompass, as appropriate, assisting relevant authorities, upon their request, in the protection of cultural heritage from destruction, illicit excavation, looting and smuggling in the context of armed conflicts, in collaboration with UNESCO, and that such operations should operate carefully when in the vicinity of cultural and historical sites.

This provision can be interpreted as a consolidation of the precedent set by the UN Multidimensional Integrated Stabilization Mission in Mali (MINUSMA) established on April 25, 2013. It was the first peacekeeping operation mandated by the Security Council through Resolution 2100 to "protect from attack the cultural and historical sites in Mali." According to Leloup (2019), heritage management can contribute to the broader ' stabilisation mandate' of UN peace operations by triggering a virtuous circle of confidence between the local population and UN staff on the ground.

After the destruction of mausoleums and damage to mosques by terrorist groups during the occupation of Northern Mali, MINUSMA undertook several quick impact projects (QIPs) to rehabilitate manuscript libraries and cultural properties in Timbuktu and Gao and also prevented pillaging of archaeological sites. Experts from UNESCO trained MINUSMA military, police and civilian staff in managing their environmental impact, especially on cultural and historical sites. Thus, MINUSMA's heritage management tasks contributed to the 'support activities' forming part of the operation's stabilisation mandate, aimed at 'gaining the confidence of the population.' The cultural heritage management by the Peacekeepers in Mali is a unique example of the UN stabilisation mandate till date. The major challenge arising from heritage management tasks undertaken by UN peace operations is to include local populations and to rebuild a sense of social cohesion. An experiment in Mali demonstrated how conceiving of cultural management as a 'support' activity by a UN peace mission could contribute to the overall stabilisation. [26] However, according to Leloup

26 The MINUSMA experience, however limited in time and space, provides new insights into the debate on the 'desirability and effectiveness' of quick impact projects (QIPs) within the stabilization mandates of UN peacekeeping operations. This is of particular interest at a time when Para 19 of Resolution 2347 of 2017 has left the door open for more systematic integration of cultural heritage protection within the mandates of future peace operations. Leloup Mathilde, Heritage Protection as Stabilization, the Emergence of a New 'Mandated Task' for UN Peace Operations, *International Peacekeeping*, Vol. 26(4), 2019, pp. 408–430; While MINUSMA's civilian component, as discussed above, did launch useful projects to assist its peacekeepers and local communities in the rehabilitation of Timbuktu, described further below, the United

(2019), this contribution is unreliable and may even trigger a vicious circle at a time when the blurred nature of stabilisation mandates' wording can lead to very different interpretations on the ground.[27]

The protection of cultural property by the UN peacekeeping missions will help create goodwill with the local community and thus win hearts and minds at the local level. This is particularly relevant to peacekeeping missions in light of the core principle of neutrality based on which they are expected to operate. Cultural property-inclusive peacekeeping missions are more likely to garner local support than a mission which does not incorporate cultural property in its mandate. They are more likely to be perceived as apolitical and thereby be seen as less imposing on the host state's sovereignty. Where cultural property in the area where peacekeepers are to be deployed is assessed to be at risk, cultural property needs to be on the agenda from the outset, during the planning phase and thus before deployment. To prevent its destruction, guarding exceptionally important objects of immovable cultural property should be envisaged by the mission's mandate and the rules of engagement.[28]

In March 2004, during the crisis in Kosovo, Albanian rioters attacked a series of Serb communities and religious sites, including Serbian Orthodox churches dating back to the fourteenth century. However, the German peacekeeping contingent stationed in Prizren was unable or unwilling to protect this heritage. Reportedly German soldiers stepped away from their checkpoint positions as mobs approached. Troops guarding one of Prizren's religious buildings asked a mob for time to remove their equipment from it before the mob burned it down. The violence left the pearl and Jerusalem of Kosovo' a disfigured, mutilated and blackened remnant.[29] Similarly in

States persuaded other Security Council members in 2018 that this was no longer a priority, and it was cut from the mandate. Gowan Richard, "Peace Operations and the Protection of Cultural Heritage," in Cuno James, and Thomas G. Weiss, (eds.), 2022, *Cultural Heritage and Mass Atrocities*, Los Angeles: Getty Publications, pp. 517-530.

27 Leloup Mathilde, Heritage Protection as Stabilization, the Emergence of a New 'Mandated Task' for UN Peace Operations, *International Peacekeeping*, Vol. 26(4), 2019, pp. 408–430.

28 Petrovic Jadranka, "The Cultural Dimension of Peace Operations: Peacekeeping and Cultural Property," in Campbell Andrew H., (2018), Global Leadership Initiatives for Conflict Resolution and Peacebuilding, IGI Global, pp. 84-115.

29 In Prizren, local people said a more determined effort by German KFOR could have prevented the destruction of churches, monasteries and seminaries. There were reports of soldiers stepping away from their checkpoint positions as mobs approached. According to one persistent rumour, troops guarding one of Prizren's religious

Afghanistan and Iraq, the US and its allies proved unwilling to secure museums and heritage sites from epidemics of looting after intervening in 2001 and 2003, respectively. In January 2008, peacekeepers of the UN Mission for the Referendum in Western Sahara vandalised a prehistoric site containing 6,000-year-old rock paintings. Hopefully, in the future, such incidents of failure to protect cultural heritage by international forces will be reduced.

UN officials have highlighted three main priorities for peace operations: (i) Saving civilians facing imminent violence and, where possible, deterring such violence before it begins; (ii) Creating the best possible conditions for conflict parties to compromise; and (iii) Community-level engagement to rebuild fractured societies. It is in this context that the case for treating the protection of cultural heritage as a priority must be made. If peace operations can offer only limited physical protection for cultural heritage, they may also facilitate more political approaches to the problem. The case of Mali also offers evidence that peacekeeping missions can take a more people-centred approach to heritage protection.[30]

Responsibility of the UN for acts by its Peacekeeping Missions: The UN Secretariat has taken a clear position that, as a general matter, when a UN peacekeeping operation is under UN command and control and is engaged in military operations, the UN is responsible for violations of IHL committed by members of that mission.[31] However, as UN peacekeeping missions consist of troops contributed by member states, a question has arisen as to whether troop-contributing countries could also be responsible for the acts of their troops serving in UN peacekeeping missions. In 2013, this issue was considered in the courts of the Netherlands. These courts examined certain actions carried out by the Dutch Battalion while it was serving in the UN peacekeeping mission in the former Yugoslavia in the

buildings asked a mob for time to remove their equipment from it before the mob burned it down. The violence left "the pearl and Jerusalem of Kosovo" a disfigured, mutilated and blackened remnant. *Collapse in Kosovo*, Brussels: International Crisis Group (ICG), April 22, 2004, p. 20.

30 Gowan Richard, "Peace Operations and the Protection of Cultural Heritage," in Cuno James, and Thomas G. Weiss, (eds.), 2022, Cultural Heritage and Mass Atrocities, Los Angeles: Getty Publications, pp. 517-530.

31 Report of the Secretary-General on Financing of the United Nations Protection Force, the United Nations Confidence Restoration Operation in Croatia, the United Nations Preventive Deployment Force and the United Nations Peace Forces Headquarters, UN GAOR, 55th sess, Agenda Items 129 and 140(a), UN Doc A/51/389, September 20, 1996.

1990s. In particular, the courts examined whether the Netherlands was responsible for the deaths of three persons who were asked to leave the Dutch compound in Srebrenica, and who were subsequently killed by the Bosnian Serb forces. The Supreme Court of the Netherlands ruled that the Netherlands had effective control over the Dutch Battalion and was, therefore, responsible for the deaths of the individuals concerned. This case illustrates that not all actions by troops serving in a UN peacekeeping operation are attributable to the UN and that certain specific actions could be attributed to a state. It also illustrates that the question of attribution should be approached on a case-by-case basis and that the facts of the specific case should be examined carefully.[32]

UN Peacekeeping missions have evolved from early boots-on-the-ground operations, being non-inclusive of cultural property considerations, to complex missions, whose mandate in future must explicitly include the protection of cultural property. That peacekeepers are under obligation to protect cultural property is well entrenched in international law.[33] Today, peace operations play an important role a vitally important role in managing armed conflict, supporting stable peace and protecting endangered population and their cultural heritage.[34] Cultural property has a crucial role to play in the reconciliation and unification of the nation in the aftermath of conflict. An inscription on the National Museum in Afghanistan reminds us, "A nation stays alive when its culture stays alive."[35] Culture is inseparable from what it means to be a human being. We all must respect and protect cultural property. Due to its dual nature, i.e., comprising both 'national' and 'international. aspects, cultural property presupposes the responsibility of all peoples to protect it across space and across time. It is, therefore, essential that during peacetime, the armed forces are trained on the contents of the 1954 Hague Convention on the

32 *Netherlands v Nuhanovic*, Hoge Raad, Supreme Court of the Netherlands, Case No 12/03324, September 6, 2013.

33 Petrovic Jadranka, "The Cultural Dimension of Peace Operations: Peacekeeping and Cultural Property," in Campbell Andrew H., (2018), *Global Leadership Initiatives for Conflict Resolution and Peacebuilding*, IGI Global, pp. 84-115.

34 Williams Paul D. and Bellamy Alex J., 2021, *Understanding Peacekeeping*, UK: Polity Press, pp. 474.

35 Jachec-Neale Agnieszka, After Palmyra, What Can the World Do to Protect Cultural Treasures? *The Conversation*, September 2, 2015.

protection of cultural property and its two Protocols. This training is essential regardless of command level, role, or mission phase.[36]

Impact of Social Media

Social media has become one of the most popular spaces to express people's opinions. It enhances the connection between people and heritage by making it more accessible. It can be used to share information about cultural heritage events and activities, promote local cultural heritage sites, or provide a space for community members to share their personal stories and experiences related to cultural heritage.[37] However, social media also has a negative side. Due to its global reach, social media has a substantial impact on cultural heritage and its protection. During the occupation, a key challenge for foreign militaries in the protection of cultural heritage is that social media facilitates the immediate dissemination of an armed group's message to its intended audiences. The non-state armed groups destroy cultural heritage to expunge the identity of perceived enemies and sow fear throughout the population. Information is used as a weapon of war and it becomes vital to the success of military operations.

The videos of the destruction of cultural heritage by the Islamic State of Iraq and Syria (or Da'esh) were their most popular posts, as evidenced by the number of views. The rapid circulation of messages creates a dangerous environment for foreign militaries or peacekeepers in a host country. The destruction of the Bamiyan Buddhas in Afghanistan illustrates the impact of modern communication on cultural heritage destruction. The Taliban's manipulation of the media by encouraging the photographing and documentation of the demolition reflects its profound understanding of social media's value in achieving its strategic objectives. The ability of armed groups to manipulate messages through social media with strategic

36 Cunliffe Emma, et al. (ed.), The Protection of Cultural Property in the Event of Armed Conflict: Unnecessary Distraction or Mission-Relevant Priority? NATO OPEN Publications, Volume 2, No. 4, Summer 2018, p. 29.

37 The term 'social media' refers to any digital tool that allows users to quickly create and share content with the public, encompassing a wide range of websites and apps such as the following: (1) photo-sharing apps like Instagram, Flickr; (2) video and audio sharing apps like YouTube; (3) short written message sharing apps like Facebook, Twitter; (4) and other apps designed for geo-location sharing with social interaction functions. Social media apps contribute significantly to collective community memory through storytelling practices and cultural expression by mapping. Liang Xiaoxu, Lu Yanjun and John Martin, A Review of the Role of Social-Media for the Cultural Heritage Sustainability, *Sustainability*, Vol. 13, 2021, pp. 1055-1073.

consequences impacts the efficacy of foreign forces and creates diplomatic tensions in a host country. Governments often perceive foreign forces as protectors of cultural sites and blame them for their destruction, even when foreign forces are nowhere involved in it.

A perception exists that using precision missiles should negate the possibility of ever hitting cultural heritage. In an armed conflict, there could be several occasions when a munition misses its intended target and inadvertently destroys a cultural site. Cell phones capture the devastation and photographic evidence in a selected form circulates the globe instantaneously. Modern networked communication permits individuals to process events and express diverse opinions when sharing the incident through Facebook, Twitter, and other social media platforms. For foreign forces, even when their military manuals set rules for cultural heritage protection, uncertainty and fog of war during operations may lead to mistakes. Due to the rapidity with which the ramifications of these errors are captured by social media, occupation forces lack time to ameliorate the fallout.[38]

The Destruction of Cultural Property as a Weapon of War

Throughout history, all types of cultural heritage have been used as a weapon and a method of influence. Buildings and monuments have become collateral damage in some cases; at the same time, the artwork and artefacts have also been looted in several conflicts. In some cases, cultural sites and objects have also been deliberately targeted and destroyed. For instance, in 70AD, the future Emperor Titus conquered Jerusalem from Juden rebel factions and carried the golden Monarch from the Temple.[39] One of the most well-known examples of cultural heritage being purposefully targeted occurred during the Second World War when the Nazi regime systematically looted and destroyed art and cultural objects across Europe. Hitler also intended to eliminate Polish higher culture to make the nation easier to enslave. Campaigns against cultural heritage are also part of the contemporary armed conflicts. After the destruction of the Bamiyan Buddha by the Taliban in March 2001, deliberate and systematic destruction

38 Beitler Ruth Margolies and Dexter W. Dugan, "Practicing the Art of War While Protecting Cultural Heritage: A Military Perspective," in Cuno James and Thomas G. Weiss, 2022, *Cultural Heritage and Mass Atrocities*, Los Angeles: Getty Publications, pp. 500-516.

39 British Army Review, Special Report: Culture in Conflict (containing papers given at the Realising Culture and Human Dimension Symposium on June 12-14, 2018), p. 130.

of cultural heritage has spread to a considerable extent.[40] Cultural property has increasingly become a target and a means of war used by extremists. The destruction, looting and pillage of cultural property have been used as a weapon of war in several recent armed conflicts.

During the 1990s conflicts in the former Yugoslavia, cultural property was used as a weapon of war by inflicting widespread attacks against cultural heritage. Armed conflict in the former Yugoslavia popularised the term' ethnic cleansing' to describe the concerted operations to cause widespread violence and mass atrocities. Perpetrators sought not only to clear territories of other ethnic and religious groups but their cultural heritage as well. They aimed to wipe away symbols of the long history of cultural diversity and coexistence in the destroyed territories.[41]

During the wars in the former Yugoslavia, criminal campaigns were unleashed to cleanse captured territories of ethnic and religious minorities. Attacks were undertaken to create an ethnically pure state to remove all indications of a multi-cultural past. Well-planned and systematic attacks were executed to destroy identity and cultural heritage. This destroyed the cultural heritage of all major religious denominations in the contested areas. The Catholics, Muslims, and Orthodox Christian populations as well as cultural property common to all three suffered during the war. The most

40 In March 2001, the international community watched in dismay as the Taliban in Afghanistan destroyed the Buddhas of Bamiyan, built-in 507-554 CE, in an attempt to crack down on "un-Islamic" segments of Afghan society. Mullah Mohammad Omar, a Taliban militia leader, explained the destruction as follows: "Based on the verdict of the clergymen and the decision of the supreme court of the Islamic emirate all the statues around Afghanistan must be destroyed. … Because God is one God and these statues are there to be worshipped and that is wrong. They should be destroyed so that they are not worshipped now or in the future." Mullah Omar's order was only one amongst a long line of such decrees implemented by the Taliban at the time. According to the Online Centre of Afghan Studies, the destruction of the two Buddhas was not an isolated incident, but a carefully planned systematic move to eradicate ancient Afghan cultural heritage in its entirety. Francesco Francioni & Federico Lenzerini, "The Obligation to Prevent and Avoid Destruction of Cultural Heritage: From Bamiyan to Iraq", in Barbara T. Hoffman (ed.), 2006, *Art and Cultural Heritage: Law, Policy and Practice*, Cambridge: Cambridge University Press, p. 32.

41 Brammertz Serge, Kevin C. Hughes, Alison Kipp and William B. Tomljanovich, Attacks against Cultural Heritage as a Weapon of War: Prosecutions at the ICTY, *Journal of International Criminal Justice*, Vol. 14, No. 5, December 2016, pp. 1143-1174.

widespread crime of cultural destruction was the obliteration of houses of worship.[42]

From 1991 until 1995, widespread ethnic cleansing took place throughout Yugoslavia, directed against Bosnian Muslims. The Bosnian Muslims were brutally killed and attacked throughout the country, and "their places of worship, museums, libraries and archives" were destroyed. When the Bosnian-Serb Army came through Sarajevo in Bosnia-Herzegovina, it specifically targeted mosques, Catholic churches, the National Library, and the Oriental Institute. During these attacks, there was no military action, therefore the destruction of cultural sites cannot be attributed to collateral damage. The attacks were planned and coordinated to defeat and eliminate a particular group within the society, effectively cleansing that society of that group forever. The vast majority of all intentional destruction was done by quasi-state extremist groups as a central component in ethnic and/or cultural cleansing. Both terrorists, government troops and civilians use looting as a source of income, something which prolongs armed conflicts.[43]

Between 1998 and 1999, nearly 225 mosques in Kosovo were either destroyed or damaged. Islamic religious schools and libraries, traditional stone mansions and three out of four Ottoman historic centres in the Kosovo cities were extensively damaged. In 1993, the *Stari Most* (Old Bridge) of Mostar of Balkan, a symbol of the coexistence of diverse cultural, ethnic and religious communities, was destroyed by artillery fire. Serb forces laying siege to Sarajevo shelled and destroyed the National and University Library of Sarajevo, and also attacked the Gazi Husrev Beg Library. Behind the zone of conflict, far away from fighting, minority populations were expelled, and the cultural property associated with them was deliberately destroyed. In several cases, even the ruins were razed, and religious sites were further desecrated by being used as garbage dumps, markets or temporary parking areas.

42 Between 1992 and 1995 in Bosnia and Herzegovina, 1,200 mosques, 150 churches, four synagogues and over 1,000 other cultural institutions such as major museums, libraries, archives and manuscript collections were systemically targeted and severely damaged or destroyed. Riedlmayer A., Libraries Are Not for Burning: International Librarianship and the Recovery of the Destroyed Heritage of Bosnia and Herzegovina, Paper Presented at the 61st International Federation of Library Associations General Conference, August 20-25, 1995.

43 Lindhagen Adam, *War on Memory: International Law and the Destruction of Cultural Property in Armed Conflict 1979-2018*, Master Thesis, University of Oslo, 2018, p. 125.

In the armed conflict in Syria, the ancient Syrian city of Palmyra[44]-A heritage city declared by UNESCO in 1980--was captured by Daesh in May 2015. Daesh claimed that it would not harm the historic city; however, it gave notice that it would 'break idols that the infidels used to worship.' Within a few months, Daesh began a campaign of attacks[45] against cultural property in Palmyra to systematically erase its history. Ancient monuments in the Valley of the Tombs were destroyed in August 2015. The Temple of Baalshamin was dynamited and levelled on 24 August. Days later, the Temple of Bel,[46] one of Palmyra's primary sites and among the most important remaining ancient religious monuments in the Middle East was reduced to rubble. Finally, the ancient Roman Triumphal Arch was destroyed in October 2015. The destruction of monuments appears to have been only part of Daesh's attack against Palmyra's rich and diverse cultural heritage.[47] The jihadis have carried out a sustained campaign of destruction against heritage sites in areas under their control in Syria and also in Iraq.[48]

44 Known as the Pearl of the Desert, Palmyra – which means the City of Palms – lies 210 km northeast of Damascus. Before the Syrian conflict erupted in 2011, more than 150,000 tourists visited Palmyra every year.

45 The use of the term 'attack' against cultural property connotes the international crime of damaging or destroying cultural property as established in the jurisprudence of the International Criminal Tribunal for the former Yugoslavia (ICTY). This crime is often described as 'cultural destruction', 'heritage destruction', the 'destruction of cultural heritage' or the 'destruction of cultural property'.

46 The Temple of Bel at Palmyra has been the most important site and the most important temple in the Middle East alongside Baalbek in Lebanon. Before the arrival of Christianity in the second century, Palmyra worshipped the Semitic god, Bel, along with the sun god Yarhibol and the lunar god Aglibol. Construction on the temple began in 32 BC and ended in the second century. It later served as a church and a mosque.

47 Campaigns against cultural heritage, such as in Syria and elsewhere are not unique in contemporary conflicts. Daesh's methods are just one example of a distinctly modern practice of cultural cleansing as part of attacks against civilian populations based on religion, nationality, ethnicity and/or race. The first step in liquidating a people is to erase its memory and destroy its books, its culture, and its history. Kundera Milan, 1999, *The Book of Laughter and Forgetting*, Knopf Press, p. 320.

48 Brammertz Serge, Kevin C. Hughes, Alison Kipp and William B. Tomljanovich, Attacks against Cultural Heritage as a Weapon of War: Prosecutions at the ICTY, *Journal of International Criminal Justice*, Vol. 14, No. 5, December 2016, pp. 1143-1174. Also see Barnard Anne and Saad Hwaida, ISIS Fighters Seize Control of Syrian City of Palmyra, and Ancient Ruins, *The New York Times*, May 20, 2015; Shaheen K, Syria: ISIS Releases Footage of Palmyra Ruins Intact and "Will Not Destroy Them", *The Guardian*, May 27, 2015; Shaheen K, ISIS Destroys Ancient Tombs in Palmyra, *The Guardian*, September 4, 2015; and Shaheen K, Islamic State Releases Images Said to Show Destruction of Palmyra Temple, *The Guardian*, August 25, 2015.

There are allegations that Russia, in a clear violation of international law, has tried to weaponise cultural heritage in Ukraine. Whether the result of deliberate targeting or indiscriminate shelling, numerous sites of cultural significance for Ukraine have been partially or destroyed by the Russian military.[49] Shultz (2022) is of the view that by weaponising narratives around cultural heritage and history to further its geopolitical ambitions, Russia has actively engaged in cultural heritage exploitation.[50]

According to Dunkley (2018), cultural heritage is being weaponised by Russia in three principal ways: (i) Public diplomacy, primarily with the help of various organisations, events, forums, and conferences as a means of extending soft power; (ii) Media influence, especially through the mobilisation of international resources available to news network; and (iii) Protection of the Russian minorities/compatriots abroad, including access to appropriate culture, ideological and patriotic information/ education, through the application of hard power. The current trend indicates the escalation of the weaponisation of culture as a part of a long-term strategy to preserve and promote the cultural heritage and the identity of the peoples of Russia, and to extend its influence and strategy. By weaponising cultural heritage, the Russian Federation is seeking to secure its future.[51]

There are also allegations that in the ongoing armed conflict, Israel is wiping out facets of Palestinian culture on the besieged territory.[52] The extensive

49 These sites include religious sites such as churches and cemeteries – particularly those belonging to the Ukrainian Orthodox Church, museums, monuments and memorials, universities, as well as libraries and archives. As of February 2024, UNESCO had confirmed damage to 343 cultural sites. UNESCO, Damaged cultural sites in Ukraine verified by UNESCO, UNESCO, February 7, 2024.

50 Shultz, Daniel and Jasparro, Christopher, How Does Russia Exploit History and Cultural Heritage for Information Warfare? Recommendations for NATO, Antiquities Coalition, April 2022.

51 Dunkley Mark, Russian Weaponization of Cultural Heritage, British Army Review, Special Report: Culture in Conflict (containing papers given at the *Realising Culture and Human Dimension Symposium* on June 12-14, 2018), pp. 18-31.

52 Israel's large-scale operation was in response to the Hamas-led attack of October 7, 2023, which caused an unprecedented number of casualties in a one-day attack in Israel. In May 2024, the fatalities in the Gaza Strip were estimated to have exceeded 34,800 killed. Of them, 24,682, including 7,356 children and 5,419 women, were identified as of 30 April 2024. Detailed findings on the military operations and attacks carried out in the Occupied Palestinian Territory from 7 October to 31 December 2023: Independent International Commission of Inquiry on the Occupied Palestinian Territory, including East Jerusalem, and Israel, Human Rights Council, A/HRC/56/ CRP.4 dated June 10, 2024.

use of explosive weapons with wide area effects in populated areas [53] by Israeli forces is the primary cause of this damage. For instance, airstrikes by Israeli forces destroyed the ancient port of Anthedon Harbour, which is on the Tentative List of UNESCO World Heritage Sites.[54] In December 2023, the use of explosive weapons by Israeli forces destroyed the Great Omari Mosque, Gaza's oldest mosque, first constructed in the 7th century and rebuilt multiple times since. Images show the mosque's courtyard full of rubble surrounded by crumbling walls.[55]

Organised looting has been a systematic feature of most historic armed conflicts around the world. Most European nations were involved in large-scale acts of looting at the end of the 19th as well as 20th Centuries. The East India Company and later the officials of the British Government in India were involved theft and looting of cultural property, sometimes in the form of prize money which was subsequently transferred to Britain.[56]

53 Explosive weapons' blasts, fragmentation, and secondary fires inflict direct effects on the full range of cultural heritage sites at the time of the attack. The blast produced by detonations on or near cultural heritage can bend and break the structural elements of a building, even concrete and steel, leading to the collapse of part or all of an entire edifice.160 Explosive weapons use is particularly harmful to cultural heritage because sites are often old or made of more vulnerable materials, such as "unreinforced masonry," clay, stone, or wood. Furthermore, attempts to pre-emptively protect heritage can be very difficult, expensive, or unachievable. Even though reinforcement frameworks may not withstand explosive weapons, actions to temporarily relocate portable cultural heritage are much more difficult during wartime, and efforts to protect cultural heritage can sometimes damage it. Armament Research Services, Explosive Weapons in Populated Areas: Technical Considerations Relevant to their Use and Effects, May 2016; National Research Council, Protecting Buildings from Bomb Damage: Transfer of Blast-Effect Mitigation Strategies from Military to Civilian Applications, Washington D.C.: The National Academies Press, 1995, p. 30.

54 As reported, the archaeological site of Blakhiyya, identified as Anthedon Harbour, Gaza's ancient seaport dating from 800 BCE - 1100, has been largely damaged by airstrikes and military activities, as shown in a report by Forensic Architecture. Excavated by a Palestinian–French expedition (1995-2005), it is one of three Gaza sites on UNESCO's World Heritage Tentative List. There is also a fear that artefacts will be looted or illicitly transferred to Israel. Mahmoud Hawari, Israel Destroys Palestinian Cultural Heritage Sites in Gaza, February 28, 2024, available at: https://www.palestine-studies.org/en/node/1655264.

55 Destroying Cultural Heritage: Explosive Weapons' Effects in Armed Conflict and Measures to Strengthen Protection, Human Rights Watch, Harvard Law School, International Human Rights Clinic, April 2024, p. 87.

56 The officials of the East India Company committed large-scale plunder and looting of property including cultural objects in the conquered provinces in India. They took back the valuables to their own countries, sold them or decorated their gardens and living rooms with those antiquities. Later when the British Government took over

Looting of cultural property affects both, wealthy as well as poor countries. Ethnographic studies in many countries demonstrate that looters loot during times of armed conflict and political instability, as well as during peacetime, and are motivated primarily by the profit they earn. Looting activities respond to market demand for particular types of artefacts, and looting has moved from an occasional, opportunistic activity to a sophisticated, well-funded, well-organised business in many countries.[57]

Theft, looting, and pillage of cultural objects during conflict are complex acts and are interwoven with notions of revenge, economic gains, and tropism. Primarily the acts of looting lead to a loss of cultural heritage and historical knowledge. In both Iraq and Syria, the terrorist organisation, knowing the market value of these objects, engaged in the methodical and massive looting of museums and archaeological sites in the areas it controlled. It even introduced a tax on the value of the looted items. This makes the trafficking of cultural goods one of the most important means of financing terrorism, along with the trafficking of oil resources.

The recent strategic destruction and theft of cultural property in Iraq and Syria further validate the fact that cultural property is important to the survival of a nation. Perhaps, this is the main reason why it is being attacked. In an attempt to destroy the state, the people, and their history, IS has systemically attacked religious and other pre-Islamic sites, looted these sites to finance its reign of terror and destroyed them for propaganda value and attention. The extremist groups that are looting and destroying cultural property/heritage in war zones are exercising what they see as their divine right to destroy other cultures.[58]

In recent decades, cultural heritage and goods have been at the forefront of armed conflicts. By undermining the identity of populations, looting and illicit trafficking contribute to the profound destabilisation of conflict-torn

---

the control of India, many Indian valuables were transported to England under the pretext of better preservation there. In the perceptions of colonisers, the Indians were inferior and incapable of conserving their heritage. Today, British museums shine because of the loot from India. Available at: https://indianculture.gov.in/stories/looted-recovered-and-awaited-stories-indias-stolen-antiques.

57 Watson Peter and Cecilia Todeschini, 2006, *The Medici Conspiracy: The Illicit Journey of Looted Antiquities—From Italy's Tomb Raiders to the World's Greatest Museums*, Italy: PublicAffairs, pp. 379; Atwood Roger, 2004, *Stealing History: Tomb Robbers, Smugglers, and the Looting of the Ancient World*, Peru: St Martin's Press, p. 368.

58 Almukhtar Sarah, The Strategy Behind the Islamic State's Destruction of Ancient Sites, *New York Times*, March 28, 2016.

regions. As a source of financing for terrorism, they are acting as weapons of war. The loot is taken out of the site, sold, and taken across borders to art markets, where it is sold again, and ends up in an art gallery or private collection. This whole process requires extensive networks, which are often vast and well-established. It is well-known that these networks – dealing in weapons, drugs, antiquities, and even humans – are all connected.[59] Attacks on cultural heritage are not simply attacks on inanimate objects; they are attacks on the identity, past, and future of entire communities. Attacks on cultural heritage target the very soul of communities, damaging their sense of cohesion and unity. Overall, these attacks violate the fundamental principle of human dignity.

Today, cultural heritage remains a strategic target in war and conflict. There are, in fact, many reasons why these attacks occur. They are often intended to impact self-identity and denude the will to fight, or they can be the means to punish an adversary. Other motivators include iconoclasm, the removal of symbols of legitimacy and authority; generation of publicity to provoke support, outrage, or other response, such as the Taliban's ruination of the Bamiyan Buddhas, 2001; wanting to gain access to spoils; and opportunistic and organised looting, including thefts from the museums. During war, there is often also considerable collateral, inadvertent, and neglectful damage caused by armed forces.[60]

According to Dzerowich (2024), in the last two decades or so, the weaponisation of cultural heritage has specifically served four main purposes.[61] First, the destruction of cultural property is exploited by armed actors to coerce, dominate, and destabilise an opponent. Aware of its symbolic and emotional value, some belligerents have sought to purposefully target cultural property to weaken their adversaries in the context of military campaigns. In Myanmar, for instance, the military junta has been deliberately destroying and looting cultural sites in areas with

59 For example, ISIS attacked and destroyed major monuments like the Temple of Bel in Palmyra, and the contents of the museum in Mosul, Iraq, as part of a concerted propaganda campaign to demonstrate their power to act with impunity – and the impotence of the local authorities and the international community to stop them. We must punish the looters, but also the buyers, UNESCO, October 16, 2023.

60 Clack Timothy, Cultural Heritage on the Frontline: the destruction of peoples and identities in war, October 4, 2022. Available at: https://www.ox.ac.uk/news/2022-10-04-cultural-heritage-frontline-destruction-peoples-and-identities-war.

61 Dzerowich Julie, History and Identity Under Attack: Protecting Cultural Heritage in Conflict, Committee in Democracy and Security (CDS), NATO Parliamentary Assembly, Preliminary Draft Special Report, March 29, 2024, p. 17.

strong resistance forces.[62] These attacks are part of a broader military effort to terrorise and break the resistance of populations.

Second, the intentional and systematic destruction of cultural heritage as a form of "cultural cleansing" has occurred in the context of sectarian or identity-driven conflicts. By engaging in such acts, belligerents seek to dehumanise, delegitimise, or erase the presence of an entire group, often from a disputed territory. According to UNESCO, in Syria and Iraq, Daesh/ISIS systematically destroyed cultural sites and artefacts relating to pre-Islamic civilisations and religious minorities as part of its plans to erase the countries' long history of cultural diversity and pluralism and impose its extremist vision of society and the world via the creation of its so-called caliphate.[63] The deliberate destruction of cultural heritage has also been linked with genocide or ethnic cleansing. In the region of Darfur, the massacres perpetrated by the Sudanese government and affiliated Arab militia groups against non-Arab ethnic tribes from 2003 onwards were preceded and accompanied by systematic attacks on their intangible cultural heritage. Under President al-Bashir, Arab political elites actively sought to erase non-Arab history and languages from the Sudanese public space. [64]

Third, armed and terrorist groups instrumentalise cultural property for strategic communication purposes.[65] The destruction of cultural property is used as a tool to provoke outrage or generate support and thus amplify propaganda. This is facilitated by the widespread use of social media and other means of modern technology. The intentional destruction of the UNESCO-protected Bamiyan Buddhas in Afghanistan in 2001, the ancient

62 Foster Malcolm, Looting and destroying, junta declares war on Myanmar's cultural sites and artefacts, Radio Free Asia, May 24, 2023.

63 UNESCO, Reinforcement of UNESCO's action for the protection of culture and the promotion of cultural pluralism in the event of armed conflict, UNESCO, 2015.

64 Since its independence in 1956, Sudan has been ravaged by war. For residents of the westernmost state in the country, Darfur, the war has led to ethnic cleansing on a massive scale. During the peak years of the war, 2003–2005, the Sudanese Air Force struck villages using assault helicopters and Russian-made Antonov bombers. Ground forces followed aerial attacks with infantry assaults, targeting ethnic tribes that the Sudanese government accused of supporting rebel resistance movements. Three ethnic tribes received the brunt of these assaults: the Fur, Massalit and Zaghawa. ACCORD (African Centre for the Constructive Resolution of Disputes), "Ideology and Cultural Violence in Darfur", ACCORD, 19 October 2016.

65 Rosen Frederik, NATO and Cultural Property: Embracing New Challenges in the Era of Identity Wars, Nordic Centre for Cultural Heritage and Armed Conflict (CHAC), 2017.

city of Palmyra in Syria in 2015 and 2016, and the Timbuktu shrines in Mali in 2012 are among the most infamous examples. These destructions were largely staged as publicity stunts designed to draw worldwide attention. These calculated attacks on cultural heritage sites sought to demonstrate the groups' strength; prove their dedication to their belief system in the eyes of their followers while helping to attract potential recruits from all around the world; and provoke opponents through the broadcasting of images of destruction.

Lastly, the belligerents exploiting cultural property are increasingly motivated by financial gain. This is facilitated by the high commercial value of cultural artefacts in international markets and the breakdown of the rule of law during armed conflicts. Looting and illegally trafficking cultural property can help armed actors finance and sustain their operations on the battlefield. Cultural goods, alongside drugs and petrol, were a crucial source of funding for Daesh/ISIS's terrorist activities between 2014 and 2017. At its height, the group engaged in large-scale artefact looting and illegal archaeological excavations in Syria and Iraq. Artefacts were then trafficked out of the two countries with the help of organised crime networks. The group is estimated to have made millions of dollars from these activities[66]

Cultural heritage has increasingly become the target of intentional attacks by belligerents and its deliberate destruction is the hallmark of recent conflicts across the world The systematic destruction of heritage often forms part of strategic acts of 'culturecide'. The destruction and theft of cultural heritage from areas under conflict is aimed to dehumanise and delegitimise entire ethnicities. In a few recent cases, cultural cleansing was accompanied by extreme physical and sexual violence. In Syria and Iraq, women were brutalised. Attacks on both tangible (buildings, monuments, and artefacts) and intangible (practices, customs, and knowledge) heritage are not only forms of propaganda by deed but serve to deny people their very identities.

The protection of cultural property is important for the long-term security agenda because history and culture are important ingredients in nation-building. Culture is essential to the survival of a society and integral to its renewal.[67] Protecting cultural objects serves to support a nation's efforts to

66 Rose-Greenland Fiona, How much money has ISIS made selling antiquities? More than enough to fund its attacks, *The Washington Post*, June 3, 2016.

67 Turku Helga, When Cultural Property Becomes a Tool of Warfare: Law, Politics, and International Security, *Inter Gentes*, Vol. 1, issue 2, 2017, pp. 5-23.

restore its national identity. Citizens of all ethnicities, faiths, backgrounds, and economic stations can feel the pride and sense of national unity that comes with that.[68]

Several recent armed conflicts demonstrate that cultural heritage is increasingly weaponised by armed actors. The protection of cultural heritage must not be viewed exclusively as a legal requirement but is also treated as a security concern in its own right. The 1954 Hague Convention for the Protection of Cultural Property in the Event of Armed Conflict requires states to ensure heritage is not damaged or misappropriated in war. The Convention was further reinforced by two Protocols in 1954 and 1999. Direct and intentional attacks on cultural property may constitute a crime under international criminal law. The Second Protocol of 1999 specifies a range of serious violations of the Protocol and the Convention amounting to war crimes. The Convention builds and expands on relevant provisions contained in the Conventions of the Hague of 1899 and 1907, as well as on the Geneva Conventions of 1949. The 1977 Additional Protocols I and II to the Geneva Conventions also include relevant articles applicable to, respectively, international and non-international conflicts. The aforementioned instruments as well as customary international humanitarian law set clear obligations for parties to an armed conflict. State Parties are obliged to respect cultural property within their territory and the territory of other State Parties. Directly targeting cultural property and using it or its surroundings for military purposes – thereby exposing it to destruction or damage, is prohibited. The obligation to respect such property can only be waived in cases of imperative military necessity. But even then, the general humanitarian principles of distinction, proportionality, and precaution apply. The exception to such protection is military necessity. Thus, forces are permitted to damage heritage, if an adversary is utilising it to present a threat. It is legitimate, for example, for a military force to use proportionate means to neutralise a sniper in a church spire.

Furthermore, the Rome Statute of 1998 confers upon the International Criminal Court (ICC) jurisdiction over crimes against or affecting cultural heritage. Under Article 8(2)(b)(ix) and 8(2)(e)(iv), which respectively apply to international and non-international conflicts, intentionally directing attacks against, among other objects, buildings and monuments that fall within the broad definition of cultural property and that are not being

68 Anne C Richard, Remarks delivered at the Launch of the International Council of Museums, *Emergency Red List of Syrian Cultural Objects at Risk*, September 25, 2013.

used for military purposes constitutes a war crime. Attacks against cultural heritage may also represent a crime against humanity under Article 7(1)(h) if found to amount to persecution, which is when systematic and widespread attacks are committed against a specific group on racial, national, ethnic, cultural or religious grounds. Heritage is also a human rights issue, insofar as it relates to freedom of expression, thought, conscience, and religion. Protecting heritage can, thereby, play a prominent role in safeguarding human security and the return to 'normality' in the aftermath of conflict. Heritage can help people find a home again.

Cultural Property Versus Combatant Lives in War

In an armed conflict, if both human life and heritage are at risk; a military commander may face a dilemma, whether he should save human lives or cultural heritage. For the armed forces, hard battlefield choices arise because the protection of civilians, troops and cultural heritage all are given importance in the IHL and military ethics. The armed forces may also encounter cultural heritage when fighting desperately to protect their civilians, or to limit the number of deaths among their troops in the process. Some defenders may feel the need to fight to the end in places which are most important to them, risking massive destruction in the process and dying with their heritage in an ultimately meaningful way. The issue thus comes up: Would it be better to surrender to a vicious foe to avoid the destruction of their heritage?[69] The matter becomes more crucial for the commander of a UN peacekeeping force, whose mandate includes protecting cultural property. In the context of IHL, the protection of cultural property is essentially inseparable from the protection of people and their human rights.

Deliberate and premeditated destruction of cultural heritage in war is ethically and legally wrong. However, recent times have witnessed widespread destruction of cultural property. The protection of cultural property is crucial to the preservation of civilisations' historical experiences. Even if a state is not a party to a treaty governing the protection of cultural property in armed conflict, it is still bound by obligations imposed by customary international law. On a battlefield, attackers may feel a pressing military necessity to target combatants inside or around important cultural heritage and so destroy large parts of it. Instead, they may prolong the

69 Slim Hugo, "Choosing between Human Life and Cultural Heritage in War," in Cuno James and Thomas G. Weiss (ed.), 2022, *Cultural Heritage and Mass Atrocities*, Los Angeles: Getty Images, p. 299-308.

fight, extend people's suffering and risk more lives among their troops as they carefully avoid damage to cultural heritage and delay victory. Can a military commander use maximum force against a ruthless enemy because the latter's forces are held up within an area rich in cultural heritage in which they continue to impose harsh treatment and significant suffering on an occupied population? In these situations, when soldiers are faced with saving people or cultural property, the ethics embedded in the IHL, which say that human life and human culture are equally valuable, are put to the test. While both life and cultural property are held to be valuable, the law itself does not answer as to which should be given priority in the face of military necessity. Therefore, a military planner or commander has to make a hard choice between the preservation of human life and cultural property in armed conflict.

Article 7 of the 1999 Second Protocol lists certain precautions which should be taken in an attack.[70] In IHL "attack" is an act of violence against the adversary, whether in offence or defence and in whatever territory is conducted. While conducting operations, a military commander must do everything feasible to verify that the objectives to be attacked are not cultural property protected under Article 4 of the 1954 Convention. He must take all feasible precautions in the choice of means and methods of attack to avoid, and in any event to minimise, incidental damage to cultural property. He must also refrain from deciding to launch any attack which may be expected to cause incidental damage to cultural property, which would be excessive about the concrete and direct military advantage anticipated. He should cancel or suspend an attack if it becomes apparent: that the objective is to protect cultural property and the attack may be expected to cause incidental damage to cultural property protected which would be excessive about the concrete and direct military advantage anticipated.

Modern IHL accepts that harm, destruction, and death can be lawful during armed conflict. The principle of military necessity requires that a party to an armed conflict may only resort to those means and methods that are necessary to achieve the legitimate purpose of a conflict, i.e. 'to weaken the military forces of the enemy'. The principle of humanity imposes certain limits on the means and methods of warfare. It seeks to limit suffering, injury, and destruction during armed conflict; its purpose is to protect life and health and to ensure respect for the human being. This principle

70 This provision is a copy of Article 57 of the 1977 Additional Protocol I to the Geneva Conventions of 1949.

precludes the assumption that anything that is not explicitly prohibited by specific IHL rules is therefore permitted. To end a conflict as quickly as possible whilst minimising the loss of lives of both civilians and soldiers, the possibility of the loss of cultural heritage cannot be ruled out.

Prioritising Human Lives

The main aim of the principle of humanity[71] is to prevent and alleviate human suffering wherever it may be found. Its purpose is to protect life and health and to ensure respect for the human being.[72] IHL places significant emphasis on the importance of protecting human lives as well as cultural heritage. The way the laws are written seems to give human lives and cultural heritage ethical parity. A bomber pilot must avoid destroying both as much as he can. In emphasising parity between life and culture, the law declares that cultural heritage is a vital part of human life and that certain artefacts that we make with our hands and our machines are essential to being human.

Human beings are not simply a process of flesh, blood flow and breathing. It is also about being a particular person with a life of one's own that is lived with others in a shared sense of meaning and custom that are represented in things made around us and ideas believed between us.[73]5 This includes the things we have in common: our homes, our cultural buildings, our books of learning, our ideals, our gods, our religious artefacts, our games, our clothes, our manners, and our art, etc. thus, our cultural assets do not just give us creative refreshment and social life as an emotional public good, they are woven into the very fabric of our particular identity as a

71 At the Hague Peace Conference of 1899, a Russian diplomat, Fyodor F. Martens, introduced the "Marten's clause" into the preamble of the Hague Convention II, from which the principle of humanity is derived. It reads, "The inhabitants and the belligerents remain under the protection and the rule of the principles of the law of nations, as they result from the usages established among civilized peoples, from the laws of humanity and the dictates of public conscience." However, the issue remains that the term "public conscience' is very vague. For instance, the public conscience may be startled by selective cases of humanity, in which some are included, and others are excluded from our notions of humanity. Indeed, war itself requires an appeal to exclusive humanity for one party to the conflict and the dehumanisation of the other side to enable violence.

72 Humanity, impartiality, neutrality, independence, voluntary service, unity and universality: these seven Fundamental Principles of the International Red Cross and Red Crescent Movement.

73 Hugo Slim, 2015, *Humanitarian Ethics: A Guide to the Morality of Aid in War and Disaster*, New York: Oxford University Press, pp. 46–49.

human being. Every civilisation embodies some truth about human life and experience in its culture. This is why the destruction of Buddha statues in Afghanistan, classical Greek and Roman ruins in Iraq and Syria, and mosques in Rakhine State, Myanmar, are deemed crimes under IHL. It therefore remains crucial that how we should deal with human life and cultural heritage—blood and bricks—under IHL.[74]

The law insists it is right to protect both human life and cultural heritage in the conduct of hostilities, but this may not be possible in certain instances of war and does not resolve which should take precedence. Even so, when the progress of war throws up a choice between blood and bricks, it is clear that human life should trump cultural heritage as the more important object of protection. It is always better to save lives instead of buildings or paintings when both cannot be saved. In any comparison between the value of a work of art and a human being, the human is in the great majority of cases inherently more valuable. Though cultural heritage is a part of us, the potential of our lives and the importance of our ethics mean more to us than a cultural heritage which we can carry within us and realise anew in a different place. In the long run, it is better to have a remnant of a human community than it is to have the remains of buildings without people. If saved, human beings can create and build again. Cultural heritage is irreplaceable, but it is renewable. The following two examples support this view.

City of Venice

One of the richest cultural sites in the world today, Venice, was founded in 421 AD by thousands of displaced persons fleeing the Germanic invasions of northern Italy. Running from their invaders and their cultural heritage, they hid in marshlands bordering the Adriatic, where their conquerors decided not to follow. Venice was thus founded by the Venti refugees fleeing Vandal invaders, and in the following years were joined by those escaping Lombard attackers. At that time Venice's coastal lagoons were home only to small fishing communities. Here, they huddled together and, over many years, building on small islands and around lagoons, they slowly became a people of the sea.[75]

74 Slim Hugo, "Choosing between Human Life and Cultural Heritage in War," in Cuno James and Thomas G. Weiss (ed.), 2022, Cultural Heritage and Mass Atrocities, Los Angeles: Getty Images, p. 299-308.

75 In 828, two Venetian merchants, visiting Alexandria, smuggled the supposed body of Saint Mark to boost the standing of their home city. Hidden in a case of pork, the saint's relics went unnoticed by the Muslim customs officers and were subsequently

Cambridge University

The University of Cambridge had its origins in 1209. In England in the late twelfth century a group of scholars decided they could no longer tolerate the endemic urban violence and unlawful reprisals that plagued medieval Oxford: its murders, robbery, rape, and arbitrary hangings. A group of scholars decided to flee, escaping riots and disorder, carrying as many manuscripts as they could. Heading northeast they settled by the River Cam and founded Cambridge University. At first, the scholars lived in rented hostels, and gradually they evolved a distinct organisation with Masters and other officials. In time, the hostels gave way to 'Halls' and 'Houses' that began to define the form and function of the colleges that characterise the University to this day. The establishment of Peterhouse marks the opening of the first of three great phases of college foundations in the history of the University.

Gestalt

IHL aims to impose limits on the destruction and distress caused by armed conflict and is essentially a compromise between two fundamental principles, of humanity and military necessity. The principle of military necessity permits force required to achieve the legitimate purpose of a conflict, and the principle of humanity forbids the infliction of all suffering, injury or destruction not necessary for achieving the legitimate purpose of a conflict. All other rules of IHL are constructed on these principles. According to Slim Hugo (2022), human life should always trump cultural heritage in extreme circumstances even though it is always important to mitigate cultural losses in two ways: by letting some individuals stay with their cultural heritage if they wish; and by trying very hard to save some part of peoples' heritage during or after the fight, while primarily prioritising human life. However, advocates for heritage protection are of the view that the protection of cultural heritage is inseparable from the protection of people and, further, that protecting cultural heritage can result in saved lives.[76]

---

interred in the city's great new church, the Basilica di San Marco. This first Basilica was destroyed by fire in 976, but today's cathedral, consecrated in 1094, stands on the same site. Saint Mark became the city's patron saint and his emblem, the winged lion, became the symbol of the Republic and decorated its standard.

76 Wise Paul H., "Saving Stones and Saving Lives: A Humanitarian Perspective on Protecting Cultural Heritage in War," in Cuno James and Thomas G. Weiss (ed.), 2022, *Cultural Heritage and Mass Atrocities*, Los Angeles: Getty Images, p. 309-322.

Even though remote sensing technology, especially satellite Earth observation, was not originally designed and established for archaeological purposes, it can be an indispensable and powerful tool in archaeological and cultural heritage protection. Google Earth provides advanced new tools and procedures for carrying out archaeological prospection and assisting cultural heritage management.[77] For instance, the Endangered Archaeology of the Middle East and North Africa (EAMENA) Project is documenting archaeological sites and the threats posed to them in an online database that spans 20 countries (an area of roughly 10,000,000 square km). The scale of heritage recording initiatives again varies, from highly detailed assessments of single sites to threats to archaeological sites across the entire MENA region, from Mauritania to Iran. In addition, using fieldwork to validate remote recording methods is crucial to increasing the accuracy of the process of assigning interpretation.[78]

Despite the plethora of laws, cultural property remains under serious threat in the event of armed conflict. The destruction of cultural property in the ongoing armed conflict in Syria, Ukraine and Palestine has continued to exhibit a serious shortcoming in the treaty regime. The next chapter, therefore makes certain recommendations relating to an increase in ratification, the enhancement of the implementation by the states and monitoring and sanctioning mechanisms.

77 Luo Lei, et al., Google Earth as a Powerful Tool for Archaeological and Cultural Heritage Applications: A Review, *Remote Sensing*, Vol. 10(10), 2018, pp. 1558-1590.

78 The project uses two main methodological approaches, both designed to promote the recording, protection and understanding of cultural heritage at risk across the MENA region as a whole. First, accessible, user-friendly and open-source remote sensing technologies and tools. Second, to enhance our data and understanding of risk/damage to sites with more specific analyses using high-resolution data where possible. Rayne Louise et al., From Above and on the Ground: Geospatial Methods for Recording Endangered Archaeology in the Middle East and North Africa, *Geosciences*, Vol. 7(4), 2017, pp. 100-130.

Chapter 9

The Final Words

The cultural property is a unique resource that is important for learning about the diversity of human history and cultures. It helps to provide communities with a sense of place, identity, and belonging. The destruction of cultural property during armed conflict is not new. It was common in the earlier days when victors took important cultural property as spoils of war or symbols of victory. During the late 17th and early 18th centuries, Napoleon was renowned for his theft of art and antiquities in conquered lands, returning to France with his "spoils of war." It was also prevalent for cultural property to be lost through pillage, misapplication, and vandalism.[1] Deliberate destruction of cultural property was also perpetrated as an instrument of war to demoralise the enemy. Places of worship were not spared as some were converted from a particular type of religion to another. Several Hindu temples were forcibly converted into mosques after the conquest. There was massive destruction of cultural property during World War I and II. The destruction continued even after the UN was formed on October 24, 1945, with the hope that an international organisation would promote peace, justice, and better living for all humankind.

1 In 1849, after the conquest of the Punjab by the British forces, the properties of the Sikh Empire were confiscated. The Koh-I-Noor was transferred to the treasury of the British East India Company in Lahore. In 1851, Dalhousie arranged that the Kohinoor diamond should be presented by Ranjit Singh's successor, Duleep Singh, to Queen Victoria, the Empress of India. In 1852, Prince Albert ordered that the Koh-I-Noor diamond be re-cut from 186 carats to its current 105 carats thus increasing its brilliance. The Koh-I-Noor diamond was mounted in a crown with more than two thousand other diamonds. The Koh-I-Noor diamond is now a centrepiece of the crown (set in a Maltese cross at the front of the crown) of the British Queens/ Kings. Kaur Jasvinder, Koh-I-Noor "Mountain of Light," *International Journal of Science and Research*, Vol. 3, Issue 8, August 2014, pp. 729-732.

Attempts to protect cultural property date back several centuries. Customary international law provides for the protection of cultural property. Each party to an armed conflict must avoid damage to property of great importance to cultural heritage unless they are military objectives. In addition, it prohibits acts of seizure or damages to institutions dedicated to cultural property. The Rule also prohibits any form of theft, misappropriation or vandalism directed against property of great importance to cultural heritage. The occupying power must also prevent the illegal export of cultural property from the occupied territory.[2]

The 1954 Hague Convention for the Protection of Cultural Property in the Event of Armed Conflict and its First Protocol is the major international instrument for the protection of cultural property during armed conflicts. Cultural property includes museums, libraries, archives, archaeological sites and monuments of architecture, art, or history, whether religious or secular. It was adopted following the enormous devastation and pillage of cultural property in the Second World War. It has also been asserted that the basic principles of the 1954 Convention have acquired the character of customary international law.[3] The effectiveness of the 1954 Convention became a subject of general concern in the early nineties, during the Gulf War and the war in the former Yugoslavia. In 1999, the Second Protocol to the 1954 Hague Convention was adopted which enhances protection of cultural property in armed conflict and renders individuals who destroy them criminally responsible. The 1999 Second Protocol, which supplements the 1954 Convention; however, failed to deter individuals, groups or governments determined to destroy cultural objects during armed conflict or in times of peace.

There could be the following risks to cultural property during an armed conflict: [4] (i) It may not be considered important enough to be included

2 Rules 38 to 41, Customary International Humanitarian Law; Henckaerts Jean-Marie and Louise Doswald-Beck, *Customary International Humanitarian Law*, Vol. I Rules, ICRC/ Cambridge University Press, pp. 621.

3 Archibong James E., Destruction of cultural property as a war crime: Breaking new ground in the quest for accountability, *International Journal of Law*, Vol. 5, Issue 2, March 2019, pp. 126-132; Henckaerts Jean-Marie, New rules for the protection of cultural property in armed conflict: The significance of the Second Protocol to the 1954 Hague Convention for the Protection of Cultural Property in the Event of Armed Conflict, Protection of Cultural Property in the Event of Armed Conflict, Report of the Meeting of Experts, 2000, pp. 27-32.

4 Stone Peter, The Seven Risks to Cultural Property in Armed Conflict, British Army Review, Special Report—Culture in Conflict, Great Britain. Ministry of Defence, 2019,

in national and local emergency response systems or during the pre-conflict stage; (ii) war and political instability may create unfortunate opportunities for the theft of art and cultural objects as well as the pillage of archaeological sites; (iii) apart from theft, the cultural object may be exposed to mutilation arising from rough handling such as dragging, piling and other abuses, in addition to their exposure to inclement weather; (iv) military personnel may lack expertise in the importance and location of cultural heritage;[5] (v) possibility of its collateral damage due to the use of explosive weapons remains high;[6] (vi) as compared to human casualties in the conflict, cultural property may not get any prioritised attention and could be neglected; (vii) there may be hampering of routine maintenance, preservation and safety of cultural sites due to armed conflict and lack of finances; (viii) local civilians and low paid employees could be lured by the criminal network for committing theft of cultural property;[7] and (ix) cultural sites and repositories may themselves be the intended targets in armed conflict.[8]

Peacetime Measures

Under Article 3 of the 1954 Convention, States undertake to prepare in time of peace for the safeguarding of cultural property against the foreseeable effects of an armed conflict, "by taking such measures as they consider

pp. 102-113.

5 It may be extremely difficult for the Ministry of Culture to convince the military, particularly in South Asian countries, to include the importance of cultural heritage as part of their training sessions.

6 NATO bombed the Federal Republic of Yugoslavia (Republic of Serbia and Republic of Montenegro) for three months in 1999, from March 23 until June 10. During this time, a great deal of cultural heritage in Serbia (objects, buildings, cultural landscapes) was damaged or destroyed as a result of direct hits, or as collateral damage.

7 Regular support also discourages excessive risk-taking by reducing the likelihood that cultural workers would feel compelled to place their lives in harm's way to be paid for a special project. Such support requires strong collaborative partnerships between cultural workers on the ground and organized consortia of international cultural institutions willing to adopt a long-term view.

8 In Swat Valley, during the military operation against the Taliban in 2007 and afterwards, several suicide attacks and bombings occurred in the surrounding areas, and as a result badly damaged the museum building along with adjoining areas (sites called Butkara and Barikot) where relics of Gandhara civilization such as stupas, monasteries and Buddhist arts existed. These sites were either damaged, looted or vandalized. Geo-strategically, this region has a key position because it shares boundaries with China, Afghanistan and Russia. The valley proudly witnessed the footprints of Alexander, Mehmood Ghaznavi and King Ashoka.

appropriate." However, the Convention does not provide any further details on measures states should take. The 1999 Second Protocol aims to provide more guidance in this respect, as it provides specific examples of concrete measures to be taken in times of peace; which include the preparation of inventories, the planning of emergency measures for protection against fire or structural collapse; the preparation for the removal of movable cultural property or the provision of adequate in situ protection of such property; the designation of competent authorities responsible for the safeguarding of cultural property. These measures are of great practical importance for the protection of cultural property in the event of armed conflict.

In addition, the Second Protocol expands on the rather general provision concerning dissemination contained in the 1954 Convention. It lists specific examples of concrete dissemination measures, especially for the military and civilian authorities who assume responsibilities concerning the application of the Second Protocol. The states parties must (a) Incorporate guidelines and instructions on the protection of cultural property in their military regulations; (ii) Develop and implement, in cooperation with UNESCO and relevant governmental and non-governmental organisations, peacetime training and educational programmes; (iii) Communicate to one another, through the Director-General of UNESCO, information on laws, administrative provisions and measures taken under the preceding paragraphs; and (iv) Communicate to one another, through the Director-General, the laws and administrative provisions which they may adopt to ensure the application of the Protocol.[9]

There are four essential elements relating to the protection of cultural property, binding for all states during armed conflicts whether they acceded to or acknowledged the legal framework, or not. First, the obligation of each party to the conflict is to respect cultural property. Special care must be taken in military operations to avoid damage to buildings dedicated to religion, art, science, education or charitable purposes and historic monuments unless they are essential military objectives. Property of great importance to the cultural heritage of every people must not be the object of attack unless imperatively required by military necessity. Second, the prohibition to use of cultural property of great importance for purposes which are likely to expose it to destruction or damage, unless imperatively

9 Henckaerts Jean-Marie, New rules for the protection of cultural property in armed conflict: The significance of the Second Protocol to the 1954 Hague Convention for the Protection of Cultural Property in the Event of Armed Conflict, Protection of Cultural Property in the Event of Armed Conflict, Report of the Meeting of Experts, 2000, pp. 27-32.

required by military necessity. Third, the obligation of each party to the conflict is to protect cultural property. All seizure of or destruction of or wilful damage done to institutions dedicated to religion, charity, education, the arts and sciences, historic monuments and works of art and science is prohibited. Any form of theft, pillage, or misappropriation of, and any acts of vandalism directed against, property of great importance to the cultural heritage of every people is prohibited. Fourth, the obligation of the occupying power to prevent the illicit export of cultural property from the occupied territory and to return illicitly exported property to the competent authorities of the occupied territory. The first three elements are applicable both in international and non-international armed conflicts while the fourth is only in international armed conflicts.

Loopholes in the Law

The 1954 Hague Convention and its Protocols have certain shortcomings. The Convention and its First Protocol fail to provide any procedures to keep track of 'international cultural heritage,' especially in armed-conflict regions. The 1954 Convention requires that in times of armed conflict, each state must act to safeguard its cultural property. It relies heavily upon national institutions for the protection of cultural heritage in an emergency.[10] It fails to provide any measures when a country becomes incapable of protecting cultural heritage. There are no measures when the occupying power does not adhere to the general obligations under the 1999 Second Protocol. In addition, the exceptions provided under "military necessity" give impetus for an aggressive party to the armed conflict to exploit the situation. There is no set standard as to what constitutes military necessity thereby placing cultural properties under danger.

On the other hand, 'cultural heritage' gets a higher level of protection from both the state where it is situated and from the international actors concerned with the preservation of cultural items. The 1972 World Heritage

10 When cultural property is at stake, the state is obliged to identify the object concerned, provide measures to protect it from harm, and impose penalties for infractions. It also enjoys an ample degree of discretion in implementing these tasks, since it is generally believed that these measures are principally for the state's benefit. Under all the treaties that use the concept of cultural property (the 1954 Hague Convention, its 1999 Protocol, the 1970 UNESCO Convention and the 1995 UNIDROIT Convention) states are called on to make their selection of cultural objects and guard them against the forceable effects of armed conflict, occupation or illicit trafficking. Lostal Marina, 2017, *International Cultural Heritage Law in Armed Conflict: Case-Studies of Syria, Libya, Mali, the Invasion of Iraq, and the Buddhas of Bamiyan*, Cambridge: Cambridge University Press, p.61.

Convention[11] also establishes a system of international cooperation and assistance to support the state parties in conserving cultural heritage. a state may request assistance from other state parties and/or UNESCO when it finds it cannot meet the obligation alone. In the event of a state failing to preserve such heritage, the World Heritage Committee retain the prerogative to place the site on the List of World Heritage in Danger and activate certain emergency measures, until such time it is eventually deleted from the list.[12] Under the 1999 Second Protocol, the enhanced regime of protection can only be requested for "cultural heritage of the greatest importance for humanity."[13] Under Article 16(1)(c) of the Protocol, crime against such cultural heritage is subject to universal criminal jurisdiction.

The 1999 Second Protocol defines five types of intentional conduct as serious violations.[14] These are as follows:

(i) Making cultural property under enhanced protection the object of attack;

(ii) Using cultural property under enhanced protection or its immediate surroundings in support of military action;

(iii) Extensive destruction or appropriation of cultural property protected under the Convention and this Protocol;

(iv) Making cultural property protected under the Convention and this Protocol the object of attack;

(v) Theft, pillage, or misappropriation of, or acts of vandalism directed against cultural property protected under the Convention.

11 On May 18, 2023, Tuvalu became the 195th State Party to the 1972 Convention concerning the Protection of the World Cultural and Natural Heritage. With this new ratification, the UNESCO World Heritage Convention nears universal recognition, as one of the most ratified legal instruments in the world.

12 The List of World Heritage in Danger is designed to inform the international community of conditions which threaten the very characteristics for which a property was inscribed on the World Heritage List and to encourage corrective action. The World Heritage Committee has decided to include 56 properties on the List of World Heritage in Danger by Article 11(4) of the 1972 World Heritage Convention. In 2003, the Cultural Landscape and Archaeological Remains of the Bamiyan Valley in Afghanistan was placed on the list of World Heritage Under Danger. See: https://whc.unesco.org/en/danger/.

13 Article 10(a), the 1999 Second Protocol.

14 Article 15, the 1999 Second Protocol.

The states must establish criminal sanctions against all these violations. When violations fall under the first three kinds of conduct) i.e., in the case of enhanced protection or there is extensive destruction of cultural property), there is an additional obligation either to extradite or to prosecute the offender, establishing universal criminal jurisdiction. After the destruction of the Buddhas of Bamiyan,[15] in 2003 UNESCO passed a Declaration and encouraged the states to provide effective criminal sanctions against those persons who commit, or order to be committed, acts of international destruction of cultural heritage of great importance to humanity.[16] Even after a lapse of 21 years, no one has acted on this recommendation. The empty niches of the giant Buddhas in the Bamiyan Valley of Afghanistan are a perpetual reminder of our duty to protect cultural heritage, and what future generations stand to lose if we do not.[17] The international community must unite to fight against terrorist acts of the deliberate eradication of iconic world cultural heritage.

15 The fanatical Islamic group used dynamite to destroy the Bamiyan Buddhas over several weeks and in multiple stages. They first used anti-aircraft guns and artillery with the help of anti-tank mines to damage the statues and later obliterated them by lowering local Hazara men down the cliff face to place explosives into holes in the Buddhas. Even if the Taliban based their decision on religion and even though they had control of the land at the time of the destruction, they had a moral obligation to the rest of the world to preserve the Buddhas as objects of our universal cultural heritage.

16 UNESCO Declaration Concerning the Intentional Destruction of Cultural Heritage Paris, October 17, 2003. Article VII of the Declaration dealing with Individual criminal responsibility provided: "States should take all appropriate measures, by international law, to establish jurisdiction over, and provide effective criminal sanctions against, those persons who commit, or order to be committed, acts of intentional destruction of cultural heritage of great importance for humanity, whether or not it is inscribed on a list maintained by UNESCO or another international organization."

17 There is another point of view that the "treatment of Buddha was not governed by the laws of armed conflict." Taliban decided to dynamite the Buddhist statues in 2001 after a fatwa was issued by the Afghan Supreme Court proclaiming that the idols had been gods of the infidels, and the real God is only Allah, and all other false gods should be removed. UNESCO was also not certain whether customary rules providing clear obligations to protect cultural heritage from intentional destruction in times of peace existed. However, such an event was covered by the World Heritage Convention in Article 6(3) and Article 4 (taken together), which prohibits deliberate measures leading to the damage and destruction of world heritage situated in the state's territory. Lostal Marina, 2017, *International Cultural Heritage Law in Armed Conflict: Case-Studies of Syria, Libya, Mali, the Invasion of Iraq, and the Buddhas of Bamiyan*, Cambridge: Cambridge University Press, pp. 158-159.

Military Measures

The protection of cultural property in times of conflict is not possible without the involvement of the armed forces, as practically the military tends to be the only group with access to a conflict area. Military personnel are usually the first ones to be present on the scene and damage to cultural property is often sustained during the early phases of a conflict, their role is of critical importance.[18] Article 7 of the 1954 Hague Convention provides for the obligations of the state parties about the training of the armed forces to ensure compliance with the Convention. The states must also establish within their armed forces, specialist personnel whose purpose will be to secure respect for cultural property and to co-operate with the civilian authorities responsible for safeguarding such property. These are obligations to be implemented in times of peace. The states therefore must ensure their military manuals on the law of war include their obligations relating to the protection of cultural property during armed conflict.

Pre-deployment Training: Prevention of pillage and looting of cultural property and trafficking should be part of pre-deployment training. The looting and illicit trade of cultural property look different in each conflict and may affect the success of each mission differently. Before departure, soldiers should receive information on what type of cultural property they can expect to encounter in what places. Military personnel should be trained in recognising cultural property in operations. For instance, military personnel may be provided with booklets containing pictures and descriptions of the cultural property they may encounter during armed conflict. Pre-deployment training can also address what sites might be vulnerable to looting and by whom. In pre-deployment training, members of the armed forces can also be informed of any relevant mission-specific procedures regarding cultural property trafficking and reporting procedures, if necessary.

The subject of cultural property is very sensitive. The protection of cultural property must be part of military planning. The military personnel must be made aware of the prohibition on pillage and looting cultural property. This includes the various situations in which military personnel may find themselves during their deployment. If a soldier is found to have taken cultural property, the commander should ensure that appropriate disciplinary action is taken against him. Given the complex network of

18 Kila Joris D., Cultural Property Protection in the Context of Military Operations: The Case of Uruk, Iraq, *Conservation and Management of Archaeological Sites*, Vol. 13, No. 4, November 2011, pp. 311-333.

legal obligations that underlies the issue of taking cultural property, commanders should consult a judge advocate if a member of the armed forces is associated with the misappropriated cultural property.

To avoid or at least minimise harm to civilians, their property and cultural heritage from the use of explosive weapons, the armed forces must review their military policies, training curricula and practices to incorporate the following good practices: (i) identify protection of civilians as a strategic objective at the highest level before military operations and incorporate it in all military orders, and (ii) explicitly limit the types of weapons and munitions that may be used in such areas, (iii) ensure that all those involved in the targeting process are trained to identify cultural objects, and (iv) ensure effective maintenance and storage of explosive weapons and munitions, and do not deploy poorly maintained or stored weapons or munitions in operations in areas having cultural objects.[19]

The military occupation of cultural heritage sites, such as monuments and museums, must always be avoided. Their presence constitutes a serious threat to their preservation. Even when the military is positioned to preserve a specific site, the occupation puts the site in danger of direct aggression by the insurgents and non-state actors. International conventions highlight how cultural heritage sites should be necessarily defended by a third party and not by the armed forces of one of the parties to the conflict. During the occupation, military personnel should engage with the local population, as they have the most information on the location of cultural property which requires protection or could be looted. For instance, at the end of January 2004, a patrol from the Dutch Army (Marines) visited Uruk (modern-day Warka) in Iraq. While receiving a guided tour, they saw people digging in the far distance. It was informed to the Duch army that these were plunderers. The patrol and the Bedouin guard rushed to the area, arrested the thieves, and returned the stolen goods that had been taken from an illegally opened grave. Only minor damages to the cultural property were reported. The Uruk case study contains several important elements that play a role when implementing cultural property protection in the context of military operations. Both Iraq and the Netherlands are parties to the Hague Convention of 1954, so there was a legal obligation for cultural property protection in line with IHL.[20]

19 Explosive Weapons with Wide Area Effects: A Deadly Choice in Populated Areas, ICRC, Geneva, January 2022, p. 152.

20 In 2003, during the Dutch deployment in Iraq, the ancient site of Uruk (Warka) was situated in their area of responsibility. Before the war broke out, the site was guarded by

Military commanders at all levels bear operational responsibility for ensuring that military forces abide by the rules of IHL and adopt best practices for the protection of cultural property in armed conflict.[21] These best military practices can be drawn from a range of sources. Besides the 1954 Convention and its Protocols, non-binding instruments such as declarations, recommendations and guidelines adopted by international organisations and treaty bodies [22] can provide general principles of use to military forces in the protection of cultural property in armed conflict. For

a local Bedouin tribe. The tribe received payments from the German Archaeological Institute, which was in charge of excavating the site. The German Archaeologists left when the conflict started, and the German payments stopped in 2003. The Bedouin tribe still felt responsible for guarding the site but were unable to do so without money for transport, food and water. The Dutch Army (Marines) arranged a solution. The tribe could continue to guard the site in return for a payment of approximately $70 per month. In interviews, the locals were positive about the arrangement; the financial rewards for looting during wartime are quite low and barely enough to make a living. By paying the locals to guard the site, the cultural property was preserved, and the locals had a consistent source of income. When the Dutch forces left, the payments again stopped. In 2006, Japan funded a new fence to surround the site. Kila Joris D., Cultural Property Protection in the Context of Military Operations: The Case of Uruk, Iraq, *Conservation and Management of Archaeological Sites*, Vol. 13, No. 4, November 2011, pp. 311-333.

21 History provides numerous examples of orders, directives and the like from senior commanders directed towards the protection of cultural property during a campaign. On December 29, 1943, a few weeks before the Allied landings at Anzio, General Eisenhower, then Allied Commander in the Mediterranean, issued General Order No 68 (Historical Monuments), spelling out detailed instructions concerning the military use and prevention of looting of historic buildings in the Italian campaign and emphasizing that the seriousness of offences against cultural property was to be impressed by commanders on all Allied personnel. General Order No 68, which put in more emphatic form a similar order issued by Allied Force Headquarters in April 1943, bore a covering memorandum in which Eisenhower emphasized that he did not want military necessity 'to cloak slackness or indifference' and placed the responsibility on all commanders to ensure compliance with his orders. Eisenhower reiterated these points as Supreme Commander of, the Allied Expeditionary Force, in a directive and memorandum of May 26, 1944, just before the Normandy landings, in which he instructed commanders to preserve centres and objects of historical and cultural significance 'through the exercise of restraint and discipline'. General Alexander, Supreme Commander of the Allied Forces Headquarters in the Mediterranean theatre, issued a similar directive on January 12, 1945.

22 For instance, the UNESCO Declaration concerning the Intentional Destruction of Cultural Heritage, adopted by the Organization's General Conference in 2003; the Recommendation for the Protection of Movable Cultural Property, adopted by the General Conference of UNESCO in 1978, and the Recommendation on International Principles Applicable to Archaeological Excavations, adopted by the UNESCO General Conference in 1956.

the armed forces of those states, not parties to the 1954 Hague Convention or either or both of its two Protocols, the provisions of these three treaties, of the 1999 Second Protocol, may provide instructive guidance for the protection of cultural property in armed conflict.

Field experience shows that cultural property protection is necessary in all different phases of a conflict, including the early stages. Currently, a big challenge for training the military on cultural property protection is the fact that the subject is not considered important by the armed forces. The subject is given low priority by the military echelon and even by the ministries of defence. Training and teaching military personnel is different from attending a seminar on the subject. Backgrounds, language, and intellectual levels vary, so methods to transfer knowledge must be tailor-made for the target group. [23] Cultural property protection could also be a part of military exercises.[24] Recent examples of successful UN peacekeeping operations in Mali show that it is possible to embed cultural heritage protection into military operations. The Security Council resolution 2347 linked the protection of cultural heritage to the maintenance of peace and security, suggesting that peacekeeping operations could be mandated to carry out such tasks.

UNESCO has been working to address the weakness of the present system of international heritage protection and has launched several significant initiatives. However, awareness-raising is undoubtedly not adequate to increase heritage protection during conflict. The existing mechanisms need to be substantially reinforced through a more systematic integration of cultural protection into humanitarian interventions and a greater involvement of the armed forces. UNESCO, under Article 23(2) of the 1954 Hague Convention, must make proposals to the state parties to bring

23 The cultural property protection expertise is complicated and multidisciplinary. Therefore, first, a basic introduction to art history and archaeology is essential. The next step is to introduce legal, political, and military implications. Important tools for the training are the use of practical examples, anecdotes, discussions, working groups such as syndicates, guest lecturers, simulations, and visits to places like museums and libraries. Due to the scarcity of military in-house legal experts, it is necessary to establish a team of experts to deal with subjects like compliance mechanisms with existing rules, treaties, and military issues. Kila Joris D., Cultural Property Protection in the Context of Military Operations: The Case of Uruk, Iraq, *Conservation and Management of Archaeological Sites*, Vol. 13, No. 4, November 2011, p. 327.

24 Edmondson Scott M., Patricia L. Fogarty, and Elizabeth L. B. Peifer, Planning for Culture: Incorporating Cultural Property Protection into a Large-Scale, Multi-Domain Exercise, *Military Review*, November-December 2021, pp. 16-30.

out the laws of war manual incorporating provisions for the protection of cultural property in the event of armed conflict.[25]

The destruction of cultural property in the recent armed conflict or otherwise has been continuing. The list is long and includes the deliberate destruction of the 1,700 years old statues of Buddha in Afghanistan; systematic destruction and looting of cultural property in Iraq; destruction and theft of cultural property in Syria; looting and destruction of cultural goods in Libya; the devastation of cultural property in Yemen; the destruction of ancient monuments in Timbuktu, Mali; the destruction of cultural property in ongoing Israel-Hamas War, and damage and destruction to nearly 400 buildings of historical and/or artistic interest, museums, and monuments in ongoing Russia-Ukraine War.[26]

The illicit antiquities market has become increasingly complex in the globalised twenty-first century. It has been infiltrated by sophisticated and destructive terrorist organisations.[27] International conventions are

25 Article 23 of the 1954 Hague Convention provides: 1. The High Contracting Parties may call upon UNESCO for technical assistance in organizing the protection of their cultural property, or in connection with any other problem arising out of the application of the present Convention or the Regulations for its execution. UNESCO shall accord such assistance within the limits fixed by its programme and by its resources. 2. UNESCO is authorized to make, on its initiative, proposals on this matter to the High Contracting Parties.

26 Damaged cultural sites in Ukraine verified by UNESCO: As of June 12, 2024, UNESCO has verified damage to 412 sites since 24 February 2022; this includes 137 religious sites, 201 buildings of historical and/or artistic interest, 31 museums, 27 monuments, 15 libraries, 1 archive. Available at: https://www.unesco.org/en/articles/damaged-cultural-sites-ukraine-verified-unesco.

27 The illicit antiquities trade is a transnational grey market--it is a market with both licit and illicit elements. While how antiquities are obtained may be illegal (e.g., fed by looting at archaeological sites); on the demand end of the market, trading in antiquities is perfectly legal. Owning an antiquity thus becomes illegal only when it has been stolen, smuggled, or illicitly exported. Therefore, to be profitable, the illicit means by which antiquities are obtained must be disguised to be profitable. The trade-in of illicitly obtained antiquities involves local, small-scale thieves, larger groups of looters, and international connections with auction houses, galleries, museums, dealers, and collectors. With the help of middlemen, antiquities looted from archaeological sites are generally smuggled transnationally, laundered, and end up in the open, legal antiquities market. Advancements in technology have increased the destructiveness of illegal digging, and archaeological sites are scavenging at an increasingly accelerated pace. The existence of a grey antiquities market facilitated by legal loopholes and fed by theft from archaeological sites has led several scholars to conclude that the looting situation has reached epidemic proportions and that the world's archaeological resources are vanishing at an alarming rate. Passas Nikos and Blythe Bowman Proulx,

largely inept because they lack force and universal applicability. Similarly, legal actions at national criminal courts are highly underutilised and ill-adjusted to address cultural property disputes. In the wake of the continuous plundering and destruction of cultural property, monitoring mechanisms must be improved to reduce the availability of illicit goods in online venues, marketplaces, auction houses, and other commercial platforms. Additionally, legal enforcement tools must be implemented to punish complicit persons and deter potential actors.[28]

The bombing and shelling of cities and towns produce foreseeable and wide-ranging humanitarian consequences. The existing IHL provides the legal framework to regulate the conduct of armed conflict. It applies to the use of explosive weapons in all situations of armed conflict, and all parties to an armed conflict, including both State and non-state armed groups. The Political Declaration on Strengthening the Protection of Civilians from the Humanitarian Consequences Arising from the Use of Explosive Weapons in Populated Areas is an international political commitment developed to address the devastating humanitarian consequences resulting from the use of explosive weapons in populated areas and to strengthen the protection of civilians in armed conflict. It is the first formal international recognition that the use of explosive weapons in populated areas has severe humanitarian consequences that must be addressed by states. The Political Declaration was endorsed by 83 states at the Dublin Conference in November 2022. Between then and April 12, 2024, three new states joined – Montenegro, North Macedonia, and Jordan – bringing the total number of endorser states to 86, including the UK and the USA.[29] The Political Declaration has the potential to strengthen the protection of civilians in armed conflict and to mitigate and address the harm to civilians and their properties caused using explosive weapons in populated areas, including cultural properties. This requires endorser states to review, develop and implement national policies to operationalise the Declaration's commitments and to bring about changes in practice. Implementation is an ongoing process and endorser states will move through it at different speeds and with different approaches, depending on their national context and capacity.

"Overview of Crimes and Antiquities," in Manacorda Stefano and Chappell Duncan, (eds.), 2011, *Crime in the Art and Antiquities World: Illegal Trafficking in Cultural Property*, New York: Springer, pp. 51-68.

28 Willett Hannah D., Ill-Gotten Gains: A Response to the Islamic State's Profits from the Illicit Antiquities Market, *Arizona Law Review*, Vol. 58, 2016, pp. 831-865.

29 The Explosive Weapons Monitor 2023, The International Network on Explosive Weapons (INEW), April 2024, p. 68.

The states, whether party to the Declaration or otherwise, must review military doctrine, such as about targeting and urban operations, as well as military manuals, standing and operation-specific rules of engagement (ROE)[30] to follow their obligations under the 1954 Hague Convention and its Protocols.

The statute of the International Criminal Court (ICC) prohibits the destruction and looting of cultural property. Perpetrators can be prosecuted for war crimes,[31] and for crimes against humanity, when the destruction of cultural property was widespread when it happened systematically, and when it was carried out within the context of persecution for political, racial, or religious reasons. By the principle of complementarity, the ICC exercises jurisdiction only when a state is effectively unable to prosecute alleged war criminals within its jurisdiction or does not want to do so. Consequently, to ensure that penal sanctions are imposed on war crimes at the national level, states should enact legislation enabling them to bring the perpetrators of such crimes to justice. The following measures are necessary to do so: (i) Criminal legislation must be adapted to include the crimes listed in the Statute; (ii) The jurisdiction of the courts over such crimes must be defined; (iii) Rules on mutual legal assistance with the ICC must be drawn up; and (iv) Extradition agreements must be drawn up or other criteria must be set for the hand-over of the alleged perpetrators of the acts specified.

According to O'Keefe (2007), contrary to common assumption, the protection of cultural property in armed conflict using international law is not a hopelessly unrealistic proposition.[32] No doubt, there are some shortcomings in the international legal system for the protection of cultural property during armed conflict, but contemporary jurisdiction

30 The rules of engagement (ROE) are directions endorsed by the Government and issued by commanders, which delineate the circumstances, and limitations within which military force may be applied to achieve military objectives. They do not inhibit or replace but are part of the command function. ROE may be framed to limit certain actions; alternatively, they may authorise actions to the full extent permissible under domestic and international law.

31 Article 8 of the Rome Statute establishes the jurisdiction of the ICC in respect of War Crimes. Regarding cultural property, Article 8(2)(b)(ix) and 8(2)(e)(iv), state that "intentionally directing attacks against buildings dedicated to religion, education, art, science or charitable purposes, historic monuments, hospitals and places where the sick and wounded are collected, provided they are not military objectives", constitutes a war crime.

32 O'Keefe Roger, 2006, The Protection of Cultural Property in Armed Conflict, *Amicus Curiae*, Issue 71, Autumn 2007, pp. 3-7.

demonstrates that the international law on the protection of cultural property during armed conflict is continuously progressing. The existing lacunae can be addressed, not by adding instruments, but by improving ratification and implementation of the existing treaty system by the states. Serious monitoring measures by international organisations are needed to facilitate states parties to improve their implementation mechanism.

Bibliography

Abtahi Hirad, The Protection of Cultural Property in Times of Armed Conflict: The Practice of the International Criminal Tribunal for the Former Yugoslavia, *Harvard Human Rights Journal*, Vol. 14, 2001, pp. 1-32.

Aghlani Sasan, Patricia Lewis and Beyza Unal, Nuclear Disarmament and the Protection of Cultural Heritage, Chatham House, International Security Department, October 2017, pp. 14.

Alcala Ronald, Cultural evolution: Protecting "digital cultural property" in armed conflict, *International Review of the Red Cross*, Vol. 104, No. 919, 2022, pp. 1083–1119.

Alcala Ronald T.P., Babylon Revisited: Re-establishing a Corps of Specialists for the Protection of Cultural Property in Armed Conflict, *Harvard National Security Journal*, Vol. 6, 2015, p. 206-254.

Archibong James E., Destruction of cultural property as a war crime: Breaking new ground in the quest for accountability, *International Journal of Law*, Vol. 5, Issue 2, March 2019, pp. 126-132.

Arnal Victoria, Destructive trends in contemporary armed conflicts and the overlooked aspect of intangible cultural heritage: A critical comparison of the protection of cultural heritage under IHL and the Islamic law of armed conflict, *International Review of the Red Cross*, Vol. 102, No. 914, pp. 539-558.

Arimastu Louise and Mohbuba Choudhury, Protecting Cultural Property in Non-International Armed Conflicts: Syria and Iraq, *International Law Studies*, Vol. 91, 2015, pp. 641-698.

Auwera Sigrid Van der, International Law and the Protection of Cultural Property in the Event of Armed Conflict: Actual Problems and Challenges, *The Journal of Arts Management, Law, and Society*, Vol. 43:4, 2013, pp. 175-190.

Ba Oumar, Governing the souls and community: why do Islamists destroy world heritage sites? *Cambridge Review of International Affairs*, 2020, pp. 1-18.

Beitler Ruth Margolies and Dexter W. Dugan, "Practicing the Art of War While Protecting Cultural Heritage: A Military Perspective," in Cuno James and Thomas G. Weiss (ed), 2022, *Cultural Heritage and Mass Atrocities*, Los Angeles: Getty Publications, pp. 500-516.

Belder Lucky, 2014, *The Legal Protection of cultural heritage in international law, and its implementation in Dutch Law*, pp. 369.

Berend Jolien, Cultural Property Protection Makes Sense, Civil-Military Cooperation Centre of Excellence (CCOE), The Hague, 2020, pp. 80.

Brodie Neil, Why is no one talking about Libya's Cultural Destruction? *NEAR Eastern Archeology*, Vol. 78:3, 2015, pp. 212-217.

Burns Ross, Weaponizing Monuments, *International Review of the Red Cross*, Vol. 99(3), 2017, pp. 937–957.

Campfens Evelien, Andrzej Jakubowski, Kristin Hausler and Elke Selter, Protecting cultural heritage from armed conflicts in Ukraine and beyond, European Union, 2023, pp. 103.

Cassar Brendan and Sara Noshadi, 2015, Keeping *History Alive: Safeguarding Cultural Heritage in Post-Conflict Afghanistan*, UNESCO, pp. 253.

Chauhan Khushboo, Rethinking the Concept of Cultural Genocide under International Law, Paper presented at the 7th Annual International Conference on Genocide, organized by the International Network of Genocide Scholars in 2020, pp. 22.

Clapperton Matthew, et.al., Iconoclasm and strategic thought: Islamic State and cultural heritage in Iraq and Syria, *International Affairs*, Vol. 93, No. 5, 2017, pp. 1205-1231.

Corliss Cody, Prosecuting Members of ISIS for the destruction of Cultural Property, *Florida State University Law Review*, Vol. 45, 2017, pp. 183-223.

Cultural Genocide: On the expansion of terminology, Lund University, Department of Political Science, pp. 31.

Cunliffe Emma, Fox Paul and Peter Stones, The Protection of Cultural Property in the Event of Armed Conflict: Unnecessary Distraction or Mission-Relevant Priority? NATO Open Publication 2018, pp. 22.

Cunliffe Emma, Muhesen Nibal and Marina Lostal, The Destruction of Cultural Property in the Syrian Conflict: Legal Implications and Obligations, *International Journal of Cultural Property*, Vol. 23, No. 1, 2016, pp. 1– 31.

Cuno James and Thomas G. Weiss (ed), 2022, *Cultural Heritage and Mass Atrocities*, Los Angeles: Getty Publications, pp. 619.

Moffett Luke, Dacia Viejo Rose & Robin Hickey, Shifting the Paradigm on Cultural Property and Heritage in International Law and Armed Conflict: Time to Talk about Reparations? *International Journal of Heritage Studies*, Volume 26, Issue 7, 2020, pp. 619-634.

Davidaviciute Rasa, Cultural Heritage, Genocide, and Normative Agency, Journal of Applied Philosophy, Vol. 38, No. 4, August 2012, pp. 599-614.

Destroying Cultural Heritage: Explosive Weapons' Effects in Armed Conflict and Measures to Strengthen Protection, Human Rights Watch, 2024, pp. 97.

Diatta Ismaila, Protecting Cultural Heritage in Times of Conflict, International Centre for the Study of the Preservation and Restoration of Cultural Property, pp. 109.

Drazewska Berenika, 2022, *Military Necessity in International Cultural Heritage Law*, Boston: Brill/ Nijhoff, pp. 365.

Drumbl Mark A., From Timbuktu to The Hague and Beyond: The War Crime of Intentionally Attacking Cultural Property, *Journal of Int'l Criminal Justice.*, Vol 17, 2019, pp, 77-99.

Dulti Maria Teresa, Protection of Cultural Property in the Event of Armed Conflict, Report on the Meeting of Experts, Geneva: ICRC, 5-6 October 2000, pp. 226.

Elekyabi Salwa Youssef, Enhancing International Law with Respect to the Protection of Cultural Property in Times of Armed Conflict: A Comparative Analysis, *JLAW*, Vol. 10, Issue 8, 2021, pp. 2515-2594.

Ellis Mark S., The ICC's Role in Combatting the Destruction of Cultural Heritage, *Case Western Reserve Jour of International Law*, Vol. 49, Issue 1, 2017, pp. 23-61.

Fay Kathryn O. and George W. Calfas, Endangered Cultural Heritage: Global Mapping of Protected and Heritage Sites, US Army Corps of Engineers, Final Report, July 2017, pp. 29.

Foliant Major Yvette, Cultural Property Protection Makes Sense: A Way to Improve Your Mission, Civil Military Cooperation Centre of Excellence (CCOE), 2015, pp. 75.

Forrest Craig J.S., The Doctrine of Military Necessity and the Protection of Cultural Property During Armed Conflict, *California Western International Law Journal*, Vol. 37, No. 2, Spring 2007, pp. 177-219.

Forsyth Marion, Casualties of War: The Destruction of Iraq's Cultural Heritage as a Result of US Action During and After the 1991 Gulf War, *DePaul Journal of Art, Technology and Intellectual Property Law*, Vol. 14, issue 1, 2004, pp. 73-108.

Francioni Francesco and Ana Filipa Vrdoljak, (ed.), 2020, Oxford Handbook of International Cultural Heritage Law, Oxford: OUP, pp. 1012.

Frulli Micaela, The Criminalization of Offences against Cultural Heritage in Times of Armed Conflict: The Quest for Consistency, *The European Journal of International Law*, Vol. 22, No. 1, 2011, pp. 203-217.

Gerstenblith Patty, The Destruction of Cultural Heritage: A Crime Against Property or a Crime Against People? *The John Marshall Review of Intellectual Property Law*, Vol. 15, 2016, pp. 337-393.

Gerstenblith Patty, From Bamiyan to Baghdad: Warfare and the Preservation of Cultural Heritage at the Beginning of the 21st Century, *Georgetown Journal of International Law*, Vol. 37, 2005-2006, pp. 249-351.

Gottlieb Yaron, Attacks Against Cultural Heritage as a Crime Against Humanity, *Case W. Res. J. Int'l L.*, Vol. 52, 2020, pp. 287-330.

Gowan Richard, "Peace Operations and the Protection of Cultural Heritage," in Cuno James and Thomas G. Weiss (ed), 2022, *Cultural Heritage and Mass Atrocities*, Los Angeles: Getty Publications, pp. 517-530.

Han Junhi (ed.), 2015, Safeguarding the Cultural Heritage of Afghanistan, UNESCO, pp, 110.

Hassner Ron E., "Protecting Cultural Heritage on the Battlefield: The Hard Case of Religion," in Cuno James and Thomas G. Weiss (ed), 2022, *Cultural Heritage and Mass Atrocities*, Los Angeles: Getty Publications, pp. 471-484.

Hausler Kristin, Cultural Heritage and the Security Council: Why Resolution 2347 matters, *Question of International Law*, Vol. 48, 2018, pp. 5-19.

Hausler Kristin, Cultural under Attack: The Destruction of Cultural Heritage by Non-State Armed Groups, *Santander Art and Culture Law Review*, Vol. 2(1), 2015, pp. 117-146.

Higgins Marrissa E., Fortification of the International Defence of Cultural Property Trapped in Areas of Armed Conflict, Master's Thesis, The Honors College, University of Maine, Spring 2015, pp. 99.

Hill Caitlin V., Killing a Culture: The Intentional Destruction of Cultural Heritage in Iraq and Syria under International Law, *Georgia Journal of International and Comparative Law*, Vol. 45, 2016, pp, 191-220.

Hladik Jan, Protection of Cultural Property: Legal Aspects, *International Law Studies*, Vol. 80, pp. 319-329.

Howe Zoe, Can the 1954 Hague Convention Apply to Non-state Actors? A Study of Iraq and Libya, *Texas International Law Journal*, Vol. 47, Issue 2, 2012, pp. 403-425.

ICC Reparations Award for Destruction of Cultural Heritage in Mali, Queen's University Belfast, Human Rights Centre, August 17, 2017, pp. 2.

Jayaraman Shiva, The Destruction of Cultural Property at the International Criminal Court: *The Prosecutor v. Al Mahdi*, International Immersion Program Papers, 2017, pp. 16.

Kelly Luke, Lessons learned on cultural heriJiritage protection in conflict and protracted crisis, April 27, 2021.

Keane David, The Failure to Protect Cultural Property in Wartime, *DePaul J. Art, Tech. & Intellectual Property Law*, Vol. 14, 2004, pp. 1-38.

Kila Joris D. and Christopher V. Herndon, Military Involvement in Cultural Property Protection: An Overview, *JFQ*, Vol. 74, October 2014, p. 116-123.

Klesmith Elizabeth A., Nigeria and Mali: The Case for Repatriation and Protection of Cultural Heritage in Post-Colonial Africa, *Notre Dame Journal of International & Comparative Law*, Vol. 4, Issue 1, pp. 45-76.

Layton Robert, Peter G. Stone and Julian Thomas (ed.), 2004, *Destruction and Conservation of Cultural Property*, London: Routledge, pp. 329.

Leloup Mathilde, Heritage Protection as Stabilization, the Emergence of a New 'Mandated Task' for UN Peace Operations, *International Peacekeeping*, Vol. 26(4), 2019, pp. 408–430.

Lenger Mattias, The protection of movable cultural property in wartime: Pre-conflict planning in Sweden, *International Journal of Cultural Property*, Vol. 29, 2022, pp. 265–281.

Losson Pierre, Does the International Trafficking of Cultural Heritage Really Fuel Military Conflicts? *Studies in Conflict and Terrorism*, Vol. 40, No. 6, 2017, pp. 484-495.

Lostal Marina, 2017, *International Cultural Heritage Law in Armed Conflict: Case-Studies of Syria, Libya, Mali, the Invasion of Iraq, and the Buddhas of Bamiyan*, Cambridge: Cambridge University Press, pp. 198.

Luck Edward C., Cultural Genocide and the Protection of Cultural Heritage, J Paul Getty Trust Occasional Papers in Cultural Heritage Policy, No. 2, 2018, pp. 35.

Luo Lei, et al., Google Earth as a Powerful Tool for Archaeological and Cultural Heritage Applications: A Review, *Remote Sensing*, Vol. 10(10), 2018, pp. 1558-1590.

Manacorda Stefano, Duncan Chappell (Ed.), 2011, *Crime in the Art and Antiquities World: Illegal Trafficking in Cultural Property*, New York: Springer, pp. 453.

Margottini Claudio (ed.), 2009, *After the Destruction of Giant Buddha Statues in Bamiyan (Afghanistan) in 2001: A UNESCO's Emergency Activity for the Recovering and Rehabilitation of Cliff and Niches*, Italy: Springer, pp. 293.

McDonald David, Culture under Fire: Armed Non-State Actors and Cultural Heritage in Wartime, Geneva Call, October 2018, pp. 62.

Milligan Ashlyn, Targeting Cultural Property: The Role of International Law, Ch 5, pp. 91-116.

Mohammadi Atiyah Rad and Shams Ahmad. Domestic and International Obligations of the Government in Preserving and Managing the Cultural Heritage, *Int J Sci Stud*, Vol. 5(4), 2017, pp. 460-467.

Mucci Federica, Intentional destruction of cultural heritage by ISIS: the reaction of the International Community against this specific aspect of the aggression to peace and human rights, *Peace Processes*, Vol. 2 No. 1, Winter-Spring 2016, pp. 15.

Muscat Marcie M., Legal Frameworks for Protecting Cultural Heritage in Conflict Zones, Master's Thesis, May 2020, City College of New York, pp. 76.

Nahlik Stanislaw E., International Law and the Protection of Cultural Property in Armed Conflicts, *The Hastings Law Journal*, Vol. 27, 1976, pp. 1069-1087.

Nersessian David, "The Current Status of Cultural Genocide Under International Law," in Bachman Jeffrey (ed), 2019, *Cultural Genocide: Law Politics and Global Manifestation*, Routledge, pp. 38.

Nuzban Yulia, For private or personal use": The meaning of the special intent requirement in the war crime of pillage under the Rome Statute of the International Criminal Court, *International Review of the Red Cross*, Vol. 102, No. 915, pp. 1249-1272.

Oblivion or Prosecution? The Search for the International Legal Framework on Individual Criminal Responsibility for Cultural Heritage Crimes in Armed Conflict, Master Thesis, Katholieke University Leuven, 2017-2018, pp. 125.

O'Keefe Roger, et.al., Protection of Cultural Property: Military Manual, UNESCO, 2016, pp. 91.

O'Keefe Roger, 2006, *The Protection of Cultural Property in Armed Conflict*, Cambridge University Press, pp. 404.

O'Keefe Roger, Protection of Cultural Property under International Criminal Law, *Melbourne Journal of International Law*, Vol. 11, 2010, pp. 1-54.

O'Keefe Roger, The meaning of 'Cultural Property' under the 1954 Hague Convention, *Netherlands International Law Review*, Vol. 46, 1999, pp. 26-56.

Penal Protection of Cultural Property, UNESCO, 2017, pp. 21.

Petrovic Jadranka, "The Cultural Dimension of Peace Operations: Peacekeeping and Cultural Property," in Campbell Andrew H., (2018), *Global Leadership Initiatives for Conflict Resolution and Peacebuilding*, IGI Global, pp. 84-115.

Policy on Cultural Heritage, The Office of the Prosecutor, International Criminal Court, June 2021, pp. 48.

Pollard Nigel, 2020, *Bombing Pompeii: World Heritage and Military Necessity*, University of Michigan Press, pp. 321.

Protecting Cultural Property, International Conference on the 20th anniversary of the1999 Second Protocol of the 1954 Hague Convention, Conference Proceedings, 25-26 April 2019, pp. 142.

Rayne Louise et al., From Above and on the Ground: Geospatial Methods for Recording Endangered Archaeology in the Middle East and North Africa, *Geosciences*, Vol. 7(4), 2017, pp. 100-130.

Request by the Government of Libya to the Government of the United States of America for Imposing Import Restrictions to Protect its Cultural Patrimony under Article 9 of the UNESCO Convention (1970), pp.8.

Ristoldo Filippo, Attacks against Cultural Property as a weapon of war: An exploratory case study, Student Paper Series, 2016-2017, pp. 28.

Rossi Laura, The Politics of Selective Preservation: a Study of Causes and Consequences of Cultural Heritage Destruction during Peace, The Cases of Afghanistan, Egypt and Libya, Master of Arts Thesis, Graduate School of New Brunswick, 2013, pp. 92.

Rothfield Lawrence, 2009, *The Rape of Mesopotamia: Behind the Looting of the Iraq Museum*, University of Chicago Press, pp. 228.

Rush Laurie W., Cultural Property Protection as a Force Multiplier in Stability Operations, *Military Review*, Vol. 92, No. 2, March–April 2012, pp. 36–43.

Ryska Ivan, Military Necessity and Cultural Protection in Laws of War: Historical Overview, *ICLR*, Vol. 21, No. 2, 2021, pp. 187-211.

Sagan Scott D., “From Kyoto to Baghdad to Tehran: Leadership, Law, and the Protection of Cultural Heritage,” in Cuno James and Thomas G. Weiss (ed), 2022, *Cultural Heritage and Mass Atrocities*, Los Angeles: Getty Publications, pp. 485-499.

Salman Reem, Emotional Aspects of Cultural Heritage Destruction During War Conflicts, Master’s Thesis, Charles University, Budapest, 2023, pp. 119.

Schabas William, Al Mahdi Has Been Convicted of a Crime He Did Not Commit, *Case W. Res. J. Int’l L.*, Vol. 49, 2017, pp. 75-102.

Silverman Helaine and Ruggles D. Fairchild, 2007, *Cultural Heritage and Human Rights*, USA: Springer, pp. 205.

Smith Claire, Social-media and the destruction of World Heritage as global propaganda, Proceedings of the II Internacional Conference on Best Practices in World Heritage, pp. 27-49.

Suber David Leone, et al., Antiquities trafficking in conflict countries: A crime-mapping approach, *International Journal of Cultural Property*, Vol. 29, 2022, pp. 531–561.

Thurlow Matthew D., Protecting Cultural Property in Iraq: How American Military Policy Comports with International Law, *Yale Human Rights & Development Law Journal*, Vol. 8, 2005, pp. 153-187.

Toman Jiri, 1996, *The Protection of Cultural Property in the Event of Armed Conflict, Commentary on 1954 Convention*, Ashgate, UNESCO, pp. 525.

Toman Jiri, 2009, *Cultural Property in War: Improvement in Protection, Commentary on the 1999 Second Protocol to the Hague Convention*, UNESCO, pp. 892.

Turku Helga, When Cultural Property Becomes a Tool of Warfare: Law, Politics, and International Security, *Inter Gentes*, Vol. 1, Issue 2, 2017, pp. 3-23.

Varner Elizabeth, The Art of Armed Conflicts: An Analysis of the United States' Legal Requirements towards Cultural Property under the 1954 Hague Convention, *Creighton Law Review*, Vol. 44, 2011, pp. 1187-1243.

Vrdoljak Ana Filipa, The Criminalization of the Intentional Destruction of Cultural Heritage, University of Technology, Sydney, 2016, pp. 28.

United Nations Human Rights Council Resolution A/HRC/33/L.21, dated September 27, 2016.

United Nations Security Council Resolution 2347 (2017), S/RES/2347 (2017), dated March 24, 2017.

Walasek Helen (ed), 2017, *Bosnia and the Destruction of Cultural Heritage*, London: Routledge, pp. 399.

Walasek Helen, Cultural heritage and memory after ethnic cleansing in post-conflict Bosnia-Herzegovina, *International Review of the Red Cross*, Vol. 101(1), 2019, pp. 273-294.

Weiss Thomas and Connelly Nina, Protecting cultural heritage in war zones, *Third World Quarterly*, Vol. 40(1), 2018, pp. 1-18.

Willett Hannah D., Ill-Gotten Gains: A Response to the Islamic State's Profits from the Illicit Antiquities Market, *Arizona Law Review*, Vol. 58, 2016, pp. 831-865.

Williams Paul R. and Coster Christian, Blood Antiquities: Addressing a Culture of Impunity in the Antiquities Market, *Case Western Reserve Journal of International Law*, Vol. 49, 2017, pp. 103-114.

Willett Hannah D., Ill-Gotten Gains: A Response to the Islamic State's Profits from the Illicit Antiquities Market, *Arizona Law Review*, Vol. 58, 2016, pp. 831-865.

Index

www.ingramcontent.com/pod-product-compliance
Lightning Source LLC
Chambersburg PA
CBHW031341230926
51848CB00002B/330